THE FALL
OF THE
HOUSE OF SAVOY

Also by Robert Katz:

DEATH IN ROME

BLACK SABBATH

THE FALL
OF THE
HOUSE OF SAVOY

A study in the relevance of the commonplace

or the vulgarity of history

BY

Robert Katz

THE MACMILLAN COMPANY · *New York, New York*

To Beverly

CONTENTS

(Illustrations following page 202)

(Maps on pages 9, 138–139, 265, 325)

AUTHOR'S NOTE   xiii

PROLOGUE   WHEN A KING DIES   xv

PART I

*THE TRIUMPH OF THE HOUSE OF SAVOY
—A FAMILY ALBUM (1000–1878)*

PART II

HUMBERT and MARGHERITA (1878–1900)

1 A FUNERAL IN ROME   43

2 LOVE IN TURIN   49

3 ROMA CAPITALE   56

4 "THE HEIRS TO THE CAESARS"   63

5 THE ITALIANS (INFERIOR, IDEAL, AND SUPERIOR)   70

6 "HUMBERT FOR PRESIDENT"   80

7 A KISS IN VIENNA   90

8 THE GAY EIGHTIES   104

9 THE RISE AND FALL OF "A CERTAIN MR. CRISPI"   119

10 THE BEGGARS' REVOLT   133

11 A CRIME OF A CENTURY   145

PART III

THE LITTLE KING (1900–1922)

12 VICTOR AND ELENA   157

13 THE "SOCIALIST MONARCHY"   169

14 ROMA DEMOCRATICA   178

15 A "NECESSARY" WAR   191

16 A GREAT WAR   198

17 THE WARRIOR KING   208

18 "BLOODY CHRISTMAS"   214

19 "A NEW WAVE . . . OF SAINT-JUSTS"   223

20 VICTOR AND BENITO   229

21 THE OCTOBER REVOLUTION, OR "IF GIOLITTI
RETURNS WE'RE . . ."   238

PART IV

THE FALL OF THE HOUSE OF SAVOY (1922–1946)

22 "SEPARATE BEDS": THE DIARCHY   255

23 MURDER IN ROME   263

24 ROMA FASCISTA   279

25 THE LITTLE EMPEROR   291

26 WAITING FOR DIO   303

27 "THE SITUATION IS GRAVE, BUT NOT
DESPERATE"   313

28 ET TU, VICTOR?   323

29 "I WILL PUBLISH TO THE WORLD
THE FULL RECORD OF THIS AFFAIR"   338

30 THE FLIGHT OF THE DAMNED   353

31 HUMBERT II THE MAY KING   365

EPILOGUE WHEN A MONARCHY DIES   380

APPENDIX I GENEALOGICAL TABLE OF THE HOUSE OF SAVOY   386

APPENDIX II THE ROYAL PREROGATIVES   388

NOTES   389

BIBLIOGRAPHY   417

INDEX   427

The army returned in safety
After it had hacked up the
  land of the Sand Dwellers . . .
After it had thrown down
  its enclosures . . .
After it had cut down its fig
  trees and vines . . .
After it had cast fire into
  all its dwellings . . .
After it had killed troops in
  it by many ten-thousand

—STELE FROM THE TIME OF PHARAOH
PEPI I OF THE SIXTH DYNASTY,
THE AGE OF THE BUILDERS

AUTHOR'S NOTE

The House of Savoy arose as a powerful family around the year 1000. It remained so until its inglorious fall in 1946. Counts, then dukes, then princes and kings, and at last king-emperors of all Italy and her ill-won foreign lands, the Savoys in the fullness of their reign laid legitimate claim to being the oldest ruling house in Europe. Indeed, they held sway over one or another domain longer than the Shang dynasty in China, longer than the pharaohs of the Old Kingdom, and, by the calculations in the Book of Kings, longer than the House of David.

It is, therefore, surprising that few people, apart from their admirers and beneficiaries, ever paid them much mind. They were almost always regarded as comical, insignificant, and weighing nothing on the balance of history. The readers of this book may find, as I did, many things amusing about the House of Savoy; they may agree that the family was petty and small in every sense of the word. From the foregoing review of the dynasty's fall, however, it would seem difficult to conclude that it ought not to have been taken seriously, if only for the circumstances of its longevity.

History, it is often lamented, is a repetitive phenomenon. Vico saw it as the rise of great nations on a foundation of primitive sociability only to decline and fall on "the custom of each man thinking only of his own private interests," and then, "like the phoenix, they rise again." Voltaire and Gibbon concurred that history was little else than the register of crimes by and against humanity. Marx and Engels had it as the record of class struggles, and others have viewed it, perhaps in its roundest dimension, as merely the story of man's intentions. Where better to attempt to grasp these elusive truths than inside the tiny confines of a single, relatively stable, rather simple-minded institution that influenced the lives of ever larger numbers of people for nearly a thousand years? That something so little, often clownish, and always mediocre could have presided over some greatness and have endured so much folly and misfortune, in which its own role was supreme, seems worthy of attention all the more.

But of course this is only a story of Italians and should not necessarily be construed as being relevant to your nation and to mine.

R. K.
Rome, September 12, 1970

WHEN A KING DIES

WHEN VICTOR EMMANUEL II OF SAVOY, THE FIRST KING OF MODERN ITALY, CAUGHT COLD ON NEW Year's Day of 1878, no one even remotely suspected that in a little more than a week he would be dead. He was a robust, vigorous man of fifty-seven who displayed the very essence of virility and life. Embodying the spirit of his times, he had raised aloft the banners of nation and crown; yet they remained to be firmly implanted and it seemed this only he could do. Thus the national and dynastic crisis brought on by an unfortunate chill was extremely grave.

He had been to the Apollo Theater in Rome on that first evening of the year. On the way home he felt uncomfortably hot and feverish, and once alone in his palace bedroom, he stripped off his kingly clothes, threw open the tall, paneled windows, and, never having read the ancient caveats of Aristotle, he drank several glasses of melted snow. Then he lighted a long cigar, settled himself on the windowsill, and let the damp, wintry air cool him down.

The next day he went hunting at his great reserve by the sea, hoping, as he himself said, "to shake" a general feeling of illness which persisted. On the third day he was tired, tremulous, and cold. On the fourth day (it was a Friday) he took to his bed, and against his better judgment, summoned the palace doctor. His temperature was 103° and his lungs were congested. The royal specialists were called by telegraph from Turin, Florence, and Pisa. On Sunday they assembled in the capital, and after examining the king, they agreed he had pneumonia.

They gave him quinine to prevent complications from the chronic malaria he had contracted in the marshy southlands while fighting for his country's independence. They applied freshwater leeches to his flesh in order that the "bad" blood might be sucked away, and, in spite of the king's forbiddings, they opened the veins in his arm, expecting that the letting of blood would facilitate his arduous breathing. That afternoon they predicted that by Tuesday the malady would pass through a crisis which they told those closest to the patient would either be "good or sad."[1]

News that the beloved monarch was ailing began to spread, as medical bulletins were issued periodically to the press. There was great consternation throughout the land. Even Pope Pius IX, who considered himself Victor Emmanuel's prisoner and had been his arch enemy in the struggle for nationhood, said a prayer for the king. The scheming Count Alessandro Guiccioli, a member of the right wing opposition, wrote in his diary that weekend, "The state of the king's health is disquieting. . . . If a tragedy were to occur, it would be a national tragedy, especially at this moment. I am very worried about this."[2]

In the meantime the king remained absolutely calm, unperturbed. But on Tuesday the expected crisis took place and it was not "good." Early the following morning, the ninth, he began to fade, and the first medical notice of the day was considered alarming, which caused the Rome stock market to fall.

The doctors saw death coming on and someone rushed through the palace whispering the news. The royal family, the court, and the ministers gathered. The king had to be told he was going to die, it was decided, and Lorenzo Bruno, the court physician who had come from Turin, took it upon himself to so inform him. With a trembling voice, it is said, he asked his majesty whether he would care to receive the comforts of religion.

"Then my illness must be quite serious," said Victor Emmanuel with surprise. Until now, notwithstanding his discomfort, he had believed he would certainly recover. "All right, let's have it," he said. "I feel no remorse; nor do I have anything to repent. Whatever I have done, it has been in the service of my country, never with any intention of offending religion or its leader."[3]

When the rites had been administered it was about noon and the king was experiencing increasing difficulty in respiring. Pure oxygen —a luxury at the time—had been prepared for him at a laboratory in the University of Rome, but even that brought scant relief. Instead he got out of bed and stood by the window, saying he could breathe more easily in a standing position. He repeatedly asked to smoke a cigar, feeling that too might help, but the doctors forbade it, insisting that he return to his bed. How could he die if he were on his feet? He climbed between the ample bedclothes scarcely in time to receive his deathbed visitors, who had concluded that the terrible hour of the last farewell was at hand. There were tears in their eyes. The crown princess, Margherita, wearing a delicate black veil, could barely remain on her feet. She and Prince Humbert, who would shortly himself be king, entered the chamber carrying lighted candles. The flames raised ghostly, quivering shadows on the yellow-papered walls as the royal couple kneeled at the side of the bed. The mood and the trappings were such that Victor Emmanuel could not doubt that the end was near. Those who were there say he was perfectly resigned and from this moment on he played his part "like a hero."[4]

The king's bedroom, which was rapidly being filled to the stifling point with would-be mourners, was a rather austere little cubicle. It was on the ground floor in the west wing of the Quirinal. His iron bed faced a window. A pocket watch and a gold chain dangled above his head from a hook, upon which he hung the timepiece every night before retiring. There was a mirror in a gilded frame above a fireplace; a small desk stood off to one side near a well-worn easy chair which was coming unstitched at the seams. A patch rug of red, white, and green squares—the colors of the Italian flag—lay on the floor, and glistening stars made of thin metal were set in the squares. There were stars of various shapes and sizes throughout the room. They were made not only of metal, but of silver paper and embroidered cloth, and others were painted on the ceiling and walls—a veritable galaxy. It was like a boy's room, the feeling being enhanced by the presence of two large stuffed birds dressed like men, which were appended to the walls. They possessed enormous beaks, and one wore a Piedmontese peasant costume, the other top hat and tails. The king had nicknamed this latter creature The Diplomat.

"You see that diplomat over there," he used to say to visitors, "he's the best of all the ambassadors accredited to my court." Or, when a distinguished political leader would call, he would wait for the most serious moment, suddenly cast his eyes at the bird and cry, "Look! A secret agent from the left," which never failed to frighten even those on whom the joke had often been played.[5]

Someone in the death chamber thought the comical bird unseemly for this sad occasion and tried to at least turn its head away. But the king looked up and said, "Leave him in peace. If I am to die, he will watch over my final sleep."[6]

Princess Margherita could not bear the anguish. She rushed from the room, and when she reached her apartment, she fainted.

Victor Emmanuel's bastard son, Emmanuel, arrived. He asked permission of his half-brother Humbert to go to his father's side. The request was granted, for Humbert knew how great the king's love was for his former mistress and now morganatic wife, "La Rosina," and their two grown children. Once, nearly fourteen years earlier, when Victor Emmanuel was already a widower, he had written a long letter about La Rosina to his legitimate daughter Princess Clotilde. She had married a nephew of Napoleon and was finding her father's behavior a source of embarrassment. It is a rare, moving, pathetic, white-lying letter by this gruff hunter-king, this semiliterate warrior who in more ways than one was the father of his country. The letter has only recently come to light; it reads in part:

Dear Kekina,

I have worked up the courage and I am writing to you. You will think that I waited too long, but to tell you the truth I was too frightened by the first part of your letter, in which you gave your miserable old papa an old-fashioned tongue-lashing. But in the second part you said that my Kekina forgives me and that she still loves me, which gives me the courage to undertake this labor, trusting myself to your good will and, in knowing that, I will speak to you of everything.

Listen, dear Clotilde, I have suffered much in my life because of that affair, but I believe I have paid for whatever harm I have caused, and now I would like to have a little peace. Put yourself in my shoes and imagine yourself in the stormy life I lead. I believe there no longer is anything for which I must reproach myself and I feel that what I have done is not such a terrible thing. . .

In this world I have loved only your sainted mother and then this woman, with whom a terrible destiny and a great love on both our parts has united me. I sought, we sought, both of us, from the very beginning, many times, to separate from one another, but strange circumstances always reunited us in spite of ourselves. I knew this woman when I was fourteen years old. She used to accompany her father, a horseman and captain of my Father's royal guards at Racconigi, and wherever my Father went her father came along too because my Father loved him, particularly for his great courage, and he often spoke with him. In this way I used to see her always. She loved me very much and I saw in her, even though she was very young, a great beauty, and wonderful qualities of mind and heart, so rare in a girl so young. That's how the thing began. . . .

Now, dear Kekina, here is the situation I find myself in. The censures, if I were to ask the Pope, would surely be lifted; I am ready to marry her, but I can't, unless it is done secretly, because here everyone thinks we have already been married for a long time, at least I am forced to allow many people to believe that. . . . I am, as I said, ready to do all, but I must proceed very prudently because . . . my reputation would be at stake if the thing were to come out as something new.

Now I must tell you still another thing which will seem strange to you, but that's the way it is: La Rosina, guided by sentiments of the highest delicacy, has never spoken to me of marriage. . . .

Now, dear Clotilde, I have opened my heart and I assure you it has taken great pains. Do not think badly of me and have a little pity for your poor old papa . . .

I have suffered much in my life; I have had many family misfortunes, have passed many years in war. I lost my father in exile; my head was ruined by too much serious thinking . . . I wish to be able to die in tranquility. I need therefore to be united with that person who for seventeen years was my inseparable companion in all my pain and in all my labors for the fatherland, my companion in all my long sufferings.*

Excuse me if I have exhausted you, my dear daughter. Write me something good, something to cheer me. I need that. *Ciao*, love and kisses . . .

Your miserable father,
Victor, known as
the unfortunate . . .[7]

The old wolf, with his devilishly pointed beard and his great waxed mustaches which swung up with the authority of the arms of an anchor, was always getting into trouble over women. As heir to the throne, he was quite proper, almost under obligation, in having had "discreet adventures" before marriage with women of every rank, with princesses and maids, with the wives of the rising, ambitious bourgeoisie, with the peasants he passed on the way to the hunt. But he had married at twenty-two and was king at twenty-nine, too young to relinquish his "rights" to princely pleasures, and in that sense he would never grow old. He was a crude, rotund man, who liked to keep one thumb in his pocket, talk horses, guns, and chase *pupu*, a word he invented to describe an amorous palace dame, and one which he later employed generically. "Physically," said the sculptor Marrocchetti, describing the monarch at thirty, "there is something savage in him, picturesque, reminiscent of a barbarian king."[8] He was incorrigible. His poor wife, beautiful, fragile, angelic Maria Adelaide, literally died from the labors of love, consumed like a fire stoked too hard at the age of thirty-three, giving birth to her eighth child.

---

* In 1869, believing erroneously that he was deathly sick and about to die, he married her, properly and religiously (see genealogical table in Appendix I).

He was always disappearing. At royal festivals and balls, he would slip away early pleading *travail de nuit*. Once, on one such laborious evening, coming out on a quiet street after passing several hours in the home of a young lady, he was accosted by three ruffians. They knew where the king had been and sought to blackmail him. He beat them to the ground with his walking stick and one of them never got up, a brutal deed which required a great deal of money to still.

He loved La Rosina passionately; even Maria Adelaide knew that. She never reproached him for she thought him reasonably regardful and he loved *her*, too. Indeed he cherished, worshiped her, but she was always pregnant and so delicate.

They say Rosina was as wild as he. The daughter, not of the captain of the guards, but of the royal drummer, she was radiantly beautiful, with flashing eyes, wholly feminine, earthy, and not at all taken with his loftiness. ("Love me half as much as I love you," he had pleaded; his must indeed have been a great love.) If Maria Adelaide said nothing, the nobility and the clergy were far less generous. The abbot Giacomo Margotti filled the columns of the reactionary journal *Armonia* with nasty cruelties aimed at the libertine king. A violent man himself, Don Margotti was found dead one day, lying in a puddle of his own blood. The murderer was never identified, but among the possessions of the king a package would years later be found, a highly suggestive but not conclusive piece of evidence labeled in Victor Emmanuel's own hand: "walking stick broken on the back of Don Margotti in gratitude for what he wrote about Rosina."[9]

It was a love, like many royal affairs, which altered the course of history. When Maria Adelaide died in 1855, a new queen was sought for the king. Italy was convulsed in revolution and the cause of national unity was still but a dream in a long and tortured sleep. Victor Emmanuel's kingdom extended only from Piedmont, in the northwest corner of the Italian peninsula, to the island of Sardinia. The rest of Italy was still, as it had been for centuries, fragmented in petty states, ruled by the Hapsburgs, the Bourbons, and the popes. A king's marriage was always an opportunity to advance dynastic and national ambitions, but in this time and place it was a golden opportunity.

All the royal houses of Europe, each of them pursuing aims of its own, put forth their most alluring candidates. The ever ready matchmaker Queen Victoria offered the hand of the princess of Cambridge, Napoleon III recommended a Hohenzollern, and the kaleidoscope of German royalty was eager to provide any one of six princesses of varying beauty. But Victor Emmanuel's prime minister, the Great Statemaker Cavour, had his cunning heart set on the Duchess of

Leuchtenberg, Maria Nicolajevna, sister of Czar Alexander II. The Russians could be a useful ally in the very likely event of an imminent war between Piedmont and the imperial Hapsburgs. The king himself, however, would have only Rosina, and all the logic in the world could not subdue his passion for the drummer's daughter.

Cavour, who knew his Boccaccio as well as his Machiavelli, conceived of a plan. He had Rosina followed everywhere and before long he discovered or invented the royal mistress's "other lover," a dark, unworthy figure, a young and handsome jeweler. Cavour went straight to the king with news of Rosina's alleged deceit. Marco Minghetti, who one day was to succeed Cavour, was present at this encounter. He later wrote that Victor Emmanuel "became livid with rage and summoned the woman before him, wanting to confront her in his [Cavour's] presence. But the woman did not lose her composure in the slightest. The only argument she adduced in her own behalf was that so great was Victor Emmanuel's passion and so frequent were his embraces, that she was continually exhausted. The only thing further she ever yearned for was a little rest. . . ."[10]

Nevertheless, after she had gone, the king proposed, and Cavour accepted, that Urbano Rattazzi, Cavour's chief aide, investigate the matter. This assignment was duly discharged and Rattazzi, after completing his researches, reported to the king that the jeweler in question was indeed engaged in a clandestine love affair, but not with Rosina. The court gossipers say that when Cavour heard this his anger knew no limits, and, as he was quite capable of doing, he politically emasculated Rattazzi, stripping him of power and prestige. "The day Rattazzi could no longer serve Cavour's purposes," said the king's close friend and another future premier, General Lamarmora, "he found himself transformed into a vulgar, ambitious, inept, insignificant man, and was deprived of all influence. He was left with nothing."[11] This, it is said, proved to be a serious mistake, reaching across half a century. It contributed to the failure of Cavour's political party, which is generally recognized as one of the major causes of the ultimate collapse of the parliamentary system in Italy and the consequential advent of Mussolini. All because of Rosina? It is fetching far to say so, but there is truth in it, and such is the stuff of history.

The last moments were rushing in. Old friends filed past the bed and the king said *addio* to them all. Then he spoke to the crown prince. Humbert had remained kneeling at his father's side, sobbing without surcease. The king embraced him. "Oh, Humbert," he is said to have invoked his son, "I entreat you to be strong, to love your country, and to love freedom."[12]

He had been and done all of those things. He was known throughout the land as the *re galantuomo*, the gentlemanly, honest, upright king. No one seemed to notice the implication that in the House of Savoy there had been few or no such kings before him, and in many ways he was less so than his forebears. But he had fought valiantly for his country and the House of Savoy, and, more important for dynasties and nations, he had fought successfully. The moral inferior of his father, King Charles Albert, he had taken the one step which the older man had been incapable of. Victor Emmanuel, throwing absolutism, legitimism, and the worn-out class structure to the winds, which were blowing them anyway into the past, had linked the fate of his ancient house with a pack of wild-eyed, bourgeois revolutionaries and hardheaded liberals; men such as the prophet Mazzini, who was full of madness and folly, the beautifully simple Garibaldi, all heart and sword, and the unscrupulous genius Cavour, a son of Satan himself. It had been an all or nothing gamble and he knew it. As he put it: either king of all of Italy or "*monsù* Savoy."[13]

Never had any of the thirty-seven reigning princes of Savoy who had preceded him dared to envision himself as king of all the Italians. For nearly nine hundred years the oldest ruling house in Europe had religiously followed the rule of the artichoke, which viewed Italy as having to be "eaten leaf by leaf."[14] But Victor Emmanuel II, who could say with Mazzini, "We do but translate the thought of the Age,"[15] was prepared to gobble. Who could know his house would choke on it?

According to the official version of Victor Emmanuel's death, Dr. Bruno now announced to everyone present in the chamber that the "extreme hour" had arrived. "It was a moment of intense agony for all. The King, making a slight movement with his lips, breathed his last at the stroke of 2:30 in the afternoon as if he were falling off to sleep."[16]

He was gone. Dr. Bruno confirmed it: "The first king of Italy is dead; he seems asleep, resting after a long and glorious labor."[17]

Everybody burst into tears, although someone had the presence of mind to take note of the stars on the ceiling and walls and recall the motto of Amadeus VI, a fourteenth-century Savoyard prince: "*J'attends mon astre.*" It seemed just the right bit of poetry for the moment. In retrospect it was a black prophecy, for the long awaited star was on its way indeed, already twinkling in the Italian sky: the star of the Republic.

PART I

The Triumph of the House of Savoy— A Family Album (1000-1878)

O, Sir John, do you remember since we lay
all night in the windmill in Saint George's Fields?

No more of that, good Master Shallow, no more of that.

Ha, it was a merry night. And is Jane Nightwork alive?

She lives, Master Shallow. . . .

By the mass, I could anger her to the heart. She
was then a bona-roba. Doth she hold her own well?

Old, old, Master Shallow.

Nay, she must be old; she cannot choose but be old;
certain she's old; and had Robin Nightwork, by old Nightwork, before I came to Clement's-inn.

That's fifty-five year ago.

Ha, Cousin Silence, that thou hadst seen that that
this knight and I have seen!—Ha, Sir John, said I well?

We have heard the chimes at midnight, Master Shallow.

That we have, that we have; in faith,
Sir John, we have: our watchword was, *Hem, boys!*—
Come let's to dinner:—O, the days that we have seen!
—come, come.

—SECOND PART OF KING HENRY THE IV,
ACT 3, SCENE 2

THE FALL OF ANCIENT ROME WAS A CATASTRO-
PHE ON THE SCALE OF THE FLOOD OR A NUCLEAR
war. The world had to be remade and the Dark Ages were like a
seething, primordial sea from which the new humanity would emerge.
Yet not everything had gone down with Rome. A great and terrible
truth, which the Romans had not discovered but had elevated to its
then highest stage, had survived. It taught that the breadth of mankind far exceeded its wealth, and only in the principle of divine
kingship could these scarce riches best be preserved and augmented.

Emperors and kings, in their association with the gods, were the
great unifiers of a social organization which arose on the backs of the
men it forcibly enslaved. As a result of the universal dearth men had
long before found their way to this the most fruitful of all possible
social systems. Like today, these societies in whatever time or place
were pyramidally shaped, with the have-nots at the bottom and the
haves on high. This unity was capable of unleashing power of an un-
imaginable dimension and the lesson of Imperial Rome had been
that the greater the unity the greater the power, which was the
fundamental source of all wealth in almost every sense of the word.

Thus virtually all societies pursued a larger unity, and as a consequence, when they did so contemporaneously, sooner or later they
found themselves locked in conflict with one another. These were
struggles which could be resolved in many ways, but primarily and
most decisively in war.

In the centuries that followed the tragedy of Rome, Europe became
an immense battlefield for such wars, which took place in countless
numbers. Kings and their kingdoms rose and fell like the waves on
the sea, and when a new empire was at last achieved by Charlemagne, it too collapsed in the clash of differing unities. After each

3

collapse the fortunes of men and social groups were revised. Those who had improved their condition sought at first to stabilize and protect this new position, and later to enhance it. The newly mighty allied with the more mighty and, through the agency of the Church, with the Almighty.

Unable to achieve the larger unity, men in possession of varying measures of social power evolved a pattern of allegiances, and with the passage of time it took hold and hardened in feudal institutions. These institutions, insofar as they remained intact, assured the perpetuity of a new order of social cohesion, and those most deeply entrenched in it began now to yearn hardest for peace, for law and order.

To the extent that peace was restored and disorder suppressed, the feudalists were more or less content. They grew conservative, wary of change. The new order aged and stiffened; its institutions became brittle, and they were assailed by men whose mark had not yet been made, men who dreamed of the elusive unity, or at least of elevating themselves on the ossifying social scale. They represented the forces of change, and those among them who had the greatest lust, the most irrepressible greed, the sharpest sword, and the largest measure of good fortune sometimes succeeded.

It was under such circumstances that around the year 1000 there emerged from long and bloody strife a newly powerful family, to be known in history as the House of Savoy.

About one hundred years earlier an assembly of feudal lords had convened in an already ancient monastery on an Alpine watch over the Rhone. As a result of the definitive dismemberment of Charlemagne's empire, they had come into possession of a kingdom which extended beyond the Valaisian Alps to Val d'Aosta in Italy. Offering the crown to a certain marquis named Rudolf, the recoverers of this realm, a large part of the land of the Burgundians, invested him with the mission of making peace with their neighbors and creating stability at home.

Rudolf and his successors, Rudolfs II and III, were ambitious men, however, they too heady with the imperial dream. But in truth not one of them was master of his crown. For the Rudolfs had been reified by the true proprietors of power—the landed feudalists—who

wished to legitimize the gains they enjoyed from the breakup of Carolingian rule. In reestablishing the institution of kingship, however,
they had again turned loose its concomitant forces, as the new kings
sought to found all power in themselves.

When the childless Rudolf III ("the Lazy") died, a war of succession
broke out between the supporters of the Old Order and the modernist
German Emperor Conrad II ("the Salic"), who laid claim to the
throne. On Easter, 1034, Conrad assembled a council of war, attended
by rebellious Burgundians and Italians, most of them in a secondary or
tertiary stratum of the prevailing social order. They were ready to
take up arms against the Establishment and fight for the New Society
with all the inherent benefits that entailed. Military plans for the
decisive campaign were drawn.

The emperor and his iron men came down from the north armed
with spiked and flanged maces which could turn a human head to
pulp in a single blow. All that summer long they engaged the feudal
militia of the lords of both land and church in protracted, inconclusive, skull-cracking combat. In the meantime, according to Conrad's
Easter plan, reinforcements—an entire army of Italians—were arriving
from the south. They were commanded by a fearless and audacious
nobleman of recent prominence whose name was Humbert. Tradition
says his hands were as white as snow.

Leading the Italians through the Great Saint Bernard pass in the
Alps, Humbert arrived at Conrad's side at the most melodramatic
moment, and in the face of such overwhelming military power the
old proprietors surrendered, did homage to the emperor, and recognized him as king.

There was peace in the Alpine land, and the rewards of the New
Society, which of course was but a nuance of the old, were manifold,
if only for the victors. For his services to the Good Cause, the heroic
Humbert won vast feudal dominions on both sides of the Alps, in
Italian Aosta, part of Maurienne, the Tarantaise, Belley, the Chablais,
and the small county of Savoy, which bore with it the title of count.
With these territories he commanded three of the most important
Alpine passes, the Mont Cenis and the two Saint Bernards.

Count Humbert the Whitehanded was the founder of the millenary dynasty of Savoy.[1]

Scholars of the Savoy* phenomenon, a vanishing breed of dedicated men who for at least six centuries have been combing the archives of Europe in search of the "secret" of the dynasty's astounding successes, are no longer willing to climb the genealogical tree any higher than Humbert the Whitehanded. They, as will be seen, have more than once fallen badly from such a rarified altitude. But we need not be afraid; the documents, if not explicit, are sturdy enough for the ascent, and the panorama it affords is worth the risk.

In all probability the family, somewhere along the line, is descended from an indigenous barbarian tribe, perhaps one of those which the Romans found in "swarms" in the valleys and on the banks of the Rhone when they came as conquerors under Caesar.

The Romans, of course, disappeared, and the Alpine peoples whom they had subjugated came to rule themselves in the image but not the substance of their fallen masters. We shall not be too far from the truth in placing the benighted ancesters of the Savoys among the victorious barbarians.

The first glimmer of light to focus on the actual individuals who, among other accomplishments, fathered Humbert the Whitehanded begins to come through about the year 976. Domenico Carutti, a faithful student of the royal house, exactly nine hundred years later discerned what appears as an early family tradition of naming the firstborn of alternate generations Humbert and Amadeus, respectively. On this basis he was able to find some evidence of Humbert the Whitehanded's forebears, a Savoyard family of Amadeuses and Humberts. They were vassals who became prominent in the second half of the tenth century as a result of their participation in a struggle to expel an invasion of Saracens. "Destruction and massacres came

* Savoy itself becomes known to us for the first time in the fourth century A.D. through the eyes of that wandering Roman historian Amaianus Marcellinus. Describing the tortuous course of the Rhone as it issues from Lake Geneva, Amaianus wrote that "without losing any of its majesty, it flows through Sapaudia and the land of the Sequani. . . ." [2] Sapaudia, or Sabaudia, is what we call Savoy, a word whose origins are somewhat obscure. One school traces it to *Sapp-Wann*, Celtic for "the land where the pine trees grow"; another to *Sapp-Aud*, "the land of the many waters." But fourteenth-century Savoyard princes, apparently unsatisfied with such pacific and pastoral images, made their Savoy originate from *Salva via* [3] ("save the way"), which held fast for centuries, although it was, presumably unwittingly, close to the roots of *savage*. Such etymological fictions and, as we will see, genealogical fables as well, helped to saturate the generations with a sense of mission and hold them steady on the course of aggression.

first," said Carutti, "then a victorious war, changes in property ownership, and advantages to the victorious soldiers."[4]

Be that as it may, there can be no doubt as to the origins of the dynasty's power, since all social groups which cleave mankind asunder and set men above men derive their power in one way or another from the sword and the will to cut it loose from the weak.

As evidence in this instance we have the sworn testimony of Humbert the Whitehanded himself. He tells us a great deal about the mode of power accumulation in that long ago time. At the Council of Anse in 1025, the vassal Count Humbert had taken an oath of loyalty to the old feudal order, which of course he secretly opposed in its existing form. The higher lords and the ecclesiastical powers had sought to put an end to the ceaseless daily struggles rife within their class, and called on the entire nobility to maintain the peace of God. Humbert, it is known (and doubtless many other noblemen), went before the symbols of Christ and Church and made a vow to that which he would refrain from doing in the future. From this we may surmise something of what he had been doing in the past, and, by his deeds in the rebellious war of succession—a repudiation of both the Old Order and the oath—what he never ceased for a moment to do. Humbert swore, with a number of explicit qualifications:

> I will not assault or imprison ecclesiastics or monks who do not bear arms, nor those who may be traveling with them without lance or shield; and I will not rob their horses, as long as they commit no flagrant offense.
>
> I will not take as booty cattle, horses, and other animals. I will not arrest peasants and merchants; neither will I steal their money, nor force them to pay blackmail. I will not seize other people's horses and mules while they are at pasture, as long as they cause me no damages; and I will uphold this from the first of March to the first of November.
>
> I will not raze or otherwise destroy houses, as long as there are no thieves nor one or more of my enemies inside. I will not cut, tear down, or uproot vines, willows, and fruit trees. I will not destroy mills and neither will I steal the grain inside them. . . .
>
> I will not assault merchants and pilgrims, and I will not steal their things, as long as they are not guilty of any offense. . . .
>
> I will not assault a noblewoman or anyone who travels with her. I will not arrest or kill a man when he is traveling with a noblewoman. I will also conduct myself in this manner with ecclesiastics and widows. . . . I will not attack an unarmed horseman, during Lent.[5]

Of Humbert the Whitehanded and his barbarian forefathers we may say with Gibbon, while questioning his final two words, "Such were those savage ancestors whose imaginary virtues have sometimes excited the praise and envy of civilized ages."[6]

The true beneficiary of the passing of the turbulent era of the three Rudolfs was not the distant Emperor Conrad, but the entirely refurbished class of patricians, the newly enfeoffed lords and bishops in whom all regional power had been reinvested. Since they were but the heirs of the class they so rudely displaced, they necessarily found themselves with many of the old desires and needs. Foremost among them: law and order.

They had succeeded where their predecessors had failed—in casting off the ambitious Rudolfian monarchy—but had done so at the price of imperial rule. This was a yoke, the new barons almost universally agreed, which had to be lifted. No one among them was placed more favorably to make a contribution in this regard than Humbert the Whitehanded, now a veritable king of the Alps. As an imperial vassal of Conrad, a distinction the Savoys were to exalt for centuries, Humbert began at once to undermine the recently acquired strengths of his lord.

The time-sculpted form of the mountains themselves lent sinew to his endeavors. Ridged up in grandiose folds, as if a great thumb had pushed against the pliant firmament of primeval Italy, the Alps were an awesome barrier to the temporal and spiritual kingdom it overlooked. Only in the passes lay the gateways to Italy and papal Rome, and Conrad, as emperor of the West, had given them to Humbert in order that they might lie in faithful, trustworthy hands. But the moment the Savoyard took possession of such a powerful position, the loosening of "foreign" domination became his first labor, mastery of his own house his primary goal. Neither he nor his neighbors of equivalent social rank would find these tasks less than formidable. The bonds of feudal loyalties were ample and the punishments for infidelity severe.

The great mountains also etched the policies of the House of Savoy, which from the beginning were a compounding of duplicities, and as the Alps were eternal so would be that which they determined. Thus while he cultivated his pretended service to the German emperor, Humbert went about organizing his own autonomy. This was performed by reinforcing his ties with the highest circles of the lay and

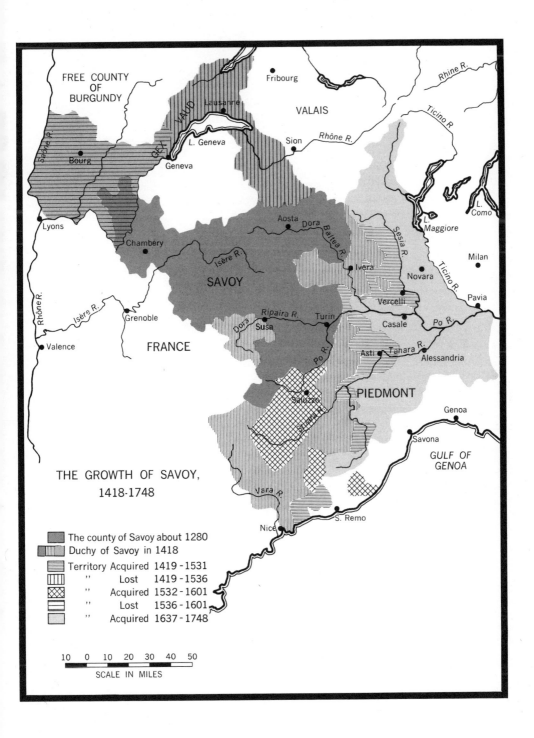

FREE COUNTY
OF
BURGUNDY

Fribourg

VALAIS

VAUD

Lausanne

Rhine R.

Saône R.

L. Geneva

Sion

Rhône R.

Ticino R.

Bourg

Geneva

Lyons

Aosta

Dora

Baltea R.

Sesia R.

L.
Maggiore

L.
Como

Chambéry

Isère R.

SAVOY

Ivera

Novara

Milan

Ticino R.

Vercelli

Pavia

Rhône R.

Isère R.

Grenoble

Ripaira R.

Turin

Casale

Po R.

Valence

Dora

Susa

Po R.

Asti

Tanara R.

Alessandria

FRANCE

PIEDMONT

Saluzzo

Genoa

Savona

GULF OF
GENOA

THE GROWTH OF SAVOY,
1418-1748

Vara R.

Nice

S. Remo

The county of Savoy about 1280
Duchy of Savoy in 1418
Territory Acquired 1419-1531
    ''   Lost   1419-1536
    ''   Acquired 1532-1601
    ''   Lost   1536-1601
    ''   Acquired 1637-1748

10   0   10   20   30   40   50

SCALE IN MILES

religious local nobility. It was immeasurably enhanced by Conrad's successor, Henry III ("the Black"), to whom Humbert seems to have proffered even greater "loyalties" at a time when other feudal powers rebelled. Pious Henry, the aboriginal hangman of the heretical Cathari, was anxious about his lines of communication with the pope. He desired that the "devoted" House of Savoy exercise even greater control over the passageways to Rome, and therefore arranged for the marriage of the youngest of Humbert's sons, Oddone, to the incomparable Adelaide, thrice married heiress to all of Turin and most of the lands of Piedmont.

This turned out to be of crucial importance to the dynasty, for untimely deaths in the family caused Humbert's rule to pass not to his firstborn son but his fourth, Oddone. This took place on Humbert's own death, believed to have occurred in 1056. Aside from his wealth and power, Humbert the Whitehanded left an intellectual legacy gained from his turbulent life experience. It was to steer the family through the centuries, and has been well formulated by Francesco Cognasso, the most sensible of the family's scholarly admirers. He has Humbert's enduring counsel as follows:

> Never ally yourself completely to one side, to one faction, to one policy. Conserve intact, neither taut nor slack, all our bonds of friendship, family ties, and political relationships. Remain faithful to your stipulated word, honestly and scrupulously . . . while at the same time guaranteeing your own complete freedom of thought and action.[7]

This fortune-cookie advice, so often adhered to by the Savoyard generations, is politics in its most vulgar and familiar form. It is also quite suitable for the survival of the less fit in the everlasting wilds of divided mankind.

The three hundred and fifty years from the death of Humbert the Whitehanded to the elevation by imperial edict of Amadeus VIII as the first duke of Savoy (1416) were marked by the slow and steady, tentacular expansion of the dynasty's power.

In exquisite touch with their times, they relaxed their obsolescent feudalism where necessary and transformed themselves into true princes, developing the young and powerful muscles of statecraft. They grew, at the expense of all that encircled them, to hold sway over a million souls. They came down the banks of the rivers, along the roads built by Rome; a few square miles at a time, two steps forward, one back, two forward again. They gained most of Adelaide's Piedmont and extended their rule from Neuchâtel to Nice, from the Rhone to the Po.

They did so behind the shield of the Savoyard black eagle and in a manner worthy of a bird of prey, not excluding the carrion. They had followed the first Humbert's credo well. High in their Alpine nest, they watched the shifting of historic circumstance with an aquiline eye, ever ready to fly with the mighty and devour the moribund. It was an age which knew no peace and they were on everyone's side, opposed to the enemies of all.

Free of the burdens of ideology and convictions, there was little they could not do or profit by. Against the pagans and heretics of the world they hurled the fury of the Church. Against the Church, they brandished the lance of the emperor. Against the emperor they stood behind monarchical power in France. Against the French ruling House of Capet, they backed the Plantagenets of England, and married into the families of both. Here where the empire grew strong, they hailed the emperor and labored quietly for the greatness of the pope. There where the commune began to rise, they offered a friendly hand, and tightened their feudal clasp upon the soil. Sometimes Ghibelline, sometimes Guelph, they were more often both; they changed the eagle for the cross and honed the cross into a sword.

But theirs was not merely a performance in basely exploiting the helpless and the downtrodden; or even in simply benefiting from the inevitable weaknesses of the mighty. It was all that, but something more. Theirs was that painstaking activity of dreaming small, the low art of striking that proper balance, the mundane skill of walking the tightrope of opportunity. Of the many who would seek to define this quality (and among them were multitudes who wished to ennoble such unscrupulousness), the Marquis of San Tommaso, himself a royal minister of Savoy, was to express it best of all in 1726:

> The interests of the House of Savoy are to derive gain from all occasions and to aggrandize itself by all just means; and since it cannot make war on its own, it has no other means than to profit by the conflicts of others, and therein draw its advantages.[8]

In this way, while lesser, younger dynasties who had welded their destinies to a burning cause rushed by them on a path to ephemeral grandeur or the gallows, the leaf-eating, tortoiselike House of Savoy, with irritating sure-footedness, just grew. They went forward writing the motto which so many centuries later would be embraced and vaunted by Queen Margherita: *"Sempre avanti Savoia!"*

The pandering tragedian will find little material in the closets of the House of Savoy. They were, as might be expected of plodders, pious, rough, spartan, ignorant, and dull. The Visconti continuously murdered their enemies by torture and hanging; the Medici poisoned and stabbed; and the popes sent men, women, and children to the stake. The Savoys killed "cleanly," in endless petty wars, and unlike many dynasts they were only infrequent parricides. Their tyrants were few and yet to come. For the most part, they were ordinary men. Their tragedy is mankind's.

Amadeus VIII, the future Pope Felix V, was called "the Peaceful," an appellation he scarcely merited, since a great part of his life, was spent in war or the preparation thereof.

He was the family's first real prince, in the Italian *Quattrocento* sense of the word, devoting much of himself to the business of state-making. This was the age of the petty despots and their bloody struggles for greater masteries in the general decline of feudalism. When Amadeus acceded to the Savoyard throne, at the tender age of eight, the grandest despot of the day, Gian Galeazzo Visconti, ruled neighboring Milan and the vast dominions he had brought together with every conceivable kind of violence. The Savoys were suspicious, if not envious, of the flamboyant and ostentatious family next door. As a boy, Amadeus's person had been zealously protected by a company of master archers, and it was doubtless this precarious general state of affairs which turned him to a life's labor of organizing, modernizing, and fortifying the Savoy domains. In a reign of half a century, he was to lay the foundations of a ponderous bureaucracy, features of which, unhappily, live still in Italy today.

One of the very first things Amadeus set out to do was that which had long been overdue: the formal ennobling of his family. The House of Savoy was already one of the oldest in Europe. Its then living members, however, did not know how old. The vogue was such that all of the princely families were continually searching for glorious ancestors in the ever more distant past. The counts of Geneva claimed descent from the twelve paladins of Charlemagne and the Visconti did not deny extravagant affirmations that theirs was the oldest house because it could easily trace its origins to Aeneas, that heroic son of the goddess Venus.

The Savoys of the twelfth century had by rather dubious means made some efforts in this regard, but these had been completely forgotten. Now they could remember only as far back as Amadeus III, who, according to family tradition, died in 1148, on his way home from the Second Crusade, in which he fought magnificently.* Impressive though this was, it meant nothing to the "ancient" Visconti (whose sovereignty actually went back only to 1277), a family into which the Savoys hoped to marry. The moment Amadeus VIII was made a duke (Gian Galeazzo had been granted that title twenty years earlier), he set himself to the task of enshrining his past and ensuring the sacrosanctity of his posterity. To do this he hired and brought to fame a writer, called Jean d'Orreville, otherwise known as Cabaret. He was retained by Amadeus VIII on February 27, 1417, to *"préparer quelques écritures pour le Duc . . ."* and over the next three years he was given various "advances," as they were called, totaling twenty small-weight florins—a minuscule sum compared with the annual salary of 100 gold florins Amadeus paid his munitions and weapons expert. On completion of his studies Cabaret composed, in an admirably readable style, the following delectable tale:

The founder of the House of Savoy, wrote Cabaret, was not Amadeus III, not even Humbert the Whitehanded. He was instead a valiant knight of more olden times named "Berold." This Berold, "duke of Saxony," was descended from imperial ancestry, Cabaret discovered, and he lived at the court of his uncle, Otto III, an emperor who had succeeded Charlemagne.

One fateful day, good Berold set out on a long journey with the emperor and his party. Several hours after their departure, old Otto was reminded that he had forgot his ring, and as no self-respecting emperor traveled so lightly, he sent Berold back to the imperial palace to retrieve it from its place of safekeeping: under his pillow.

Our hero rode hard and swift all day, and by nightfall he reached the emperor's bedroom, into which he silently stole. Groping in the darkness for the pillow, Cabaret revealed, Berold's hand fell upon a

---

* In truth he did not participate at all in that disastrous and humiliating expedition. He died in Nicosia, Cyprus, on April 1, 1147, on his way to the front, after having pawned much of the family's wealth to help finance the Crusade. (The pawnbrokers of Savoy, by the way, were the local ecclesiastic proprietors.) Most histories, however, continue even today to relate the more generous, medieval version of Amadeus III's death.[9]

sleeping figure. It took no more than the slightest touch to learn that whoever was in the emperor's bed was the owner of a great big beard. Berold demanded that the intruder identify himself, whereupon the empress, who was lying in the very same bed, replied indignantly that her companion was only one of her ladies-in-waiting. But Berold had never met a lady with a beard of quite such dimensions, and he suspected the empress was lying. Indeed he felt he had cause enough to unsheath his sword and run both the empress and her hirsute bed-mate through, which is precisely what he did.

Otto, of course, when he learned of Berold's gallant deed, was exceedingly grateful to his nephew for having defended his honor, and he formally knighted him. But the slain empress's father, a nearby king, sought revenge, and to prevent further bloodshed Berold agreed to go into exile for ten years. The good knight passed the time as a warrior in the service of Christendom and kings, including Boso of Arles, who rewarded Berold's matchless courage with territories in and around Savoy. When the ten years had gone by, Berold wrote to his uncle Otto and told him of his good fortunes. He said he no longer wished to return, and asked for his wife and son, as well as Otto's blessing, all of which were at once forthcoming. Berold, who, said Cabaret, eventually reigned wisely over all of Burgundy, had begat a certain Humbert, who begat a certain Amadeus, who begat another Humbert, known as the Whitehanded.

Cabaret's book was far from being entirely concocted from the *chansons de geste* or the knightly tales which were still popular reading in his time.* In the first place, he had traveled widely in Savoy searching the archives of monasteries and abbeys. In one of them, on Lake Bourget, he had found the bare outlines for his story in a dusty collection of obituary notices. Monks under the tutelage of Humbert III ("the Blessed") had at the request of their Savoyard lord recorded the deaths and deeds of "members" of the family some two hundred and fifty years earlier. First there had been a "Gerard," who had served King Boso, then came a lord of Burgundy, then came *Humbertus blancis manibus* (the first known use of the epithet), who had married an Adelaide (sic) of Italy. These "records" went on voluminously, with the clear purpose of establishing the family's claim in many territories.

Basing his work on the old "documents," Cabaret must have sensed

---

* Some of it, however, probably had precisely such origins. Picardy, from where Cabaret had come, was a leading book center of thirteenth-century Europe. Handmade, illustrated romances—recounting the legends of King Arthur, Sir Lancelot, *et al*—were produced there in abundance.

their true purpose, for, in the second place, his story, on close analysis, reveals the precise political program of his prince-employer Amadeus VIII. Making the worthy Berold a duke of the house of the imperial Ottos not only proved the high origins of the Savoys, but also that Amadeus's ducal title was merely a recognition of rights long possessed and not something newly bestowed, as with the Visconti. As descendants of the emperor (and defenders of royal honor), the Savoys were as noble as the noblest and had to be juridically regarded as such. The history of their past possessions proved their right to expand territorially in almost every direction of the compass, particularly in the old kingdoms of Burgundy and Arles, and in the former marks of Italy—exactly the lands Amadeus wished to annex.

There would be nothing exceptional about the Caberet-Amadeus fabrication were it not for its extraordinarily successful sojourn in the realm of accepted truth. At one time it was considered the only dependable source for serious scholars, many of the most illustrious of whom were continually turning up "corroborative" evidence. Indeed, they were able to trace Berold, who before long had his noble "likeness" struck on the coins of the Savoyard kingdom, back to the Saxon hero Vitikund, archenemy of Charlemagne.

No one believed harder in these "histories" than the rulers of Savoy themselves. The alterations made from time to time—right into the twentieth century—were as attributable to "new findings" as they were to the changing needs of the dynasty's foreign and domestic policies. That this was an odd coincidence was somehow never noticed, and even the enemies of Savoy believed the most up-to-date account, although they often resisted such truth with weapons and unconscionable lies.[10]

To the claustral, reflective Amadeus VIII the family owes not only the immortality of its origins, but also the institutionalization of its princely rule. The latter, from the dynasty's point of view, was the far greater gift. Even at the dawn of the fifteenth century western civilization was entering into the present egalitarian age where it matters less who you were than who you might become; and history knows of no case of either prince or common man becoming something more than he was without mastery of some degree of the social power inherent in his institutions.

Amadeus was no prophet, though. His foresightedness was the result of a workaday assessment of existing social realities, something being undertaken by princes everywhere.

Medieval feudalism was dying; chivalry, as the saying went, was dead. The duke's grandfather, Amadeus VI, the Green Count, could in 1362 still found the Order of the Collar of the Annunziata as an expression of knightly love and devotion to the noblewoman; bearing the motto *fert* ("support"), it represented the collar of a dog and the wearer's slavish loyalty and readiness to support a lady in every distress. But when for reasons of statesmanship Amadeus VIII in 1409 revived the order of the collar (which Mussolini was one day to wear so proudly), no one any longer recalled its meaning. In keeping with the times, the duke gave it a military and religious character, which it was to retain.

Now, for this Amadeus, the knight was but the callous, faithless *condottiero*, and the ties of loyalty were very loose indeed. The emerging society was to find its common bond in the confines of the state.

The Savoyard state, as the supreme social institution of the realm, rose up, as states often do, on the swell of growing and otherwise irrepressible fears. First there was the external threat to the society as a whole—present almost at all times, but now especially great—of being engulfed by "foreign" power. Second was the internal ferment brought on by an irreconcilable contest of antagonisms between the feudal nobility and the mercantile class. Thus, in order that the warring parties might neither devour each other nor be eaten together by someone stronger than both of them, the territories of Savoy, which had hitherto been an agglomeration of baronial manors and towns, after a century of labor gave birth to a full-term state.

On that occasion Amadeus VIII handed down the law—with Mosaic pretensions, five books and all. The law, promulgated in 1430, was called the "Universal Reform of Savoy." It was high-sounding enough, and it replaced all existing law—a mere babel of contradictory customs, mixed and competing jurisdictions, and a means by which the local nobleman extorted money and other things of value from the local poor. But in effect Amadeus's law changed little other than to concentrate judicial power in his own hands and relegate the native Jews, about whom he was "somewhat superstitious," to a ghetto.

Before the universal reform, there was hardly a crime, including murder, which could not be amended in gold florins. Such funds went directly to the judge and the local baron who employed him. Now, however, they went to the officials of the state and to Amadeus of Savoy. For the overwhelming majority, who could not pay, punishment was cruel and usual. Counterfeiters were burned or thrown in boiling oil, thieves were hanged, and convicted Jews were hung by one foot until death. Minor offenses meant a simple fine, but a fine unpaid brought the severance of a hand, an ear, a nose, or all three.

But the young state was less interested in meting out sentences than in acquiring incontestable rule. Thus some offenses were ruled too heinous to be atoned for in cash, as when in 1446 a prominent citizen was thrown into a lake with a heavy weight around his neck—"universal nobility laughing and applauding." He had been charged with intriguing against the state.[11]

The state and its machinelike parts grew. The new evils drove out the old. The people learned with the passage of time that the sum of their private hardships rose and fell at no greater rate than before. Indeed the state was not all gloom. The protection from external intrusion it offered to the people in general, as well as the codification of custom, encouraged domestic prosperity. It did not quite succeed as an arbitrator between classes, but in manifesting its potential power it showed the leading social groups that only in alliance with the state could their position of dominance be secured. As for the dominated, there were philosophers and poets among them who began to see in the concentrated power of the state, if taken captive, a new and effective means of setting the oppressed man free. That freedom, such as it was, would be a long time coming.

The House of Savoy had to wait more than a hundred years for the arrival of its next great founding father: the perfect despot, Emmanuel Philibert the Iron Head.

In the meantime state and dynasty fared poorly, and for a while it seemed all was about to vanish. As a result of neglect of Humbert's credo, due to folly and unbridled avarice, the duchy fell under French hegemony after the Hundred Years' War, and in 1536 France occupied Savoy, Piedmont, and the precious Alpine passes—a dreadful humiliation which held for a generation.

When Emmanuel Philibert ascended the ducal throne in 1553 little remained in his control. Serving as a general in the armies of Spain, however, he defeated the French at Saint Quentin. It was one of those decisive, "brilliant" victories with which the living witnesses like to mark the start of new times; and it brought on the famous peace of Cateau-Cambrésis. The accompanying treaty provided for the restoration of an independent Savoy-Piedmont as a buffer state between France and Spain, created, unfortunately, at the cost of harsh Spanish rule for most of the remaining part of Italy.

The new times were those of absolutism, and Emmanuel Philibert was more absolutist than Hobbes, but hardly a fraction as wise. He found the state in terrible repair: rusty, corroded, and covered with the mold of long-term corruption. Moving the capital to Turin, he scraped, oiled, tightened, fumigated, and remodeled the state apparatus, fashioning a sturdy, showcase monarchy of unrelieved intolerance. He was inexhaustible, and, to many, insufferable. The Venetian ambassador to his court, Francesco Morosini, drew a superbly indulgent and amusing portrait of the fussy duke in a report sent home in 1570 to the *Serenissima*:

> He is a little man of light complexion, blond hair, and his legs are somewhat bowed, but taken together his appearance gives him a graceful, amiable aspect. There is not a single gray hair on either his head or his beard, although he is forty-two years old, having been born in '28 on the eighth of July. His health is excellent, except for a tendency toward depression, and at times he suffers from kidney stones. . . .
>
> From the moment he gets out of bed until he retires, he never sits, save at meal times, and as soon as he fills himself with food he gets up. He transacts his affairs always on his feet, walking in his garden . . . his excellency declaring that it is much better to be in the open air, even in fog, than in one of those rooms [in the palace] where so many people come in and out, filling it up with their breath which is often infected with various maladies. . . .
>
> The Duke of Savoy has a keen understanding of every science, but has not applied himself to the field of letters with the same diligence, which he freely admits to anyone who cares to know, since his principal profession is the craft of making war. . . .[12]

Emmanuel Philibert, who was also an amateur alchemist and a mixer of health potions, gave the dynasty, the state, and the people their first professional army.

Raising a standing infantry of 23,000 men, he armed them with lances and halberds, and an elite few with the latest weapon of war, the musket.

The new army, he told his countrymen in words of a familiar ring, "has to be furnished with every need and prepared for every eventuality. One does not live by chance. In all honesty, only in this way can the peace be best negotiated and war avoided."[13]

After he made the army, he made the navy, the first ministry of war, an extensive system of fortifications, and finally the first police force, a branch of which was charged with breaking up illicit organizations, dispersing public assemblies, and keeping an eye on foreigners. Above all, he forbade politics.

Fearing the spread of Protestantism and all other heresies, he turned education over to the Jesuits, censored the press, and banned all writings contrary to the faith, including the poetry of Ovid. He persecuted native Waldenses and Jews, and would have executed his order for the expulsion of the latter had he not made the tiresome "discovery" that they made excellent bankers and pawnbrokers, and could be mulcted of princely fortunes.

He did "good," too. He limited serfdom, rationalized state finances, legislated in favor of commerce, industry, and mining, and in 1572 sent one of his most prominent Jews on a mission to Constantinople "to obtain the right to trade freely with the Ottoman countries."[14] This final touch of liberalism, which came only months after he had participated in a religious-racist-imperialist war against the Turks, was dipped in irony. Who but the forces of free trade were the bane of the absolutists?

As an autocrat of the early Counter Reformation, Emmanuel Philibert was typical, predictable, and barely more than mediocre. He was single of purpose and plural in his wants. Yet compared with his contemporaries, such as Ivan the Terrible, and the royal massacrers of the Huguenots, he was flexible, malleable, even mild. He mimicked the style of the French, admired the Spanish, and, in spite of the myths, was indifferent to the Italians. He abhorred all that was unconventional, honored everything that appeared durable, and believed in the true divinities, including his own sovereignty.

These were Emmanuel Philibert's contributions to his house. Without them it is difficult to see how the dynasty would have survived the crises of his times. They should be borne in mind by all who wish to know the old secrets of success.

In absolutism lay the glory and the ruin of most of the royal houses of Europe; among the exceptions was the first family of Savoy. They remained absolutist—ambitiously so—until the limits that time would allow, but, being small, whatever inclinations they had for abandon and grandeur were mercilessly crushed by the great powers around them. This was the tempering of their substance, necessary now, for their sons grew restless, weary of the low road.

Charles Emmanuel the Great, Emmanuel Philibert's only son, was impatient in this way, and in his fifty years of rule spoiled much of what his father had built. His greatness was in his extravagant desires, which could not be quenched in either repetitious defeat or grievous discomfiture.

Setting out on wars of conquest, he imposed very heavy taxes on his people, not the least of which had to be paid in blood. He sought to persuade them that their sacrifices were, in the third-person words of his own decree, "for the defense of the state, the person, the wealth, and the *ancient freedoms* of his beloved subjects, for whom he is forced to arm himself anew and go beyond our frontiers risking his own life and lives of our children."[15]

He fought at least as valiantly and as treacherously as his enemies, but he failed in almost every endeavor and in the end he had neither gained nor lost very much, save the hapless armies of the dead, the wreck of the state machine, evil and vice, and poverty so vast that even the House of Savoy was virtually penniless for a while. Their royal robes were shabby and torn, their pockets literally empty. So numerous were Charles Emmanuel's frustrations that he was driven to writing the kind of poetry that burns in the hearts of adolescents. He had tried to make a Savoyard kingdom in northern Italy and when that had been thwarted by superior foreign power, he composed a love song of many verses to the Italians.* This was published and clandestinely distributed throughout the peninsula by his agents, but with little effect. One Italian, surveying the Savoyard prince as a would-be liberator, said at the time: "He returned as he came: beside himself with fervid cravings. He risked much, wanted all, and got nothing."[17]

At the death of Charles Emmanuel in 1630, Savoy became, under Victor Amadeus I and Charles Emmanuel II, a battleground for the continual clashes of arms between Spain and the France of Cardinal Richelieu, and later, a civil war among the people of the duchy themselves. It was not until the close of the century that the Savoyard princes could begin to free themselves from subjugation and every kind of physical and spiritual exhaustion.

---

* A stanza of which read: O, *Italy*, fear not, do not believe/those who say I send warriors to your damage./Your burden is what I desire to relieve/not against you to conspire. *Hope, have courage.*[16]

Yet, though it appeared at the time that they were losing ground, they were instead moving short-leggedly to always greater glories. Their very insistence on their own dynastic survival, in spite of its cost in human suffering, convinced even their enemies that they were not without rights, and their place in the arena of the major struggles of the day assured that they would not be forgotten.

They were to be best remembered in this period for their slaughter of their native Protestants, the Waldenses, under the young Charles Emmanuel II. In a moment of quietude in the Franco-Spanish wars, the Savoyard duke descended on the sect, excusing such conduct by the need to neutralize a threat to his sovereignty. The massacre of the Waldenses, beginning on Easter 1655, aroused the ire of Protestant Europe and stirred Milton to write his sonnet "On the Late Massacre in Piedmont." The Swiss and the Dutch intervened, and in June of that year the Lord Protector Oliver Cromwell led his armies against the duke.

The moment in which Charles Emmanuel II (and his supremely influential mother, Christine) realized he had caused such an international to-do, he yielded easily. The traditional, by now almost instinctive, family aversion to principles of any kind was the one inviolable tenet by which they lived.

Only when Cromwell disappeared and the Catholic James II was on the English throne; only when Louis XIV revoked all that the Protestants had gained, did the House of Savoy, in the person of Charles Emmanuel's son and successor, Victor Amadeus II, pick up the cudgel of religious persecution. But they could arouse in themselves no particular malice. To please France, Victor Amadeus readily expelled the Waldenses from their homes and chased them over the borders of Savoy. To defy France (after joining the new European coalition of powers against Louis XIV), with equal facility, he permitted their return and rendered honor to their name. That only 327 persons of several thousands survived the severities of the forced exodus and the difficult repatriation was a misfortune lamented by all.

The irascible Victor Amadeus II, one-time jailer of the Man in the Iron Mask, ruled for fifty-five years. Sometimes he fought with France; sometimes opposed; and in the War of Spanish Succession, both for and against. Voltaire, in a head-scratching way, made it sound almost virtuous: "Victor Amadeus . . . he would sooner take his own side . . . than break his commitments for his interests."[18]

His dynastic achievements, in the shadow of Louis XIV and the rise of Russian, Prussian, and above all British power in Europe, made all that had gone before him seem but the small parts of a grand design. In 1713, for his valor in the latest war, he was elevated by monarchs greater than he to a throne which bore the long-wished-for title and crown of king.

The gift was only the island kingdom of Sicily, far more distant from Savoy than from North Africa, but a kingdom nonetheless.

Indeed the island proved to be too handsome a prize for its king and the greater powers very soon had second thoughts. During the next war, which followed the last peace by only a few years, Sicily was taken from Victor Amadeus, who was given instead the punier island of Sardinia. This was legitimized in 1720, and for the next one hundred and forty years or so the island, "united" with Savoy and Piedmont, and all the little lands around them, enclosing some 2,500,000 rather ill-cared-for people, were to be universally called simply the Kingdom of Sardinia—an improbable realm whose name alone was cause enough to impel its rulers on to bigger things.

In 1730 Victor Amadeus II abdicated in favor of his son, Charles Emmanuel, leaving the throne to pursue an affair of the heart. Charles Emmanuel III will forever be remembered for his prowess in war and for having coined the aphorism about his family's predilection for eating Italy like an artichoke. His son and successor was Victor Amadeus III.

In the absence of a suitable war, this prince employed the brief respite in undertaking a wide reform of the state institutions, notably the army, which he restyled at backbreaking expense *alla prussiana*. Actually it was his grandfather and namesake who had begun this cycle of reforms, which was aimed at reducing the wickedness of the aristocracy, and raising the restless plebeians from the depths of poverty. A new equilibrium was being sought in order to alleviate internal stresses which were growing rapidly throughout most of Europe and of course especially in France. Now Victor Amadeus III carried on the process to the extent that when Gibbon, who was a far more astute observer of the past than the present, passed through the kingdom in the latter part of the century, he could write, at least of the court, that the Savoyards lived "with decent and splendid economy."

Life at court was said to be simple now—as simple as might be expected from a sovereign served by 330 noblemen and 625 domestics. Meals were spartan. The king took a daily walk through the neatly laid out, lamp-posted streets of Turin. Every Saturday he received a delegation of his humblest subjects. In June, 1775, he went to the opening of Alfieri's first tragedy, "Cleopatra," at the Carignano Theater. At carnival time he threw a masquerade ball and on every Holy Thursday he washed the feet of twelve poor men and gave them some supper money, a family generosity inaugurated by the Green Count in 1353.

All of these niceties and many more, for rich and poor alike, came under supreme threat from the French Revolution. The third Victor Amadeus supported the royalists. He was quick to unleash his Prussianized army on the side of the Austrians against the French republicans, only to suffer bitter and costly defeat at the hands of the young Napoleon. The revolutionaries in 1796 cut Savoy loose from the kingdom of Sardinia and took it for themselves. Victor Amadeus died that year leaving his multiple woes to his firstborn, Charles Emmanuel IV.

This Charles Emmanuel was an unlucky wretch. He took the role of an executioner of revolutionaries and after six dark years abdicated in order to enlist in the Society of Jesus. These were years in which the despised ideas of the Jacobins and their types whipped through Piedmont dazzling the long-pressed populace with all the latest, straight-from-Paris notions of freedom and the "inalienable" Rights of Man. Although it is not often remembered, Charles Emmanuel IV even had to suffer from his more ungrateful subjects a kind of mock war crimes trial in absentia, the likes of which befell no other Savoyard prince past or future. But the record endures.

The burdens, the oppression, and the injustices imposed by the House of Savoy, said the Piedmontese rebels and republicans who were responsible for this document,[19] were too many to be recounted in full. Even gallant, fictitious Berold was singled out and accused of rapine and massacres in Piedmont. The marriage of Turin's own Adelaide into the family had been made under duress, it was said, and Emmanuel Philibert had burned the archives of Turin so that the abolished rights of the Piedmontese, set forth in ancient agreements, would be forgotten.

As this merciless indictment came closer to the living experience of its authors, it came closer to the truth. Their view of the past months, in which Victor Amadeus III had died and Charles Emmanuel IV had acceded to the throne, merits quotation. The late king's exalted wars, they wrote, had caused the "extermination of a hundred thousand men" and had "cost the state seven times more than their worth." But the name of Victor Amadeus III, they said with the overestimation men cede to the present, would be execrated for all time for having turned the people of Piedmont into bloodthirsty barbarians. . . ."

He had therefore ruined the nation, they said, and Charles Emmanuel had already proved his "*mal talento*" with "arbitrary arrests and bloody executions." They concluded, as was the fashion then, with a declaration of independence, somewhat reminiscent of one which enjoyed greater success in that age.

These bold men were forgotten, but their cause would prove mighty and would triumph in the great revolutionary movement, which was now being born everywhere in Italy: the Risorgimento. The New Times were coming hard, and in the vanguard of the victors, standing first among the first, would be the House of Savoy.

The bourgeois, nationalist revolution in Italy, or the Risorgimento, which is a romantic way of putting it in any language, was a long and bloody exercise in class transformation. It was an all-peninsular affair in which the House of Savoy played a leading role and in the process was itself transformed. The Risorgimento was the dynasty's— and Italy's—greatest crossroad on the unlighted path of history.

Some scholars of the period are offended by those who date the beginning of the Risorgimento with the French Revolution. They recall the poetic hopes of Dante and Machiavelli for Italian nationhood. But the truth is that in the two hundred years from the sunset of the Renaissance, which may be conveniently dated with the burning of Giordano Bruno in 1600, until the dawn of the Risorgimento, the Italians lived in a dark age over the Styx, where the idea of national unity was as foreign as their many rulers. The peninsula, as we have glimpsed, was the arena of other peoples' ghastly struggles, in which the Italians were scarcely involved. Whatever loyalties they had were attached to family, Church, and *paese*, a geo-emotional concept which never extended much further than the eye could see.

To be sure, there were glimmers of the new liberalism and nationalism among the people. The Enlightenment beyond the Alps was mighty. But it was not until Napoleon, carrying the new ideas on the shoulders of his invading armies, rammed them straight to the sole of the Italian boot that the giant really stirred.

Napoleon did all kinds of mischief in Italy. First he crushed Charles Emmanuel IV; then he ran the king's brother and successor, Victor Emmanuel I, from the mainland into exile in Sardinia. With fire and blood, Napoleon created small republics from north to south in Italy, including one in Naples and yet one more in Rome, where he arrested and deported the pope.

He absorbed Piedmont, turned some of his republics into kingdoms, and was at times a president, and at others a sovereign with a crown. When the Bourbon-Neapolitan kingdom of the Two Sicilies was restored by the barbarous cardinal-warrior Ruffo,* Napoleon returned to Naples to drive out the Bourbons for a second time and placed his brother Joseph Bonaparte on the throne.

This reel of activity, all of which took place in less than a score of years, in many ways effected as much social change in Italy as had occurred in the last score of centuries. Napoleonic rule, although hated in many quarters and abounding in forces destructive of Italian independence and nationalism, at the same time introduced the mighty principles of the French revolution, which were perfectly attuned to the burgeoning desires of the oppressed bourgeois class. The liberal Code Napoléon, removal of internal customs barriers, road construction, rapid expansion of industry, sudden access to world markets, the breaking of the iron rigidity of the old nobility, centralization and administrative efficiency; in short, the lifting of a half-forgotten, backward people to the breast of the modern world, which held out the promise of untold wealth and power to all, were precious gifts that could never be forsaken.

True enough, when Napoleon fell the Old Order was restored virtually to the last detail and rendered more harsh than ever. But class relationships had been altered irrevocably and a wide sector of the Italian social structure, extending from the middle classes high into the aristocracy and penetrating to the roots of the nascent proletariat, realized for the first time in history what the prize of nationalist unity really meant. *Liberté, égalité, fraternité* were the fine words which spelled opportunity, influence, and riches to the men of the new class; many of them had made fortunes under Napoleon's rule and it would be these very fortunes which would pay for the coming fight for justice and freedom for all—who joined them.

Not that the Risorgimento was without high ideals and untainted,

---

* This was the era of the bestial Fra Diavolo, who fought in Cardinal Ruffo's bandit army of the "Holy Faith," and the renegade Neapolitan Mammone, who liked to drink from a human skull and had a reputation of never eating a meal without a freshly severed head gracing his table.

selfless, heroic men prepared to die for them. On the contrary, they were legion, and even today it tears the heart to relive their early, violent deaths for a cause so soon to reveal itself as having ever been deprived of any meaning in the human sense; men such as Carlo Pisacane, hideously slain by the very peasants he had come to free.

But a core of high ideals and valiant men lives in every generation, drowsing where an equal measure of evil lies. It is only when one or the other quality corresponds to the real needs of the times that they are summoned forth to work their magic on the mind. The Risorgimento was such a moment in history, an epoch in which a society was bursting apart for want of a revolutionary change in social relations among men, something, as we shall see, quite different from their yearning to be free. The Risorgimento, sad to say, was nothing but the advance of the New Oppression.

No one better exemplifies this than the movement's supreme ideologist-activist, Giuseppe Mazzini To his eternal grief, the Apostle, as he is known still, sent more young idealists to a glorious but meaningless death than perhaps any other man in history save Stalin—wrenching his pure heart and soul.

"He and he alone," wrote one of his best and fairest critics, Salvemini, "was responsible for that psychological preparation . . . from which . . . sprang Italian unity."[20]

Further, his influence on everything Italian, at least until the fall of Mussolini and the House of Savoy, was probably greater than any other man's, and as it is necessary for our purposes to examine the nature of the Risorgimento it is imperative to know Mazzini.

Born in 1805 to an upper middle-class Genoese family, he fell under the rule of the Savoys at the age of ten, when Napoleon's defeated Republic of Genoa was acquired by the Kingdom of Sardinia. Mazzini was ignorant of the rest of Italy. He had traveled no farther than Tuscany before going into early and endless exile. He knew nothing of the Italian peasant masses and even less of the aristocracy. In spite of this, or because of it, he did indeed, as he claimed, "translate the thought of the Age." He fought a lifelong battle against the Marxists, but he was a perverse kind of Christian socialist, who believed in to each according to his needs and from each according to his ability, and wished to establish a community on earth of just and moral men inspired by God.

This could only be realized by a family of nations, which he viewed as the highest form of social organization, since people were eternally divided from one another by "natural" frontiers. These obstacles had been drawn on earth by the hand of God, in the rivers, the mountains, and the seas. It was a concept that was self-evidently false, but viewed from the Italian peninsula, which was bounded by the Alps and the waters of the Adriatic and the Mediterranean, it had a ring of truth and gave a new identity to a disparate people.

In truth, the cause of national unity could work no greater wonders than release the material and psychological benefits blocked by national disunity—and then only to a minority. But the Apostle, like all apostles, had a dream, and in order that men might make it true, he did what apostles often do. He called up that age-old abstraction of many names, which, since the time it was employed by the first pharaoh, Menes, who forcibly unified Upper and Lower Egypt, until its latter day use in the glorification of the working classes as the bearers of the new society, has created nothing but the *abattoirs* of mankind.

Preaching that Italian is best and beautiful, he invested his unfortunate people with a Sacred Purpose; the Italians and only the Italians were destined to issue forth a "third world," a "Third Rome." The pagan and Christian worlds, that is, the first and second worlds, which Mazzini saw as having been rendered putrescent by materialism and the papacy, "await a third world, more vast and sublime than the first two, arising on their mighty ruins." He continued:

> And this is the Trinity of History, of which the Word is Rome. Tyrants and false prophets may delay the incarnation of the Word; none can prevent it. Many cities have perished from the earth, all can perish, but Rome; by the design of Providence, divined by the people, Rome is the *Eternal City*. . . . As the *Rome of the Caesars*, which unified much of Europe by Action, gave way to the *Rome of the Popes*, which by Thought unified Europe and America, so will the *Rome of the People* replace the other two, to unify, by the Faith of Thought and Action, Europe, America, and the rest of the terrestial world.[21]

These nationalist dialectics would one day be the cornerstone of Fascist philosophy.[22]

Thousands of young men were slaughtered on the battlefields of the so-called Risorgimento. They helped make Italy, but not the Third Rome of an idealist whose naïveté was unwittingly more cruel than the *Realpolitik* of Bismarck or the ruthlessness of Robespierre. They helped make the Italy that was laboring to be born, a United Italy in the image of the United Kingdom, that free-trading, self-loving, smooth-running, liberal, imperialist, nation-state-machine, which was the paragon of the times. It broke Mazzini's heart, and like all men who give their life to a vain illusion and receive only the possible, he felt betrayed. In the hour of his death he damned the land he loved, and declared it dead. But no one heard, for the drum of Mazzinian nationalism had been taken up in other hands, and it beat louder every day.

The new unity, whatever was to be its vivacity, was an artifact that came from Piedmont and the "old, greedy, timorous ambition of the House of Savoy," as Mazzini called it.[23] But the House of Savoy had first to undergo profound change, of which, to be sure, it was eminently capable.

At the time of Napoleon's fall, when the early hopes for Italian unity were crushed by the emergence of the arch-reactionary Metternich as the Big Man of Europe, few regimes remained as backward-looking, absolutist, and legitimist as the Kingdom of Sardinia of the first Victor Emmanuel. He was a lame-brained figure who bore the aquiline nose of the direct line of his house, which had been passed down through the centuries like a family heirloom. When the Restoration of 1815 returned to Savoyard rule all the lands annexed by Napoleon and more, Victor Emmanuel came back to Piedmont, from seventeen years on primitive Sardinia. He made a tragicomic entry into Turin, wearing clothes two decades out of fashion and ordering all but the calendar returned to 1798.

"The only exception," noted a contemporary aristocrat, "was the taxes, which the French occupation had tripled."[24] The administration was reorganized by the court almanac in use at the time of the king's flight. Hereditary positions were redistributed accordingly, causing some difficulty, as in the case of the former court page boys, who were now in their forties and had to resume their places among children scarcely fifteen years old.

The restored reign of Victor Emmanuel I was an extended effort to trample down the embers of liberalism. This ushered in the era of café conspiracies and secret societies, notably the Carbonari with its oaths, rituals, initiatory chambers, and other spooks, calculated to make the cause of unity and independence at least as awesome, and hence as respectable, as the established social order. Unrest was rife throughout the kingdom, even in the army—a bad sign for any society. The Piedmontese asked not only for liberty, but had specific demands, such as a constitution and a war against the Austrians, who ruled their brother Italians in Milan, Venice, and elsewhere.

In 1821 a military mutiny took place and the rebels seized the citadel of Turin. Rather than grant a single concession Victor Emmanuel abdicated in favor of his manic-depressive brother Charles Felix. Ranting about hangings and shootings, the new king, with the help of a German army, put down the insurgents and lapsed into a cloistral, melancholy existence, during which everyone, including himself, awaited his death. This occurred in 1831, shortly after he had emerged momentarily from his personal darkness to instruct his successor, Charles Albert.* His instructions were: "Hate Austria."[25]

Charles Albert the Magnanimous is Italy's Hamlet. He was torn between a will for national independence and a religious dedication to absolutism and dynastic ambitions. His life was passed swaying from one side to the other, tormented by the mental clanging of sentiment and principle, such as it was. As a youth he had played with the fire of the Carbonari and had even served, treasonously, in Napoleon's imperial dragoons. Yet there were times when he found even Metternich a radical, and he sought to make himself the Don Quixote of legitimism everywhere. Hated by the liberals as a traitor, it was he, however, who began the remaking of Piedmont into a modern state. He introduced liberal reforms, and in 1848 "magnanimously" gave the new class its much longed-for constitution, which in turn made him an anathema to European reaction from Madrid to St. Petersburg. He nevertheless remained a negation of himself to the last, and as such was capable of saying to a nationalist virtually on the eve of proclaiming the constitution, "I, as you do, want the liberation of Italy, and it is for this very reason that I can assure you that I will never give a constitution to my people."[26]

Observing the Italian revolutionary scene, the young Marx and Engels wrote of the king of Sardinia:

Among the indigenous princes, the number one enemy of Italian freedom was and is Charles Albert. The Italians should bear in mind and repeat every hour the old saying: "God watch over my friends, so that I can watch over my enemies!" From Ferdinand of the House of Bourbon, there is nothing to fear; he has for a long time been discredited. Charles

* The gloomy brothers Charles Emmanuel IV, Victor Emmanuel I, and Charles Felix were unable to produce a single male offspring among them, and family rule now passed from the direct to the cadet, Carignano line of the house. Charles Albert was descended from the younger son of Charles Emmanuel I (see Appendix I).

Albert, on the other hand . . . calls himself pompously the "liberator of Italy," while on the very people he is supposed to be liberating he imposes as a condition the yoke of his rule.[27]

This was true. He had taken Charles Felix's advice and hated Austria—but only to the extent that it served the House of Savoy. With characteristic hesitation, he fought the Hapsburgs in the revolutionary year of 1848. He dared to dream of driving them from northern Italy and founding the greatest Italian kingdom the Savoys had ever known, although he never thought of "liberating" the entire peninsula.

When the people of Milan, Venice, and the northern provinces rose up against the Austrians, he posed as the sword of Italian independence. What really moved him, however, was the fear that the neighboring Italians might succeed without the Savoys and establish a republic extending to his front door.[28] He marched east from Piedmont pre-empting the republican threat by absorbing the revolutionaries under his crown. But indecisive men make bad soldiers. The old Austrian veteran Field Marshal Radetzky routed Charles Albert at Custozza and again at Novara, among the most disastrous engagements of the oft-defeated armies of Italy. Radetzky imposed "unacceptable" conditions, which forced Charles Albert to abdicate in favor of his roguish young son, the Duke of Savoy, Victor Emmanuel II.

King Victor Emmanuel found Camillo Cavour, and what followed, the high Risorgimento, is in great measure a monument to Cavour and his singular art of witchcraft as statecraft.

Born in 1810, Cavour was the House of Savoy's greatest servant. He taught the dynasty how the shackles of the past could be cast off and how the immortal principles of the French Revolution, as he called them, might be turned for a handsome profit.

"Free institutions," he instructed, "tend to make people richer."[29]

The New Times were unstoppable, and all power to them. They were, as Cavour knew better than anyone else, the best guarantee of continued class rule. Freedom, believe it or not, was slavery. "You will see, gentlemen," he told a meeting of his less sanguine peers, "how reforms carried out in time, instead of weakening authority, reinforce it; instead of precipitating revolution, they prevent it."[30]

Preaching liberalism and practicing despotism, he presided over and directed the final liquidation of the *ancien régime*. Heartlessly, without the slightest heed to tradition or sentiment, he fashioned the new monarchy, hewed the new state, and installed the new class in the seats of power. In the span of years between the aftermath of the revolutionary events of 1848 and the proclamation of a united Italian nation in 1861, Cavour gathered up and burst a hurricane of human energy, rarely matched in all the turbulence of history. He remade Piedmont into a prototype of a modern welfare-warfare state, turned it loose in every direction, and won the crown of Italy for his master. Then he died.

Yet he cared little about Italian nationalism and even less about Italians in general. He could scarcely speak the language, the French of the court at Turin being his mother tongue, and he was more at home in Paris and London than in Rome. He despised Mazzini, had no faith in the moral "mission" of his people, and believed to the last that the political unification of Italy was, in the words of his fellow Piedmontese aristocrat Cesare Balbo, "a puerile idea, held at the most by pettifogging students of rhetoric, common rhymesters and café politicians."[31]

His deepest concern was the fabrication of a prosperous, flourishing, powerful, expansionist Piedmont. His highest aim was to win the long-sought prize of Milan and Venice for the House of Savoy. Such greatness could only be achieved, he never ceased to argue, by imposing all the latest ideas of freedom.

Thus, while others, including the House of Savoy, were preoccupied with the republican revolutionary threat, Cavour was able to go about his self-given tasks in relative transquillity. These activities, as Victor Emmanuel II's prime minister, consisted of effecting in Piedmont the very material and administrative changes which Mazzini found so needed everywhere in Italy. At the same time he undertook that which seems always to step lively with the march of progress: preparing the nation for war.

The war came in 1859. Cavour had been among the first to realize that the greater Piedmont created by Metternich in 1815 as a buffer between Austria and France stood more to gain from an aggressive foreign policy than from one which pursued the cause of peace. As long as Piedmont made Austria her natural enemy, she could count not only on the support of the Italians under Hapsburg rule, but, more important, on the other great powers. They believed the Austrian empire already too big for a properly balanced "Concert of Europe," as they liked to think of it. When France re-emerged as a big power under Louis Napoleon, Cavour thought the time had come for a Piedmontese-inspired, Italian war of "independence" against Austria, with the French doing most of the fighting.

He showed Napoleon III why it would be proper for France to attack Austria: in order to drive out the Hapsburgs and establish a north Italian kingdom ruled from Turin and friendly to Paris. The emperor hesitated. Cavour offered him Nice and even Savoy, and later his king's own daughter as a bride for Napoleon's nephew Jerome. The emperor could no longer resist. Victor Emmanuel was heartbroken at the thought of losing ancient and precious Savoy (which contained his best hunting grounds), but he was selfless nonetheless. "Kekina," fifteen years old, was too. Unwillingly, but epically, she surrendered her heart to Prince Napoleon, "true to the sense of duty which stamped the House of Savoy," said Cavour.[32]

On January 1, 1859, Napoleon made his famous remark about how sorry he was that his relations with Austria were "not so good," which caused the stock markets of Europe to slump and the Hapsburgs to shake. Victor Emmanuel publicly lamented that he could no longer remain insensitive to the cries for help raised by his brother Italians under Austrian tyranny. Then Cavour sent an unacceptable ultimatum to Vienna, and the war was on.

Old Radetzky had died carrying the Austrian military star with him to the grave. The French moved into Lombardy, and early in June Victor Emmanuel, with Napoleon at his side, entered Milan, taking the city which had been coveted by the House of Savoy since the time of Adelaide.* Austria still held Venice, but Piedmont swiftly annexed the lesser Italian states of Parma, Modena, and Tuscany, as well as the province of Romagna, which had during the war broken away from the papal fiefs.

These rapid changes excited the activity of the Mazzinians and all the nationalist revolutionaries throughout Italy. Mazzini himself would have nothing to do with what he called Cavour's "treasonous"

---

* It was not all glory. Covering the peace conference at Villafranca, the correspondent of the *New York Tribune*, Karl Marx, wrote on August 4, 1859: "There was a war between a Hapsburg and a Bonaparte. It was not an Italian war. Victor Emmanuel was only an instrument and is therefore being excluded. . . . He is not even receiving the honors conceded to the German prince in the peace of 1815; just a poor relative who is being permitted to devour in silence the crumbs that fall from the table of his rich and powerful cousin. Italian independence has been transformed into the dependence of Lombardy on Piedmont and the dependence of Piedmont on France. . . . The king of Sardinia has concluded a dynastic affair. . . ."[33]

aggrandizement of the House of Savoy, but most of his followers, anxious for cathartic victories of any kind, left his side and gathered around the handsome figure of Garibaldi. He too had forsaken the lead of the Apostle, but not his slavish devotion to the Mazzinian ideal of Italian unity.

Garibaldi and his "Thousand" remained mesmerized by the rhetoric of the Third Rome. They conceded, however, that only under Victor Emmanuel could the goal be reached, and in the fever of recent events they could scarcely contain themselves for another day. Their brethren in Sicily were rising up against Bourbon rule and on May 5, 1860, driven to hysterical ecstasies by the blood and thunder of idealist nationalism, they set sail under a starry sky to free them. ("Oh, night of the fifth of May," Garibaldi was to sing, "lit up with the fire of a thousand lamps with which the Omnipotent has adorned the Infinite. Beautiful, tranquil, solemn with that solemnity which swells the hearts of generous men when they go forth to free the slave. Such were the Thousand . . . and I, proud of their trust in me, felt myself capable of attempting anything.")[34]

While Cavour disapproved of the expedition and did all that was politically possible to prevent it, Victor Emmanuel was secretly working with the already legendary adventurer. The king was anxious to aid Garibaldi and his revolutionaries, who were fighting under the motto "Italy and Victor Emmanuel," although he was equally prepared to disown them should they fail. But the Thousand succeeded overwhelmingly, driving the Bourbons not only from Sicily but also from their throne in Naples. Garibaldi proclaimed himself *duce* of the conquered territories and assumed dictatorial rule. In spite of his professed loyalties to the House of Savoy there were doubts for a while as to whether he would surrender his own rule to his king. When it seemed he might march right on to papal Rome, the greatest prize of all to the nationalists, the king moved down from the north. Both he and Cavour feared that the revolutionaries might take everything. Leading the Piedmont armies in a blitzkrieg, Victor Emmanuel invaded and annexed the papal states of the Marches and Umbria. He marched on, well to the east of Rome, an assault on which was fraught with the dangers of foreign intervention. Then he crossed the Abruzzi to link up with (and neutralize) Garibaldi and his Thousand at Teano, on the outskirts of Naples.

The meeting of monarch and revolutionary at Teano was one of those unforgettable moments in history upon which anonymous Italian artists used to thrive, depicting the stuff of prints that hung on the walls of barber shops and pizza parlors for a hundred years.

All the trial and error, all the misdeeds, the guns, and the blood since the English and French revolutions spread their messages of freedom and free trade to the oppressed bourgeois classes in Italy, found their symbol in that encounter of October 26, 1860, between the man who wanted Italy and the man who had it to give away. Until then the tall question—whether Garibaldi, the old Mazzinian republican, would obey the will of the monarchy—frightened the king and even Cavour. Cavour never trusted Garibaldi. But Garibaldi trusted Cavour, and at Teano, where the red-shirted knight did obeisance to his prince, he gave all, asking for nothing.

There have been many accounts of that event at a crossroads due north of Naples, most of them painted in the colors of the flag. Perhaps the following eyewitness report is best, if only for its honesty:

> Garibaldi arrived first.
> The king, in a general's uniform, wearing a beret, was riding a grey Arab and was followed by a line of generals, chamberlains, and servants.
> . . . Everyone approached Garibaldi, that plebeian giver of kingdoms. . . .
> The king extended his hand, saying, "Greetings, my dear Garibaldi. How are you?"
> Garibaldi: "Fine, your majesty, and you?"
> The king: "Great!"

Here was the moment, it seemed to many who were then alive, for which the thousand-year struggle of the House of Savoy had been endured. Papal Rome was still under the protection of the French, and Venice remained in Austria's grip, but this was an age in which men could believe in Destiny, in preordained greatness written in a Book. A vast kingdom of twenty-two million Italians had been won. A single flag unfurled from the foothills of the Alps to the shores of North Africa, and such was the thrust of the times that the whole world knew that Rome and Venice could not hold out for long.

That Italy which had been shattered and plundered by the Vandals and the Goths; held asunder by the emperors and the popes; deflowered and enfeebled by the *condottieri* and their lords; mangled by princes and prophets, by war, by peace, and even by nature; that Italy was now to be joined together in Victor Emmanuel's hands. People and governments, from elegant St. Petersburg to gold-crazed California rejoiced.

The eyewitness describes that historic, memorable moment:

> Victor Emmanuel, stepping aside so that the troops might pass, talked for a while with the general [Garibaldi]. I placed myself inconspicuously near the two of them, seeking to hear for the first time how kings really

speak, to verify whether their high rank corresponds with the heights of brilliance and thought. The situation was epic . . . with images of the consuls of Rome, of Hannibal . . . of a prince receiver and a common man, donor of the crown; the transformation of a petty ruler into the king of Italy.

His majesty discoursed on the fine weather and the bad roads, interspersing these observations with raucous admonitions to his restless, noble charger. Then they moved on.

They mounted their horses and rode off, the motley red-shirts coming up behind Garibaldi and the splendidly outfitted Piedmont regulars following their king. The peasants came out to acclaim them, although they had barely an inkling of who they might be. They had heard of a soldier "Galibardo," and they applauded the troops, hailing, "Long live Galibardo!" The disillusioned eyewitness continues:

> Garibaldi tried to divert that applause to the king . . . "Here is Victor Emmanuel, the king, our king, the king of Italy. Long may *he* live!"
>
> The peasants grew still and listened, but they could not understand all that and began again the chants, "Long live Galibardo!"
>
> It was torture for the general. He sweated blood, knowing how much the prince loved ovations and how his own popularity had always irritated him. He would have gladly given him a second kingdom if he could only snatch from the lips of those apolitical rustics a "Long live the king of Italy!" or even a simple "Long live the king!" But the difficulty quickly disappeared because Victor Emmanuel put his horse at a gallop.[35]

The triumphant entry into Naples some days later was no better. There were terrible winds and a torrential downpour which ruined the specially constructed arches and allegorical decorations. The rain pelted the procession so hard that ink-blue drops ran from Victor Emmanuel's dyed hair, mustaches, and beard, ruining his uniform. The *lazzaroni* who lined the Via Roma had been coached to shout, "Long live the king and the constitution!" Instead, without malice but in simple ignorance, they cried, "Long live the king and his uniform!"*

---

* The Risorgimento never reached the common people. Even Garibaldi, who was supposed to be the incarnation of the masses in a single, glorious soul, knew which side his Risorgimento was buttered on. When he had landed in Sicily, he appealed for the support of the peasants, who were rioting against the hated Old Order. He decreed that the land would be given to the people and food would be cheap and abundant for all. But when the Bourbons fled he discovered that only the owners of property had a stake in restoring law and order, in political stability as he knew it. He turned to them and in exchange for their backing he carried out their demands, rounding up the "communists" and shooting them in an open field.[36]

In the Palazzo Reale at Turin, Victor Emmanuel, on February 18, 1861, assembled a collection of men of appropriate mind, rank, and character from the newly subject Italian states. They mingled around him in the oblong Sala del Trono, scuffing the highly polished, squeaky parquet floors, which had been laid at the command of his forefathers. The king of Sardinia took his place on the squat, parlor-chair throne and proposed himself "King of Italy," a title to be passed on to eternity through his legitimate descendants. The protests of the princes he had dispossessed, and of those he intended to deal with in a like manner—that is, the emperor of Austria and the pope himself—did nothing to alter his inclinations.

There being no other audible objections, the king's proposal was soon afterward confirmed by the Sardinian parliament. At that time, however, he agreed that the foundation of his power was not only by the grace of God, but also "by the will of the nation." This was a universally deplorable and fatal concession from the point of view of kingship, weakening the institution of Divine Right everywhere. But it was also the necessary recognition of the arrival of the liberal ethic, and Victor Emmanuel assuaged his personal lamentations by spitefully refusing to tamper with the dynastic enumeration of his name. Speaking firmly and in the royal third person he declared of himself that "he absolutely insists on being called Victor Emmanuel *the second* and not *the first*, because it seems to him that if he were to assume the latter title, he would commit an ingratitude toward his glorious ancestors, who with their wisdom and their sword prepared from afar the very crown which today encircles his head."[37] It was a poor argument, which was to come under endless criticism by those who were to say that the House of Savoy was more interested in its long buried relatives than in the Italians. But so it was.

In any event it was one thing to rejoin in pomp and legal fittings the pieces of conquered Italy and quite another to hold them together. All kinds of rope and glue would be needed.

Cavour and his bunch now proceeded with the forced Piedmontization of the united peninsula. They strapped to the Italian boot the entire collection of institutions which had accumulated in the cellars, attics, and salons of the House of Savoy since the time of Humbert the Whitehanded, junking nothing that was still being used. It was in this way that the new Italy acquired the first Humbert's foreign policy, Charles Albert's constitution, the Green Count's Collar of the Annunziata, Amadeus VIII's conscript army, Emmanuel Philibert's Church-dominated school system, and weightiest of all, Victor Amadeus II's czarist-style bureaucracy, with its tax stamps, rubber stamps, seals and counterseals, and the infernal paper buffer between government and people which remains extant today, known then and now as the *carta bollata.*

The effect of all this on much of the non-Piedmont part of Italy, and particularly on the south, was disastrous. The liberated peoples of the former Kingdom of Naples and Sicily suffered most of all, far more so than under the corrupt and degenerate Bourbons. Unheard-of taxes were slapped down on the peasants, while the application of free-trade dogma depressed the price value of their products. Worse, the entire ecology of the south was rudely disturbed and permanently damaged when the new regime permitted the deforestation and savage exploitation of the vast estates seized from the Church and the princes of the annexed territories. To acquire both financial and political capital, these lands were given away as patronage or sold cheaply to speculators.

The *Mezzogiorno* was, in fact, turned into a classic nineteenth-century colony. The blind extraction of raw materials and cheap labor in order to promote the rapid industrialization of the north was the principal feature of the first period following unification.

Such conditions helped to bring on a north-south civil war. It coincided with the years in which the American civil war was fought and in some ways was affected by it.* Turin called the reaction in the south treason against the Italian union and set its armies against the rebels. In reality it was a counterrevolution of monks and bandits, organized by the papacy, the cast-out Bourbon king, and his cantankerous entourage of royal émigrés, senile generals, and former policemen now down and out in Rome. Needless to say, their efforts were in vain, in spite of the considerable support received from the southern peasants who saw in the ignoble rebels and brigands the only means of protest against the new misery. The government was determined to pacify what Cavour called "the most corrupt part of Italy."[38] It was thus a pacification prosecuted with unmeasured brutality, and as Denis Mack Smith has pointed out, "More people perished in it than were killed in all the other wars of the Risorgimento put together."[39]

---

* Cotton and cotton-related industries in the Italian north were depressed when their American-supplied raw materials were suddenly cut off. This in turn created additional exploitative pressure on the Mezzogiorno and internal enmities.

In the meantime Cavour died and Victor Emmanuel II took up added responsibilities, particularly in readying his family and his nation for the next war. There was little doubt as to what that might be. The winning of Rome and Venice was a historical imperative— although Cavour before dying had delusions of allying with the United States in the conquest of Great Britain. The king himself had visions of dynastic possession of the thrones of Portugal and Greece, but the insistence of his subjects, above all Mazzini and Garibaldi, turned his attentions toward Venetia.

An opportunity arose during the Austro-Prussian War of 1866. Italy sent army and navy into battle on the side of Bismarck, which Victor Emmanuel claimed was the side of justice, order, and civilization. Austria had been willing to surrender Venetia peacefully if the Italians had remained neutral. But the king's government refused. It was searching for a great victory to patriotize its factious population and show the world the timber of the new Italy.

Victor Emmanuel and his sons, Humbert and Amadeus, took the field at the head of the royal troops. "I have no other ambition than to be the first soldier of Italian independence," he had said in the last war against Austria, and now he repeated his commitment ("I *still* want to be the first soldier . . .").[40] The king, however, like his father and his sons, was a bad soldier, or at least a bad first soldier. His generals, particularly his prime minister, General Lamarmora, tried to convince him to remain at home rather than risk his royal life. But Victor Emmanuel was fearless.

The army was routed—at Custozza again—by half as many Austrian troops, and the navy was defeated in the waters of Lissa by half as many Austrian ships. But Italy won Venetia, that is, Bismarck did and allowed the "crumb" to fall from the peace table to the omnivorous House of Savoy.

After Venice it seemed that only a march on Rome could redeem the national honor. The aging Garibaldi, almost as embittered as Mazzini, called up his red-shirt volunteers, led them to the papal frontier, and incited the Romans to insurrection. Victor Emmanuel, although pledged to France to protect the pope's territory, did little to stop Garibaldi. Greedily, he nourished the secret hope that the irregulars would repeat their Sicilian success. Garibaldi advanced, but the Romans failed to rise and the French easily overpowered the red-shirts, which sent Victor Emmanuel rushing artlessly to proclaim France his true friend and Garibaldi an outlaw.

In 1870 the outbreak of the Franco-Prussian War between the House of Hohenzollern and the Second Empire of Napoleon III brightened the prospects of ambitious men. Italians of such genre were hesitant at first about which position to take, since it was not immediately apparent how best to profit from this misfortune. But soon enough it became clear that France was going to lose and everyone knew that the turn of Rome had come.

In August the French withdrew their much needed troops from the Holy City, removing the pope's sole protection. At the beginning of September came the news of the German victory at Sedan, where 20,000 Frenchmen were killed in about twenty-four hours (as well as 7,000 Germans), and Napoleon himself was taken prisoner by the Prussian king. Victor Emmanuel sent an aide to Paris to rescue his daughter "Kekina," and as soon as his ministers were certain that France could not get up again they dispatched their troops against the tiny papal army.

Once again the Romans did not rally to the new freedom, and the pope's forces put up spunky resistance, suffering less than half as many losses as the Italians: nineteen Swiss Guards to forty-nine nationalists.

On September 20, Rome and all the earthly powers of the Roman Church fell to Victor Emmanuel of Savoy and his liberation army, which was welcomed at the gates of the city by about twenty newly emancipated souls.

A few weeks later a plebiscite was held to show the world that the Romans really wanted to be free and part of "Italy one and indivisible." There had been plebiscites in all of the annexed territories and they had always approved of the new order by an invariable majority of 99 percent. This was because the plebiscites were fraudulent. They fooled none but the dimmest wit, and least of all the voters. They were often led to the polls under duress, and more often were unaware of what they were electing. Thus the Romans, too, approved—by 99 percent.

Few people celebrated; there was instead a great deal of discomfiture and an awful feeling of anticlimax. Melancholia overtook the nation which had dreamed so boundlessly of greatness. The "heroic" period, as Vico had taught, was over, and where there had been "poetry" there would now and forever be only prose. Many, Croce has written, felt that the best years of their lives had passed and that Italy had suddenly grown old before ever having been young.

The hundred-year war of the Risorgimento was over and there

had been not a moment of glory, as it was known then. Not a single great unifying action had occurred, other than the forced imposition of Savoyard rule. The nation had been made by its own defeats and the fortunes of foreign powers, and there were still large numbers of people in the peninsula who did not know the meaning of the word *Italia*, while others thought it the name of the king's wife. Mazzini declared in utter disgust: "I had thought to evoke the soul of Italy, but all I find before me is its corpse."[41]

That Italians and others thought that the manner in which the unity had been accomplished was in some way shameful would urge the new state into a blind pursuit of pride and conquest, and ultimately, as will be seen, turn it straight on the road to fascism.

In the meantime, someone, in spite of the lack of general enthusiasm, had to toast the triumph of the Risorgimento, and of course it fell to King Victor Emmanuel II. He declared shortly after the Roman plebiscite:

> At last the arduous work is done. The word *Rome*, the greatest sound on the lips of man, is today rejoined with that of *Italy*, the word dearest to my heart. The decision of the plebiscite, pronounced with such marvelous concord by the people of Rome and received with joyful unanimity by all . . . shows once again that if we owe not a little to good fortune we owe very much more to the evident justice of our cause. The free consent of the people; the sincere exchange of faith and promises; these, in my opinion, are the powers which made Italy, and which have brought it to fulfillment.
>
> Now the Italians are truly the masters of their own destiny. As they, after a dispersion of so many centuries, gather in the city that was once the capital of the world, they will, without doubt, know how to draw from the vestiges of the ancient greatness the auspices of a new and real greatness.[42]

The Third Rome had arisen, erected by the dullards and servants of the House of Savoy. Herein—if there can be a beginning other than the very beginning—their fall commences.

PART II

Humbert and Margherita (1878-1900)

HUMBERT: I feel in my breast a heart which beats in unison with my people's.[1]

MARGHERITA: The King *has many fine qualities* and . . . in the course of time he will acquire even greater confidence in his own opinions, which are always exceedingly fair.[2]

HUMBERT: [I am] convinced that my reign is founded on the love of the people.[3]

MARGHERITA: The people are good; a pity the politically minded take the limelight, intrude everywhere, foul everything, and discredit the country, which has many good and vital forces![4]

HUMBERT: Upon me shines the ambition to unite my name with the economic and intellectual revival of the land.[5]

MARGHERITA: We must put a stop to the encroaching hordes who want to have their share of the wealth of this world . . . without paying mind to the havoc and violence they incur in obtaining it.[6]

HUMBERT: The Italian monarchy welcomes every reform intended for the good of the people, whose love is the base of the throne.[7]

MARGHERITA: They killed you, you who so loved our people! You were so good; you brought harm to no one and they killed you! This is the crime of the century![8]

1

A FUNERAL IN ROME

FOR THOSE WHO FEARED FOR THE SAVOYARD MONARCHY AND JERRYBUILT UNIFIED ITALY, THE death of Victor Emmanuel II in 1878 was a particularly terrible blow, and so the mourning would have to be especially hard. When a king dies, the enemies within and outside tighten down on the established order, and the men who loved him and what he stood for feel lost and under siege. That is why when a king dies he is a long time being buried. The solemnities, the funeral, and the period of national bereavement are the elements of the moratorium during which the men of state recover their balance and face their foes with the old equanimity.

Thirty-three-year-old Humbert, who had never really believed he would one day be king, was in a state of shock, and it fell to the government of the party in power, the ministry of the so-called left, to dress the nation in black. The one man who did most of the work was Minister of the Interior Francesco Crispi, the turncoat republican who was to make most of Italy's tragic *fin de siècle* history. Rules for disposing of the royal dead had been decreed by Charles Albert in 1832, but Crispi took scarce note of them. When the monarch exhaled his last breath the minister rushed from the room and made one of those tidy statements to the press which read as if nothing at all has happened and every child is well tucked in his bed. The king had not even really died, according to Crispi; he had only "ceased to live today at 2:30 in the afternoon"—but not before "receiving the comforts of religion." The throne had not for a moment been empty, for his "august Son" had quickly ascended, while simultaneously reconfirming in office all the current ministers.

43

In the next moment, Crispi convinced the tremulous Humbert to call himself the "First" and not Humbert IV, which according to family tradition he should have been.* Crispi then drew up Humbert I's maiden proclamation, issued that same day, in which the following words were made to utter from the new king's mustachio-covered lips:

> Italians, the greatest misfortune has unexpectedly struck us. Victor Emmanuel II, founder of the Kingdom of Italy, establisher of national unity, has been taken away. I have heard his last words and his last wish. They were for the nation and for the happiness of his people, to whom he gave both freedom and glory. His paternal voice imposes upon me the necessity to overcome my suffering and shows me where my duty lies. . . .
>
> I will guard the heritage he has left me: devotion to the fatherland, an active love of progress, and an unshakable faith in those free institutions which were granted by my August Grandfather King Charles Albert and religiously defended and expanded by my Father, and which are the pride and strength of my House. As a soldier like them in the struggle for national independence, I will be its most vigilant defender. To merit the love of my people, in the manner of my August Parent, will be my only ambition.
>
> Italians! Your first King is dead; his successor will prove to you that your institutions will not die. . . .[2]

The institutions ground on. Those who controlled them used them now like artillery in order to provide safe passage for the state in this period of transition. The press was fielded like infantry, consciously dispensing myths between such lines as these: "In the great palaces of the city and in the humblest hovels people everywhere are recounting the heroic deeds and the sublime virtues of the *Re Galantuomo*."[3]

People *were* genuinely moved by Victor Emmanuel's death. As the news spread, shops, restaurants, and cafés closed their doors spontaneously, and between 6:30 and 7:30 that evening the eighty telegraph messengers of Rome delivered more than 5,000 telegrams to the Quirinal. But few adult Italians harbored more than the usual

---

* Crispi had been outspoken in opposing Victor Emmanuel II's decision against calling himself the "First." On that occasion, Crispi, the "dangerous" Mazzinian and Garibaldi's former secretary, had been more monarchist than the monarch. Victor Emmanuel, he had declared, had nothing in common with the old counts of Savoy or the kings of absolutist Sardinia. "The monarchy which you have founded," he told the sovereign, "has no precedent in history; it has its genesis in the revolution. . . ." Victor Emmanuel knew better.[1]

illusions about their king, likable scoundrel that he was.* The myths were for what others thought and the generations yet to come.

As the funeral arrangements were being made, the people were spared nothing except the word *death*.

"The King has not yet been moved from the room and from the bed in which he expired," wrote the conservative Rome daily *Opinione* two days after the event. "He lies with his face turned slightly to the left. His eyes are closed and his appearance, maintaining a certain look of pride, has taken on an aspect of calm, which is enhanced by the natural pallidness. . . . At seven o'clock this evening the embalming of the royal corpse will begin. We have learned that it will be effected with a new process which assures the conservation of the body for a very long time. We cannot as yet give the details of this process, but we can state confidently that the mortal remains and the appearance of our beloved sovereign will be conserved for the benefit of posterity**. . . . After the preparation of the cadaver, it will be dressed in the uniform of a general."[5]

In the meantime a three-way fight over the body broke out in public. The city fathers of Turin wanted Victor Emmanuel to be buried at Superga, the magnificent mountaintop tomb of the Savoys situated just outside the Piedmontese capital. The government, which was itself divided on where to deposit the defunct king, would have nothing of it. The ministers of the left, who in the case of poor Garibaldi were to show what they really thought about the dead,† were decided that Victor Emmanuel had to stay in Rome in order that his bones might serve as the eternal cornerstone of the new state; but they were not of one mind as to where to break ground.

Crispi insisted on the Pantheon and others, who thought that a "pagan idea," wanted a basilica. "Remember," said Cesare Correnti, a powerful voice on the left, "the prelates know how to handle these

---

* Most would have agreed with the London *Times,* which wrote then: "Victor Emmanuel was the man in whom Italy had the greatest trust. The nation was not unaware of his private errors and did not attribute to him the genius of his great ministers. His prestige did not stem from an exaggeration of his qualities. It was based on the secure knowledge that at all costs he would be faithful to Italy . . ."[4]

** The "process" turned out to be singularly inefficient, leading to the unusually early onset of decomposition.

† Garibaldi had made elaborate arrangements to assure his simple cremation (on a pile of aromatic woods) and the burial of a fistful of his ashes "in any urn whatever" beside his two daughters who had died in childhood. But by the time the old warrior succumbed, in 1882, the government, which consisted of many ex-Garibaldian radicals, had grown too respectable for such sentimentality. A more conventional burial of the body intact, under an appropriate national monument, was deemed politically necessary, and done.

things best of all. These solemnities, if they do not address the heart and the senses, turn out to be a vulgarity and a joke." The pope, however, would not concede access to his basilicas (although he offered any ordinary church, which was considered as auguring well for future Church-state relations), and Crispi won. Turin staged a riot, but the royal troops were sent in to crush it, and the matter was brought to a close.[6]

On January 16, a full week after his death, the mortal remains of Victor Emmanuel II still lay exposed in a general's uniform waiting for interment. Stanley, the American who found Livingstone, had passed through Rome (he was given a banquet and a picture of Humbert I) and the Russo-Turkish war had replaced the home news on the front pages, but the late king was in no danger of being forgotten.

Rome had got over the shock of the king's demise, and now the city, brimming with tourists and foreign and domestic dignitaries of the first order, was full of not entirely unhappy excitement in anticipation of the royal funeral, to take place on the following day. "The crowds grow larger by the hour," Count Guiccioli wrote in his diary. "You see people everywhere with luggage in their hands, unable to find lodging."[7] The first, second, and third class *trattorie* had been bared to the cupboards, and people in all those classes of restaurants were seen eating salami and cheese bought by their owners in nearby grocery stores. The souvenir sellers did a thriving business, the museums were packed, and one enterprising printer ran an eighth of a page advertisement announcing the availability of a "beautiful portrait" of Victor Emmanuel II, cheap.

A panoply of European royalty had come, too. The queen of Portugal, Victor Emmanuel's youngest daughter, arrived with her son, the crown prince, who was dressed in the uniform of a hussar. Amadeus of Savoy, the former king of Spain and the departed king's second legitimate son, had been among the early arrivals, as had the Archduke Ranier of Hapsburg. It was the sign of the times, however, that the greatest attention and awe were given the representative of the House of Hohenzollern, the heir apparent, Imperial Prince Fredrick Wilhelm. His appearance was regarded by the grateful Italian leaders as a token of the greatest respect and that the mighty Italophobe Bismarck was not without a soft spot in his iron heart. The prince was met at the station by an embarrassingly large delegation of fawning politicians, many of whom, it has been reliably recorded, lost their ability in the presence of the German lord to straighten the column of their backs. These were uncertain men and only a true aristocrat like Guiccioli could say, "I see no need in taking so servile an attitude toward the foreign prince; but in Italy this is not understood. One must have lived abroad to understand what is said about us there. . . ."[8]

On the day of the funeral there was greater reserve. The weather may have had something to do with it. The sky was painted in a dark monotonous shade of gray, and a humid wind blew steadily from the north. It was a good day to entomb a king. From very early in the morning—as soon as the newspapers came out with a diagram of the route the royal cortege would follow—the proper streets were crowded with people in black; straining necks turned in a single direction.

Yet the government was unsure of its people, afraid of an embarrassing outbreak of disorders before the full view of its distinguished foreign guests. By eight o'clock that morning the crowd of onlookers (numbering about 100,000) had been quietly surrounded by a large contingent of royal troops in ceremonial blues, but armed nonetheless.

The men and women who were to march or ride in the cortege assembled in the main halls of the Quirinal at nine. Crispi, assisted by Correnti, was busy assuring that everyone was in his proper place. Correnti, who had worried about the danger of the funeral turning out to be "a joke," cut a most ludicrous figure when he took his self-given position in line. Holding aloft the iron crown of Monza—a sacred religious relic—on a red cushion, the well-known former atheist, Freemason, and outspoken republican led the clerical section of the column, and followed directly behind the carriage containing the body of the monarch. That he could do so was meant to be a sign to foreign and domestic spectators alike that the nation was terribly united.

At ten o'clock a starting cannon shot was heard throughout the city and the procession began to move. A cavalry regiment in a column of fours led the somber march past the statues of the Four Horsemen and down the incline that bends away from the great piazza of the Quirinal. There were some shuffling and disorganization at first, but before long everyone—man and horse—stepped well, forming an imposing spectacle before the waiting citizens of Rome.

The magistrates wore togas of black velvet, the ministers, deputies, and senators wore stovepipes and tails, and the foreign nobility wore well-stitched uniforms with buttons of gold and sashes of colored silks, purples and reds which spoke a silent language now forgotten. The gilded hearse was drawn by eight white horses draped in black and harnessed in leather and bronze. Black and white panaches fluttered on their heads and every horse had a footman in mourning clothes to guide it along the way. The carriage wheels rumbled on the cobbles, jostling the fine coffin, but this could scarcely be observed, for the hearse was covered with wreaths of myrtle and cypress leaves which were themselves becoming hidden under the rain of flowers descending from the hands of people on the roofs of the funeral route.

Victor Emmanuel's first aide-de-camp, mounted on horseback, led the hearse. He carried his master's unsheathed sword erect and point down in the saddle. Beside him, the saddle sadly empty, moved the dead king's famous war horse, his sturdy gray Arab, now grown old. The flags of the many wars in which the monarch and his charger had fought stiffened in the wind. The people stared in silent and respectful awe. Above all, their leaders noted, they were orderly.

"The crowd was immense; order perfect," Count Guiccioli wrote that evening, after having marched in the cortege. "The entire solemn ceremony could not have gone better. Neither could the behavior of the crowd have been more perfect."

> Rome [he went on] has given Italy the best proof that it truly knows how to carry out its mission. And Italy has shown the world that it is a serious country, whose institutions have their most solid foundations in the links which unite the Dynasty with the people. All this proves once again how the Monarchy makes it possible for the nation to proceed sure-footedly and smoothly along the road to progress. (I have written a banal sentence . . . but the thought is right.) In Italy the monarchical regime is the best guarantee of our future.[9]

By dusk the funeral was over, the crowds broke up, and the sky, too, suddenly cleared. Romans still milled around the Pantheon and although during the night the coffin would be moved to a room-sized vault inside, there was nothing further to be seen. Many visitors, hoping for an early start, were already leaving the city. This was lamented by the shopkeepers, who hastened to take out last minute ads, such as the following: "To all ladies and gentlemen who are at this moment visiting Rome and want to acquire some of the very latest novelties to give as gifts, we recommend the stores of the Münster Brothers, on the Corso, 162–163."

2

LOVE IN TURIN

ON JANUARY 19 THE NEW KING WAS SWORN IN. IT WAS A BEAUTIFUL, SUNNY DAY, BEARING THE kind of January freshness Romans wait the year for. The crowds came out again, this time to Piazza Montecitorio, site of the Bernini palace which had lately become united Italy's Chamber of Deputies. The king and queen—Italy's first queen—arrived in a shiny, brand-new carriage. It was two o'clock on the latest French pocket watches possessed by many of the new upper class who had come out to greet the king; it was two o'clock by the stark shadow of the sundial obelisk which stood in the center of the piazza, taken from Heliopolis a long time ago.

The king was received at the *palazzo* door by a delegation of deputies. He was visibly nervous. When he shook hands, his were felt by others to be clammy and trembling. Indeed during the morning he had been so overcome with stage fright that his aides were certain the ceremony would never be able to be performed that day. But he had gathered up some of his courage, and now he stood before 630 admiring and enthusiastic senators and deputies, taking the solemn oath of office, albeit in a broken, squeaky voice.

In his acceptance speech, written by Crispi, he paid tribute to the nation's past, promised to pursue peace and progress, and said that he would bring up his son, the prince of Naples (the fragile eight-year-old boy who one day was to be Victor Emmanuel III), to follow the example of Victor Emmanuel II. Above all he wished to be guided by parliament, which represented the will of his people. His only desire was that it be said of him, "He was worthy of his father." The speech brought thunderous applause at the end of each

49

sentence, and when it was over, all but the handful of republicans exploded in a cathartic ovation. The king would never be nervous again.

His return to the Quirinal was an endless triumph. Once inside the palace, the king and queen and the visiting princes went out on the balcony to receive the best wishes of the people, who cheered literally for hours. By all appearances they were aptly rewarded when Prince Frederick Wilhelm lifted little Victor Emmanuel in his arms and showed the handsome *principino* to the throng. The German kissed him on the cheek, and Humbert and beautiful Margherita smiled jubilantly, as the Romans cried, "Long live Italy!" "Long live the House of Savoy!"[1]

Those were the sweetest moments of their troubled, violent reign.

The new king and queen were first cousins, both of them grandchildren of Charles Albert. Humbert had not wanted to marry her (nor she him). He had been destined for a princess of Austria. His father had married a Hapsburg, as had Charles Albert, and in view of the recent disastrous wars with Austria it seemed to everyone but Humbert that a continuation of the tradition might heal the new wounds.

Count Cibrario, Victor Emmanuel II's man in Vienna, was instructed in 1867 to shop for a bride, and he chose the exceptionally beautiful Mathilde, daughter of Archduke Albrecht, who had whipped the Italians at Custozza only the year before. "At our meeting," Cibrario wrote to his master, "Princess Mathilde seemed quite good, affectionate, and healthy. She will have twenty-five million. The Emperor [Franz Josef] would be happy to give her away. . . ."[2]

Twenty-three-year-old Humbert was not at all pleased. If it had to be Hapsburg, the dark-eyed prince of Piedmont had his heart set on the princess of Este. She, however, let it be known that she "cordially hated" both Humbert and his father—her sensibilities having been offended by the late Piedmont aggressions—and Franz Josef said that he did not wish to use "moral violence" to force her consent.[3] It would have to be Mathilde, who, still a teen-ager, presumably was too young to have formed such strong prejudices.

Humbert was furious. He took it upon himself to telegraph Cibrario: "I want absolute freedom of action." That meant nothing. Victor Emmanuel ordered the boy to take a trip to Paris so that "these ideas will pass," and the negotiations for the marriage proceeded.[4] But tragedy, so much a part of the Hapsburg phenomenon, intervened.

One evening in 1867, enchanting, fair-skinned Mathilde was dressing for a ball. Whenever the princess went out, all the eyes of Vienna were on her, and this night, it seemed, was to be no exception. A beautiful new party dress lay carefully stretched out before her, as she stood in her delicate underthings alone in her palace bedroom. She had just got into her crinolines when, realizing she was unattended, she decided to risk a forbidden pleasure. From a secret place she withdrew a cigarette—doubtless it was stolen—lighted it, and defying a lifetime of royal rearing and all in the world that was prudish, she began to smoke. In walked her governess, who, it is clear, was a severe and intolerant disciplinarian. The young princess tried to conceal the cigarette behind her back and for a moment deceived the intruder. But her crinolines began to issue smoke and suddenly burst into flames. Mathilde was enveloped in fire. The governess shrieked and ran for help. The fire was eventually smothered, but that night the princess died of her burns in "atrocious spasms."[5]

The effect of this on young Humbert is unknown; he wrote his father from Paris, but the message was entirely illegible. ("Thanks for your letter," Victor Emmanuel wrote back. "But I want you to know that we couldn't read it. If you have anything to say to me, send a telegram . . .")[6] In the meantime a new bride had to be found, more so than before. Garibaldi's defeat at Rome's doorstep in November of that year and Victor Emmanuel's duplicities toward both the red-shirts and the French had pushed the prestige of the monarchy to a new low. This was viewed as a problem in public relations which might be lightened by the heartstrings of a well-played royal romance.

The prime minister, General Menabrea, suggested Margherita of Savoy, the daughter of the king's late brother. Victor Emmanuel had half forgotten who she was and anyway thought her still a child. She was a very eligible sixteen, he was told, gracious, virtuous, and extremely patriotic. "Is she pretty? Does she have any physical defects?" the king wished to know. She was sound, and, more than pretty, she had the face of an angel, but one had to act quickly for the king of Rumania was seeking her hand.

That settled it. Humbert came home from Paris toward the end of the year and was given the news. He was adamantly opposed and terribly upset. He ran off to Milan and into the arms of his true love, the coquettish and somewhat promiscuous young Duchess Litta. His marriage to her, however, was unthinkable and expressedly forbidden. "*Ce n'est pas une femme pour mon fils,*" Victor Emmanuel is said to have cried on hearing of the liasion, "*c'est bon pour moi . . ."*[7] But the needs of dynasty and state had to be served, and so they prevailed. Early in January the king wrote to his fretting son:

> You will make this sacrifice. I am certain of it because, although you are young, you have shown yourself to understand that the Princes must be the first to sacrifice themselves for their country.[8]

Margherita, who liked to write romantic verse and paint in water colors, was to understand this, too. The king went to Turin and burst into her bedroom in the Palazzo Chiablese. The poor girl was terrified. She sat motionless in her dressing gown, and while her handmaid combed her blond tresses, she was instructed by her uncle.

On January 28, 1868, Humbert, having come from Milan, proposed. "Margherita, do you want to be my wife?" he asked.

"You know how proud I am to belong to the House of Savoy," she replied. "I will be so all the more, becoming your wife."[9]

It was a long way from saying *yes*, but the matter was closed.

The next night they went to the Royal Theater where they were acclaimed. Victor Emmanuel told his ministers that it was useless to try to keep their love a secret; *"tout le monde en parle,"* he said, and the wedding, forthcoming in April, was dutifully and officially announced.

They were married in Turin to console the old capital, which was swiftly and bad-humoredly losing its supremacy in the throes of eclectic national growth. The ceremonies took two days and the celebrations five more. Dynastic popularity went up like bullish stock. Everyone was happy, even, it seems, the bride and groom. "Princess Margherita," remarked her friend the Baroness Olimpia Savio, "was graceful, smiling, vivacious, close to her Humbert, both of them happy with one another and pleasing to the eye and to the soul."[10]

Her Humbert was born in 1844, on the very same day and month as his father twenty-four years before. His brother Amadeus was born the following year, and the boys were inseparable throughout their insulated youth. They were motherless at an early age and rarely saw their father. Their education, supervised by the militarist courtiers of Turin, was extremely parochial; they were taught to be little toy Savoyard soldiers, cast in solid gold.

Humbert knew little about anything and next to nothing about most things. The prince's intellectual poverty shocked Victor Emmanuel's learned minister Silvio Spaventa, who accompanied the youth on a trip through the Abbruzzi. ". . . Unfortunately, the young man is ignorant," Spaventa confided to a friend. "That is to say, he does not possess a level of culture necessary for the times and for his rank."[11] It showed then in that empty, inscrutable face which was to follow him to the bier, and it shows still today in those haunting, uncomprehending dog eyes which stare out from the labels of countless olive-oil cans in supermarkets all over America.

One day Humbert grew up. His father called him aside for a talk and when it was over, Victor Emmanuel said to General Menabrea, "Now I know Humbert. He's a fine young man. He's sensible and he has a good heart. He'll do well."[12]

The king, who was a torrent of emotions, used to cry when he received properly affectionate letters from Humbert. He was especially moved when on the eve of the war of 1866 the prince wrote him from Naples requesting that he be given an important command. Nevertheless, with great pain, he had to reprimand his son, to teach him a lesson in royal maturity. "I can't at a moment's notice change the large commands for your pleasure," Victor Emmanuel replied to the prince, declaring that he would have to wait patiently. "That's what happened when I was the Duke of Savoy, and I always did my duty joyfully. . . . I hope you will understand, my dear son."[13]

When the war actually broke out, Humbert was sent into the field, bearing the ribbons, braids, and epaulets of a general. According to the primary school textbooks of the next generation, but not the documents, he proved himself an expert in military science and an "intrepid, valorous warrior."[14] He was fired on at Villafranca by attacking uhlan cavalry, and when the smoke cleared he was still in the saddle, a feat to which cries of *"Viva Savoia!"* resounded from the troops.

In peacetime he was appointed president of the Italian commission for the 1867 world's fair at Paris. He hunted hare with six fine hounds given to his father by the bey of Tunisia, and he took up residence in the royal villa at Milan, where his mother had once lived and where he could be near the Duchess Litta. Then he married Margherita.

Margherita of Savoy had a much more interesting childhood than her consort's. Her father, the duke of Genoa, died when she was scarcely four years old. Her mother, Elizabeth of Saxony, turned out to be an ungrateful woman, running off with one of her lowborn employees, a palace major seventh in command and the brother of a Genoese pharmacist. This of course created a scandal of continental proportions; the German princess, following the death of Victor

Emmanuel's wife, had become the highest ranking woman at court, with all the privileges and responsibilities of a queen. She was banished from court by the enraged king, posing a threat to future Italian-German relations. Only on the intervention of the Russian czar's Saxon mother did the crisis end in reconciliation.

Victor Emmanuel, following Cavour's counsel, forgave Elizabeth and made her husband a marquis—on the condition that they have separate bedrooms, that he continue to treat his wife in public as her subordinate and that he enter the palace only through the service entrance. The terms were accepted and matters calmed, but the effects of this marriage on young Margherita may be fairly surmised as having been unsalutary.

From another point of view, she reaped a lifetime of profit. In the absence of a "normal" princely home life, the child was drawn close to her Austrian governess, Rosa Arbesser, a gentle, loving teacher who seems to have been a woman of superior education and refinements. She succeeded in bringing a measure of culture into the philistine House of Savoy, imparting to her charge, with the aid of a number of tutors, a love of learning, if not the learning itself. Margherita read Dante before grammar, studied art, spoke French and German flawlessly, and even developed a taste for music—the daughter of Zeus most notoriously detested in the House of Savoy. To be sure, she would never truly master the language of her own country (not even its almost purely phonetic spelling) and her knowledge was to be of the most superficial character, a mixture of acquired class prejudices and half-remembered facts, all of them colored with an excess of religious zeal. But Margherita was ever to be considered as the family's most accomplished intellectual. During her reign, as we shall see, she was to capture the hearts and minds of Italy's real intellectuals—much to the damage of the nation—scholars and poets of deserved international repute unable to maintain their integrity in the scent of her queenly charms.

But Margherita the child wished only to be called "little mouse" when Madame Arbesser tucked her into bed. She liked to play house in the little forest hut built for her and her brother. She was a stubborn, strong-minded youngster, and the anecdotal annals, which accompany all kings and queens to eternity, record that one day she was scolded for having shaken the hand of a noble lady when she ought properly to have greeted her with a curtsy. "For now I shall obey," Margherita is supposed to have said, "but when I grow up I will offer my hand to whomever I feel is worthy of it."

When she did grow up, she did nothing of the sort, of course. She did as she was told. She married cousin Humbert.[15]

They were married but eighteen months when a child was born, their only offspring in a marriage that was to endure for thirty more years. The expectant mother had come to Naples to have her baby. The managers of dynastic-national politics were staging what was to be yet another triumph in winning the people. The "most corrupt" part of Italy was still alien to the Piedmontese monarchy; nostalgia for the old Bourbons ran high. Were a prince of Savoy to be born in *Naples*, however, would not the last hostile heart melt in national pride? In any event, such was the reasoning.

That the teen-aged crown princess was pregnant and would have her child in the former capital of the Two Sicilies was announced about five months before the event. Naples responded warmly. A commission of physicians was formed to choose the baby's wet-nurse from among the common people. Working with the Neapolitan police, they selected a lactiferous woman from the countryside, whose general constitution and, in particular, whose mammae were judged eminently capable of giving the royal infant a healthy push into life. The *popolana*, not to mention her kinfolk, neighbors, and fellow Neapolitans, was exultant, and when she was introduced to the future mother she was overcome with emotion when the princess, in dismissing her, kissed her on the forehead.

The city fathers of Naples gave the crib, an elaborate gift designed by a committee of artists headed by Morelli. In a country of unrelieved poverty, it was, aside from being an ornate monstrosity, offensive to any sense of propriety. So great was the joy of at least the most articulate Neapolitans, however, that even Luigi Settembrini, the former revolutionary, wrote a little book about the *crib*. How had Morelli created such a masterpiece? he asked. He had been inspired by "two magic words: Art and Margherita."[16]

The baby was born, with some medical difficulties, on November 11, 1869, in the Bourbon Palazzo Reale. The cannons on the ramparts of Sant'Elmo fired one hundred and one times. The number meant it was a boy. He was baptized Victor Emmanuel and titled prince of Naples. Tiny and frail, he was immediately recognizable as an inferior product of inbreeding. Many believed he would die young. But Victor Emmanuel III was to reign for forty-six years, during which time his principal achievements would include, as will be seen, both the installation and the tardy dismissal of Benito Mussolini.

3

ROMA CAPITALE

A LITTLE MORE THAN A YEAR LATER, WITH THE FALL OF PAPAL ROME TO THE NATIONALISTS, Prince Humbert and Princess Margherita made their triumphant entry into the new capital. Victor Emmanuel II, for superstitious reasons, had been hesitant about going there himself. A gypsy hag had told him long ago that he would die in the Quirinal. Though hardly afraid of death, he was convinced that the prophecy would be fulfilled, and with so much of his work undone he did not wish to hasten the inevitable end.* So he sent the young couple in his stead.

The palace itself, which had been the official residence of the popes for the past three centuries, had been sealed by Pius IX. He had done so when, in retreat from the nationalist assault on Rome, he had decided to take himself "prisoner" behind the walls of the Vatican sanctuary. The town police, however, passing into the service of the new state, had employed a locksmith to pick open Bernini's fine door, giving to the king and all his men entry to the memory-haunted *palazzo*, as well as its priceless treasures.

The royal couple, the little *principino*, and their entourage arrived under a driving January rain. Nevertheless the Romans came out to greet them warmly. It was a show of affection which found its reward when Margherita commanded that her carriage be uncov-

---

* Three weeks prior to the arrival of Humbert and Margherita, the king had visited Rome and the Quirinal, but only for a few hours. Toward the end of December, 1870, the city had been struck with a disastrous flooding of the Tiber (viewed by many in Rome as the result of God's and the pope's anger at the Piedmontese "usurpation"). Victor Emmanuel, on the final day of that year, came to give solace and sustenance to the victims. He did not make his official entry into the city until six months later on July 2.

ered in spite of the downpour in order that she might stand and be seen by all who had braved the weather to glimpse her.

They moved into an apartment in the Quirinal. Humbert was given command of the armed forces in Rome, but in name only. He and his popular wife had been assigned a far more important task by the new governing class. Italy, as D'Azeglio had said, was made, but what remained to be done was to make the Italians. The land and the nation were of a people divided and no people were more divided than the Romans.

Every class among them, but most of all the aristocracy, was split into two hostile camps, as in the olden age of Guelph and Ghibelline. Now there were nationalist and papalist factions called, respectively, "whites" and "blacks." For more than twenty years, since the shattering events of 1848, Rome's sixty first families had been coming apart, from one another as well as internally. The very richest of them, invariably the offspring and relatives of cardinals and popes, had made their fortunes through the nepotism of the Church. For the time being, most of them remained faithfully black. But, as the whites understood, there were greater fortunes inhering in the New Times, if only the "Roman Question"—the political effect of the offended papacy's resistance*—were reconciled. To do so, the blacks would have to be won.

Rough and *goffo* Victor Emmanuel, wedded of late to the drummer's daughter Rosina, was an abomination to the black nobility, and he knew it. Not that they, with the exception of a very few, were any less ignorant than he; it was only their arrogance and their metropolitanism, which was known throughout aristocratic Europe (as was their reputed idleness), that permitted them to look upon the king as an unsophisticated boor. In any event Victor Emmanuel had neither the inclination nor the temperament to deal with the blacks himself. That was the job entrusted to Humbert and Margherita, es-

* More precisely, the "Roman Question," which was to play so important a part in Italian political and diplomatic life until the Lateran treaties of 1929, may be explained as follows: With the capture of Rome, the new government passed the so-called law of guarantees, in order that Church and State might coexist. It recognized the inviolability of the Vatican and the sovereignty of the pope, who was to be accorded the same rights as a chief of state. But Pius IX and his successors rejected any such settlement, hoping at first for a restoration of the *status quo ante* and maintaining an attitude of nonrecognition of Italy and its self-drawn boundaries with regard to Rome. Moreover, they actively opposed the unified kingdom, seeking alliances with foreign powers and barring Catholics from partaking in Italian public affairs. These policies posed a real threat to the new state for a while, but they became increasingly ineffective and inoperative, as the coincidence of interests of both parties continually expanded.

pecially to the gracious Margherita, irresistible to all, yet twice as much a Savoy as anyone else (save the tiny *principino*).

From these origins the new court began to take form, and from therein arose Margherita's internationally celebrated circle of friends, a court within the court. It was a slow process. The teachings of the revolution had to pass through many thicknesses before it could be understood.

The Rome which had fallen to the House of Savoy was little more than a complacent provincial capital. There where the urban movement of a million ancient Romans had been so great that Caesar had had to ban all daytime traffic, Rome had been reduced to pastoral sublimity. Two-thirds of the area enclosed by the Aurelian walls was covered with vineyards, orchards, and farmland. Where the Via Veneto lies today, wood and bush stood then. The Barberini Palace was on the outskirts of the town. The ruins of Imperial Rome were covered with the hovels and shacks of the extra-urban poor. Rome was the Rome of the baroque, a corner of the city which lay between Saint Peter's and the Quirinal, between the heights of the Pincio and the low, unpaved streets of the Jewish ghetto on the muddy banks of the Tiber.

The census taken in 1871 by the new government enumerated 220,000 Romans, but related little about their condition. As always, there were rich and there were poor, but in Rome and the countryside these were social groups of rather disproportionate dimension. In the city, one per cent of the people owned 100 percent of the private buildings. One-fourth of the population lived in one-twelfth of the habitable space—twelve people to a three-room flat.

One family, however, the Borghese (descendent relatives of Pope Paul V), owned land in the city and its environs enclosing eighty-four square miles—an area thirty times larger than nineteenth-century Rome itself. More or less contiguous land still six times greater in size than the Borghese's was divided among one-twentieth of one percent of the Romans, latifundia on which 15,000 peasants lived in caves. Beyond lay the malaria-ridden marshes. Indeed, at the time of the "usurpation," these *beati possedenti* and the Church, it may be fairly concluded, owned *everything*.[1] But only about half of them could be considered as truly belonging to the Roman aristocracy, membership in which came by virtue of services and tributes to the papal court.

The oldest of the true aristocratic families were of medieval origin: the feudal Colonna, the Orsini, the Barberini, and the storied Cenci.

The richest, as has been said, were the more recent beneficiaries of nepotism: the Borghese, the Chigi, the Boncompagni. The newest were the merchants and the bankers, some of whom had made their fortunes under brief Napoleonic rule and would be the first to go over to the whites. These were descendants of the families such as the Torlonia, whose founder had been a peddler-turned-money-changer-turned-banker-turned-grainseller to the Bonapartist armies. Even now members of the family began to rebel—although, in deference to the pope, black Prince Alessandro Torlonia rushed to change the colors of his livery, which had too closely resembled the House of Savoy's.

When Humbert and Margherita came to town, the blacks went into a kind of conspicuous mourning, protesting their solidarity with the injured Holy Father. The dearest rituals of their social intercourse were abstained from. No more did their ladies take their daily *passeggiata* along the Corso (except in the summer months when the whites went on their holiday). The endless rounds of gala balls were virtually suspended. Receptions at the Quirinal were boycotted, and, now that the Savoyard liberals had torn down the walls of the ghetto, the blacks no longer slummed for *carciofi alla giudea*—the fried artichoke specialty of the Roman Jews.

Yet from the start there was common ground. Fox hunting, perhaps because it was too new an activity to have graved a tight tradition, offered a mixing place for noblemen of every shade, notably for Prince Humbert, fine horseman that he was. It was from feather-touch relations such as this one that the House of Savoy, as it had always done before, began to make inroads. During the social season of 1871–72, a few private balls were held. The royal couple were invited and attended those in the palaces of the duke of Sermoneta and other Roman princes. They were all whites, to be sure, but mere sympathizers attended, too, and it was clear the blacks were losing ground. By carnival time of the following year the *feste* of the Roman nobility had picked up their old gaiety, the lines of separation always slightly less clearly drawn.

The court of Savoy, for the first time in at least a hundred years, had abandoned its spartan military demeanor and taken on color and flourish. On the last Wednesday of every month gentlemen and their ladies danced at the venerable Quirinal now. Where there had been images of saints and the portraits of popes, heroic, bigger-than-life paintings of the Risorgimento's greatest moments replaced them. The walls of the grand ballroom had been brightened with yellow damask and adorned with a portrait of an eternally confident and gracious Princess Margherita.

Costume balls became the fashion. At one of them Humbert and Margherita came dressed as Charles Emmanuel the Great and his fecund wife, Catherine of Austria. The Baron de Renzis, one-time rival-in-love of Victor Emmanuel, was Cola di Rienzo, and Donna Laura Acton Minghetti, wife of the prime minister, wore the scant dress of a squaw. The salons reopened; Donna Laura's was literary and political, and in the privacy of the home of the de Renzis noblemen and women, indiscriminate of political color, performed the latest *comédies* of Paris. The barrier would be a long time in breaking down entirely, but at the carnival of 1876 black and white danced with one another in the Palazzo Torlonia apartment of George Wurts, secretary of the United States legation at the Quirinal.

Around young Humbert and Margherita and the bright lights of modern times, Rome too was brought up to date. The government, in coming to the city, had requested of the proprietors 40,000 rooms to house its functionaries, but only 500 had been offered to let. Moreover thousands of other people were making their way to the new capital: diplomats and job-hunters, businessmen and workmen, poets and thieves. To accommodate them a vast building and urbanization program was undertaken. Its costs were hardly considered, and grace was sacrificed to speed.

First the city was dusted and cleaned for the new people. The German medievalist Gregorovius, who had been living in Rome and keeping a diary for the past twenty years, observed the changes with an insightful eye. In June, 1871, he wrote in what was to be his *Römische Tagebücher*:

> Rome has become a whitewashed tomb. They have whitewashed the buildings, even the venerable old *palazzi*; they have scraped away the rust of centuries and have thus shown Rome to be architecturally ugly. . . . [They] have even shaved the Colosseum, that is, stripped it of all the plants that adorned it so well, and have thus destroyed the flora of the Colosseum, about which the Englishman Deakin had published an entire volume some years ago. . . . Monasteries and convents have been transformed into office buildings. The claustral windows have been thrown open; the walls and the doors have been redone. . . . The monks and the nuns who still reside there are being driven out like dogs. It is shocking to see them wandering about in the corridors and in the cells like ghosts, but some of them must be happy to have their freedom. The sun has set on old Rome. In twenty years a new world will have arisen here.[2]

There was some, but not much, poetic justice to it. "This transformation of the holy city into a modern city," Gregorovius remarked with scarce satisfaction, "is the other side of that time when pagan Rome was transmuted with equal fervor into spiritual Rome."[3] The early popes had carried off the stone of the Colosseum to build their churches; the Barberini had stolen the bronze of the Pantheon to make their cannons.

But philosophy and phenomenology were rudely cast aside. There were fortunes to be made (and lost). Cardinals and Roman noblemen, who posed as the keepers of the precious past, rushed into the marketplace to compete with one another for whatever properties they might obtain in order that they could be resold at a tremendous profit to the anxious builders from the north. When the builders ran low on funds taxes went up. The head tax on the people of Rome was soon five times higher than it had been under papal rule. Greed made the building bad. During the 1870s, thousands of Roman workers were injured or killed in construction site collapses and landslides. What remained standing were tasteless buildings of oppressive stone which would very soon turn blacker than the ancient pillars of Octavia's portico.

The newcomers were called *buzzurri*. The word is close to huckster, but one of lesser elegance than a peep-show barker. They did not succeed—although the effort was made—in replacing the monuments to Peter and Paul with likenesses of Mazzini and Garibaldi, but in their scarring of Rome they were able to extract further irony from the old lampoon, *quod non fecerunt barberi, fecerunt Barberini*—what the barbarians did not do, the Barberini did. Of these years, Augustus Hare would write that the liberals from the north did more damage to Rome than the centuries of Visigoth and Vandal plunder.[4]

Nevertheless the new look in Rome and in the House of Savoy reinforced the king's government and monarchical state. The court at the Quirinal became the temple in which all who supported or approved of the new times might express their faith.

Domestically this was symbolized not only by the steady gains made on the blacks, in spite of their show of disdain, but also on the "reds." Margherita would forever complain that the left had two left feet, but when she danced the opening quadrille of the season of 1875 with the arch-republican member of parliament Nicotera (a vulgar brute soon to be a perfect prototype of a Fascist chieftain), it was a picture worth ten thousand words. Shortly afterward Nicotera swore undying allegiance to the monarchy in a famous speech at Sapri—where he once had fought for classless socialism with Pisacane.

Abroad, by 1876, the new Italy had been recognized by the French, the Germans, and Great Britain, all of whom had elevated their legations in Rome to embassy status. Queen Victoria's son, the duke of Connaught, danced with Margherita, the ambassador from Berlin played four-handed piano with her, and the London *Times* wrote that the Savoys were now sovereigns of one of the great states of Europe. They were no longer parvenu monarchs, judged the *Times*, but the equals of all who were mighty.[5]

The House of Savoy had come far since the upstart Victor Emmanuel II, visiting Queen Victoria in 1855, had impressed her as a "bizarre relic of a bygone age."* [6]

---

* Victoria's biographer Elizabeth Longford records that encounter: "The burly, eccentric *roué* with eyes so wildly rolling that they looked as if they would drop out and a head carried high like an untamed horse, confessed to Queen Victoria that he did not like 'the business of king,' so if he could not make war he would become a monk. . . . The English lips were pursed and the blue eyes frosty. Kings must be sure that wars were *just*, she said severely, for they would have to answer for men's lives before God. One must certainly aim at a just war, agreed Victor Emmanuel, but God will always pardon a mistake."[7]

4

"THE HEIRS TO THE CAESARS"

INDEED THE OLD MAN HAD BECOME JUST SUCH A RELIC. TORMENTED BY RECURRENT MALARIAL fevers, he had good cause to dislike unhealthy Rome and good reason for his frequent absences from court.

When in the capital, he would often disappear at dawn. He would tear away from the palace in an unmarked victoria, driving the horses to a frenzy. With the calash thrown back, he would be seen, though not often recognized, as a solitary figure bent over the reins, his hunting dogs barking at the wind as it rustled through the tattered clothes he loved to wear. He would strike out along the ancient Nomentana following the arrow-straight route from the Quirinal to the villa he had bought Rosina beyond the city walls. Breathless and heady with the rush of air, he would greet his old lover with fresh if fleeting excitements and pass the day with her in turbid daydreams of crowning his life with a final great victory for his armies.

The new class had elevated itself to pre-eminence on the myth that Italy was destined to great things, and no one had believed this more fervently than Victor Emmanuel. "It is true," he confided in 1873, "I have always had faith in the destiny and the greatness of Italy . . . even when others doubted it, this faith never abandoned me."[1] Now, however, glory seemed far away. He had become constitutional master of a troubled land and a backward people he hardly understood. He could concur with the conservative journal *Nuova Antologia*, which concluded in those years of disillusionment, "The Italy which became master of itself learned that it was very different from the one it believed itself to be trusting the descriptions of its poets."[2]

The real Italy was a rocky, dusty place, where eight of every ten Italians could neither read nor write. It was a country of wretched, landless peasants and a meager industrial labor force: less than 400,000 workers, of whom 200,000 were women and 100,000 were pitiful children of both sexes under fourteen years of age. Italy lacked fuel and ore, was deficient in transportation, and medieval in sanitation. It possessed problems requiring a century of honest labor to overcome, but as men and kings by past and present definition want glory now, there has rarely been such a golden age.

Thus it was not the national condition which disturbed the new regime as much as the fact that the high pitch of the Risorgimento had awakened the people. Their plight, common men had discovered by the old teachings of their new rulers, was unacceptable. They grew restless and demanding. This seemed ominous to the men in power. They wished to give something to their people, and so allowed the passage, in 1876, from the conservative-liberal right to the liberal-conservative left—while, for their own well-being, they hastened the repair of the public force.

The left came to power on many promises, not to recall a rigged election. Standing before the voters, its grandfatherly leader Agostino Depretis told the people he would urge on the era of the common man by only passing laws "emanating from the public consciousness." To the establishment he said, quite correctly, that there was "nothing to fear" in his idea of public consciousness.[3] Victor Emmanuel was convinced of this, and although he was not constitutionally obligated to empower the popularly elected left majority, he perceived the short-term worth of accepting this so-called "ministry of progressives" in hopes of assuaging the daily disappointments of his people.

The left was needed to work the same magic on the masses, and especially their representatives, that Humbert and Margherita were effecting on the divided aristocracy. No one in Italy was more suited for this labor than the hirsute Depretis. Although sincere in his desire for a better world, he embodied all that was wicked in Italy.

Born in Piedmont in 1813, he had come up through the ranks of revolutionary republicanism, only to yield to the mastery of the House of Savoy.[4] A former gunrunner for Mazzini, and an agent of Garibaldi, his principal contribution to the national life of his country was to develop a political mill in which every humane principle and every high ideal could be mashed and ground into a fine white powder and dispersed in the winds of the *tramontana.*

History assigns to Depretis the insidious political invention called *trasformismo*—the transformation of opposition to support by whatever means; government based on the usually valid notion that every man has his price. Credit for this achievement should really go to Cavour, still better, to Humbert the Whitehanded, but Depretis was the man who in the long years of his parliamentary dictatorship was to hone *trasformismo* into an instrument as sharp and as effective as the guillotine.

Depretis was an austere man whose only extravagance was a great white beard. Even as prime minister he lived in a furnished room which he rented in the home of a French *coiffeuse*, and it was there, when laid up with the gout, that he would often receive his friends from parliament, as well as ambassadors and princes. He himself was incorruptible, but he possessed a kind of Midas touch with which he corrupted all that was in his reach: right and left, rich and poor. Depretis, said the right-wing deputy Silvio Spaventa, was like a public toilet "which remains clean while all sorts of refuse passes through."[5]

His talent was for compromise. He shunned all rigid stands, was drawn to anything manipulative, and sacrificed with sweet reasonableness or with violence whatever stood in his way. He loved administration, despised art and ideas, and he never tired of saying that the people he hated most were the world's professors. His motto was "Excelsior!" In short, a perfect servant for the House of Savoy.

In the once-fearsome left, Victor Emmanuel, to his surprise, found many men close to his adventurous heart, such as the southern radicals Nicotera and Crispi. Baron Nicotera, defined by Count Guiccioli as a "colossus arisen from a sea of dung," was given the ministry of the interior.[6] This former fighter for justice and democracy set out at once to police the nation. He clubbed down protest, wiped out constitutional rights, closed up newspapers, and was among the first to pioneer in the brand new police technique of illegal wire-tapping.

Crispi, on the other hand, was given a job requiring the greatest finesse. He was sent abroad by the king on a mission so secret it remains to this day clouded in mystery, although its substance may be deduced from the surviving documents.[7] Crispi's mission was the start of a great, never-to-be-finished work conceived in Victor Emmanuel's audacious eye, his final reach for an immortality far greater than he now enjoys. As such, and as measure of the man and his men, it seems worthy of review.

The king had always exercised his royal prerogatives in the sphere of foreign policy, often entering into negotiations without the knowledge of his ministers even when Cavour was alive. Now, in the closing months of his life, he was virtually his own foreign minister. Depretis had no interest in diplomacy (his regard for diplomats, he used to say, was second only to his esteem for professors). Humbert, who received not the slightest training in either domestic or international affairs, was useful, in his father's judgment, only in the Quirinal ballrooms and on the battlefield. But Crispi, who believed in maintaining the peacetime army on a wartime footing "in anticipation of mighty events,"[8] was a chip off the king's old block.

Crispi was born in Sicily in 1819. He was a conspirator, a lusty brawler, a Mazzinian, and a Garibaldian red. Lacking in education, he nevertheless had a flair with words and when it became wise to embrace the House of Savoy it was Crispi who coined the slogan of the Thousand, "Italy and Victor Emmanuel." It was Crispi too who wrote the famous phrase, in a letter to the master, Mazzini, "The monarchy unites us, the republic would divide us"[9]—a formula which was to ease many a conscience-stricken idealist into swift conversion. In this way, Victor Emmanuel was able to place an ever greater trust in Crispi until, in the end, he was able to say to him, "Your ideas are in perfect agreement with mine."[10]

The ambitions of Crispi and his master were boundless. Crispi was to live another quarter of a century, long enough, as will be seen, to do inestimable harm to his country and his people. But Victor Emmanuel had little time remaining to him and he seemed to know that better than anyone else. In the closing months of his life, though not yet fifty-eight years old, he sensed the end was near. More and more he would slip into depressions, overcome with melancholy. His dynastic hopes since the conquest of Rome had been wrecked by unhappy circumstance. His daughter Maria Pia had become queen of Portugal, but France had gone the way of the Third Republic, striking down his desires for an imperial throne for "Kekina." His second son, Amadeus, a living portrait of Charles Albert, was crowned king of Spain in 1870, only to be forced to abdicate in 1873, barely escaping an assassination attempt. Yet his frustrations and disappointments were less persistent than his fantasies, and though the clouds were gathering up around him, he still hoped to die with iron in his hands. "I'm an old scoundrel," he was heard to say near the end, "but I cannot die badly. She [Maria Adelaide], up there, won't let that happen."[11] Such was the faith behind Crispi's mission.

On the mornings of August 26 and 27, 1877, Crispi, prior to his departure abroad, met at length with the king at Turin. One purpose of his task was to somehow derive gain from the Russo-Turkish war, which was then being fought. Crispi was to seek approval from Great Britain, Germany, and Austria for Italian territorial compensation in the "unredeemed lands" of the Trentino and Trieste in the likely event of Austrian expansion into the shaky Ottoman Empire.* If such compensation were to be denied, Italy, Crispi would argue, should be given territories somewhere else—anywhere, but preferably colonial domination of parts of North Africa.

But the king had little faith in the kindliness of the Great Powers. Only in strength and through the agency of war could Italy's aims be realized, he believed. Crispi, in his talks with Victor Emmanuel, agreed, and in this way a secret project, formulated as the "other operation," was given priority in connection with his journey. On taking leave of the sovereign, Crispi, adopting the jargon of a traveling salesman, wrote to Depretis:

> His Majesty . . . has no hope in making a deal as a consequence of the war in the East. He too believes it is too late and that there is no place for us. Nevertheless he urged me to do everything possible in order that we may realize some profit from it. His language was very different with regard to the other operation, which is the real purpose of my trip. The king feels the need to crown his days with a victory which will give our army the power and prestige it lacks in the eyes of the world.[13]

The "other operation," the "real purpose" of his travels was to be nothing less than an offer to Germany for a cooperative endeavor in cutting up Austria like a cheese from Parma or a Westphalian pig: the Germans were to get an *Anschluss*, the Italians the *terre irredente*. But that was not all. Berlin, according to what is known of the "other operation," would be asked to join Rome in the dismantling of eastern France. Crispi would proffer the provinces of Champagne, Franche-Compte, and Burgundy to Bismarck, taking for his master Provence and the Dauphine, which contained the old Piedmont territories of Nice and cherished, venerable Savoy (with its fine hunting grounds).[14]

With such visions in his red-rimmed eyes, Crispi departed. He

---

* These Italian-speaking territories were still part of the Austrian empire. The king's government had officially repudiated its claims there, but desiring them nonetheless, it secretly subsidized the Italian Irredentists, who clamored that the work of the Risorgimento could not be considered complete until their brothers in *Italia Irredenta* were freed of Hapsburg rule. The government hoped that the movement's threats against Austria might bring some concessions.[12]

learned quickly that Victor Emmanuel had been right in forecasting hopelessness about "making a deal" on the war in the east. In England, he found Disraeli entirely opposed to the idea of Italian compensation. If it was territory the Italians wanted, Crispi said he was told, "take Albania."[15] In Austria he failed to even bring up the question of compensation. It seemed utterly futile, since Minister Andrassy, before Crispi could speak, threatened an immediate attack on Italy at the first sign of an Italian policy of annexing Trieste or the Trentino. "Do you want other territories?" Andrassy, not entirely insensitive, asked Crispi. "Tell us about it. It is a policy we understand."[16]

In Germany, Crispi took up the "other operation." With scant ingenuousness, he said he had come in search of a conventional alliance with Berlin in order that Italy might be protected from French and Austrian power. But when, after some difficulty in arranging an appointment, he met with his latter-day idol, Prince Bismarck, he broached the Italian-hatched plot. The meeting took place in Gastein, a town near the Austrian border, and Crispi, putting on his best diplomacy, used this fact in adding touches of "subtlety" to so delicate a matter. It is interesting to examine his notion of a tactful choice of words. The Italian envoy said to the German chancellor:

> Permit me to observe that German unity is not yet complete; from 1866 to 1870 you made miracles, but there remain many German populations outside the territory of your Empire—and certainly, sooner or later, you will find a way to win them. . . . Austrian territory does not displease you. Every year you come here to Gastein, which along with the Alps, marks the true frontier of Germany. This seems very significant to me. Perhaps it is even a prediction of the future. . . .[17]

He then went on to outline his scheme, which of course meant a new major war in Europe. He was later to admit that on completion of his presentation Bismarck responded with an unhesitating no. The German would say subsequently that it was all he could do to keep himself from throwing Crispi out. Not that Bismarck was any more scrupulous than Victor Emmanuel's emissary, but the absurdity of the proposal convinced him that he was dealing with a man, a government, and a royal house of shocking ignorance. If Crispi or anyone in Rome had read the reports of their own ambassadors (and there is evidence that they did not), they would have known that Bismarck, who was trying hardest of all to strike a more or less permanent balance in Europe, would be the last person to approach with a plan, the effects of which, even if successfully executed, would render the continent unstable for a century or more.

Bismarck for years after Crispi's mission was to inveigh against the Italians, breaking into tirades and diatribes at every opportunity, which of course was to do them no good. "The politics of Italy today," he later told the French ambassador, "is that of a sick man, who suffers in his bed and wants to occupy the next bed to see if it will bring him some relief." On another occasion he said that the Italians had the "sick aspirations of a corrupt race, which thinks of itself as the heirs of the Caesars, forgetting that the last of them was Romulus Augustus." Finally, in a garrulous moment in 1880, he could not resist confiding the substance of his encounter with the Italian:

> The mission in which they [the Italians] sent a certain Mr. Crispi to see me about four years ago made the estrangement I feel toward them complete. This man, with the cynicism of a malefactor, came to offer me the most disgraceful deals. He proposed the outright mutilation of France and Austria. . . . This courtier followed me around shamelessly for three days with his importunities until I thought I would have to show him to the door.[18]

Crispi came home empty handed. He had a long talk with the king, in which he told him several half-truths and not a few lies. The king wrote to Depretis and said that he was "satisfied."[19] But that was far from his true state of mind. A few weeks later, on New Year's Day, 1878, he told a delegation of deputies who had come to bid him well, "It is necessary that Italy make herself respected and feared."[20] Eight days later he was dead.

5

THE ITALIANS (INFERIOR, IDEAL, AND SUPERIOR)

THE STATE OF THE MONARCHY AND THE UNION BEQUEATHED TO HUMBERT AND MARGHERITA was one of poor repair. The death of Pope Pius IX less than one month after Victor Emmanuel appeared to many as the passing of an entire age. Only crotchety old Garibaldi, fighting windmills at home and abroad, remained of yesterday's heroes. The new times were hard times, and times still harder stood knocking at the door. Some men implored the new class to take stock of itself and change before too late.

The republicans, macabrely reanimated by the disappearance of Victor Emmanuel, were already announcing the fall of the House of Savoy, "an institution which has described the arc of the extreme limits assigned to it by history."[1]

With greater persuasiveness Agostino Bertani, a sociologist and a left-wing member of parliament who had succeeded in resisting *trasformismo*, argued in a new book titled *Italy Waits* that the Savoyard monarchy had reached a point where it could survive only if it were to undertake universal and fundamental reforms.[2]

On the right, serious liberals accused the government of callous shortsightedness. "The Italian revolution," said Baron Sonnino, "has been exploited by the well-to-do classes. The lower classes have received none of the benefits." Indeed, their social position had deteriorated and their rulers were indifferent to their "cries of pain." The reason for this was, said the future conservative prime minister, anticipating the very language of Lenin, that "the Italian State is not the representative of all of the social interests; it is the instrument of domination in the hands of a single class."[3]

The great literary critic De Sanctis was only slightly more generous. His fascinating account of a visit to his home town, Morra Irpino, after a long absence was a "bestseller" among the literate few. Tradition had it that Hannibal, camping on the side of a mountain near Naples, had founded Morra. But the truth was, said De Sanctis, his ancestral *paese* was a feudal territory which had no history—at least until the revolution.

> With the new times [he wrote] more has been done than in centuries. . . . But I cannot say that truly civilized life has begun there. I still see on those streets bands of tattered and idle urchins running between my legs like stray dogs, and it pains me to think that there is not yet a single kindergarten in Morra. The old plague of money-lending has not been cleaned up and I do not see any institution which might facilitate the purchase of the tools of labor and agriculture.
>
> I see jealousy more than fraternity among men, and there is no center of community life, no sign of cooperation. The ancient barrier of disdain and suspicion between the gentry and the peasant class still remains, and little attention is given to education, nothing to good upbringing. . . . So that if in times gone by, we had vestiges of a feudal Morra and a medievally religious Morra, we still do not have a civilized Morra, but only its shadow and a coat of paint. In Morra there is vanity, not pride, and much is given to what seems, little to what is.[4]

Another successful writer told of a visit *from* his *paesani*. They were better off before the revolution, they lamented. "What freedom?" they asked. "What Italy? Those are just words. Speak rather of oppression, ambition, plunder, irreligion. And that's not all. Still higher taxes. It can only end in a general conflagration."[5]

The dismal conditions learned from first-hand reports had impelled Bertani, for one, to fight for a more disciplined investigation of Italy's condition. His attention was focused on the state of the nation's agriculture, by far its most important activity. He had slowly gained support from both the right and the left with startling and unsettling accounts of abominable misery. A commission headed by the conservative Count Jacini had begun its work shortly before Victor Emmanuel's death. It had had little success at first, as the peasants were generally reluctant to speak with investigators who for good reason were believed to be tax collectors. But now the probe was making headway, painting a picture darker than anyone had imagined.

This *inchiesta agraria* would be a labor of eight years. Its fifteen-volume report is a classic study of the depths of poverty, which at

last told some of the bitter truth about united Italy in the first quarter-
century of Risorgimentalist rule.[6]

The Italy which pretended to great power was a nation, apart from
its small elite, of *braccianti*, day laborers, sickly, half-starved farm
hands and their pathetic broods, an entire people unthought of, unheard from, and unseen. "Wherever you turn," wrote the Jacini
commission, "agricultural Italy reveals herself to feel impoverished
and looks with alarm toward a future which threatens to grow worse
than the present. . . . The word *Ireland* is on the lips of many."[7]

The popular rightist deputy De Zerbi, who was to conclude that
Italy needed a "bath of blood" to rejuvenate itself, nevertheless drew
a masterful portrait of one aspect of peasant life. He wrote:

> In Calabria you have to be a married man in order to sleep in a bed.
> A baby, until he is two years old, sleeps in the miserable manger in which
> he saw the light of day. When his brother is born, he is moved over
> to the foot of the bed. When the third child is born, he moves from the
> bed to sleep on a wooden box and finds himself sleeping by the fireplace.
> Then he grows a little. In the winter he passes his nights on a pile of
> straw beside the mule and in summer he sleeps by the road outdoors,
> sleep taken with the fevers.[8]

The fevers referred to are malaria, in Italy thought to be a natural
condition of man. The disease, which had helped to kill even the
king, had inadvertently been turned loose on the people as one of
the effects of ecological disturbances caused by the greedy deforestation following unification. Pellagra, a diet deficiency disease which
takes its name from the Italian, was shown to be on the increase, too.
It was moving down from the north, while malaria spread everywhere.
Almost everyone in the Agro Romano had the latter malady and
medical testimony revealed that in one central region the entire
peasant population wore the *abito pellagroso*, the sick-skin cloak
which marks the onset of that nightmarish disease.[9]

The report of the Jacini commission ended with a warning to the
ruling class. There was a new religion spreading among the people,
said the investigators. The masses were no longer resigned. This is
what was being said among them: "The time has come for you to put
an end to the state of inferiority in which you have been kept for
centuries."[10]

> That [the report went on] is the new word. . . . It has penetrated the
> huts and gathering places of the people of the countryside. The word
> is founded in undeniable fact and is replete with vague and implicit
> promises. No one is saying precisely in what way the rural people will

be redeemed from their state of inferiority. But it is this very allure of the vague which is awakening instincts that once lay dormant. . . .[11]

This phenomenon explained the newly manifested desire of the Italians to emigrate to distant shores, said the commission. It also accounted for recent strikes and peasant uprisings in which the lands of the owners were occupied. Further, it was the cause of a profound discontent directed against the ruling classes, and even improvements which in past generations would have been regarded as worthy accomplishments, were today being scoffed at.

Indeed, what had happened in England of the seventeenth century, in France of the eighteenth, was now taking place in Italy of the nineteenth. The overthrow of the old orders had brought forth the new freedoms, only to give motion to the causes of radical disturbances in social relations. The promised well-being had been promised to *all*, and if in the new times there were enough to go around for only the members of the highest class, that would be their misfortune. For the promise unfulfilled and the shifting of social power were giving rise to a new ethic. Marx and Engels in 1848 had seen it as the specter of communism. But with hindsight, other apparitions may also be seen. Not only were the ideas of socialism being summoned, but those too of fascism.

The socialist movement was first to gain ground in Savoyard Italy. Now the nature of capitalism required that large amounts of capital be withdrawn from the countryside to pay for the industrial power being created in the cities. This, in turn, was calling up from the impoverished farm lands the men, women, and children who were to form the Italian proletariat—the requisite human material for early capitalist production and presocialist organizing. So rapidly was this taking place in Italy that to many the country seemed ripening for the new revolution. Men such as the Russian anarchist Bakunin hurried there to hasten the day of "inevitable" socialism. They welcomed the sufferings of the Italian peasants as added impetus for the coming of still newer times. There were thousands of young people in Italy, Bakunin had written as early as 1873, disillusioned with the establishment and even with republicanism. The best of them, according to him, were ready to die for the Good Cause.* But the struggle

* To his credit Marx, who had already broken with Bakunin and his perverse ideas of humanism, held a more accurate view of the same people referred to by the Russian. "[They] are but a gang of drifters," said Marx," the refuse of the bourgeoisie. All the so-called sections of the International in Italy are led by lawyers without clients, doctors with neither patients nor medical knowledge, students adept at playing billiards, traveling salesmen and clerks, and particularly journalists for minor newspapers of more or less dubious fame."[12]

for socialism in a capitalist society has its own dynamic, and in Italy, just as many of the greatest republicans had become the most loyal monarchists, so too, we will see, many of the most loyal socialists would become the greatest Fascists.

The dangers of amorphous restiveness in the countryside and growing socialist agitation in the cities were not taken lightly by the governors of Humbert's Italy. They genuinely wished to concede the demanded reforms in order that the pressure on the poor might ease somewhat. But they were simply unable to afford them. The wars of the Risorgimento were as yet unpaid for, and the drain of industrialization on the state budget was exhausting. Further, the new government had committed itself to the repeal of the loathsome *macinato*, a deliberate, soak-the-poor tax on bread and almost everything else in the mealy diet of the malnourished masses. This measure, which would take years to put through, was in itself a major improvement. But the vast loss of revenue which its repeal entailed was irrecoverable elsewhere, and accordingly the problems of state were to deepen.*

The apparent absence of any remedy for the contradictions of nationhood led the king and his ministers to embrace the new prejudices growing like moss on the social realities. Some believed Italy's woes were good for her. Even Humbert, whose complete works of recorded utterances and known writings would have difficulty filling the pages of a dime scratch pad, had something to say in this regard. He found the Roman question, for example, felicitous "because it permits the maturing of the historical process which will lead to a solution of this discord."[14] Humbert, Margherita, and the court took comfort in the notions of the mythmakers, men such as the former revolutionary Pasquale Turiello, whose book *Government and Governed* was popular political "science" reading of the day.[15]

Turiello proved to the satisfaction of many of the few who could read that the trouble with Italy lay in the national character of the governed and the failure of the government to establish institutions conforming to the presumed nature of the Italians. As this was a fail-

---

* Some saw an evil to the poor in the abolition of the *macinato* greater than in maintaining it. Oddly enough, given the harsh realities, they were probably right. According to the recent theories of Rosario Romeo, it was only the crude exploitation of the peasant classes which could provide the nation's industrial base—that indispensable foundation for the future "progress" of the entire people.[13] The removal of the *macinato*, however, forced a much heavier tax burden on the rich, depleting capital and hence slowing development for all. Whatever the validity of this now fashionable argument, it certainly illustrates the true worth of the social structure.

ure easily corrected, Turiello's science was joyously welcomed at court, and Margherita began to remark with enduring repetitiveness that the institution Italians needed most was one which would make frequent use of the *bastone*, or the club.[16]

The nation's difficulties, Turiello theorized, arose not from its social structure but solely from a lack of recognition that the common man was like a child growing spoiled for sparing the rod. Naturally this was presented nondisparagingly, in the sensible language of the times.

> The Italian [he wrote], left alone in Europe for fourteen centuries without the discipline of a powerful State, feels within himself a keen sense of his own individuality . . . he uses the *I* much more than the *we*. . . . The Italian never reflects, is never doubtful, and even when knowing himself wrong, he is certain. . . . German and English individualism opposes itself to religious or political tyranny and is therefore social; [undisciplined] Italic individualism is opposed to anything it believes equal or inferior to itself, and is therefore backward . . .[17]

All sorts of venerable authorities were subpoenaed from past and present to give evidential testimony: from Machiavelli to Tasso (*"Alla virtù latina / O nulla manca o sol la disciplina"*); from Burckhardt to Garibaldi ("It has long been my belief, and I am always more persuaded of its truth, that to get us Italians to agree, what is needed is the club, and nothing less.").

Turiello's theories "explained" why the homicide rate in Italy, which was giving so much cause for alarm to the establishment, was the highest in Europe, six times that of France and eight times that of the English. Turiello said that this "special inclination" of every Italian came not only from his individualism but more so from the nation's laws being flaccid, its penalties too mild.

Everyone in the new Italy had hostility for his neighbor, said Turiello, agreeing with D'Azeglio's remark that there was "a little bit of civil war in the heart of each Italian." This enmity began beyond the northernmost border, he went on in an entertaining manner, writing:

> The Provençal is accustomed to imputing, until it is proved otherwise, all blood crimes of unknown authorship to the numerous Piedmontese workers who go abroad to find jobs in Provence. Then the Lombard and the Venetian fear the knife of the Romagnan more than their fellow citizens. The Tuscan has the Roman as being bloodthirsty. The Neapolitan often fears the Calabrian for the same reason, and the Calabrian

the Sicilian. Each one regards as more dangerous his more southern neighbor.[18]

The northerners' belief about the south as the homeland of a narrow, sluggish, ill-washed people of blackguards was known throughout the world, but as a Neapolitan Turiello spoke with authority when he asserted that the southerners thought even less of their fellow Italians up north. To the Sicilian, the Neapolitan, or the Calabrian it often seemed

> that outside the southern provinces of Italy less honor was given to the family because there the women go about with greater freedom. . . . The southerner, after a brief trip through other parts of Italy, returns to his home town with impressions recounted in frankness. He tells of the stench of the canals and the beggars of Venice, the meanness and the small stature of the Tuscans, and of the drunkenness and the open roughness of the common people of Milan and Turin.[19]

Italy, he concluded, was a place where almost everyone felt that the new state would run best if he himself were permitted to run it. From this the real rulers had to learn that they could no longer delay "the establishment of kindly, educative institutions which at the same time, however, organize and limit individualism."[20] Fortunately, one such institution already existed: the army. Only through military discipline could the "Italic man" be taught cooperation and obedience, and that was why the nation's most "appropriate elements" almost always came from the military. It was a good thing that the army was continually educating more Italians and it was a bad thing that there had been so long a period of peace since the war of 1866.[21]

Humbert, reared by generals and colonels, could not but agree. He and Margherita believed wholeheartedly in the philosophy of Angelo Camillo De Meis, whose little book *The Sovereign*, first published in 1868, gave the new monarchy a rationalist *raison d'être* on a par with the most dialectical thinking of the day.[22] De Meis, a professor at the University of Bologna, claimed to be a disciple of Bruno, Vico, and Hegel. He taught the history of medicine, but he had "discovered" the general laws of human society in their most beautiful simplicity. They proved beyond all doubt that the constitutional rule of the House of Savoy was not only good, but was the sole means of achieving true democracy.

His logic was silly but tight. It proceeded along the following line. In antiquity, as Vico had taught, there was but one people, all of whom took part in a world of poetry and passion. Modern times, the age of thought, knew two kinds of people: the masses, who were still of the ancient world because they lived by sentiment and custom, and the truly modern people, those who lived by thinking. The modern people think what the masses have no consciousness of, and are, therefore, the latter's natural and legitimate rulers, but, as such, they seek to transform the masses, to modernize them. But as it is unnatural for the masses to be anything other than what they are, the modern people create a situation in which the two groups are opposed to one another. They can be reconciled only through the agency of a certain kind of rare human being: a sovereign who embodies the mind and soul of both groups. Now the true sovereign of all the people is the philosopher, because he does nothing else but think; for that very reason however, he is the least acceptable to the non-thinking people. Indeed for them the philosopher as sovereign is a tyrant and his rule is thus unstable. Similarly, a sovereign who does not think would be unacceptable to the thinking people. Then what manner of man or institution, asked De Meis, was to be sovereign in Modern Times? It was clear that he had to be a "living compromise between the mass of people who feel and the few people who think." He then went on to give his celebrated description of the ideal sovereign:

> He must be an individual. Further, he must be that kind of individual who is as stately, handsome, and strong as possible, who is magnificent, conspicuous, and ever so slightly sensual, a matter however, where he does not fear to sin on the side of caution. But above all other things it is necessary that he be religious, and if he does not feel it in his heart, he must give the impression that he does, and moreover it is essential that he so conduct himself in his public life to the point of ostentation. All this is necessary in order that the lower classes recognize themselves, see in him their own facsimile and thus their natural defender against their natural enemy: the superior people.
>
> But at the same time the sovereign-mediator must be a friend of progress and ideas. He must be passionate in his will for national independence, unity, and the greatness of the fatherland, ready to shed his own blood for this cause—and so much the better if he is seen more than once actually shedding it. Above all he must be impartial, and with regard to religion, possess a wideness of views—if he has any at all. . . . [All this] is indispensable in order that the superior people, that is, the ruling people, recognize in him the representative of their own principles, their arm and their shield against the clerical-demagogic class, and, more or less, the entire lower people.[23]

De Meis's ideal sovereign was sculpted as a historical man of a particular moment in societal development, an immortal, universal being, who had served one or another society in the past and would so serve in the future (indeed, De Meis saw the "poetic" ante-bellum Americans as having divided into two opposed peoples, who would soon have need of a sovereign-mediator). He did little, however, to conceal that the model for this timeless figure had been Victor Emmanuel II—the living proof of his sociology. The Bourbon king of Naples, he explained, had fallen "on the day when the superior people no longer saw in him the shadow of themselves." But when the new sovereign, Victor Emmanuel, took his place, civil war erupted because as the Bourbons had been a tyranny of the inferior people, the Savoys represented a tyranny of the superior people and Victor Emmanuel the "king of the bourgeoisie."* This had been a sorry but inevitable episode, and law and order were not restored until "the inferior people, with the passage of time, grew to recognize in the sovereign of the superior people something of themselves, the traces of their sentiments, the image of their own consciousness—if one can speak of consciousness among such people. . . . It was then that the Bourbonite people . . . opened their eyes and welcomed the sovereign of the bourgeoisie as their rightful and legitimate sovereign."[24]

Unfortunately there remained some Italians who had as yet failed to accept the sovereignty of the House of Savoy. They were, said De Meis, the republicans, students, and demagogues who were the cause of all the evil in Italy as a result of their violation of the rule of reason. There was nothing intrinsically wrong with a republic; it was just unsuitable for the Italians. It was a system for a lower stage in society, for a people who had not yet begun to think, like the virtuous, "sub-sub-medieval" Americans, he said, hoping not to offend anyone ("It is a fact that the Americans have never passed for a thinking people").

The House of Savoy, on the other hand, was the most up-to-date thing in the world, De Meis said; old as it was, it had undergone a radical change. Unlike other dynasties, founded on the divine right of kings, a concept repugnant to modern times, the House of Savoy did

---

* In nineteenth-century Italian the phrase had the ring of irony. De Meis's sentence read: "*Egli* [the inferior people] *nel* re galantuomo *non vide il suo re, ma solo il* re dei galantuomini" (emphasis in the original). The *re galantuomo*, of course, was Victor Emmanuel's epithet, but the word *galantuomo* in the Bourbon kingdom had a meaning quite different from how it was understood in the rest of Italy. Instead of *honest* or *upright*, it meant simply *bourgeois*, its plural, *galantuomini*, as used above.

not exist by virtue of blood or blind tradition, but by the divine right of law and the will of the people, spoken in free elections, he said. Its roots, therefore, said De Meis, ran much deeper than the old-fashioned dynasties and it had a much greater reason for being.[25]

Much of what De Meis, Turiello, and the other sophists, empiricists, and metaphysicians were saying was undeniable, which only shows how variegated is the rainbow of the truth men say about an event and how little it weighs on the event itself. Such was the case in Humbert's Italy. The influence of the new ideologists, especially De Meis, on the "superior people" was inestimable, but that changed little in unified Italy. Margherita, we are told by her most objective biographer, accepted "without reserve" De Meis's definition of the ideal sovereign,[26] and Humbert, who, as we have already heard him remark, wished nothing more than to be like his father, was to pass the remainder of his life trying to become the living symbol of De Meis's catechism. Croce relates that Italy's then most renowned living poet and its most respected and ardent republican, Giosuè Carducci, who was to be De Meis's loudest critic, was in the end won over by the latter's intellectual prowess. Carducci's abjuration, in the first year of Humbert's rule, was one of the House of Savoy's sweetest triumphs. Yet it did not heal a single pellagrous child or raise a worker's wages, and for such deficiencies it only hastened the dynasty's fall.

In this period of post-Risorgimento soul-searching the policies of the Humbertine era began to take shape. Incapable of alleviating the stress on the population through substantive reforms, the men in power alleviated the stress on themselves by giving their faith and their all to the new ideology. If the Italians were an undisciplined, self-centered breed and if the army and the House of Savoy were believed to be the most modern veterinary medicine for this sorry condition, it seemed the sensible thing to do was to go ahead with the treatment. It was to be a policy of up with the new institutions, down with chaos.

6

"HUMBERT FOR PRESIDENT"

FIRST CAME THE INSTITUTIONS. THE INITIAL POLITICAL ACT OF THE NEW KING AND QUEEN was to set out on a good-will journey throughout the land. The "inferior people" were to be given the opportunity to see for themselves that the sovereignty invested in the royal couple was their own. The tour would be filled with successes, but climaxed in near disaster, due partly, it would be said, to the following situation, which arose prior to their departure.

About a month after Victor Emmanuel's funeral, Crispi, who had replaced Nicotera as minister of the interior, was accused by his vindictive predecessor of bigamy.[1] Crispi defended himself by saying that his first marriage had not been legal. The priest who had performed it, he said, had not had the proper religious credentials. Moreover, as the woman had become an alcoholic and increasingly lax in her inhibitions, he had taken a more proper spouse in order to legitimize and give a mother to a child born of the first union. But this "moral question" could not be put aside. Rumor had it that there was a third Mrs. Crispi, and Humbert and Margherita, in spite of the minister's monarchist devotions, gasped loudest of all in flushed indignation. Crispi stood firm, but according to his friend and biographer, William J. Stillman, "The Court was perhaps the most violent and unscrupulous element amongst those hostile to Crispi and even royalty was moved beyond serenity."[2] In the end he was forced to resign, a conclusion which was seen by the right as a sign of the nation's growing moral consciousness.

In the meantime, however, the Depretis regime had fallen on a minor issue. This opened the way for the formation of a new government even further to the left, which took on aspects of a reaction against Depretis and Crispi. Brought to power were the genuinely liberal idealist Benedetto Cairoli as prime minister, and the anti-Depretis, leftist reformer Zanardelli, who was given Crispi's vacated post. They had always been unwelcome at court and were acceptable to the king now only because he was hoping that the next governmental failure would create circumstances favorable for a restoration of the rule of the right.

In this unstable condition Humbert and Margherita with Cairoli and Zanardelli at their side undertook their grand tour of Italy that summer. The first stop was at the coastal town La Spezia for the launching of the warship *Dandolo*. The crowds were exceptionally warm and enthusiastic; the royal couple and the nine-year-old heir to the throne wore elegant whites, and the bishop of Sarzana blessed the 350-foot pride of the Italian navy. The ropes were taken up, the hawsers undone, and the queen broke a bottle of *spumante* on the port side. Then, amid thunderous applause, the ship slid gracefully toward the sea, puffing white steam to the sky. It was a mighty beginning, but it seemed no event in unified Italy could escape falling into farce. About two-thirds of the way down the ramp, before the massive bow could dampen in the sea, the great ship came to an embarrassing halt. Workmen ran to her rescue in hopes of somehow nudging her into the deep, and when that did not succeed, explanations about technical difficulties were all that could be advanced. "The fact is," commented Count Guiccioli, who had accompanied the king and queen, "the ship remained stationary and we remained grieved and disconcerted."[3]

To console themselves, the royal party left the bogged down *Dandolo* to inspect her sister ship, the *Duilio*, which was still under construction. Spirits brightened as Humbert and Margherita watched enormous cranes move the ship's cannons into place. "A true instrument of war," Count Guiccioli remarked of *Duilio* with its armor installed, "the most powerful ever seen."

Nevertheless this illusion too soured abruptly, turned to irony by an intrusion of ever denied reality. News from abroad, which reached the king that day, brought fresh gloom to the royal party. The Congress of Berlin was in session with Bismarck balancing southeastern Europe, redistributing spoils of the Ottoman Empire. Italy, for all her imagined power, was to get nothing, it was learned. Cairoli had been too lacking in guile for the vivisection of other people's lands, and he had sent his unschooled foreign minister to the conference with instructions to uphold a policy of "clean hands."

It was a noble gesture, even if a result of national adolescence and inexperience. It was hardly appreciated at home, however, especially since the other powers were eagerly dipping their hands in the imperialist mire and fishing out enviable prizes. The results, to the despair of the king and queen, were as follows: Britain got Cyprus, France was given *carte blanche* in Tunisia, and Austria won ill-fated Bosnia and Herzegovina. But when the Italian idea of compensation in the Trentino had been timidly broached, one of the powers, imperial Russia, brushed it aside with the sarcastic remark that if Italy were asking to annex another territory it must mean that her army had suffered another spectacular defeat in the field. The Italians had been told to take an "island or a port" somewhere, but there was no place of consequence remaining.[4]

"It's useless," said Guiccioli, reflecting the mood of the court that day. "In order for your policies to succeed, you must have the means and the will to go to war if need be. Words have meaning only insofar as they are backed by material force. Even the force of morality is often nothing more than the threat of material force behind it."

Two days later the *Dandolo* finally got into the water and the road fortunes of Humbert and Margherita improved. In Turin, the people of their home city were delirious with joy: the royal couple were acclaimed by the Milanese, too, and in Venice serenaded on the Grand Canal. The convictions of the stoniest socialists and republicans began to melt in all this warmth, and when Zanardelli chanced to meet Carducci during the tour, he impressed the republican poet, remarking that the queen had committed his verses to memory. She cared nothing of his political beliefs, and indeed, the minister intimated, wished to give him a royal decoration, the Civil Order of Savoy. Carducci was tempted, but when he learned that in accepting the honor, it was *de rigueur* to kneel and swear faith on the Gospels to the king, the poet was utterly repelled, and refused.

But Carducci had never yet seen beautiful Margherita. This occurred shortly after his encounter with Zanardelli, when the king and queen visited his home city of Bologna. It was one of those moments in which men fall captive to things bigger than themselves. "I was in the crowd which was pushing and milling in the arcades," the forty-three-year-old poet who would one day win the Nobel prize later recounted, "and in that confusion the white and blond figure of the Queen passed before me like a romantic image in the midst of a realistic narrative, powerful if you will, but endless and boring."[5] It was an image which haunted Carducci, and he found himself thinking nice things about the monarchy.

Margherita pursued him. "Mind you well," she instructed, "by whatever means I wish to see Professor Carducci." It was therefore arranged that he be invited by another man of letters to a reception for the sovereigns given during their stay in Bologna. With some trepidation and accompanied by a friend to shore up his courage, he approached the palace where the king and queen were being feted. In the antechamber he saw on one side of the room officers in dress uniforms, their medals scintillating in the gaslight; on the other side were men wearing shiny silk top hats, diplomats and high civil servants. Carducci says it was this symbolic picture of national divisions which made him realize that only "the head of the family of Savoy represented Italy and the State."

"All right, long live Italy!" he said, turning to his friend. "Valletti, lift aside the drapes and let us go and kneel before the king."[6]

Inside, the king was moving about from group to group shaking the hands of his visitors. But all eyes were on the queen, who in her regal manner towered over everybody in the great salon. The poet was later to write:

> Among those dark suits and white ties . . . she stood out with a rare purity of line and stature and with a truly superior, simple elegance both in the jewels which adorned her and in her attire, a gown and train (the color of a turtle dove, I believe). In everything she did, in her expressions, the rare movements of her feet and her body, the nod of her head, the inflection in her voice, and in her words, she demonstrated dignity and good will, yet she never once laughed or smiled. She stared at length with her fairly tranquil but steady eyes and the blond softness of her Saxon blood seemed to temper that certain something which dominated the lower part of her forehead—I don't know just what it was; I won't say rigidity, neither would imperious do. Rather, from eyebrow to eyebrow the splendid gleam of an eaglet flashed on that pious dove. With dovelike grace and the rosiest of smiles, she who had descended from the Amadeuses and from Vitikund,* had been courteous to the people on the streets, but in the palace she was queen.[7]

Then came the poet's turn. "I am very pleased to meet you in person," said Margherita, "but I feel I know you for a very long time. I am one of your ardent admirers."

---

* The legend of Savoyard ancestry to that warrior of Carolingian times was dying hard. See above, p. 15.

Carducci bowed his head.

"I know your *Nuove poesie* quite well, but your *Odi barbare* are extremely difficult! But I have memorized them too, you know. You have found a new form, and a very splendid one for the profound poem."

Carducci was overcome. He felt easier with Humbert. "That poor king," he said later that day, "spoke to me so excitedly and emotionally . . . and he shook my hand so cordially that he seemed as if he were grateful to me."

Such gratitude did not go unrequited, for the Mazzinian poet rushed to write his famous "Ode to the Queen of Italy," with "a pen that knows the tempest."[8]

The royal conquests at Bologna, a center of the most militant republicans, were virtually complete. Even the stanchest among them were heard to say, "If the Republic comes, we'll give our vote to Humbert for President." They came out to the railroad terminal by the thousands to give a rousing send-off to the king and queen and little Victor Emmanuel, who stood clutching Cairoli's hand for fear of being swallowed by the roaring crowd. Florence was the same. Eight thousand schoolchildren gathered in the Palazzo Vecchio to sing "Happy Birthday" to the nine-year-old crown prince. But at Naples, the last turn of the journey, government by charisma came full circle.

The royal travelers entered the city on the afternoon of November 17; Naples had done everything to welcome them in a grandiose manner. Morelli had painted figures on the carpet that led up to the door of their train. The entire population had been taxed one penny each so that all might share in the honor of having contributed to the gift for Margherita. A slow procession of carriages made its way under falling flowers from the station to the Palazzo Reale, and it seemed all of Naples was there in joyous greeting. But there was a lone assassin among the people, a certain Giovanni Passanante, an unemployed cook who had once been arrested for having pasted signs on the walls of Salerno reading "Universal Revolution!"

As they entered the crowded Piazza Carrera Grande, Humbert and Margherita were sitting side by side in their open coach; Cairoli and the *principino* were facing them. Suddenly the assailant ran up to the carriage, a red cloth covering his hand. Some thought he wished to supplicate the king, but the pallid youth leaped to the running board and revealed a dagger beneath the cloth, upon which he had inscribed "Long live the universal republic!" He raised his weapon high, then thrust for Humbert of Savoy.

"Cairoli!" cried Margherita, "save the king!"

The prime minister hurled himself forward and absorbed the blow. The assassin's knife plunged into his thigh, causing a deep but not serious wound. In the meantime, while the *principino* drew back in horror, Humbert, who was slightly scratched, began to pound on Passanante's head with his sheathed sword. Margherita whipped him with a fistful of nosegay she had been holding in her lap. In a few moments Passanante was subdued by the police and taken away.

Margherita, who possessed the flair of a Lewis Carroll queen for uttering memorable inanities, declared, "The enchantment of the House of Savoy has been broken!"[9]

Humbert simply succored Cairoli like a fallen comrade on the battlefield, and he insisted the procession continue. He had nothing weighty to say, but a few days later he remarked good-humoredly in calling some guests to dinner, "Let us be seated and let's not keep the cooks waiting; you have seen, ladies and gentlemen, what they are capable of."[10]

It was clear from the start that Passanante was mad. The alienists testified as much in court, although they had reached this conclusion by arithmetic, rather than psychiatric calculations. The circumference of his skull, they discovered, was 535 millimeters, "the same as found in the criminally insane in the proportion of twenty-five percent." They estimated that his brain weighed ten grams less than average, and they "observed" what they called "the obliteration of the central canal of his spinal cord," which was why his madness was symptomless (this when Sigmund Freud was a fourth-year medical student in Vienna). Passanante claimed to represent no one but his universal republican self and said he had no accomplices. If he had, he affirmed abstrusely, he would have used not a knife but a gun and would not have failed. He refused recourse in a plea of insanity, which if upheld would preclude passage of a death sentence. The motive behind the attempted assassination, he said, was his animosity toward emperors and kings. "From what I read," he stated, "I gather that kings spend too much." The trial provoked great hilarity, mainly because of the poor man's behavior ("If you let me speak, fine; if not, I'm leaving"). In the end the jury withdrew and deliberated for a "few instants" and judging him sane returned the death penalty.[11]

The incident tended to be shrugged off at first, and there was some perverse truth in Guiccioli's comment that it had resolved itself in "a new triumph for the Monarchy."[12] But in the days that followed, revolutionary violence, or that which passed for such, erupted in Florence, Pisa, and elsewhere, and Humbert, Margherita, and the more astute politicians saw the entire affair as a unique opportunity to foster the cause of law and order.

The fair-haired courtier Count Guiccioli, who continually found himself in accord with the views of the king and queen, wrote: "This is the result of our idiot weakness toward criminals. But the country cannot remain at the mercy of these malefactors. They must be struck down with a red hot iron."[13]

Humbert, too, on hearing of the disturbances in Florence and Pisa, remarked resolutely, "These are acts which absolutely must not happen in a civilized country, and they must not be allowed to happen."[14]

It was the turn of law and order. The truth was that the most established members of the new class, right and left, had little confidence in the freewheeling system they had called into being. They believed that the thrust of the French Revolution on the continent and the idea of unity at home were driving all the way to republicanism, perhaps even to socialism. Fearing the loss of all they had gained, that is, their rule, they wished to brake those forces and *fa marcia indietro*, or back up. The multiple crises created by the precipitous unification—resulting from the social awakening of the Italians from a kind of tranquil misery and the inability of the new class to satisfy even a modicum of their demands—were now to be grouped in the age-old category of "civic disorder." The Cairoli government was to be made the scapegoat for the recent disturbances and its "failure" to maintain order was to be the pretext for reaction.

Cairoli's regime had in fact pledged itself to be vigilant in securing public order, declaring that it would suppress all disturbances. But it had gone further than any other government in promising not to prevent the exercise of such freedoms as those of speech, the press, and the right of assembly. This policy of "suppression but not prevention," enunciated by Cairoli and reiterated only a fortnight before the attempted assassination and the subsequent outbreaks in the cities, now came under bitter attack in parliament, in a "great debate" on law and order.

The slogan and the policy "suppression but not prevention" were held to be the cause of violence, and Cairoli and Zanardelli were said to be personally responsible. Not only the right assailed the government as an agent of "extreme democracy," but Crispi, as leader of the radical left, spoke for the first time in public in support of the reactionaries. Depretis, who had posed as Cairoli's best friend, found the recent incidents "a threat to our social order." He was moved to tears. As one who adored Italy, he said, "I see her in danger and, oh, gentlemen, I am afraid."[15]

The right hammered away on an imagined upsurge of republicanism and socialism, which since the advent of Cairoli was found to be spreading everywhere. The courtier scholar Ruggero Bonghi declared that Cairoli's policies had made it lawful not only to form republican associations, but also "to insult the king, the dynasty, the monarchy, and our institutions."[16]

Cairoli and Zanardelli, while defending themselves, were more or less contrite. They assumed full responsibility for past events and promised a happier, more orderly, and less radical future. But this was found unsatisfactory, especially by Humbert and Margherita, whose inexperience seems to have led them to behave slightly intemperately. The king, anxious to create the maximum effect, intimated that the wounded Cairoli was somehow personally suspect in the Passanante affair, an indiscretion which had to be dispelled by wiser men. Both Humbert and Margherita were panicking from the propaganda storm in the parliamentary teacup. Seeing the peril, which was purposely exaggerated by their supporters, as imminent and true, the royal couple hoped to reinstate the right in power as their best protection. But when the party's skilled leaders, considering the lack of electoral support, found such a move inopportune, the queen is said to have lamented, "Even [they] are abandoning us."[17]

This was far from true. What was happening was that the transformist rule of Depretis, the movement of men such as Crispi to the monarchist side, and the community of interests and fears of right and left were providing ample proof that both parties formed but a single political body standing before a mirror, and now it stood naked. A genuine brotherhood was slowly emerging, which could find less and less to oppose in itself. Its common enemies were men like Cairoli, republicans, radicals, socialists, clericals, feudalists, and, generally speaking, the people. The Cairoli-Zanardelli government fell. Depretis was voted back in. The king was counseled to agree, and on December 20, 1878, Depretis made his acceptance speech in which he rededicated himself to liberalism and the people. The deputies of right and left alike, we have it on good authority, laughed.[18]

The abortive experiment in Cairolian permissiveness was but an interlude in what is often called "the Depretis 'dictatorship,'" with the noun rendered intellectually honest by dressing it with the above punctuation. This seems fair enough, for while he continually used strong-arm methods at the polls, silenced the press and public, violated the constitution and every civil and human right, he did so without "excesses," and in a manner more reminiscent of Cavour than Mussolini.

Depretis's *trasformismo* succeeded in absorbing all but the most calcified opposition. This, the court cherished. Unrecognized, however, was that the stuff absorbed only raised the level of popular discontent. The underhanded means by which the Depretis system held up the social structure not only frustrated the governed but also disgusted the governors, who saw something vampirish in the way *trasformismo* drained the national vigor. Parliament became the institution by which electoral protest was neutralized, but it would not take very much longer for the electorate to see on its portals the Dantean inscription about abandoning hope all who enter here. In one stratum near the surface of the people's wrath lay the immediate hurt of deprivation; down deeper were the incipient reactions which were to find expression in Pareto's sociology, Mosca's political science, Croce's philosophy, D'Annunzio's nationalism, Gramsci's communism, and Mussolini's fascism—all of which, for good or for bad, were to bring still greater miseries to the Italians.

Their seething ire, which erupted regularly in ever more menacing violence, held Humbert and Margherita constantly obsessed with the fear of being suddenly overthrown. This forced the young sovereigns to continue to view their house, as their predecessors had done, as an institution wholly apart from everything else Italian. Moreover they believed their own dynastic interests to be above those of the nation. National development took on a lower priority than the security of the crown. This was rationalized by the notion that the monarchy was the sticky stuff without which turbulent Italy would fall apart.

Thus, afflicted with the limited vision for which kings are best known, Humbert and Margherita could only conclude that the finest way to absorb rising discontent was with more and more *trasformismo*. Not only did this invention—in the short run—weaken all things considered dangerous to the crown, it also permitted the sovereign to stand aloof from the workings of government and give the appearance of constitutional propriety while his ministers served not the people but the House of Savoy.

For such reasons Humbert and Margherita sought now to duplicate abroad what Depretis was doing for them at home, and it was

not by chance that efforts to conclude an alliance with the most reactionary powers in Europe coincided with the predominance of De-
pretism. The royal couple understood, better than anyone else, it
seems, that not only the Italians had to be kept at arm's length, while
they attempted to reinforce their rickety throne, but all other "encroaching hordes," as Margherita called them. It would not, however, be an easy accomplishment, and that it was done and endured
may be regarded as the youthful sovereigns' greatest contribution to
the longevity of the House of Savoy. Beleaguered by hostile forces,
they relied now on the tried and true policies of Humbert the Whitehanded.

7

A KISS IN VIENNA

THEIR INITIAL DIFFICULTY IN WINNING POWER-
FUL FRIENDS ABROAD WAS THAT NO DYNASTY
in late nineteenth-century Europe was as isolated as the House of
Savoy without Victor Emmanuel II. This was due partly to appearances which in fact were not true.

In the first place Savoyard rule felt itself and seemed to others to
be on the weakest footing. All of the monarchies were in turmoil,
facing much the same problems, internal and otherwise, as those
of Humbert and Margherita. But the others were founded in the
bedrock of their non-negotiability. Although all were younger than
the Italian dynasty, and few would outlive it, they seemed eternal.
The Hapsburgs and the king of Prussia disposed of an ancient aristocracy of feudal devotions to the crown. Even the old kings in Turin
had been sustained by a closely knit class of noblemen ready to die
for them.

United Italy's aristocracy, on the other hand, was, as has been
glimpsed, divided, ignorant, and often openly opposed to one another as well as to the House of Savoy. Moreover, the loyalty of the
new bourgeois class was untested, and in its clamorous heterogeneity
seemed untrustworthy. Appearances deceived, however. Humbert
and Margherita were simply not conscious of their power to control
the political life of the country; they were unsure of men such as
Depretis, unaware that they were in fact being admirably served.

A second cause of their insularity was the very real fact that the
other royal houses of Europe were linked to one another by ties of
blood and political alliances. The children and children's children of
Victoria were legion on the continent. By century's end more than

one hundred royal personages, in almost every house but that of Savoy, from St. Petersburg to Athens, from Stockholm to Bucharest, could call the queen of England "Auntie," "Granny," or "Mother."

The Italian royal couple were but third-cousin poor relations of Franz Josef, brother- and sister-in-law to the rather minor king of Portugal, and the only way Margherita could address Victoria was with banal jealousies, whispered behind her back (". . . that little, old, not at all aesthetic *Signora*").[1]

Further, the continental system of treaties, such as the *Dreikaiserbund* to stave off subversion from the doors of the Hohenzollerns, the Hapsburgs, and the Romanovs, drew princes even closer to one another than family ties, if only ephemerally. But Humbert and Margherita participated in none of these, and their absence was conspicuous to all, but most profoundly and painfully to themselves.

Still another reason for their isolation was Italy's basic insignificance in the scheme of big power politics. This was hardest of all to bear by a generation of Italians raised on the pabulum of their nation's manifest destiny. It was a meager consolation that in a world where might was all, they were already counting for much more than their worth, acknowledged as a kind of stepbrother big power, when in fact their power was irreparably small.

The bitter realization of their real and imagined condition turned the king and queen away from policies of "clean hands" back to the stand-bys of their house: in this case, entente with the mighty, the maintenance at whatever cost of a massive army, and expansion anywhere.

Serious talk of a treaty with Germany and Austria began during the summer of 1880 between Humbert and his ministers. They hoped to get the backing of the Central Powers for Italian expansion in the Mediterranean in exchange for a guarantee of Italy's neutrality in any war which might involve Berlin or Vienna, or both.

The Austrians seemed not unwilling to arrive at some understanding, but Bismarck was adamantly opposed. Italians in the Mediterranean would upset French interests, said the chancellor, and moreover he did not believe in the sincerity or the stability of the leaders in Rome. It was Bismarck's Europe and it was Bismarck who assayed Italy's value in the big power hierarchy, estimating it very low indeed. He was "cured of Italy," he said privately. According to the German prince, the Italians were jackals who stood behind lions in order to devour their victims. Italy even as an ally in war would be worth next to nothing.[2]

On the very day Bismarck was unraveling such feelings to French ambassador Saint Vallier, Humbert made his initial approach to the Central Powers, adopting the style of his father in keeping his own ministers uninformed. Speaking to the Austrian ambassador on November 26, 1880, Humbert expressed his apprehension about republican demonstrations which had taken place in Italy some days earlier and about the chronic weaknesses of his own rule. The ambassador reported this conversation to Vienna, which in turn informed Berlin.

In a note, passed on to Bismarck, the Austrian diplomat in Rome said that his minister "knows all too well the easily excitable and at the same time versatile character of his neighbors beyond the Alps ("and their infantile selfishness," Bismarck scratched in the margin) to attribute any special value to the currents of opinion which develop unexpectedly in Italy." The Austrians, however, desiring to turn the "versatile" Italians in any direction other than toward themselves, grew well disposed, expressing sympathy for Italian designs on Tunisia, Tripoli, and elsewhere in North Africa. But Bismarck remained impassable.[3]

Meanwhile, in May, 1881, a real crisis developed in Italy, shaking both government and crown. The French, on the pretext of protecting their nationals from the imagined assaults of the "marauding," but fictitious "Krumiri" tribes of Algeria, occupied Tunisia. They forced the bey to sign a treaty establishing a French protectorate over the territory.[4] Italy was outraged. Like France, it too had colonial desires in the same region, but had not wanted to act, for fear of alienating Paris, and now that France had struck, the Italians felt stabbed in the back.

The government in Rome fell. There were riots and demonstrations, and the tension between the two Latin countries led to brutal attacks by Frenchmen on Italian workers in Marseilles. The *Nuova Antologia* wrote at the time that the Tunisian development was a happy one because at last Italy had a "great national question," but Sonnino's *Rassegna Settimanale* saw it as a disaster, carrying with it "the destruction of Italy's future as a great Power . . . unless she regains her position by force of arms."[5]

In the absence of a government, rumors of a revolution in the making began to spread, alarming the king. Hoary Garibaldi was thought to be organizing a new invasion by sea, and Humbert tried speedily to reinstall the old right. Depretis, however, rushed to the sovereign and declared that the return of the right would bring chaos and even collapse. The Italians would no longer tolerate ministries which had "starved the people," and speaking as acting interior minister, he said he could not guarantee public order.

The king for the first time in his reign was taken with the idea of a rightist *coup d'état*, but in spite of support in some court circles, he could not get up the courage.[6] Power was returned to Depretis. He restrained all who were ready to strike back inadvisably at the French, but joined them in steaming in Italy's humbling impotence, which almost everyone by now had concluded issued from her isolation. Whatever resistance to entente with the "powers of order" Humbert and Margherita might have had at home now gave way to a united push for a triple alliance.

The alliance, once made, was to ensure all sorts of debilitating and rueful complications in the long run, but governments and monarchies are institutions which exist on the premise that the past is the present gone by and the future the now yet to come. Thus Humbert and Margherita took only the next step, which, at the time, lay before them with the cold logic of the crossties on a railroad. Although now we may wonder why, it seemed to them that a state visit to the court of the House of Hapsburg was the most important thing they ought to do.

Early on the Thursday evening of October 27, 1881, the Sudbanhof in Vienna glowed in splendor and expectation. The floors and stairways of the great railroad terminal were covered with Persian rugs and adorned with a veritable garden of tropical flowers from the greenhouses of the Schönbrunn. Austrian and Italian flags, pleated together like pigtails, hung from the damask-covered walls. A small part of the train station had been recently wired for electricity and globes of robust tungsten lights outshone the Venetian gaslamps with a radiance which was noted in awe by the hundreds of spectators, who had found time to come and see. A red carpet had been rolled out to the main platform, and a minute or so before 7:30 Emperor Franz Josef, Crown Prince Rudolf, and an accompaniment of royalty in highnesses descending like a marble staircase followed the crimson stripe to the edge to await the arrival of Humbert and Margherita. Following this little ceremony there was nothing to do but stand on the platform, peer down the road, and wonder if the Italians, due in at this very moment, would be in on time.

The specially fitted royal train, carrying the king and queen and their party, was slapping hard on the rails, six minutes out of Vienna. Margherita had just changed her toilette, freshening herself for the evening's reception at the imperial palace. She wore a dress of blue silk and lace, which she covered with an abundant traveling cape made of a dark nappy cloth. On her blond tresses sat a neat little hat of the same material, giving her a prim elegance which made her look as angelic as Florence Nightingale, and indeed the following day's *Neue Freie Presse* was to deem her "the good angel of Italy." Humbert, too, had changed, substituting a general's uniform and a plumed helmet for his normal attire, a top hat and frock coat which in his growing corpulence were beginning to give him the appearance of a caricatured capitalist. Even Depretis had put on a uniform, top heavy with ribbons and medals, in deference to the Austrian court which disdained anything bourgeois.

The travelers were exhausted and it showed. It had been a difficult journey, more for the conflict and tension than the 600 miles of narrow gauge track which lay between Rome and Vienna. The trip had been undertaken in an atmosphere of desperation and, it seemed to the king and queen, so much depended on its success. Depretis had opposed going to Vienna, and his ministers had advised that it was impolitic with regard to relations with France. Moreover they could not gain a commitment from the Hapsburg court that the emperor and empress would in turn visit Rome. In the absence of such reciprocation another humiliation would surely fall on the Savoyard crown—which in fact was to be the case. But Humbert had been intransigent, remarkably out of character. Apart from seeking alliance, he felt he had to right the wrongs that were thought about Italy, or at least about the House of Savoy. For as much as he wished to look backward, events at home were causing all of Europe to whisper about the dangerous radicalism of the Italians.

In July, there had been an ugly incident while the Vatican was transferring the remains of Pius IX from one burial place to another. A mob had taunted the procession and had threatened to throw the dead pope's body into the Tiber. Depretis, knowing that the Vatican had no voice at the polls, had defended "The People," charging the Church with a provocation. This had been followed some weeks later by republican demonstrations in Rome, supported by Garibaldi, Louis Blanc, and Victor Hugo; they had called for the abolition of the Law of Guarantees. The pope, Leo XIII, had protested to the other sovereigns of Europe and sent a personal message to Franz Josef. Self-righteousness rang all over the continent, and even Protestant England had warned the Italians that the only way they could acquire a role in the club of big powers was by the steadfast pursuit of prudence and conservatism.[7]

Humbert, of course, believed in this unquestioningly, and his discomfiture in being unable to find communion with the like-minded was reaching the temperature at which blood boils. He had wanted to go alone to his cousins in Vienna to be able to speak his mind freely about the perils of liberalism. But Depretis, in spite of his misgivings, insisted on his own presence—even if it meant wearing a uniform, downgrading his revolutionary past, and apologizing for his present-day leftism. He agreed to try to win a pledge of Austrian armed friendship in exchange for Italian support of reaction, and carried an appropriate draft treaty with him to make gain should an unexpected occasion arise.[8] The king could not but yield to such right-thinking, although he insisted in his turn that during their absence the government be left in the hands of a general to forestall any attempts at a *coup*. Depretis concurred, and then at the last minute Humbert sought to redress the imbalance created by the addition of the minister and his entourage by bringing Margherita along.

The train ride itself had caused further political woes. As the transport moved up the peninsula, it excited the activities of the radicals, notably the Austrian-hating Irredentists. Demonstrations calculated to infuriate Vienna were held in towns along the rail route, despite preventive arrests by the Italian police of known organizers. The agitation was such that the king and queen and their party were forced to travel incognito part of the way through Italy.[9] It was all very irritating to the royal couple, and when their train arrived at last in Vienna not even the Italian anthem, struck up by a tidy Austrian military band, could soften the lines of enervation in their faces.

Humbert was first to alight from the train. Everyone saluted. Franz Josef, his Collar of the Annunziata dangling from his neck, rushed to him and kissed him repeatedly. This was an episode inspiring the fiery irredentist poem, "Il bacio di Vienna," which was published immediately and disseminated at home.[10] The first kiss brought on an orgy of kisses as the queen and the rest of the Italian travelers began to step from the royal coach and even Depretis felt someone's lips pressing on the white hair on his face. The Italians found it awkward that the Austrians kissed only one cheek (as opposed to their usage of the French style) and this led to all kinds of head bumping and even more near-misses.

In the meantime the people began to cry "Long live Humbert!" in *Italian*, which was impressive, though not quite as good as the *eine wahre Heldengestalt*—a truly heroic figure—they had exclaimed in the presence of Victor Emmanuel II, when he made the trip in 1873. But no one seems to have remembered that, and the presence of Margherita, spent as she was, made up for whatever might have been lacking. One of the following morning's newspapers described the scene:

> The Emperor and Queen Margherita walked toward the royal hall. All eyes were on the Queen. She looked a little dispirited and her sweet, lovable face showed the signs of fatigue from the long journey. . . . When she reached the halfway mark of the stairway, arriving in full view of the public gathered in the vestibule, she was greeted with a cry of universal jubilance. It seemed as if her appearance had produced a magical effect. There were shouts from all sides: *"Viva Margherita!"* They waved their hats and their handkerchiefs, and the enthusiastic greeting was repeated when the Queen, visibly moved and thankful in a most friendly manner, left the vestibule.[11]

This was in striking contrast to the reception received by the ravishing Empress Elizabeth when as a young bride she and the emperor visited Austrian-ruled Venice and Milan many years before. The Italians had simply stared at her hatefully, in an enduring way which was to contribute to her later resentment of the court into which she had married and was to keep her aloof from its people. It was difficult not to take note of something reproachful of her in the warm welcome given to Margherita by the Viennese, and their press was to make much of the Italian queen's patriotism, her charisma, and all the other qualities they found lacking in poor, half-mad Elizabeth.

It was Elizabeth who greeted Humbert and Margherita at the front door of the imperial palace. The empress, at forty-four, was fifteen years the senior of the queen, but she was still the most beautiful royal figure in Europe. Never were two neighboring queens more disparate. Elizabeth flighty, intense, passionate, racing with the wind to be free of herself; Margherita the insufferable bigot, yearning to devour, to command the wind and the sea like the Fisherman's Wife.

Franz Josef, the tormented autocrat, was fourteen years older than Humbert and equally as different from him as were their spouses from one another. The emperor was a man of principles who could afford to truly believe in his own divinity. "You see in me the last Monarch of the old school," he would tell Theodore Roosevelt.[12] Humbert, who may be regarded as the first of the new school, had not a single conviction other than being true to his house. Franz Josef thought infrequently of Humbert, and when he did it was only to distrust him. Humbert worshiped the emperor. The stern, fatherly Franz Josef, who rarely stooped to politics, had little to say to the king of Italy about the relations between the two countries. Humbert, who felt himself to be the loving son, looked under every spoken phrase for a chance to edge in a word about the true purpose of his journey.

Arriving at the palace, the newspaper accounts relate, Humbert and Margherita were given the opportunity to wash their hands, and then they supped with the Hapsburgs. They retired at an early hour, shown to separate bedrooms, pink for the queen, the color of lilacs for the king. Humbert's suite adjoined that of his aide-de-camp.

The Italians spent a long weekend—four full days—in Vienna. On Friday Humbert and Margherita reviewed the troops in the Schmelz: two full divisions of Germans, Slovenes, Magyars, Little Russians, and every other nationality of the empire had been gathered up in a vast open field covered with an icy fog which had barreled in from the north.

Margherita, bundled in black velvet, looking like a painting by Rubens, drew up in her carriage, and both emperor and king galloped to her side. The Savoyard couple passed in review to the strains of the Italian Royal March. They were acclaimed by all, but especially by the cavalry, for it had been the legendary Prince Eugene of Savoy who had organized that branch of the Hapsburg forces, and in recognition of the seventeenth-century general's contribution to Austrian power, the emperor made Humbert nominal commander of the 28th Infantry Regiment with the rank of colonel in the Austrian army.

His acceptance was to be considered at home an even greater sin than his surrender to the emperor's kisses. The shock was to be infinitely compounded when Humbert showed up in church on Sunday morning and again at a concert that evening no longer in his Italian general's dress, but in the uniform of an Austrian colonel. This sort of garish manifestation of the king's inner desires seems almost humorous today, but it was an act of the grossest insensitivity, an insult to the thousands of Italians then alive whose fathers or sons had been tortured and slain under Austrian rule and in the wars against them. The king's point was well taken by friend and foe alike, and only the emperor and his ministers pretended not to see the forest for the olive branches.

The visitors—each in his own way—tried their best to bring up the subject of the alliance without, for the same reasons a proper guest does not ask to be regaled, actually mentioning it. Depretis and Foreign Minister Mancini pursued their counterparts, the king played colonel, and the queen did everything to appear lacking in nothing. She wore diamonds in her hair, olive-sized pearls on her ear lobes, and lace on her snow-white bosom.

On Saturday, while Margherita went shopping on the Graben, the men hunted in the imperial reserve at Himberg. Nearly a thousand hare and partridges were killed that morning so long ago, 180 felled by Humbert's steady hands alone.

That evening a dinner and gala were given in honor of the royal visitors. One hundred and thirty distinguished persons dined on oysters from Oostende, *potage à la princesse*, salmon in a sauce *béarnaise*, wild boar in a sauce Cumberland, pheasant on a spit, and many other delectables including chocolate ice cream, but neither the hare nor partridge from the hunt, although a more delicate breed of the latter was served.

It was in fact just after the *petites timbales de perdreaux* that the emperor rose and proposed a toast. He thanked the king and queen for their visit and their friendship, concluding, "I drink to the health of His Majesty the King of Italy, Her Majesty the Queen, and the Royal Family." Then Humbert repeated much of the same, but could not resist adding what can only be called the commercial: "I drink to the health of His Majesty the Emperor and King, Her Majesty the Empress and Queen, and the Imperial Family, expressing the profoundest wish that the very cordial relations which fortunately exist between our people draw even closer together . . ."[13] That was his nearest approach to what was uppermost in his mind.

That night the Austrians and the Italians danced at the *Oper*. Outside it snowed.

On Sunday there was the solemn *Kaisermesse* in the morning, a midday audience with the emperor for Depretis, and in the evening, by the light of 4,000 candles, the hosts and their guests listened to Händel, Schubert, and Bellini—which as the Austrians well knew was the traditional torture for at least the male line of the House of Savoy.

On Monday the Italians departed. Humbert (in his colonel's clothes again) and Margherita were escorted by the emperor to the Sudbanhof. They exchanged *au revoirs*, and as the train pulled away from exuberant cries of *Hoch!* and *Evviva!*, Humbert and Margherita could be seen by Franz Josef and the crowds on the platform waving farewell from the window until they grew so tiny they vanished.

The train reached the frontier that evening. By then Humbert had taken off his Austrian uniform and had learned from Depretis that not a single word had been mentioned about the alliance. The royal party slipped back into Italy and continued the journey incognito.[14]

The government and the crown came home feeling more flaccid and fragile than ever. In November the fiercely republican Gambetta came to power in France, causing the Italian court to tremble. He poured vast sums of money into Italy, buying radicals and newspapers of every conviction for his side. Violent demonstrations and open terrorism were suddenly rife throughout the peninsula. France had a great mission, Gambetta declared, a part of which was the republicanization of Italy. Though Gambetta's ministry was to last but nine weeks, he looked ferocious at the time.[15]

Then, later in that same November, Bismarck made a famous speech in the Reichstag giving the kiss-of-death to the House of Savoy. This was followed by his offer to reestablish relations with the Vatican. The dynasty in Rome felt lost; the church and the republicans believed their time had come.

Bismarck's speech was a bolt from the north which rocked not only Italy but the entire continent. With Thor's thunder he fulminated against the idea of Italy's monarchy being based on a constitution. Said the chancellor:

> Gentlemen, you cannot stop the movement of forty million men once it has been set in motion. This is what happened in France. Did there perhaps not exist in France an hereditary monarchy of a thousand years standing, solidly entrenched? But did it not, with its often very reasonable constitutions . . . continuously slide from the extreme constitutional left finally into the republic? . . .
> In other countries beyond France we have seen corroboration of this historical experiment. . . . Take the example of Italy. Do we not already have there, in part, a provisional republic? I don't know if it has the general consent, but in any case the idea already has many partisans, who are more advanced than the German progressives. Would you be willing to assume any guarantees for the future, especially if God does not preserve the life of a dynasty composed of only a few persons? Are you certain that the prophecies declared by the opinionated to be false will not in fact be realized there? It is impossible to predict it. But do we not see that the road Italy has taken in the last twenty years leads

toward this purpose and this aim (I do not wish to affirm that it has already been reached). Is it not perhaps visible? Has not perhaps the center of gravity down there shifted from one ministry to the next always further to the left? Clearly it cannot keep going in this direction without sliding into a republic.[16]

This made the rulers of Italy literally beg for an alliance with the Central Powers. Humbert wrote to his fellow sovereign Kaiser Wilhelm, appealing for a reassuring word from Bismarck. The chancellor telegraphed that his speech should not be interpreted as being anything less than a show of friendship toward the House of Savoy.[17] The king was perplexed but immensely relieved.

Bismarck *was* being friendly. The wishes of the Hohenzollern dynasty, and developments at home and abroad, had in fact raised him above his personal dislike of Italians. He really believed Humbert's monarchy in danger from Gambetta's France. The loss of one kingdom meant the erosion of kingship for all.[18]

A few days prior to his speech in the Reichstag, the true purpose of which was to drive the Italians as far to the right as possible, he had privately expressed his reconsidered view of Italy. Confiding in a friendly emissary of the right who had come to call from Rome, he criticized the way in which the royal visit to the Hapsburg court had been handled as one of many lost opportunities.

Why, he is reported to have asked, had Depretis, "that old intriguer," and Foreign Minister Mancini, "that evil advocate of all evil causes," been allowed to go to Vienna? "I will have nothing to do with those kind of people. . . ."

When asked what ought now to be done, he replied: "Now there's only one thing left, that is that King Humbert do what his father did with us; that he deal with us directly, without his ministers."[19]

In December, at Humbert's bidding, the government let it be known in Vienna that if an alliance with the Central Powers were not forthcoming the monarchy would fall. Later in the month the situation grew even more desperate, in the Italian view. Berlin and Vienna were told that the government in Rome, at the expressed will of Humbert and Margherita, was ready to adhere to their kind of politics even without a formal alliance. It sought only an offer of anything that would sustain the *status quo*.[20]

Humbert, doubtless fearing the prospect of being written off entirely, tried his best not to appear *too* weak. "The important thing," he told his ministers starting the new year, 1882, "is to show that we are, and want to remain, the masters of our own house."[21]

The Austrians, convinced that the House of Savoy was "strongly weakened," were prepared to conclude an agreement, but Bismarck toyed sadistically with the Italians. He now wanted a treaty as much as anyone, but when men tell the truth there is no diplomacy.

On January 31 he was visited by the Italian ambassador to Berlin, who rehearsed the case for a treaty. The chancellor was noncommittal. It was a good idea, he said, but he noted the difference in value of guarantees tendered by a constitutional monarch burdened with a parliament, as opposed to an autocracy. He suspected the entire regime in Italy of being crypto-liberals and he offered in evidence the deplorable fact that Humbert nearly always dressed like a bourgeois rather than in military uniform. If the king were to pay more attention to his army, he would have less need of his neighbors' might, said the chancellor.[22]

This advice, unhappily, was taken very seriously in Rome. A few days earlier the Gambetta government had resigned and now it was felt that with the easing of the republican threat, Bismarck was even less interested in the Italians than before. Accordingly, the crown began at once to let down its sights still more.

Humbert no longer asked for protection against a restoration of papal rule in Rome. Irredentist ambitions were formally repudiated. All claims for recognition of Italian interest in the Mediterranean— the French violation of which in Tunisia had been the pretext by which the king in the first place had gathered internal support for a treaty with the Central Powers—were duly renounced. Indeed, the House of Savoy was willing to give all and ask for nothing more than the imagined psychological advantage an alliance portended. This, Prince Bismarck was ready to allow.

The Triple Alliance was signed in Vienna on May 20, 1882. The Italians got what at least their king and queen wanted in the rhetoric of the preamble. It declared that the Kaisers Wilhelm and Franz Josef and King Humbert had allied themselves in the desire "to increase the guarantees of the general peace, to fortify the monarchical principle, and to assure that social and political order in their States be maintained intact . . . ."[23]

The Austrians, with their eyes on the east, got what they wanted in Article Three, which provided for benevolent neutrality if one of the parties engaged in preventive war.

Bismarck got the rest. Two days after the treaty was signed he remarked coyly that he had adhered to it only as a courtesy to Austria. In fact it completed his system of alliances, with the Reich at the center, and France, its only serious threat, totally isolated. In exchange for military support from Italy in the event of a French assault on Germany—a very real possibility at the time, considering its territorial losses in the Franco-Prussian war—he contracted to reciprocate in the most improbable circumstance of an unprovoked attack by France on Italy.*

For Germany the Triple Alliance was the fill which rendered its security watertight, if only for a few years. For Austria the treaty guaranteed its Italian frontier and permitted the Hapsburgs to dream of an ever greater empire in the Orient. For Italy it was a serious liability imposing the maintenance of a military apparatus it could not afford, limiting its ability to deal with other powers, and further alienating powerful elements at home.

Yet it upheld the very weakness which was the "strength" of the monarchy, insofar as the crown staked its claim for home support as the nation's best unifying force. In this sense the Triple Alliance may be considered a triumph—the triumph of a sentiment which sought due regard for the manifold achievements of the House of Savoy.

In his history of the Triple Alliance Salvatorelli wrote that the treaty was the end result of an irrational fear. The monarchy, he said, "frightened by the danger of republicanism . . . desired support from the monarchic rock of the Central Powers. The danger was extremely exaggerated; the support extremely doubtful."[24]

He correctly traced the "decisive push" behind the Triple Alliance to Humbert, and finally, behind Humbert, to Margherita. To Margherita the iconoclast historian Fabio Cusin assigns with some appropriateness the entire "feminine" character of the Humbertine age. It was a sign of the times, says Cusin, that while the Italy of the Risorgimento had the myth of the *Re Galantuomo*, Humbert's Italy had to content itself with a kind of matriarchy, "idolizing the beautiful Lady Queen." There were many Italians in high places, among them Depretis, who regretted the Triple Alliance because it exposed the government of the left as wholly reactionary and thus gave aid and sinew to the radicals.

> The circles from where Depretis came [Cusin concludes] would have preferred the democratic monarchy which was fabled in Margherita by Carducci (he too a man who played to the gallery). But the real Mar-

---

* The Italians thought they had struck a bargain here, because both Germany and Austria agreed to come to Italy's rescue, whereas Rome had only to fight the French for Berlin (as if France could leapfrog Germany to assail the Austrians).

gherita, who looked to the feudal courts of the north and would fall to her knees in the dusty streets of Naples at the sight of the sacred images (an episode reported by Farini*) symbolized in a much better way the completely feminine destiny of "royal" Italy.[25]

* Domenico Farini was president of the senate and a confidant of the king and queen. His diaries are a rich source for viewing Italian court life in the period to be considered below.

8

THE GAY EIGHTIES

IF EVER THERE MIGHT HAVE BEEN A GOLDEN AGE IN HUMBERT'S REIGN—AND THERE WAS none—it would have spanned at least some of the years of the Eighties. The Triple Alliance was a contract which had to be renewed by all parties every five years, and in its first term and part of the second, the House of Savoy, in spite of mounting woes and unrest at home, enjoyed a prestige abroad it had never known before. Italy had the *appearance* of a big power, taking on all of its accouterments, from cannon foundries to pronunciamentos about the white man's burden. Old Depretis lived long enough to renegotiate the treaty more favorably for Italy, and in the last years of his rule his *trasformismo* turned parliament into a kind of symphony orchestra under the sway of his baton. He died in 1887. His successor, Crispi, the only Italian whom Humbert and Margherita really loved, came to wield not a baton but a *bastone* in true big power fashion.

These were years of illusory progress, when coal consumption, the old weight and measure of national power, doubled in tonnage, a pleasing statistic which made the fact that every scuttleful had to be imported easy to repress. Industry in general began to move ahead, and the publication of the Jacini report on agriculture gave the *impression* that something would surely be done to alleviate the unhappy condition of the countryside. The right to vote was extended in 1882 to more Italians than ever before, raising the enfranchised elite from 2 to 7 percent of the nation. This liberalism, coupled with the ineptitudes of the extreme left and Depretis's continual dismantling of socialist and other subversive organizations, make it *look as if* law and order were at last at hand.[1]

It was not all good, however, for the self-deluded. The signing of the *Triplice* gave the Irredentists a powerful demigod in the martyred figure of young Oberdan.*

But Oberdan was only dust in the bright eyes of the Savoyard court of the Eighties. It was cleansed with lace handkerchiefs and the joyful tears brought on by the blissful marriage the House of Savoy had made with the masculine north.

These were relatively happy years for Humbert and Margherita, although they used them to make very separate lives. It was not quite true that a matriarch ruled the House of Savoy, or that Humbert, as court gossiper Baron Petrucelli wrote at the time, was but "the prince consort of Queen Margherita."[3] Contemporary rumor had it that the king's office and the queen's bedroom were connected by a corridor in which a constant echo was heard of Humbert's beckonings to Margherita to counsel him on affairs of state. On the other hand, Crispi was to complain that the queen had absolutely no influence with Humbert, "to whom she means less than nothing; he is completely entwined in the coils of that old witch, Litta."[4] Entwined he was with the duchess, but this was Crispian hyperbole.

Margherita's ascendancy in Italian life was supreme and enduring. She towered over her people in her own right, but her influence was exercised only by virtue of her loyalty to her house. Her dynastic wish was almost always Humbert's will, but never his command. By the sheer presence of her regal self she gave spin to the curve he pursued. Humbert, retiring and taciturn, may have seemed possessed by the imperious Margherita, but in truth Italy's first "democratic" king was a tyrant *in familias*. Pietro Gerbore, a close observer of Italian aristocracy, writes:

> Humbert watches over his House with rigorous vigilance and imposes a strict discipline. The princes and princesses are denied the freedoms enjoyed by his subjects and they remain legal minors all their lives, under the guardianship of the sovereign. It is the king who decides on their marriages, on the education of their children, and when the children are

---

* Guglielmo Oberdan was a Triestian republican who sacrificed himself hoping to damage the treaty and call attention to the plight of his "unredeemed" people. He had been among those incensed by the spectacle of Humbert in the uniform of the Hapsburgs, and while others had spent their fury in demonstrations and burning "the Austrian colonel" in effigy, Oberdan set out to assassinate Franz Josef. His intentions were discovered, however, and he was arrested and executed by the Austrians. The immolation of Oberdan gave rise to a public outcry even among Italians who had never heard of Trieste. His act had profound repercussions. As Croce has observed, it spurred the nationalist ideal which was to contribute to the fall of the Hapsburgs, and, it may now be added, the House of Savoy.[2]

grown, on their marriages too. Each of them must remain in the residence assigned to him and may not go out, even for a few hours, without the permission of the king.[5]

Humbert waived no part of this privilege with regard to Margherita. On the contrary he employed it with a certain subtle sadism to which the queen submitted stoically, only to form a truly vicious circle in bearing malice and harm to men and things the king held dear. Farini's diaries tell of Margherita desiring, expecting, and preparing to accompany her husband on a visit to Queen Victoria, and only on the morning of departure did he answer her supplications, with a *no*.

Margherita had to suffer the humiliation of applying for whatever she wanted to the minister of the royal house, the bureaucrat Urbanino Rattazzi, he too under the spell of the royal mistress Litta. Unable to undo the everlasting bonds between Humbert and Litta, the queen never ceased her intrigues against Rattazzi until, with the aid of the cherished Crispi—that "dirty crook," as Rattazzi and many others had good reason to call him—she drove him from the palace.[6]

Humbert in the Eighties learned to play king with a flourish gained from experience and the example of his illustrious father. He would never understand anything but reactionary politics, but on a higher plane, as the sovereign of his people, he began slowly to acquire all the royal attributes found in De Meis's ideal prince. That he gave the "superior" people the Triple Alliance and its promise of law and order was enough to ensure their devotion. Having done so, he turned his attentions to the "inferior" masses. He sought to brighten the sordid shadows of their daily strife by giving them color and dash. More than that, he began to love them in a great fatherly way. "King Humbert adores the people," related Juliette Adam, a French *connaisseuse* of the most intimate side of the Italian court, who wrote under the name of Count Vasili. "He would like them to have both wealth and glory, above all glory."[7]

Suddenly he was Humbert the Good, *il buono*. He had, of course, been "good" all along, but somehow in these years he made it show. *"Buono, null'altro che buono,"* Farini sighed, believing that so much goodness would lead the crown and the nation to perdition.[8] "The chief characteristic of the man," Gerbore wrote, "is his good nature, and friendship is his major need." His generosity was to be legendary. It is said that he carried a little pouch filled with precious stones, and when properly moved by a charming lady or a man in need, he would draw it from his pocket and offer a ruby or a pearl like a sweet to a child. He gave almost everything away: diamonds to the queen and the women of his fancy, titles and cigars to the worthy, parks and hospitals to the people, amnesties to the political prisoners, and in 1889 he paid the expenses for Cairoli's funeral. Above all he gave from his personal resources to charity, to the poor, the sick, and the forlorn: fifteen million lire (the cost of a battleship) in a lifetime of philanthropy—more than any other sovereign in history, said an admirer who claimed to have checked the then known figures.[9]

More than kind and giving, he had courage, in its richer Italian and French meanings. According to Juliette Adam, "One could, it seems to me, sum up the character of the king of Italy in a single word which explains all his deeds, his preferences, his errors: the word *courage*." He was inscrutable on the outside, but down deep lay a maudlin soul easily moved to tears by anyone's misfortune, including his own. ("He does nothing but cry," Duchess Litta said on one occasion.) Yet he possessed the strength of heart to extend a paternal embrace at whatever the risk. "*Il adore le danger*," Juliette Adam observed with Italians of every social level, who watched their king rushing everywhere to comfort his people whenever calamity struck. Italy, strangely afflicted more than any other land with recurrent natural disasters, saw her Humbert always running to the scene of an earthquake, a volcanic eruption, or a deadly epidemic.

When Naples in 1884 was being rapidly depopulated by an outbreak of cholera, Humbert was there while others remained in Rome fearing for his life. He had been advised not to go and having been scheduled to attend an official ceremony in the town of Pordenone, he had had reason enough to stay away from the danger zone. It was on this occasion that he sent his theatrical, well-publicized, but nonetheless sincere telegram to the town's mayor: "In Pordenone one celebrates; in Naples one dies. I'm going to Naples."[10]

In a perverse way he felt close to his people when he watched and tended their agonies. "In misfortune we are all equal," he said after visiting the site of a devastating earthquake in Ischia; and in Naples, at the side of the choleric in their sickbeds, he chided the deputy who offered him a cigar as an antiseptic: "You don't smoke where people are dying."

Whatever love Margherita had for him was stirred when he wore his courage on the outside. He made her proud of Piedmont and Savoy. "There are places in Italy," she told Count Guiccioli, "where a man is not ashamed to say the word *fear*. I cannot comprehend this.

When I was a girl in Piedmont, I never heard a man confess that he felt fear." "The king did well to go," she said of her husband's decision to go to Ischia in the midst of the quakes, and when he went to Naples she was both thrilled and terrified, a gesture "so noble and so nobly executed by the King. Thank God it went well, but those were truly heart-palpitating days."[11]

The Eighties revealed him as being even more than kind, giving, and brave. He was, like De Meis's sovereign, *un po' po' sensuale*. One could not yet read in the daily press—as in the Nineties—of his imagined seraglios and his exaggerated concupiscence, but his loves were common knowledge. They were never stormy adventures like his father's, but brooding, melancholy loyalties, a breast on which a head made tired by a heavy crown might lie, an embrace to warm a king too long in the cold.

First and always there was Margherita's bête noire, Lady Litta. She was seven years his senior, fourteen Margherita's. "She looks as if she were my grandmother by now," Margherita snickered in those years.[12] But even then, at fifty, the duchess was beautiful. She had a knowing, aristocratic beauty, and, at the same time, the qualities of ingenuousness and virginity which made the composer Boito sing and inspired Vela's painting of a woman at morning prayer.

She was all of this for Humbert, too. He first met her when he was eighteen. She had already been married for several years to the Lombard duke Litta-Visconti-Arese. Her mother was known for her passion in all the courts of Europe. The older woman had traveled throughout the continent with her daughter, and of young Litta, prior to her marriage, it was said that kings and emperors were her slaves. Humbert had come from provincial, austere Turin. The duchess lived in cosmopolitan Milan, in the very palace where his revered dead mother once had dwelled. He fell in love. She was passionate, patient, and instructive. He could neither leave nor forget her.

He married Margherita, of course, but called Litta to serve as a palace dame. One afternoon, before Humbert's accession to the throne, she asked Margherita if she might be excused from accompanying her on her daily stroll. The unsuspecting Margherita went out alone and when she returned she found Litta and Humbert in her own apartment. They were properly attired, but too close for Margherita to bear. She ran to the king. She could not live with such unfaithfulness, she cried, telling of her discovery. "For this, you want to leave him?" Victor Emmanuel asked incredulously. Doubtless he gave her the same advice he had for the bride of his bastard son, Count Mirafiori: "My child, you should not have too many illusions. Know now that all the princes of the House of Savoy are rogues. But remember, all our princesses are virtuous."[13]

Margherita, virtuous and faithful at least during Humbert's lifetime, learned to abide her rival, and in rising above her condition, there were triumphs, too. There was the time, court memorialists relate, when Margherita, as queen, entered a crowded palace ballroom with Humbert on her arm, and with all eyes upon them she accosted Lady Litta. Suddenly everyone fell silent. Then:

> [She] stared icily into the eyes of the duchess, and with a sarcastic smile on her sweet lips, she bowed deeply. Litta, confused, returned the bow. Everyone was very embarrassed, while Margherita, as if the entire affair were none of her concern, walked across the full length of the hall, smiling. Both the queen and the lady were wearing the pearls given to them by the king.[14]

In the Eighties the countess of Santa Fiora came into Humbert's life. Her name was Vincenza, a widow in the illustrious Roman house of Sforza-Cesarini. He called her "Mimmi." He had discovered her in the Quirinal among the palace dames in the queen's retinue. For a while no one knew of the king's new love, but inevitably someone took note of his late night visits to the widow's *palazzo* in the Via Torino, about half a mile from the Quirinal, and before long the gossiping newspapers of Angelo Sommaruga (one aptly named *Cronaca Bizantina*) told all. Sommaruga was silenced by the authorities, but far too tardily. Litta, she too a palace dame (although the queen saw to it that she was given nothing to do), was jealous. Margherita by now was indifferent. If anything, she delighted in the aging duchess's discomfiture. Everyone else was excited, titillated. They were universally agreed that there was something special about the countess. "*La contessa fatale*," she was called by Matilde Serao, one of the most popular writers of the day, and the intriguingly ambiguous epithet (was she deadly, destined, or decisive for the king?) adhered. Juliette Adam said she did not merit Matilde Serao's enigmatic phrase. She was simply a coquette, a "professional beauty." Countess Hugo, another French witness at the Italian court, found her dull and introverted.[15]

It was her beauty upon which all argument broke up in wondrous admiration, and no one less than the young D'Annunzio immortalized her as one of the most fascinating creatures in the history of Rome—

but only to look at. He was only twenty-one, an apprentice reporter on the Rome *Tribuna*, chronicling the game of high society in an unforgettable style, when he wrote:

> Sometimes, when you turn a corner, you unexpectedly encounter that strange figure of a noblewoman on the sidewalk of a city street. It is one of those sights which linger on, somewhat disturbingly. Through her very thin veil, that pallid, irregularly beautiful face, those red lips, which at certain times appear almost as if they pained her, and those eyes of a Cyprian Venus suddenly give an impression of—shall I say—something gone wrong; someone suddenly awakened—shall I say—from a dream of mysterious and tempestuous loves. But when the countess parts those lips and speaks, she almost always makes irony of the illusion. She is rather cold, averse to sentiment, and often even caustic.[16]

Humbert liked it. The inferior people, if De Meis were correct, liked it. Litta told Humbert to call no more if he continued to frequent Santa Fiora's *palazzo*, but, as old royal mistresses do not begin life anew, she learned to share the king's affections. Nevertheless an intensely hostile rivalry of increasing significance developed between the two women. In the disastrous Nineties they were, as will be seen, to become the center of two political camps employing lubricious feminine intrigues in the making of Italian history, to the everlasting woe of the Italians.

Margherita, who was to thicken the perfume-scented web playing one camp off another, had her own men. Malicious rumor would never pause, but there is not the slightest evidence to contradict that during the years of her reign at least, her suitors were but platonic, her affairs not of the heart, but of the mind. She had grown more alluring than ever. Now in her thirties, she had lost that girlish look which had lightly veiled the full dimension of her grace. She would very soon grow fat and look more and more like a penguin, but when D'Annunzio saw her at the Apollo in 1884, standing high to applaud the first performance of *Lohengrin* in Rome, he was overcome, and he wrote in the morning *Tribuna*: "Watching her, never as last night did I feel the fascination of the *eterno femminino regale*."[17]

Juliette Adam told the French:

> After having met Queen Margherita, I knew how subtle perfumes are made: of that supreme seduction, of that mysterious and irresistible grace, of that beauty of beauties one calls charm. And charm is made of intelligence and good heart.[18]

The queen was all that and more. She set the pace for what ordinary bourgeois women wore, how they held themselves and combed their hair. The magazines of the time were filled with detailed drawings of the swiftly changing contents of the royal wardrobe, and on the Corso in Rome women could be seen strolling in the late afternoon dressed in one or another of Margherita's "hand-me-downs." But she was beautiful and well groomed in spite of herself, for it was her fancy for the intellect she wished most of all to display. Though she permitted the encomiasts and the hacks to exalt her cultural achievements, she knew and even confided that they were all too slight.

The truth was she could not write a letter without making the most elementary spelling, grammatical, and syntactical mistakes. When Croce had occasion to be received by her, after her reputation as an intellectual had been well secured, he was shocked by her ignorance, although even he was to perpetuate the myth. A half-century later, however, he confessed:

> I, who had always thought of her as she had been portrayed in Carducci's verses, and as she appeared to us then and for many years afterward, surrounded with poetry and the arts (among some papers . . . I had occasion to examine, I came across a few of Petrarch's strophes transcribed in her hand), was astonished at seeing her so extraneous to any kind of literature. She said to me: "You work a lot. The booksellers are always sending me your latest volumes."[19]

Her cultural failings gave her cause for her deepest regrets, which may be one of the reasons she began to gather to her side all the men of erudition of proper social class and inclination, and formed her celebrated *circolo*, that inner circle of continental fame. "No other nineteenth century queen surrounded herself with so many wise men and so few cavalry officers," Madame Adam commented, which only shows the superfluousness of one's calling, when it is the mistress who is served.

"Thursday by the queen," became the watchword of the learned and the lettered, and of course, the envy of the hopeful. These years were the "high season" of her life, as Croce was to say. "To her sweet piety and her enchanting smile, she joined a love of poetry and the arts, and seemed herself to be a poetic creature, incarnating in the most perfect way the ideal of a Queen of Italy, of the land of art and all things beautiful."[20]

Even as crown princess, Margherita had begun to cultivate her circle of intellectuals within the royal court. Her biographer Casalegno says she had sought to form "a group of worthy men, with whom to converse and discuss according to the best tradition, that is, the French—doubtless with the intention of emulating the French salons and of competing with Mathilde Bonaparte." He goes on:

> At the Quirinal her circle expanded and took permanent form, until little by little, it became—during the years between 1880 and 1890—that famous "*Circolo*" about which so much has been written. Although it has often been said that Margherita did not have aristocratic prejudices . . . it should not be thought that every scholar of renown and every illustrious statesman was invited to the "Thursdays by the queen." Margherita's salon always retained an "aristocratic" character in the highest sense of the word. . . .[21]

Indeed, in her club there was little place for the old nobility, especially the Roman aristocracy with its sublimely ignorant gentlemen and churlishly superstitious ladies. Margherita was indifferent to titles; it was one's service to the Muses and the House of Savoy that mattered. That all her men were diehards from the right was a strange but nonetheless authentic coincidence. Most of those in Margherita's circle agreed with their fellow member Count Guiccioli's aphorism: "Democracy [i.e., the left] is foolish when it votes, mad when it governs, but disgusting when it wants to be in high society."[22]

Thus it was the men of Croce's "spiritual aristocracy" who gained admittance to the queen's parlor: entirely forgotten but once luminous names such as *Professor* Minghetti, last prime minister of the Cavourian right (who began now to teach Margherita Latin); the philosopher-politician Bonghi, the historian Villari, the theologian Mamiani, the Egyptologist Neapolitan Baron Baracco (well-known in Parisian salons), and of course, the *cultivé* Count Guiccioli, whose father had known Lord Byron.

There is little direct evidence of what the Thursdayites discussed, but we are continually assured that whatever it was that was said was always on the highest plane. "How pleasurable he is!" Margherita exclaimed shortly after one of Villari's visits. "It is such a joy to see a man of such worth so modest and not at all pedantic, because beyond his serious conversation, which is extremely interesting, he is also very spirited."[23]

From Margherita's ninety-seven letters to her *maestro* Minghetti, written over the four year period 1882–1886, we do know that talks ranged from Horace and Tacitus to Carducci and Mommsen, from the abstract meanings of the great political moments of the day to the search for specifics in the proverbial sweet mysteries of life.

The continent took note; the enchanting Savoyard queen and her wise men made Margherita *"l'une des figures royales les plus intéressantes de l'Europe."*[24] But Humbert did not like it at all. Margherita's affectations were the very causes of the general impression about his uxorial submissiveness. Besides, he felt ill at ease in the presence of such a vast accumulation of human knowledge. Not that he ever attended a session, but he fumed outside the closed doors of her parlor with the nervousness which invariably arises when incomprehension is the one barrier to a satisfied curiosity. One evening he could no longer suffer the endless, unheard palaver, and exercising his kingly prerogative he burst into the sanctum.

"Is this the place where the arts are discussed?" he demanded of the savants and the queen.

Margherita, unruffled, parried with a cold "Yes," declining to either invite the king to join them, to leave, or to even comment further. To which Humbert, in his best roughhouse Piedmontese, replied:

"What's a good book I can read in bed?"[25]

He was sent off to bed with the romantic, popular, good-guys-and-bad-guys novelist Fogazzaro, and the group picked up its intellectual labors. One can still hear the twang of their vexation.

At least Humbert got a good book out of it. Margherita got even less. She never mastered Latin, not going very far beyond learning to sprinkle her misspelled Italian with words such as *optime* and *Italia sanctissima.* Worse, passing so many hours with the sages of her choosing only confirmed, in that dangerous way which comes from the sweetest part of a little knowledge, everything she knew all along. Her intolerance, bigotry, chauvinism, xenophobia, and religious fanaticism, her love of power and war both for their own sake and as a means of striking fear at home as well as in "distant lands"; her hatred of democracy, and her adulation of the despotic Crispi (and, in her dotage, Mussolini) grew more and more insufferable. She was a malevolent woman who raged in the vilest manner against all things which did not bow before the interests of the House of Savoy. She longed to cleanse Italians in a neo-Risorgimental purge "completely tinted in the color of blood."[26] That she was adored by the intellectuals casts shame on the intellectuals. That she was idolized by the people, who pressed marguerites between the pages of prayer books to bring good fortune, is to the shame and ignominy of the wise men even more.

The court of Rome had its summer in the Eighties, too. Black and white society remained at arm's length, but the times when they held hands in the dark were always more frequent and ever more pleasurable. Those Roman noblemen who had sought to remain aloof from bourgeois society found it increasingly difficult to maintain their independence. Capitalist economy drove prices upward, and only incomes tied to it rose accordingly. As a result, feudal wealth was rapidly being depleted, creating new cultural values which allowed slow integration into the white business and social worlds. Both worlds were regularly deplored, but their irresistible lure was nonetheless pursued and often secretly enjoyed.

Humbert and Margherita had given a new kind of splendor to Rome, bringing gay circumstance where there had been only the solemn pomp of temporal papal rule. To be sure, the Quirinal, which had been built for popes and cardinals, was a bad place for midnight suppers and for waltzing. It was a quarter-mile walk down a cloistral corridor to the buffet table, and the Swiss Hall entranceway looked more severe and forbidding than the Vatican itself. But this did nothing to lower the consumption of hors d'oeuvres and champagne. Many were the stampedes down that hall in unsung battles for the food, but even more were the backbiting struggles for an invitation to the dance. In 1881, for example, four ministers of the left publicly protested their not being invited. Depretis had to intervene to ward off a government crisis. A palace dame of the Roman nobility was made the scapegoat, forced to resign to assuage the offended left by replacing her with a bourgeois lady of their choosing. To all this, which others found so upsetting, Humbert, when asked to comment, had the good sense to remark, "Balls!"[27]

Roman society appeared odd to foreign observers. They complained of the absence of "the delicate science of social relations," of the deviations from the standards set by the older capitals of Europe, and worst of all, that "the game is played too much out in the open."[28] It was true that even the poorest, cave-dwelling Roman had only to pick up yesterday's discarded *Tribuna*, and if he could read, he would see with D'Annunzio's keen eye all the infuriating little details which occupied the lives of the privileged. On December 11, 1884, under the apt but improbable name of Happemouche, the poet wrote:

> These are lazy, bothersome days.
> The city is oppressed by a sirocco and, seen from on high, appears as an immense Pompeii buried in ash. A kind of unwholesome nervousness

invades the people: a poorly repressed irritation which manifests itself in all their gestures and their attitudes.

On the Via del Corso the Tiberine ladies, reclined in their half-closed carriages, pass at a tired trot. They are pallid, for the most part hidden behind dense veils, and submerged in the softness of their furs. They greet you slowly, smile weakly, and permit their heads to nod with the turn of the wheels. Sometimes they seem to be drowsing and shapeless, lost in the ample folds of their capes. Oh, beautiful capes of otter ornate with blond beaver! The lustrous skins open here and there mixing the smooth dark colors with the light of gold. Nothing is more nobly sensual than otter which has been worn well. Then, the skins yield to all the curves of the feminine body, but not with the light touch of silk or satin, rather with a certain heaviness not deprived of gracefulness, that gracefulness which animals endowed with rich coats show in their furtive movements. . . .

It seems to me that the longest and most magnificent fur cape belongs to Princess Venosa. Yesterday, she was at Spillmann's, asking for *bonbons*, perhaps for her five o'clock tea. She had on a tidy little hat with heron and ostrich feathers and her face was covered with a speckled veil. She was chatting with Princess Borghese, whose admirable figure—the crescents of her shoulders, her very narrow waist, and her opulently rounded hips—was entirely enveloped in otter perfumed with the odor of cypress and *sachet de veloutine*, contrasting markedly with the serious countenance, the proud matronly nobility, of her interlocutress.

Another celebrated cape is the one possessed by the Countess Santafiora. . . . She was wearing a very tall black hat of lace and jet, lightened by a bouquet of plumes. She walks with a very quick step, holds her elbows at her waist, her hands in her muff, and her muff tight against her clothes. Countess Taverna was wearing otter, too. Who is unfamiliar with the countess's heavenly pallor, her blue-black hair full of dark and undulant reflections, and her large eyes veiled with long lashes? . . . Princess d'Antuni wore a stole, befallen with a beautiful curl tied with a light blue ribbon bow. The Duchess of Magliano's jacket was thrown over her shoulders in military fashion, the sleeves dangling on her dark brown suit trimmed with *soutaches*.

All these ladies pass along the Via del Corso in their carriages between four and five in the afternoon. And, in gloomy weather, it takes no more than an otter cape to arouse in their onlookers a desire for the intimacy of love.[29]

The social season began at Christmas with Humbert lighting the tree at the palace, and ended in the paroxysm of carnival time and Mardi Gras. Humbert and Margherita gave three balls a year to an increasing number of guests, which in 1889 had risen to 1,500. The invited arrived in time for the buffet supper and mulled about near the throne room. The ladies were escorted into the ballroom by masters of ceremonies, who gave them their arm and a *carnet de bal* made of velvet and silk and stamped with the royal coat-of-arms. Gerbore describes the best moment of the gala:

> Precisely at eleven o'clock one of the two doors on the opposite side of the hall is thrown open. The orchestra intones the first bars of the royal fanfare, then falls silent. The king and the queen come in, followed by the foreign princes present in Rome . . . Then come the knights and dames of the Annunziata and the ambassadors. Everyone takes a place previously assigned to him.
>
> The queen is dressed in satin . . . the king wears tails, the Collar of the Annunziata, and the sash of the Military Order of Savoy. The ambassadors, in his honor, place a small gold button in their vest.
>
> The signal for the quadrille of honor is given. The couples, chosen in advance according to the rules of etiquette, and previously advised by the masters of ceremonies, take their places. In that ball in 1881 the queen had as her partner the future King Oscar of Sweden. The right gave its hand to the left in the persons of Marco Minghetti and Donna Amalia Depretis. The quadrille goes on for fifteen minutes, and then everyone begins to waltz.[30]

The theater season was opened by Margherita. In 1882 Sarah Bernhardt came to Rome to do *Lady of the Camellias* at the Valle. Count Guiccioli found her "very Jewish," *but* more feminine than the queen. "She is the true woman of our times, made only of nerves and eyes." Margherita stayed home; the actress was booed by the xenophobes, but the court was represented in Guiccioli who had dinner with her at Spillmann's. "Offstage she is even more pleasurable," he confessed of the queen's rival for the crown of European feminism. Her level of culture, however, was superficial, or "wholly Parisian," to use, as Guiccioli did, a then fashionable slur. "She is convinced of being the most important personality of our time," said the count, who was horrified, when Miss Bernhardt, in that year of the great pogroms, told a Russian diplomat present at Spillmann's, that the czar was "an imbecile and a coward." Guiccioli said he could never have tolerated such language, although the Russian suffered the insults in silence. "If this incident were known in Petersburg," the Count observed, "he would lose his job."[31]

But the slate of bitterness and tears was each year wiped clean at *carnevale*. The king and queen and the *principino*, who was growing older but not taller, watched all smiles from a balcony on the Corso, as their upper-class peers threw flowers and chocolates at the people, who howled with delight. At four in the afternoon the floats came down the street, and in the evening the Romans danced, drank beer, and tried to do everything from which they would pretend to abstain for six Sundays. The blacks and the whites danced together, and Humbert and Margherita stayed up until dawn.

9

THE RISE AND FALL OF
"A CERTAIN MR. CRISPI"

THE TIME WAS APPROACHING WHEN SOMEONE IN ITALY WOULD HAVE TO PAY FOR ALL THE GROWing phantasmagoria, for all the ritual and armaments, and all the belts and buckles of being a big power. For this, the nation's leaders turned to their people. But in an uncanny, fundamental way—instructive in that even the poor and the downtrodden have limited means—it was to be Humbert the Good who would discharge all debts incurred, paying, as will later be seen, with his life.

In 1887 events relatively insignificant in themselves combined in a random fashion to form the matrix, from which everything meaningful was to come for a long time ahead. The first of these occurrences took place in January. An expeditionary force of five hundred Italian soldiers was destroyed to the man at Dogali, Ethiopia, representing an early, crushing defeat for Savoyard imperialism. The royal troops had been sent to the Red Sea side of Africa to find Foreign Minister Mancini's "Keys to the Mediterranean"—that coveted dominion of ancient Roman hegemony, denied to Italy by the powers bigger than she.

The "Five Hundred" (so the victims were posthumously named) had been slaughtered by the "four highwaymen," as Mancini's successor Di Robilant had called the Ethiopian forces when warned that they were massing for the attack at Dogali. The wound, of course, cut deep into the very white matter of the Italian soul, and though many until now had opposed the colonial urges of the ruling groups, a cry for revenge was raised in one voice. The government thus won easy approval for further military operations in East Africa on a fantastic scale which foresaw an army of Italians numbering in the many millions.[1]

In February, in the midst of undertaking these new follies, the Triple Alliance, with all its pressure on the Italian economy, was renewed in terms favorable to Italian expansion in the Mediterranean, further paving the way to new adventures. Next Depretis, recovering politically from the Dogali incident, dropped the discredited Di Robilant and took on the lately imperialist, Francophobic, indeed half-crazed Crispi. Depretis promised now that his new government would reestablish Italian honor in Africa. Then, in July, this unfortunate promise yet unkept, he died.

Once again a government had to be formed. Francesco Crispi, whose service in Depretis's last cabinet, after ten years of opposition to *trasformismo*, had signified his unreserved obeisance to the crown, was called to the task. Power was not lightly extended by the king to the lowborn Sicilian. Crispi by now had proved his loyalties beyond any doubt. He concurred wholeheartedly with the commitments of faith and substance to the illusions about Italy's destiny, which had been so laboriously assumed by the king and queen. At sixty-seven years of age, Crispi had come to worship might, prestige, aristocratic honorifics, the *Junkers*, and the Triple Alliance. He had grown megalomaniacal, unscrupulous, amoral, authoritarian, and downright silly; but he had a way.[2] If Humbert the Good could have been someone else, he would have been Crispi, who had become his idol. Pious Margherita thought him sent from God.[3]

"A man has appeared," Crispi said early in his first ministry, "who considers Italy the equal of any other nation, and intends to see that her voice shall be heard and respected."[4] He ran off twice in his first year in office to see Bismarck, doubtless to instruct himself and repair the poor impression he had made when sent there a decade earlier. He told the chancellor that Italy was united and strong in its determination to engage in a war of revenge on the Abyssinians. Bismarck was no more impressed than before. "The Italians have a big appetite," he said, "but such poor teeth."[5]

Then Humbert, after receiving the new German emperor, Wilhelm II, in Rome, went to Berlin. The Italian king reviewed the troops at Templehof, muttering afterward that the best-looking soldier in his own army did not look as good as the worst-looking Prussian recruit. Crispi's military budget went up.

In the meantime Italy sank into economic depression. For years

Italian industrialists had been lobbying for a tariff barrier to protect their inefficient fledgling operations from French competition. They found allies in many of the *latifondisti* who wished to secure domination of the home market. Everyone knew that protectionism was but another crude device to further exploit the southern poor in order to build up capital in the north. Pro-French Depretis, although he yearned for the political support of the powerful protectionists, had resisted to some extent. But Crispi did not hesitate to feed his Sicilians and the rest of the south to the north. He denounced a Franco-Italian commercial treaty and virtually closed the door to French exports.

"France must now forget the history of the supremacy and influence which she once possessed on this side of the Alps," said Crispi in a kind of declaration of commercial war with the Third Republic. "She should recognize that the Italian nation is as good as herself and must now be allowed to enjoy its independence and profit from it."[6]

The independence, such as it was, was for all; the profit for somewhat less than everyone.

France, which really was a big power, with vast resources and alternatives, suffered little, and when it hit back Italy was ruined. Italian agriculture, long seething and steaming like oily rags in the nation's cellars and closets, felt the effects first and hardest. The duty placed on French grain—a political reward for the big producers in Italy, who made fortunes in this way—forced the price of bread higher than it had been at the time of the abominable grist tax. Worse, it put unbearable pressure on the native soil, destroying the poorest farms by the thousands, driving the sick and the hungry from the land into the city slums. Then France blocked off Italian oil, wine, fruits, and vegetables—the four pillars on which the entire economy stood. As a result, vineyards and orchards, which had been expanded on credit in recent years to meet French demand, now collapsed in the many hundreds. Thousands of foreclosures, aggravated by the precipitous retaliatory sale by the French of their Italian securities, caused banks to fail or engage in illegal activities, which were shortly to scandalize the nation. Overproduction, bank failures, the consequent drop in consumer buying, and a general loss of confidence in the economy brought on a full-scale depression. Depression brought revolution.

Early in the 1890s the revolutionary forces which had been building up for a generation began to explode. Sicily was first. Crispi's economic war on the French had ravaged his native island. Unemployment in the sulphur mines sent workers to compete for farm jobs, of which there were none. Sicilians were dying of hunger. The island was totally disrupted, uprooted, and livid with anger. Workers and peasants banded together in *fasci*, groups under socialist leadership, which sought to defend the islanders from the rude, unbounded oppression of their masters in Rome and at home. Grievances unheard led to strikes, and strikes to attempts at smashing them, which brought fire, destruction, and bloodshed by the barrelful.

To the owners this appeared as a disregard for law and order requiring exemplary punishment. Humbert and Margherita, though the striking peasants raised their likenesses beside the venerated saints, agreed. Crispi, the Sicilian, thought the Sicilians ungrateful, envious, and a danger to freedom. He considered them and almost all Italians "corrupted by ignorance."[7] But Crispi, whose government had resigned for tactical reasons in 1891, was out of power when the Sicilian revolts erupted. The current prime minister, Giovanni Giolitti, a somewhat less violent man of the Depretis school, refused to dissolve the *fasci*, believing that the unrest would exhaust itself of its own accord.*

The owners, the king and queen, and Crispi were incensed. Margherita beat her fists in tantrums at the government's restraint.[9] The Quirinal knew panic as the revolt spread ever farther north. The king and queen wanted Crispi returned, but Giolitti, having learned well the techniques of his predecessors, had reinforced his parliamentary position through rigged elections and apparently was firmly entrenched. In this situation, however, he was suddenly exposed as implicated in the sensational bank scandals of that year, 1893. Some of the nation's first citizens were shown to be engaging in malpractices which had enriched them by hundreds of millions of lire. Giolitti, destined to play later his primary role in Italian life, was forced to resign, and incidentally, flee to another country.

Unfortunately Crispi was no less guilty than Giolitti in his own malversations (they would go to their graves accusing one another). Like Giolitti, Crispi had drawn money from the crooked banks to

---

* Giolitti, the Piedmontese whose time of violence was yet to come, later wrote of the *fasci* rebellion of 1893: "I understood immediately that it was an economic movement, fully justified by the painful conditions to which the peasants and miners were being subjected. These had been amply shown as a result of investigations conducted by authoritive newspapers, such as the *Tribuna* and the *Corriere della Sera*, whose revelations on the wretched condition of the Sicilian workers and on the atrocious abuse of child labor in the mines had deeply impressed public opinion."[8] Crispi, it is known, never read the newspapers.

pay for his political campaigns. These were loans to be discharged not in cash but in favors which assured fortune and honor for their creditors.[10]

Thus, with Crispi so compromised, and the nation faced with a "moral question," Humbert found himself unable to turn to his preference. He was forced to call on an honest man to form a new government. The candidate selected was the untouchable Zanardelli, the old Cairolian leftist who was known for his scruples and his liberalism. In Zanardelli, the king hoped to restore public confidence in the monarchy, which, he was counseled, might help dampen the fiery rebellion licking the old wood of the House of Savoy.

But Zanardelli had complicated matters immeasurably. He had named as his foreign minister-designate, General Baratieri, a native of Austrian Trentino, who was suspected by the Hapsburg court of Irredentist leanings. Vienna had said as much to the Italian ambassador Count Nigra, who immediately telegraphed his king. Humbert had therefore concluded that the general would be unable to deal well with the cherished Hapsburg ally. Making things still worse, the Austrian *Diktat* had become public knowledge, and rejection of Zanardelli's choice would be interpreted as Italian servility to the Austrians. Humbert was paralyzed.

Sicily was in full revolt. The customs houses, symbol of the ruinous duties on French imports, were burning. City halls were being sacked and telegraph wires were down. Strikes had spread to the north, and for the first time public service employees in the capital were walking out.* The owners, the king, and the queen thought a "social republic" was at hand. There was only one man, they believed, who could save them—moral questions notwithstanding—Humbert's and Margherita's "*salvatore*," Crispi.[12]

Humbert, on December 7, 1893, dispatched a "very urgent" telegram to Crispi, who was in Naples at the time. He asked him to be at the Quirinal at nine o'clock the next morning. Crispi had just received another communication from which he had concluded that he was under a threat of assassination.

---

* This latter strike, which involved the telegraph workers, was considered most portentous of all. Crispi reveals a conversation he had with the king in this regard: "Have you spoken with the telegraph employees lately?" Humbert asked. "Yes, Your Majesty," Crispi replied. "I have spoken with them. But I did not treat them with kindness. I told them that if I had been minister, I would have had them all arrested. It would have been illegal, but I would have done it. They are employees of the State, and they cannot be allowed to strike. . . . I advised them to go back to work and I promised to study their demands and support them, if they are right." "You did very well," the king replied. "And I congratulate you."[11]

His mind half-gone, the seventy-three-year-old red-shirt was capable of believing anything. As prime minister he had created panic with an unfounded report that the French navy was about to launch a surprise attack on Italy. Regarding the Sicilian uprisings, he was convinced of a thoroughly fantastic notion that they were being financed by the United States; that the "revolutionaries" had concluded a secret treaty with Russia, and that they had won France and the pope to their side.[13]

Now he had learned from "trustworthy sources" that the French Jesuits in league with Rome had decided to eliminate him, for, according to his informant, he was "the only man Italy can depend on to get her out of the current bind."[14] An abortive attempt had already been made, Crispi was warned by the editor of his own newspaper, *La Riforma*, and the assassin had infiltrated the Crispi household. "We have not as yet been able to learn whether he is a domestic, or one of your friends," said Crispi's source, who advised: "Do not eat anything whatsoever while traveling, and exercise every possible caution at home and away against poison or any other means."[15] With this in mind, the old man departed, somewhat tardily, to answer the call from his king.

He arrived the following day, six hours late, and was rushed into the Cabinet Room, where Humbert was waiting for him. The king shook his hand and kissed him. He seemed to Crispi to be disturbed. A cameo in crisis management now began to play:

> Crispi: Here I am, Your Majesty, at your service. Your telegram was delayed and there wasn't time enough for me to catch last night's train. Don't blame me for being late.
>
> Humbert: I need you and there's still time. As you know, I had entrusted Zanardelli to form a new ministry. He seemed to have succeeded. But a difficulty, which could have been overcome, arose. Zanardelli proposed General Baratieri as foreign minister. I gave him my views about that name and the man's origins, but I was not very fortunate. . . .
>
> Crispi: And then?
>
> Humbert: Baratieri withdrew, and Zanardelli, on the pretext that he could not go before the Chamber without Baratieri, gave up the mandate. After that I asked the advice of Farini and others, and everyone said I should turn to you.
>
> Crispi: The situation is serious. . . . Today, aside from the difficulties at home, we have to consider the way Zanardelli has withdrawn. The whole country is talking about Count Nigra's telegram, interpreting it as an injunction from Austria to the king of Italy. Whatever ministry is formed will seem to have been at Vienna's pleasure.

Humbert: I understand all that. But you'll know how to get around all the difficulties and save me from the embarrassment.

Crispi: I am under your orders, Your Majesty, and would never dare refuse to render my services in these difficult moments. I pray you, however, to allow me some time for reflection as to what may be done and to seek the advice of some of my friends. We'll meet tomorrow.

Humbert: I'd like to do it quickly. Tomorrow at three P.M.?

Crispi: Excellent. Tomorrow at three, I'll be here.

The king shook his hand and kissed him once again.[16]

Crispi rescued his master by persuasion. He extracted promises from his political opponents not to embarrass either the king or the new government, which he decided to head. Those who refused were cajoled. Farini announced that Crispi, of bank scandal fame, was "the one moral force left in Italy." Whatever resistance remained crumbled when Crispi said that he was ready to rule without parliament if need be. The deputies got the point. In a few days he was able to hand Humbert his list of ministers, a collection of job-hunters who could be relied on to allow Crispi to rule as he pleased.

"The king is in better humor than he was the other day," Crispi wrote in his diary. "He approved my choices." Within the week the Crispi ministry was sworn, to the echoes of a grandiloquent speech, in which Crispi presented himself as the nation's savior.

The first order of business was the Sicilian rebellion and the restoration of law and order. Crispi, who was undoubtedly in need of psychiatric or geriatric care, was given a free hand to set the country right. He began at once to install a dictatorship which only in its duration was less severe than Mussolini's. The king relaxed. The queen rejoiced, remarking at the time:

Crispi is old; he knows that he does not have much longer to live and wants to render a final service. And he will render it, because the country feels and knows that it has at its helm someone who is *someone*. Admirable is the way in which he is master of himself. They say he is aged and enfeebled. That is a slander and I know where it comes from—*from that so-and-so who used to be with us in our own house; it is a disgrace.** It is true that Crispi has people around him who are less than pleasing, and who I have had to stomach for his sake. But he himself is *simpaticissimo*. He is a man of heart. He is a believer, and without faith nothing can be done. And, I repeat, the country knows and feels that he is someone.[17]

* Here, Margherita is speaking of the younger Rattazzi, who had just been relieved of his post as minister of the royal house, as a result of the queen's machinations. Rattazzi, kicked upstairs to senator by Humbert, now began to form an anti-Crispian cabal centered around Duchess Litta's influence in the royal bedrooms. See below, p. 135.

Crispi sent 15,000 troops to his native Sicily, declaring a state of siege and martial law. For the good of the nation, he said, it was necessary to call a "truce of God." As a "believer," he did not presume to be God Himself. He was merely assuming the powers of God in that he would tolerate nothing but unquestioning faith, at least for the unspecified duration of the "truce." Once that had been fully interpreted by his admirers, he proceeded to liquidate the sources of discord.

Military tribunals were established in Sicily with the right to conduct summary trials and executions for retrospective "crimes." One such crime, for example, had been a peasant raid on a Sicilian baron's private property, the purpose of which was to destroy a contaminated pipeline traced as the source of a cholera epidemic.[18]

Crispi dissolved the *fasci* and the Socialist party. Their leaders were arrested and persecuted. Thousands of Sicilians were imprisoned merely on suspicion, and sent to concentration camps. Every freedom was denied, every inconvenient regulation abrogated. One hundred thousand persons were stripped of the right to vote, and during the general commotion, everyone involved in the bank scandals, even those who had confessed to outright theft, was exonerated by Crispi. "Law" and order returned—briefly.

The reaction against this Neronian storm was ineffectual. A "liberty league" of socialists, republicans, and radicals was formed in Milan, with branches throughout Italy, and the old-line, liberal-conservatives, who saw the nation's institutions threatened by totalitarianism, conspired against Crispi. Giolitti returned to join them. He had appropriated government documents while in office, and now he presented a dossier before parliament documenting Crispi's criminal involvement in the "moral question" of the bank frauds. But this maneuver only brought on greater tyrannies. The heavily incriminated law-and-order interests agreed that it was unpatriotic to raise such issues when the country was in danger. The king, as Crispi noted, remained "more than affectionate" toward him, and Margherita raged against the "disgusting spectacle" of any kind of parliamentary opposition to her *someone*.[19]

Crispi claimed that in view of his age and his service to the nation he ought to be regarded as infallible, and he simply closed up parliament. Then, with arm-twisting, head-smashing violence and funds which had been appropriated for the victims of a disastrous earthquake in Calabria, he conducted an election campaign to wipe out the lingering Giolittian majority. The few remaining anti-Crispi deputies on both the left and the right launched an appeal "to the honest men of all parties" for a trial against everyone inculpated in the "moral question," not excluding the head of government. Humbert immediately sent for Crispi and declared:

> I have not read the famous libel published last night, nor do I want to read it. I have been told what is in it and there's nothing for you to worry about. You must know that this lurid press of ours can do nothing to alter my affection for you; neither can it lessen my feelings of friendship for you, which always remain the same. Do not be disturbed and go ahead with your work. I understand how this must pain you. But lies do not endure. You are strong. Continue to be calm and it will come to an end.[20]

He embraced the Sicilian and, as usual, kissed him; but very soon he would discard him.

The grip of the law-and-order elements pressed out more of the old ideology about a strong army being mankind's truest earthly friend. "Our soldiers, so valorous and so good, appear to me as the guardians of *Italic virtue*, which seems to have taken refuge entirely in the army, fleeing in indignation from that *cesspool* of politics."[21] Such were the words of Margherita and the sentiments of Humbert and the court, not to dwell on the army and its suppliers. Those who had all along favored a strong military now found invaluable support in the proprietary classes, who had concluded from the Sicilian events that the troops were needed against the ungrateful masses at home. But this gave way to an unholy paradox: the larger the army the more its incompetence, disorganization, and weakness, which, in turn, invariably led to enlarging the apparatus still further in order that it might be strengthened. Whenever man or group sought to break the spiral, the king threatened to quit. He would rather "become Mr. Savoy," he said, than see anyone tamper with the sacrosanctity of his army, whatever its inefficiency. ("Who knows where it will lead to . . . better we all leave now.")[22]

The real trouble, Humbert was told by his generals, was that the army needed a battle. The pressure of social unrest had swollen the ranks, and now, said General Cosenz to the king, the army would soon become demoralized without a war. A lightning colonial war against the push-over weak and backward would build morale fastest and best of all.[23]

The king was willing, as was the queen, who wished to be "feared in distant countries." Crispi, full of bilious vengeance, an unquenchable thirst for Italian grandeur, and the need to divert public opinion from his crimes, was more than willing. That Europe was burning with imperialist fever made it all the easier.

This was the Nineties and the scramble for empire and markets was on. The "Banjo-Bard" Kipling was singing his *Barrack-Room Ballads*, exalting brutality and barbarism. Peace was thought of as a stupefying nightmare, and war the maddening delight before which all other pleasures paled. It was the rough-riding age in which the bourgeois exporters of capital discovered the divine nature of empire and the eternal truths of vulgar Darwinism ("Oh, Evolution, what crimes have been committed in thy name," a lone voice cried out); when Rhodes saw God granting "the title-deeds of the future" to the fittest men, when Chamberlain found trade following the flag, and when Lord Rosebery gasped, "How marvelous it all is!"[24]

> In every nation of Europe [a rare contemporary critic had the good sense to say] . . . the same whisper from below the threshold sounds incessantly in men's ears: "We are the pick and flower of nations: the only nation that is really generous and brave and just. We are above all things qualified for governing others . . . The excellence of our rule abroad is proved in black and white by the books of our explorers, our missionaries, our administrators, and our soldiers, who all agree that our yoke is a pure blessing to those who bear it."[25]

And so it was in Italy.* But there existed a difference which made of what was elsewhere convenient and profitable self-deception, pure and bloody chicanery dragged through the hookah of Crispian madness and Humbertine folly.

Gramsci a generation later was among the first to see that Crispi's imperialism was but another means by which northern Italy exploited its true colony, the south. The rebellious Sicilians and the entire peasantry of the Mezzogiorno desired the land which they tilled, but that was an ancient taboo known in Humbert's time as Jacobinism and socialism. Crispi instead offered land in the colonies. Gramsci, writing in Mussolini's prisons, said:

> Crispi's was an oratorical, passionate imperialism, without any economic or financial base. . . . Italy, still underdeveloped, not only had no

___

* Following the Tunisian debacle, Italian imperialism began anew with the establishment of a small commercial enterprise in Assab, on the Red Sea. The British eventually gave the Italians a free hand there in controlling the local traffic in slavery and gunrunning. In 1882 Rome proposed to establish its sovereignty over Assab, and its occupation of this coastal enclave imposed a new set of imperatives, leading into the interior and a half-century of colonial disasters from Dogali through the African campaign of World War II.

capital to export, but required the importation of foreign capital for its most basic needs. There was, then, no real push behind Italian imperialism, and the yearning of the rural people, striving blindly for the ownership of their own land, was substituted in its place. It was a matter of having to resolve an internal political problem, postponing its real solution *ad infinitum*. Thus Crispi's [colonial] policies . . . were popular in the Mezzogiorno, for he had created the myth of the easy land.[26]

The northern capitalists, who could not see how they could make an immediate profit in Africa, opposed a colonial war, as did the Irredentists and the financial conservatives. But Crispi, with the backing of the very people he had done most to destroy, the miserable southern poor whose sons made up the largest part of the army, declared one day that Ethiopia would soon be erased from the map, and the assenting King Humbert ordered his generals to the ready. A grandiose empire was to be created, and silver coins were struck with Humbert of Savoy bearing the imperial crown. The Italians in 1895 marched against the Ethiopian emperor, Negus Menelik, whose "four highwaymen" had mortified them at Dogali. At last the revenge was to be had.

Menelik had come to power as Crispi's protégé, and the Italians regarded the negus as little more than their puppet. But Menelik, who claimed descent from a royal house far older than Humbert's— that of King Solomon and the queen of Sheba—was that much more adept at the old Savoyard ploy of playing one power off another. For years he had been writing fawning letters to Humbert, in which he invariably found space to ask for armaments ("How are you in health? I, thank God, am fine. . . . All I need today are rifles"),[27] and the king kept supplying him and his gunrunners, among whom was the poet Rimbaud. Now the negus could field a well-armed, well-trained army of 100,000 men, although Italian military intelligence would never get the figures straight, unable to count more than a "hundred thieves."

The state of the Italian army was one of many martial failings, short supply, and an overabundance of confidence in the skin color of its troops. The field commanders in Africa were divided by intramural rivalries, misguided by inaccurate maps, and the document pilferer Giolitti was to reveal that when General Baratieri requested more funds, Crispi telegraphed him to "make war like Napoleon"— meaning force the conquered peoples to pay for it.[28] Opposition was growing at home. Italians were crying "Long live Menelik!" in the streets. A resounding victory, which usually satisfies almost every opponent, had to come quickly and had to come cheap.

No Italian ever believed his country would actually *lose* the war. Discussion at home centered on the terms to be dictated when the empire was won. In December, 1895, however, Menelik's forces scored a military success at Amba Alagi, and some weeks later the Italian fortress at Macallé fell to the Abyssinians. It was clear that the negus's armies could advance at will. Rome panicked. Parliament, appropriating an additional 20 million lire for the military, united behind Crispi in a vote of confidence. Reinforcements were dispatched. Crispi waited at the teletype link with the war zone, hoping for a miracle, and the king rushed to Naples to review the fresh troops prior to their embarkation. Too late. On March 1, 1896, while Humbert was passing up and down the ranks of the men setting sail for the front, General Baratieri was leading 6,000 Italians to their death at Adowa.

Baratieri, who had learned that he was to be replaced for incompetence and lack of initiative, had launched an improperly organized attack, blindly seeking a stunning victory. He moved 15,000 men too far from his base, was cut off by the enemy, and all his forces, surrounded and outnumbered by at least five to one, were totally destroyed, either slain or imprisoned.[29]

The latest war was over. Aghast, Crispi quit, as form demanded, but he had no intention of leaving. He hoped to find a scapegoat in Baratieri, who in turn had sought one in accusing his dead troops of cowardice. Crispi expected that the king would refuse his resignation, reinstate him, and charge him with making a bigger and better war of revenge. The queen was for it, as was Carducci and others. Humbert brooded for a few days. He seemed exhausted, full of doubt, and spoke of abdication. He worried about the army, believing that public opinion would now demand a reduction in military commitments and expenditures. Then, stiffening his courage with the cardboard backing the tradition of the House of Savoy provided for such occasions, he summoned Crispi for a painful "final scene," as he called it. The monarchy had been compromised and humiliated once more. The bourgeois class, on which the entire Savoyard structure was founded, was losing faith and was in a mood to shake loose from the bungling crown. In such a situation, from the king's point of view, there could be only one scapegoat, and that was Crispi. Humbert thanked him for his services and told him he was through. There were no kisses now.

Crispi felt betrayed. His secretary later revealed the contents of

Crispi's file on the episode, on which the prime minister had scrawled, *"la grande infamia."* Documents disclosed that Crispi had had an agreement with the king that in the event of a military defeat in Africa, martial law would be declared to quell all dissent at home, and 100,000 troops would be sent to Ethiopia in a total war of conquest.[30] But the king drew back from this final insanity.

Now that Crispi had fallen into disgrace and was powerless, the nation turned against him (with the exception of his brutalized Sicilians with whom he remained popular until his death in 1901). The Fascists were later to make him a hero, but after Adowa the people scorned him and parliament censured him, a concession to those who wished to see the old man jailed for embezzlement.

10

THE BEGGARS' REVOLT

THE KING ASKED THE RED-BEARDED MARQUIS ANTONIO DI RUDINÌ TO TAKE CRISPI'S PLACE. DI Rudinì, also a Sicilian, was a right-wing conservative who had publicly opposed a big military budget and aggressive adventures abroad. He was, for those reasons, unpopular at court, and especially with the king, but clearly the man for this embarrassing moment. Reluctant at first to come to the monarchy's rescue, he finally accepted the mandate. Thanks were apparently due to the importunities of Humbert's mistress Litta. The king begrudgingly empowered him, admonishing the monocled nobleman to leave the military untouched and not to withdraw entirely from Africa. "Neither I nor the army will tolerate it," he said.[1]

Di Rudinì opened peace negotiations with Menelik and agreed to reparations, part of which were paid by melting down the silver coins bearing Humbert's head and the imperial crown. In the meantime, Countess Santa Fiora, the king's other lady friend, organized a charity to succor and gain the release of the thousands of Italian prisoners being held by the negus pending a settlement. Margherita refused to contribute (as did Crispi), saying that the prisoners should be freed by force. As the daughter of a soldiering family, she said, anything less would be dishonorable to her. Humbert, too, assumed this attitude at first, but according to Farini, after a few of his regular evening visits to the countess's *palazzo*, he changed his mind.

Toward the end of the year peace was concluded in Africa, but not at home. The fundamentally disruptive errors committed by Crispi and the king were irreparable. The Italy which had been born in the trauma of the Risorgimento was growing up wrong. It could no more be stilled than the heaving sea.

The movement of uprooted capital to the north meant the movement of uprooted people to the north, and when the north teemed, people were driven to the misery of emigration. The concentration of the masses in the industrial north turned them into a proletariat, and the social unrest of the early part of the decade became disciplined socialist unrest and agitation in the late Nineties. Compared to what was coming, the bloody woes of yesterday were to appear as innocence and bliss.

Italian socialism of the Nineties was no longer the adventurous anarchism of Bakunin or murky Mazzinian republicanism. The socialism which Marx had characterized as being the pastime of a "gang of drifters" had now become materialist and Marxist, the work of serious thinkers and activists, such as the theoretician Antonio Labriola, the young Turati and Bissolati, and the Russian *émigré* Anna Kulishov, whose salon in Milan was the socialist equivalent to Queen Margherita's. Italian socialism would never learn how to reach the peasantry and root itself in the soil, but it was a movement which captured, as Croce was to write, "the flower of the younger generation," including the early Croce himself. This generation of Italians, enraged and embittered by the unrelieved suffering of the people, understood almost to the man that Italian unity had been jerrybuilt, and they ached for social change.

They knew it in the idiom articulated by Engels in a letter written shortly before his death to Turati, who published it in his popular socialist journal *Critica sociale*:

> The bourgeoisie [wrote Engels], which came to power during and following the national independence movement could not, nor did it want to, complete its victory. It did not destroy the residue of feudalism, neither did it reorganize national production on the model of modern capitalism. Incapable of giving the nation any of the relative and temporary advantages of the capitalist system, it imposed instead all the burdens and disadvantages of the system. Not content with that, it lost whatever trust and credit it might have had left in ignominious bank scandals.
>
> The working people—peasants, artisans, laborers in industry and on the farm—are on the one hand the victims of the old abuses, inherited not only from the feudal period, but even from more ancient times (one thinks of the sharecroppers and the latifundia of the South, where man is supplanted by beast), and on the other hand, they suffer the con-

sequences of the most voracious fiscal system ever employed by a bourgeois regime.

Here too one can say with Marx: "Like everyone else in the continental West, we are not only afflicted by the development of capitalist production, but also by the lack of development. Beside the sad necessities of modern times lies an entire series of calamities; old, surviving systems of production handed down with all their anachronistic social and political relations. We suffer from not only that which is alive, but also from that which is dead. *Le mort saisit le vif.*"[2]

This was also understood, perhaps even better, in the language of the new generation of Italian poets and writers. Even D'Annunzio crossed over to the left for a while. Verga and Pirandello told of the wretchedness of the Sicilians, Mathilde Serao wrote passionately of the "daily martyrdom" of her beloved, suffering fellow Neapolitans, and Ada Negri, in her twenties, assailed the rulers of Italy, "wielding a lash that seems knotted with scorn," as one contemporary essay had it. "She scourges the dominant classes of society; we can almost hear the swish of her whip as it cuts the faces of the smug, astute bourgeois . . ."[3]—as in "*Sfida*," or "Challenge" (1892):

> O, fat, crafty, bourgeois world . . .
>   world of well-fed millionaires . . .
> O, adulterous world of plunder
>   world of hopes betrayed . . .
> O, fat world of geese and snakes
>   vile world, which you've profaned . . .
> Go, fat world, go on your merry chase
>   for prostitutes and money from another's purse
> And I, with my whip of flaming verse
>   will lash you in your ugly face[4]

There was reason for such loathing. Sardinians were eating grass to stay alive. Starvation was common. Bread prices, taxed anew, were soaring, and to some peasants the taste of salt, which was also taxed iniquitously, was barely known. One report disclosed:

Sometimes they [the peasants] will cook their *polenta* [corn gruel] in sea water, though this is an offense against the Excise, and women are still arrested or fired at if they are found drawing from the sea, and it is said that a poor child in Venetia, if given the run of the kitchen, prefers to eat salt rather than sugar.[5]

Conditions such as these opened in the last years of the reign of Humbert the Good and the "poetic creature" Margherita a period of national turbulence rarely paralleled in Italian history. What had been more or less confined to the island of Sicily in Crispi's time—the strikes, the fires, and the sight of torn flesh—now gripped the entire mainland with added fury. Violence and the royal troops were on every corner, the prisons overflowed, but no one was safe, including the king. In April, 1897, while driving peacefully to the racetrack along the Appian Way, Humbert was in fact assailed, unsuccessfully, by a would-be assassin.*

The economic morass brought on by the profligacy of the Crispian era now precluded all possibility of satisfying even the smallest measure of the people's needs. Only socialism, it seemed, had meaningful solutions, and the eminent conservative historian Villari warned that everything favored its progress. Large sections of the ruling class, aware of their predicament, were beginning to chip away from the monarchy's foundations. The next scapegoat, many of this class believed, particularly in industrial Milan, might have to be the House of Savoy itself.

"A notable portion of the Lombard bourgeoisie," one conservative deputy wrote in 1898, "is republican, and . . . it is as morally respectable, intellectually cultivated, and socially elevated as the bourgeois monarchists."[7] The economist De Viti de Marco, himself a monarchist, was more explicit. In the same year he wrote in the *Giornale degli economisti* that public opinion regarded the crown at the forefront of Italian militarism. As a result, he said, the monarchy was being more and more identified as a "military institution" opposed to liberal reforms. The growing popular sentiment against the army had therefore become equally anti-monarchist, he said.[8] Even the stanchest courtiers were beginning to grumble about Humbert's inability to master the situation, and one titled aristocrat was heard to say, "Monarchy is an excellent institution when there is a monarch."[9]

The king and the court knew they would have to work harder than ever. They talked about parliament being the source of all evil ("a disgusting spectacle," said Margherita), and Sonnino wrote a widely discussed essay appealing for "a return to the constitution."[10] This was merely a scheme for weakening parliament and establishing a more absolutist type of rule, in which the king would be the fount of

---

* His name was Pietro Acciarito. An unemployed keymaker, he made the following confession: "I had no work and I was hungry. Today, when I saw all those gentlemen, all those liveries, all that luxury, and I remembered that the king had offered 24,000 lire to the winning horse, I lost my head and I did what I did."[6]

all state power. The elections of 1897, however, reinforced the parliamentary opposition and socialism in general, which made matters worse and hastened the process of isolation enveloping the throne.

Byzantine cabals began to encrust around the uncertain Humbert. These were political intrigues linked intimately to the bigotry of Margherita and the rivalry for the king's affections between Countess Santa Fiora and Duchess Litta. The machinations of the king's mistresses were revealed by Crispi, who, half-blind and near eighty, still hoped with the queen for his recall. They were published in the Neapolitan newspaper *Il Mattino*, which spoke of two camps, the countess's gathered around Prime Minister Di Rudinì and the duchess's around the Piedmontese Minister of War General Pelloux. Italy, wrote the newspaper's editor Scarfoglio, now had a Madame Maintenon and a Marquise Pompadour.[11]

There was much truth in it, although the women themselves were probably extraneous to the political ambitions being contested. The supporters of Pelloux, a nondescript officer doggishly devoted to the king, sought to drive out Di Rudinì, who was almost as lackluster and narrow-minded as Pelloux, but obstinately independent and loyal to parliamentarianism. Di Rudinì, it was plotted, was to be supplanted by the general, who as an officer had sworn allegiance to the king. This would permit one faction of the court to institute Sonnini's program of Savoyard authoritarianism. The Crispian episode had taught nothing enduring; it was the experience of the ages from which lessons were learned.

Di Rudinì, a stubborn little man who could not comprehend the despair of the monarchy and its shortage of alternatives, felt himself personally persecuted by the court, and, as the goaded Baratieri had done in Africa, he too foolishly and recklessly tried to defend his position.

To foil the cabals of the Humbertine right, Di Rudinì fraternized with the left. He took Zanardelli into his government and won a peace and neutrality promise from the leader of the electorally reinforced *estrema*, Cavallotti. Cavallotti, the "bard," incorruptible *galantuomo* of the old-line radicals, abomination of the right and especially the queen, allowed himself to be drawn into Di Rudinì's personal resistance to the crown, by way of Countess Santa Fiora. Suddenly, to the "universal wonder" of Farini and the rest of the court, Cavallotti was receiving and accepting invitations from the lady whose private aim was to enrage Humbert the Good and slap Margherita's face.

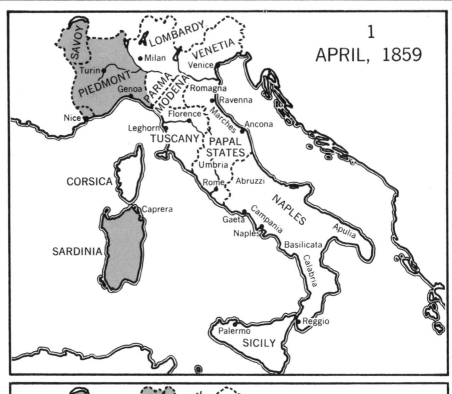

1
APRIL, 1859

SAVOY
LOMBARDY
Milan
VENETIA
Venice
Turin
PIEDMONT
PARMA
Genoa
MODENA
Romagna
Nice
Ravenna
Florence
Marches
Ancona
Leghorn
TUSCANY
PAPAL
STATES
Umbria
Rome
Abruzzi
CORSICA
Caprera
NAPLES
Gaeta
Campania
Apulia
Naples
Basilicata
SARDINIA
Calabria
Reggio
Palermo
SICILY

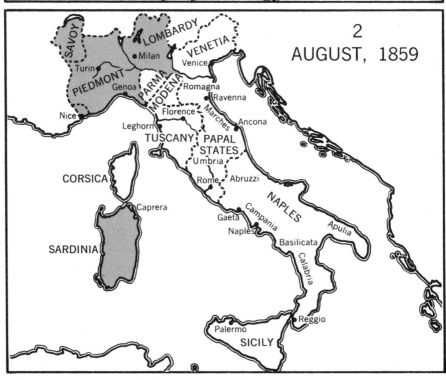

2
AUGUST, 1859

SAVOY
LOMBARDY
Milan
VENETIA
Venice
Turin
PIEDMONT
PARMA
Genoa
MODENA
Romagna
Nice
Ravenna
Florence
Marches
Ancona
Leghorn
TUSCANY
PAPAL
STATES
Umbria
Rome
Abruzzi
CORSICA
Caprera
NAPLES
Gaeta
Campania
Apulia
Naples
Basilicata
SARDINIA
Calabria
Reggio
Palermo
SICILY

3
MAY, 1860

SAVOY
LOMBARDY
Milan
VENETIA
Venice
Turin
PIEDMONT
Genoa
PARMA
MODENA
Romagna
Ravenna
Nice
Florence
Marches
Ancona
Leghorn
TUSCANY
PAPAL
STATES
CORSICA
Umbria
Rome
Abruzzi
Caprera
NAPLES
Gaeta
Campania
Naples
Apulia
SARDINIA
Basilicata
Calabria
Reggio
Palermo
SICILY

SAVOY
LOMBARDY
Milan
VENETIA
Venice
Acquired from
Austria 1866
4
NOVEMBER 1860
Turin
PIEDMONT
Genoa
PARMA
MODENA
Romagna
Ravenna
Nice
Florence
Marches
Ancona
Leghorn
TUSCANY
PAPAL
STATES
CORSICA
Umbria
Rome
Abruzzi
Caprera
NAPLES
Taken from the
Holy See 1870
Gaeta
Campania
Naples
Apulia
SARDINIA
Basilicata
Calabria
Reggio
Palermo
SICILY

This worked well for a while: the government and the *estrema* were invigorated, and the spiteful countess awakened in the king feelings that he was perhaps giving more mind to the charms of the duchess than hers. But, by luck or by plot, the time of the monarchist schemers arrived: the impetuous Cavallotti accepted a challenge from a right-wing deputy and thug named Macola, who claimed to have been somehow offended by the bard. Justice was to be done in a meadow behind Castel Sant'Angelo by dueling to the death.

Macola, a former henchman of Crispi and now a junior member of the clique around Pelloux, was a cold-blooded animal fighting his fifteenth duel. Cavallotti, who had served under Garibaldi in Sicily and was a national idol, a romantic figure adored by the people, had had thirty-one such barbaric encounters. But he was aging and myopic, and everyone sensed Macola would win—which he did, slaying the poet-politician. Cavallotti was given a hero's funeral, the nation mourned, and even Humbert, it seems, felt sad. The queen, however, was nothing less than delighted.

Margherita, speaking two months after Cavallotti's funeral, during the bloody events of May, 1898, which will shortly be described, had this to say:

> One of the most disgusting and moreover fearsome spectacles was the apotheosis of that Cavallotti. He was a very wicked and vulgar man, who had always been a doer of evil, and who died as a man who had had thirty-three [sic] duels had to die. Providence, which always does the best of all things, knew well what it was doing, causing him to die before the troubles [of May], because only he, with his energy and intelligence, would have been able to seize control of them, and would have made them much worse![12]

In truth, the disappearance of Cavallotti meant the passage of radical leadership to the socialists. It weakened Di Rudinì's relations with the *estrema*, and hence his ability to stave off the Pelloux camp, which was openly accusing the prime minister of decrepitude, insulting his family and honor. When the May disorders came, the taunted Di Rudinì, feeling his loyalty and patriotism suspect by the king, surrendered to recklessness. To save his country from the "socialist revolution," he rushed to be first to call out the royal troops, and in doing so, became responsible for the ghastly mistake which led to the slaying of about one hundred innocent civilians in Milan.

The Milanese episode of 1898 is enlightening with regard to the state of mind which had overtaken the crown and the rulers of Italy.

They were suffering from a pox on the social nervous system, a malady from which apparently no nation is immune.

On the first Saturday in May some of the workers at the Pirelli rubber plant laid down their tools and walked out in protest. They sought to show their support of Italians in other cities who in recent days had been beaten and jailed in demonstrations calling for a reduction of the price of bread. Pirelli, the former Garibaldian freedom fighter who was to live long enough to help finance Mussolini's "March on Rome," was enraged. He had boasted that his workers, most of whom were illiterate peasants, farmers' daughters, and children, were incapable of being influenced by socialist propaganda, but now he believed that the Revolution had begun, and he therefore summoned the army. A few rocks were thrown, and the infantry went on the attack.

When the other industrialists heard that the "revolution" was on, they closed their shops, throwing thousands of bewildered workers onto the streets. This made it suddenly appear as if the forces of law and order were insufficient to put down the "uprising," so the leading citizens of Milan began sending frantic telegrams to Rome for reinforcements. Rudinì obliged.

When night fell, however, the "revolutionaries" went home to sleep and calm returned. But by this time, the king, who happened to be in Turin celebrating the fiftieth anniversary of Grandfather Charles Albert's proclamation of the constitution, had heard news of sorts about Milan. Having traveled via Rome, the reports had become so garbled that Humbert and his entourage believed that the "revolution" had not only broken out in Milan, but was nationwide. The workers of the nearby Leumann factory, almost all of whom were women, were said to be marching on Turin, and the university students of Pavia, a town in Lombardy, were on their way to Milan, ready to join the front line of the fight. The royal party debated whether or not to declare a state of siege.

The following morning, while many of the "revolutionaries," who had all but forgotten about yesterday's clashes, were putting on their Sunday best and going off to church, General Bava Beccaris deployed his troops at the gates of Milan. The city had to be protected from the Pavian students. They never arrived, although some people who looked like students were shot dead in the streets. At two o'clock in the afternoon, Bava Beccaris telegraphed the king that order had been restored, but by now Humbert had received new information that bands of Italian exiles were mobilizing on the Swiss border, preparing to invade the homeland and link up with the students and workers. The foreign ministry dispatched urgent messages to Bern and other European capitals requesting their aid in preventing the invasion of the nonexistent "Swiss bands."[13] A state of siege was declared at Milan.

On Monday morning Milan was an armed camp. Bava Beccaris had given orders that the "revolutionaries" were to be shot on sight. When a group of beggars lining up at a convent for a free bowl of soup were mistaken for the enemy, the troops opened fire, the beggars fell, and the convent was occupied.

The chief editor and director of the prestigious, liberal-conservative *Corriere della Sera* of Milan, Eugenio Torelli Viollier, who realized that a terrible error was being committed, sought to alert the authorities. He went to the mayor and argued that there had not been the slightest indication of any kind of revolution, and that whatever disorders had occurred had been the result of misunderstandings. The workers were entirely unorganized and unarmed, he said, and his newsmen had seen no attempts at disrupting power lines and communications; nor were any of the known socialist leaders involved. The mayor paid no attention to him, and when he tried to persuade the other city fathers they looked on him, he said, as a "false conservative, an infidel."

In the meantime the brutal repression continued. Order was restored. Two thousand persons were arrested, the new customary touring military tribunals were set up like a tent circus, and leading republicans and socialists were sentenced to long prison terms. Turati, for example, was given twelve years, convicted of having spread socialist propaganda.

Half of Italy was placed under martial law, states of siege being declared at Bologna, Florence, Rome, Naples, and elsewhere. Universities were closed and 110 newspapers were shut down; 109 were socialist, republican, Catholic or otherwise non-monarchist, and the 110th was the pro-monarchist *Il Mattino*, which had published the articles about Humbert's extra-marital love life.

The *Corriere della Sera* was permitted to remain open, but the courageous Torelli Viollier quit. He wrote a long letter explaining his resignation to Villari. This remarkable document which has recently turned up in the Vatican archives, attributes the Milan episode to a whole people in the grip of fear. The ruling class, he wrote on June 3, 1898, had been afraid that "the great day of its liquidation had arrived." He went on:

It was fear which threw the workers of Milan onto the streets; it was fear which caused a hundred persons to be slain and several hundred more to be wounded, many seriously. Fear made all of Italy believe that our city was on the verge of a catastrophe, and fear has placed us beyond the protection of the law, bringing on the suspensions of every freedom, of every constitutional guarantee.

The fear, however, had now subsided for the class of which Torelli and Villari were prominent members.

The bourgeoisie [Torelli said] was ferocious in rejoicing over the victory obtained, as it is now ferocious in its reaction. We are in the midst of a *coup d'état* undertaken in behalf of the bourgeoisie and against the people, that is, by one class against another, by the oppressor against the oppressed.[14]

Rejoicing and reaction continued relentlessly. Di Rudinì praised Bava Beccaris for his "rigor," which, according to the prime minister, had rescued the nation from darkness. On June 6, Humbert himself sent the general, who had become the odious symbol of the repression, a telegram which proved to be most unfortunate, particularly for himself and the House of Savoy. A request had been made to give Bava Beccaris an award for his salvaging operation, and now the king replied:

I have examined the proposal . . . and in giving my approval I am happy and proud to honor the virtues of discipline, abnegation, and valor which [your troops] so admirably exemplify. To you personally I wish to confer *motu proprio* the Grand Officer's Cross of the military order of Savoy in appreciation for the services you have rendered to our institutions and to civilization. . . .[15]

That telegram, signed with "fond sentiments" and the king's personal gratitude, was published in all the remaining newspapers of Italy. It was, by chance, read by a young man named Gaetano Bresci, an Italian immigrant living in Paterson, New Jersey. Bresci had wept at what had happened in Milan, and felt that those who had been innocently killed had to be avenged. The telegram persuaded him of Humbert's responsibility for the tragedy. Bresci decided to punish him.

Those who favored totalitarian rule believed now that they had at last gained the upper hand. Even Di Rudinì, who went on committing one liberticidal act after another, had been converted to wishing for a dictatorial state, and indeed it was he who wanted now to do away with parliament and govern by royal decree. This the king would not allow, opposing the advice of his dearest counselors and the deepest yearnings of the queen. Pretenses had to be maintained; Humbert the Good was not going to go down in history as the Indian-giver of magnanimous Charles Albert's constitution.

Di Rudinì resigned in protest, which was fine with the king. He promptly entrusted General Pelloux to head a government of generals and admirals sworn to take orders from the crown. Pelloux declared his dedication to the constitution; and at the same time promised "absolute maintenance of order, the constant and jealous safeguarding of society and its institutions, and the pacification of the mind."[16]

That was a tall order. Before long, he too wanted to rule by decree law. It seemed to him the only way to govern the Italians. Humbert could not but agree, and as long as lip service were rendered to the constitution, he gave Pelloux a free hand. The repression had to continue until the nation was tamed. "If a man comes along who gives in," said Humbert, "in a short time we'll have to start all over again."[17]

That was in June, 1898. In June, 1900, nationwide elections, in spite of rigging, returned a liberal-left opposition stronger and more allied than ever before, and brought on the fall of Pelloux's military regime. The monarchists still had a parliamentary majority, but it was slight. Humbert's alternatives were running out. He seemed tired. He chose the ancient Piedmontese senator Giuseppe Saracco to defend the crown as his prime minister, and then went to Naples to review the troops departing for China to help crush the Boxer Rebellion and win glory for Italy.

11

A CRIME OF A CENTURY

THE TRIP TO NAPLES IN MID-JULY, 1900, WAS TO BE THE LAST OF THE KING'S OFFICIAL DUTIES before his summer holiday would begin. Normally Humbert and Margherita would have already departed for the royal villa at Monza, but the troops had to be properly dispatched. European imperialism had been outraged, and the Italian flag had been profaned by the "harmonious fists" of the Boxers. The Italians, as Humbert put it, had to join the international assault on the Chinese to uphold "the sacred rights of the people and all humanity, which has been tread upon."[1]

He was loved in Naples. He stood on the docks, watching the troops and the Catholic missionaries who had accompanied them sail away on the great white *Singapore* and the newly launched *Marco Minghetti*. He was visibly moved when the men gave their last salute, and only when the ships moved over the horizon did he look away. He returned to the palace in the heart of the city, and, it is said, the people of Naples celebrated his presence throughout the night.

At last the king's vacation could begin. On July 20 he stopped briefly in Rome and the following day he arrived at his residence in Monza. He and Margherita at the end of the month were to go to their Alpine retreat in Gran Paradiso, two miles high in the sky. It was to have been a glorious summer passed in the very heartland from whence the first Savoys had come. The king looked forward to hunting chamois and wild mountain goats, and the queen, who loved to look at Italy from high places, hoped to climb the most rewarding peaks.

"My holidays," Humbert had once remarked at Monza, "are the

times when I forget I wear a crown."[2] And at Gran Paradiso, where the Savoys possessed one of Europe's most bountiful hunting reserves, he could forget. Margherita had exclaimed of last year's Alpine holiday: "What a joy that in the summer there is no parliament, and that the mountains, those beautiful mountains, speak such a different language to those who know how to listen to them!"[3]

Humbert and Margherita were growing old and reflective; their joys were ever fewer. Time is cruel even to kings and queens, and the era which lay across the centurial divide was their cruelest time of all. The years had done their devastations to the royal couple. Margherita was no longer beautiful. Her bodily charms had surrendered to gravity. She had become heavy and she waddled. She looked like a proud, majestic penguin. Humbert appeared much older than his fifty-six years. Only the brooding eyes that seemed to open on a soul that had never lived remained. His hair and his flowing mustaches, which hung over his mouth like a schoolgirl's bow, had turned as white as his high stiff collar, and though his tutored bones still held him tall, in a kingly way, the flesh was falling.

Margherita's departure was scheduled for July 31, and Humbert was to follow her three days later. There were a few small matters which he had to dispose of before he could leave. One of these was that he wished to fulfill a promise he had made to the director of an athletic competition. The event was to take place at Monza July 29, and he had said that if he were at his villa he would attend. It was an insignificant engagement. The queen at lunch that day urged him not to bother with it, but Humbert insisted, saying that he had given his word, and it had to be kept. "All right," the lovers of irony record Margherita as having replied, "but at least come home early."[4]

In the meantime Gaetano Bresci had come home from Paterson. In the one hundred and some odd weeks since the May days of 1898 he had managed to put aside about one dollar and fifty cents every week from the wages he had received as a textile worker at the Hamil Booth Company, a silk factory in New Jersey. By May, 1900, he had accumulated the price of a special third-class excursion ticket to the Paris Exposition, $100 in cash, and a gun, and on May 17 he had set sail from New York on the French Line's *La Gascogne* for the eleven-day voyage across the sea. He had been to see the Exposition and then had gone on to his home town in Tuscany. On Sunday, July 29, having read of the king's scheduled public appearance at the sporting event, Bresci was in Monza.

Bresci was a strange young man, turned thirty the winter before. He was born in Prato, the youngest of a family of peasants. His brothers grew up to be ardent monarchists, one of them a captain in the royal artillery. He claimed to be a revolutionary, a socialist, and an anarchist. His neighbors knew him as a silent, bookish type, and when he was arrested in 1891 for having participated in a strike, some were convinced that he was a "dangerous fellow." After that, he found it hard to find work.

He went to America, where there were jobs for millions of Italians. He joined a revolutionary group in Paterson, and read the local Italian-language anarchist newspaper *La questione sociale*. But he found his comrades not revolutionary enough, and he became a loner. He married an Irish immigrant. They had a daughter, whom they named Maddalena. Then came 1898, Milan, and the king's telegram to General Bava Beccaris. He began to save for his return to Italy. He practiced with his gun, shooting at a target in a vacant lot. He bade farewell to his wife and child, saying he was going home to sell his share of a small piece of farm land he had inherited in common with his brothers. When he arrived in Prato he discussed the matter of the property with them, stayed a few days, shot thirty-five rounds to keep an edge on his aim, and then went away. He said he would be back in a few days. He went to Bologna and slept three nights with a woman he knew. Then he went to Milan, and, finally, to Monza, where on Friday he took a furnished room near the train station and waited for Sunday.

He was rather tall and very dark. He had black hair and mustaches, was handsome in a way, but appeared underfed and uncared for. His eyes were inscrutable. He looked not unlike the young Humbert of Savoy. He had a gold ring, a watch with an elegant chain, and a few lire in his pocket. He had one good suit, an unfrayed white collar, and a dark tie, and when he took a walk in a park that Sunday morning he looked like a gentleman of some means. No one in the world but he knew his plans.[5]

The athletic event, a competition in gymnastics, was to begin at 9:30 in the evening. The king left his villa a few minutes earlier in a two-horse landau with the top down. He paused to say good-bye to Margherita, who was resting on a terrace that looked onto her gardens. He was accompanied by two generals, Count Ponzio Vaglia, one of his dearest friends, and Count Avogardo, an aide-de-camp. There was no escort, no armed guard other than the police and *carabinieri* at the stadium. Humbert, although he had already undergone two assassination attempts, had refused all importunities that special precautions be taken for his safety. "If it is destined that I am to die like Alexander II, of what importance are precautions?" he once said, and when he had learned of an abortive assault on the life of Kaiser Wilhelm II, he had advised the younger monarch that "these are the risks of the trade." There was nothing to do but "open your eyes wide and look into the faces of your people."[6]

Arriving at the stadium, Humbert was greeted with an uproarious welcome from the crowd. He took his place on the reviewing stand, and the gymnastics began. "How I envy those agile young men," he remarked to someone beside him as he watched the display. "I am old now, but when I was a youth I used to do a lot of gymnastics, too."

Gaetano Bresci wedged his way through the crowd, inching toward the front row. His nine-caliber, short-barreled pistol was clenched in his hand, hidden in a pocket of his coat. The five-chamber weapon was loaded to the full. With a scissors he had carefully scratched the surface of each of the bullets. He had reasoned that the roughened lead would penetrate the flesh more easily and more deeply, and that bits of dirt and sweat from his hands would cling to the cut metal, provoking, should the wounds not be fatal, lethal infection.

He was calm. Earlier in the evening he had taken dinner at the boarding house in which he was staying, but he had hardly eaten, remarking that his appetite had been spoiled by the heat of the day. Now, having reached the head of the crowd, he struck up a conversation with a nearby spectator and glanced from time to time at the king.

The contest was over in an hour. The team from the Trento won the cup. The king came down from the stand, boarded his carriage, and took the seat closest to the spectators. When his aides had joined him, the vehicle began to move, but suddenly all the athletes gathered around him to send him off with a cheer. Humbert stood and said, "Thanks, boys. Thank you very much." Then he sat again. Everyone cried: "Long live the king!"

Just then, Bresci broke from the crowd, his gun held high, a stride away from his target. Three shots rang out. Some heard four. The horses lurched. The king slumped back.

"Your majesty," asked Count Avogardo, "are you hit?"

"I don't think so," said the king. "Away, away!" he commanded the driver.[7]

One bullet had entered his throat just above the collar bone. It had passed through his body in a downward direction, lodging beneath the skin behind his shoulder blade. Another bullet, having penetrated between his third and fourth ribs, had been deflected and had come to rest in his breastbone. A third bullet, which was later found in the back rest of the royal carriage, had gone through the center of his heart.[8]

As the landau raced away, an officer of the *carabinieri* seized Bresci by the collar. He had hurled the gun away and now he shouted, "I didn't do anything!"

"Kill him! Kill him!" cried some from the crowd. Others began to throttle him and beat him to the ground. But the police came to his rescue and dragged him away.

The royal coach churned the dust on the road as it made for home. The king lay in Count Ponzio's arms, rattling death in his throat, and finally, at the very moment they arrived at the villa, it seems, he blew out the last of his soul.[9]

Humbert the Good was dead. Those eyes, unseeing in life, were open wider than ever now, looking at the nighttime sky.

"The king is here," said Margherita, hearing the sound of approaching hoof beats. She had been leafing through a catalogue of the latest models of gramophones, and she put the booklet aside and went out to greet him. As she walked toward the front gate, one of the king's aides stood in her path. He wore a look of alarm, and in his hands he held Humbert's tall silk hat. Margherita knew intuitively that tragedy had struck. "I saw him before me like Christ on the Cross," she wrote some days later.[10] She ran down a flight of steps, her summer white lace robes billowing in the breeze. Ponzio Vaglia, Avogardo, and the servants who had opened the gate were carrying the slain sovereign into the house.

Margherita thought him still living. "What a crime! What a crime!" she exclaimed. "And against a man like him, who never did a bad thing to anyone." A physician arrived. "Save him for me, doctor," cried the queen. "Save him for me, for God's sake!"

A second doctor appeared, and they laid the wide-eyed corpse on a mattress which someone had placed on the ground. They stripped away the cover of clothing, and began to wash down the blood in search of the wounds. The queen ran and brought a first aid kit which she kept in her bedroom.

"Do something," she implored. "Save the king!"

They closed the eyes and covered the body with a sheet. At last Margherita understood.

"This is the crime of the century!" she thundered irresistibly.[11] The chapter headings of schoolroom history had to be written on the scene.

But, unhappily, in view of the date no one would ever really be sure which century she meant, the old or the new.

Somehow Margherita, suddenly queen mother, knew without pause how to fill in the interregnum. She was sustained by her belief that God had taken the king to spare him the "supreme bitterness . . . of knowing that the parricidal [sic] hand was Italian," and that the slaying was a supernatural event "in which the Lord wishes to test all of Italy."[12] She herself was at once prepared for so awesome a trial. Humbert was dead, but the House of Savoy and the train of imagery it had dragged through the dust of the centuries had to go forward. It was she who had coined the motto, *Sempre avanti, Savoia!* And now she lived it hard.

She cut fresh flowers from the gardens of the royal villa. She ordered that her husband's body be properly dressed and placed in the bed where he used to sleep. A flag was draped over the headboard, and during the night the room was turned into a chapel, complete with an altar torn from the floor of a nearby church. Margherita, with incredible presumptuousness, then set herself to the task of composing a liturgical prayer in the form of a rosary, adding five new "painful mysteries" concerning Humbert of Savoy to those about Jesus and Mary. She asked that the new rosary be recited in churches throughout the land, and indeed obtained the approval of the bishop of Cremona, but the pope had the good sense to overrule him.*

The body, in the midsummer heat, began at once to decompose, and a prompt burial was recommended. But Margherita would hear no counsel. The royal corpse was packed with ice, and an electric fan was brought into the bedroom to distribute the cold air in a fashion. She insisted that the dead man had to remain unmoved at least long enough for all respects to be paid. She gathered up her husband's bloodied clothes and requested possession of the bullets extracted from his wounds. These were to go into a specially made chest in order that they might be kept for posterity. With showy

---

* The prayer, if it may be so called, was a crude attempt to mythicize, if not sanctify, the dead king, insisting on his impeccable righteousness in association with God. Here is one sentence, which follows the "rosary": "Oh, Lord, he did nothing but good in this world, had malice toward no one, always forgave whoever did wrong, sacrificed his life for his duty and the good of the Fatherland; and, until his last breath, he endeavored to carry out the mission which You, oh Lord, had entrusted to him in this world."[13] The Church, having already beatified the last Humbert of Savoy (the twelfth-century count Humbert III), who was later revealed as someone scarcely saintly at all, was not going to make the same mistake twice. Nevertheless the "prayer" was a popular success. It was translated into several languages, including Hebrew, and did much to earn Humbert in death the enduring epithet concerning his goodness.

generosity she permitted Duchess Litta a few moments of solitude with her dead lover. For nearly two whole weeks, Margherita did nothing but pose for legendry and write "memorable" phrases in Italian and Latin.[14] Then she withdrew, but only for a while. She was to be Italy's emotive queen mother for even longer than she had reigned as her queen.

Desiring that the news of Humbert's death be broken in two stages, Margherita on the evening of the crime told General Ponzio to telegraph Prime Minister Saracco that the king was desperately ill. The same message was to be sent to her son, Victor Emmanuel, the new king of Italy. Ponzio obeyed, adding in his wire to the prime minister, however, that in his own "opinion" Humbert was already dead.

Victor Emmanuel, who was aboard his yacht with the Slavic princess he had married four years earlier, was located in the Aegean Sea. He received an ambiguous report by semaphore about his father's health calling on him to proceed at once to an Italian port. It had taken some thirty-six hours to find him, and by now the whole world but he and his party was aware of Humbert's fate. When, however, an Italian torpedo boat soon arrived to give escort, it was flying the tricolor at half-mast, and Victor Emmanuel, who but for a few hours was the very same age as his father's assassin, guessed at least part of the heart-rending truth.

He came ashore at Reggio Calabria and was given a sheaf of messages addressed to "His Majesty, the King of Italy." A train was waiting to take him and Italy's new queen, Elena of Montenegro, to Monza. The royal party stopped briefly in Naples, where Victor Emmanuel spoke for a moment or two with Crispi, whom he despised, and received his uncle and aunt, the duke and duchess of Ascoli. They gave him a letter from his mother, which he read in silence, except to murmur, "I feel like this is all a dream."[15]

Public reaction to the slaying was one of both apparent and genuine indignation. Even the left and the socialists took a position of sympathy for the dynasty, although the monarchists called them liars.[16] Indeed the monarchical establishment sought to marshal the feelings engendered by the brutal crime and gain a new victory for the House of Savoy and, above all, for its class.

A plot of international proportions was at once discovered, although none at all existed. The idea of a plot was accepted without question and without proof. It was a kind of social reflex, conditioned by a decade of government by grapeshot and weighted clubs. Everyone expected a new wave of official repression, and the pretexts had to be battened down. Several arrests were made. Old Crispi said that all internal enemies of the state had to be "eliminated," and at least one businessman's journal demanded that Bresci be tortured. But the fact was that government violence was aborted this time, prevented by the new king; Victor Emmanuel III, the dullest Savoy, was to be nonetheless unpredictable.

The new times were beginning. The lifeless, bullet-riddled incarnation of the Old remained to be properly disposed of, the killer had to be dealt with by justice, and the symbol of the New had yet to be sworn. That was all taken care of in August. Humbert was entombed in the Pantheon on August 9, near his illustrious father; Victor Emmanuel III signed his vows with a golden pen on the 11th (his lucky number, he would later say), and on the 29th Bresci was tried in a single day.

Of the three rituals, the final one was of the greatest contemporary interest. Bresci had asked to be defended by the socialist leader Turati. Turati, after consulting with the accused and then with his fellow socialists, had refused for the good of the party, he said. Instead, he associated himself with the anguish of the monarchists, who, showing little gratitude, accused him of shedding crocodile tears. The assassin found a halfhearted lawyer to take up his case, a former anarchist turned sociologist who claimed to be both for and against socialism.

Only Bresci's anarchist friends in New York and Paterson gave him their uncritical approval and devotion. Interviewed among a group of revolutionaries in New York, young Emma Goldman, the "queen of the anarchists," was reported to have said, "We have never plotted for the death of the monarch, but the assassin has our sympathy."*[17] Bresci's family in Italy disowned him; one of his brothers changed his identity. But the killer's wife, a young woman named Sophia Neil, stood by him, though not blindly. Her husband was affectionate and kind; he loved her and their daughter profoundly, she said, adding: "I cannot comprehend how he could have forgotten his responsibility to his child. His crime will weigh heavily on her for the rest of her life."[18]

* Asked if she would approve of assassinating the United States President McKinley, one of her comrades answered instead: "He's no better than the others." Humbert's death, and perhaps comments such as this, led to the immediate doubling of the Secret Service guard on McKinley, which of course was to no avail. Leon Czolgosz, the anarchist, had already clipped several newspaper accounts of Bresci's deed. He was shortly to begin taking them to bed with him (he felt the clippings to be something precious), and in 1901 he would kill the American president.

Bresci's trial was something less than fair. The judge, in charging the members of the jury, reminded them that in their deliberations they should think about Humbert's "very noble lady." Margherita, he instructed, "has suffered martyrdom and awaits your verdict"; "the young king of Italy, who was denied his father's last breath, awaits your justice."[19] The jury was out for nine minutes. It found Bresci guilty of murder, without any attenuating circumstances. The accused, who had remained impassive throughout the proceedings, listened silently to the reading of the verdict, wiping his forehead occasionally with a handkerchief. There being no legal capital punishment in Italy, he was given the maximum sentence of life imprisonment. He was advised that he had three days in which to appeal to a higher court. But he simply rose, put on his hat, and looking neither right nor left allowed himself to be led away. He had nothing to say. He had already declared some minutes earlier, "I shall appeal after the coming revolution."[20]

He was never seen or heard from again. Ten months later it was announced, but never demonstrated, that he had committed suicide, having hanged himself on a towel tied to a bar of his cell window.[21]

Almost nobody cared. He and his victim were all but forgotten. Social change had come to Italy. Bresci had been proved right in predicting the approach of a "socialist revolution," although he had not foreseen its content. It was being made, or preempted, as usual, by the House of Savoy. The new Victor Emmanuel was sweeping away the cluttered past, old mistresses and ministers to boot. He was tidying his house, making way for the political painters and moving men to usher in the latest, twentieth-century model in Savoyard rule: an eclectic short-lived contraption to be known as the "socialist monarchy."

So broad and so swift were the changes being made that some people were already saying that while Bresci had cut a decade from Humbert's life, his deed would lengthen the rule of the House of Savoy by a hundred years.

PART III

The Little King
(1900-1922)

VICTOR EMMANUEL III: I understand perfectly all my responsibilities and my duties, and I do not presume to be able to, on my own, remediate the present difficulties. But I am convinced that these difficulties stem from a single cause. In Italy few people carry out their duties properly. There is too much slack and too much ease. Everyone, without exception, must be strict in the observance of their obligations. I, in carrying out my duties as King, will set the example. My ministers will help me, deluding no one with vain illusions, promising nothing which cannot be maintained. Whoever does his duty and does not hesitate to risk his life in doing so will be for me the best of citizens.[1]

MUSSOLINI: What is a king anyway except by definition a useless citizen?[2]

VICTOR EMMANUEL III: This Mussolini, can he be trusted?[3]

MUSSOLINI: I think the state can be profoundly renewed, without touching the monarchical institution.[4]

VICTOR EMMANUEL III: [He is] very sensible. . . . and his proposals are not, as one might have been led to believe, overblown plans.[5]

12

VICTOR AND ELENA

VICTOR EMMANUEL III WAS THIRTY YEARS AND NINE MONTHS OLD WHEN, ON AUGUST 11, 1900, he took the same oath his father had sworn to and had so often breached. He stood five feet and not quite a quarter of an inch tall in his newest shoes. Once, in self-disgust, he had called himself a midget. This was an exaggeration indicative of his psychology, but he certainly was a shrimp.

He was the butt of countless jokes, which were invariably cruel yet always laughed at; kings are forbidden by lesser men to appear as anything but majestic. It was said that when he sat on the throne his feet did not reach the floor. This was untrue—as long as he remained at the edge of his seat. He was too short to get into the army, so in order that he might take his rightful place as commander-in-chief, the army had to lower its standard to five feet and not quite a quarter of an inch. This did not exactly swell the ranks, for it may be fairly said, in spite of many exceptions, the king was the smallest full-grown man in Italy.

It is important to dwell on his size. To the extent that men make history, this condition, in a world which he was forced to observe with a worm's-eye view, was to influence Italian history in the first half of the twentieth century at least as much as war, communism, and Mussolini. That is outrageous; it is also, as we shall see, true.

Non-Italian historians do not yet ascribe very much to Victor Emmanuel III. They will. The fact is that at every crucial turn of events from 1900 on through two world wars the king was the determining influence on the shape of all things, and all the king's influences were shaped by the tiny mold in which he had been cast.

He was not to be the last of the ruling Savoys. His son, libertine Humbert II, who would be king for a month, was to have that distinction. But he would place the greatest stigma on his house, make it fall ignominiously, and in abdication, banished from the cherished land, he would die a thousand miles from home.

He was the truest symbol of the House of Savoy, notwithstanding its occasional flirtations with flamboyancy. He embodied with uncanny perfection nine hundred years of earthbound cunning, parsimony, phlegmaticism, fragility, incredible selfishness, and all the other foxy qualities nature gives to little things.

"The Savoys reign one at a time," the family's princes used to say as if that were God-given wisdom, and so Victor Emmanuel III, like most of his predecessors, came ill-prepared for his work. There were differences, however, some of them singular.

Of his lavishly celebrated birth, the single, slim picking from a genetically tired family tree, we have already spoken.[1] The ample breasts of his Neapolitan wet nurse proved to be insufficient to invigorate the *principino*, and until the age of eight the child was reared as an invalid. His slight little body was unmistakably, although only subtly, malformed, with short, spindly legs and a top-heavy chest, giving him a storklike appearance. Yet when, as almost always, he was dressed in sailor's clothes (the child was inscribed as, and wore the uniform of, the second in command of the torpedo boat *Caracciolo*), he was a handsome lad, bearing Margherita's German blond tresses and the Carignano all-scenting nose.

He passed much of those frail years in a room in the Quirinal playing with balls of wool, his princely cousins, and the children of the palace nobility. He was envious of his playmates, who were conspicuously more robust and energetic than he, and once when engaged in a game with the daughter of Countess Villamarina, he was angered and then heard to snap, "When I grow up to be king, I shall have your head cut off!"[2] The punishment for this, decided upon by his mother, was severe: three days of "imprisonment" on a fare of bread and water.

Severity was the rule. His first teachers were a strict English governess, Margherita, and a Tuscan boy she employed as the prince's personal servant, chosen so that her son might learn the language of Dante rather than the whiny Piedmontese of his forebears. He never entirely gave up the Piedmont twang, but he did learn Dante—the hard way: The rather extinct collectors of Vittoriana tell the story of the time the child, forced to wait much past the dinner hour for his father, rudely complained of a hunger he could no longer support: to which the queen responded by lifting a copy of *The Divine Comedy* from a nearby shelf, opening it to Canto XXXIII of *The Inferno*, and pointing to the verse in which Count Ugolino is dining on the flesh of his companion Archbishop Ruggieri. "Here," she replied, "read this, and your hunger will pass":

> *The sinner raised his mouth from his grim repast*
> *and wiped it on the hair of the bloody head*
> *whose nape he had all but eaten away....*

Margherita, as the admiring Professor Morandi said in authoritatively relating this anecdote, "[was] very affectionate, but she had none of the maternal weaknesses."[3]

Humbert, in his only recorded advice to his son, once told him, "Remember, to be a king all you need to know is how to sign your name, read a newspaper, and mount a horse,"[4] but Margherita, lover of knowledge that she was, saw to it that the boy received a superior education. When he was twelve years old, his health much improved, he was given into the hands of a martinet colonel with instructions from the queen that he make a man of the boy, a king such as Italy and the Savoys had never known. The tight relationship between the prince and the forty-year-old Colonel Osio was a crushing experience which lasted for eight years. The boy was moved from his comfortable surroundings to a spartan room above his mother's library, and his all-powerful master lived almost every waking moment with his charge. "The prince can do whatever I like," Osio used to boast, and indeed, his word, the king and queen agreed, was the rule by which young Victor Emmanuel lived.[5]

Osio arranged the prince's life, Prussian style. He had been a military attaché at Berlin, and unfortunately these were the Germanophile years of the House of Savoy in which Humbert and Margherita were obsessed with the oiled and flexed muscles of the Hohenzollern physique. Victor Emmanuel until his dying day was to hate Germans indiscriminately, even when they were Italy's dearest allies.

His regimen was tough: up at six, to bed at nine, without a moment's peace. The colonel taught him history, geography, German, and the art of war. Professor Morandi taught Italian and literature; Professor Zambaldi and old Monsignor Anzino instructed him in Latin and religion. Then there were the daily lessons in fencing, military drilling, riding, and at Margherita's insistence, music and art.

The queen [writes her biographer Casalegno] had ambitious plans for her only son. She desired that he grow up to be much different from his father, more cultured, more certain in his judgments, less timid and insecure in his relationships with the personages his royal duties would require that he maintain. She wanted that his studies be serious . . . and undoubtedly they were. Perhaps they were badly imposed, too dry and mechanical for a student like Victor Emmanuel, who was almost always alone and was already deprived of imagination, but no prince of the House of Savoy had ever had such a profound and complete education.[6]

The prince rarely saw his mother or his father. He studied with the colonel, rode with the colonel, dined with the colonel, and only on Thursdays was he permitted to take lunch with his parents. Another family occasion was the year-end exams. The king and queen sat on either side of a blackboard, and in the presence of the minister of war, the army chief of staff, and the royal teachers, the prince was tried and tested, sitting for hours on a wooden chair. Times had changed since his grandfather's day, when the princes of Savoy took their lessons at will and chased *pupu* in the noonday sun.

The prince began to grow up smart, cocksure, and very anal. He collected rare coins with a watchmaker's sure-fingeredness, kept neat accounts of every penny he spent, and drew stiff watercolors of hard ships penetrating tight little inlets and coves. The colonel was not entirely pleased. Discussing the boy's superior intelligence with Professor Morandi, he remarked, "How come, with so much ability, he shows so little imagination?"[7]

But Margherita seemed eminently satisfied. "What a pleasure to see that he is becoming a man!" she exclaimed when he was almost sixteen. "That is a woman's greatest satisfaction. It is the moment in which we may rejoice in our inferiority; because we have been able to make that which we can never be! You know that I myself would like very much to be a man. . . ."[8]

Victor Emmanuel at some level of his mind must have known that. He thought little of his mother and far less of her proclivities. "When Mamma asks me things," he once confided to Professor Morandi, "she makes me feel uneasy and often confuses me."[9] When Margherita died he burned her diaries without so much as glancing through the pages. He despised nearly everything she believed in: Germans, De Meis's ideal sovereign, Crispi, music and art, high society, the pope, and religion of any persuasion. He made war and loved the army not for glory's sake, but for his own sake and that of his house. He abhorred poseurs. He passed his lifetime seeking secrecy and solitude.

At age twenty, the prince took leave of the colonel. He went to Naples to fulfill the royal requirements of a brief and fictitious military career. He was a colonel himself now, with gold-colored chevrons piled on his sleeves from his wrists to his elbows. In spite of being *piccolo* he was not at all *brutto*, and he held himself at least an inch more erect than his true height would permit bones less schooled in the ways of the titled upper class. He sported a sparse blond mustache of virgin hair, and a strong, boxlike chin, an elevated brow, and horny ears put still another false inch on his generally defiant frame.

But it was not enough. Though more hinted than discussed, a concern for the dynasty's blood began to haunt the court of Savoy. The prince was approaching the royal marrying age and it was clear to all, particularly then Prime Minister Crispi, that the political arts would have to combine with, if not yield to, the new science of eugenics. Crispi in fact had someone paste up an album of photographs displaying the physical attributes of all the princesses thought to have suitable blood, dowries, and inclinations.[10]

It was "Mamma," however, who had most to say, although in the end Victor Emmanuel, finding the entire procedure repugnant, boldly threatened not to marry at all unless the choice were his own (". . . and he would have kept his word," said Farini, "because like all little men he is firm and has a tenacious will").[11]

"No woman will enter this house, unless she is first a Catholic," Margherita insisted, winning on that point at least, and thereby narrowing the field considerably. She went on in this vein: "The Orleans bring bad luck, the Belgians too, an Austrian girl is inopportune, and there are no eligible Saxons."[12]

"Mamma" took a lively interest, to say the least, in her son's relations with the opposite sex. In one of her many "post-graduate" reports to Colonel Osio, she wrote while visiting Victor Emmanuel in Naples:

> He likes women very much—the true kind, that is. I don't know, however, who is his preferred. It seems to me they constantly vary. Perhaps he does this so that the true one will not be revealed! Beyond that I don't know anything, because *cela n'est pas mon affaire*, but I believe he has no diversions in that area in which youth makes its demands, because he is too good and has none of that dissipation in his face which so characterizes the *viveurs*, and this fact too gives me much, but very much pleasure! ! !ized[13]

This kind of talk, which began to get around in court circles receiving a rather different emphasis, did nothing to enhance the prince's reputation. Rumor had him engaged in all sorts of non-hetero-erotic social intercourse, so much so that Humbert, it seems, instructed his dear friend Rattazzi to "leak" reports on the propriety of his son's sexual demeanor. Victor Emmanuel was not "sexually frigid"; on the contrary, Rattazzi is reported to have whispered around, he was enjoying frequent relations with women in Naples, "but [had] only one true love . . . an aristocrat who went mad."[14]

It was an ingenious tale, calculated no doubt to fill the rumormongers with remorse at having spoken so evilly of the unfortunate prince, and for a while it apparently worked. But when the unwed heir to Humbert's throne approached his twenty-seventh year, the gossip began again. Humbert had married at twenty-four; Victor Emmanuel II at twenty-two; the court and "Mamma" were downright worried.

"My son," Margherita said defensively to President of the Senate Farini, "doesn't know how to decide. He does not try to avoid the question, and in fact has written me a very frank letter. Next year he will surely go on the attack. In some things my son is too wild for certain tastes. Of course he will not choose a stupid woman, nor one in inadequate health, but with regard to the physical side, he may do something strange. One year, at the races, he got himself all excited over a lady who was small, fat, and ugly—a true gnome."[15] Even young Kaiser Wilhelm tried to get the Italian to marry, but Victor Emmanuel rejected the German's advice with a fury.

The truth was, the young prince was having the time of his life in Naples, in his own austere, withdrawn kind of way. He loved the city ("I have become a Neapolitan"), and maintained a little court of his own. When his mother came to visit, he put her up at the family villa in nearby Capodimonte and saw her only at dinner hours, staying himself in town. Of his sex life, really nothing is known, but as it turned out all the fears about his wonts and his glands were to prove entirely unfounded.

He married at last in October, 1896, and his choice, as Margherita had prophesied, was indeed very strange. The bride was the Balkan princess Elena Petrovich of Montenegro, a statuesque mountain creature who towered over her prince by a head and a half.

Victor and Elena: an untold story of love. He met her in Moscow on the first day of June of that year, and when he died in 1947 he loved her still and she cherished him in life and in death to her last.

"*We meet!*" he scrawled in excited English on a page in the home-made "diary" he kept on scraps of paper throughout his life.[16] He had journeyed to the court of Nicholas II to be among the seven thousand guests at the czar's coronation. He had dined on borsch and pheasant in cream sauce amid the clamor of the bells and cannons of Moscow, and of all the princesses from Japan to England he had picked her. Queen Mary of Rumania, who was there, tells how it all began:

> For the various official ceremonies the royal guests had been coupled according to a protocol. My partner was Victor Emmanuel . . . He carried out the formalities being neither overly friendly nor eager to do so. A man of few words, he spoke in brief, staccato sentences, thrusting his jaw forward with a pugnacious air. We found little to say to one another, but I was very interested in the budding romance between him and his future wife, Elena of Montenegro, who because of my partner showed great friendship toward me. Feigning a sudden jealousy for my company, she constantly sought me out, but I understood at once the significance of this innocent subterfuge, and I knew that I was not the true attraction. Elena was a beautiful girl, vivacious, full of joy, and not at all timid or shy. Her eyes were superb and she dressed quite pleasingly. . . . I do not well recall how young Victor Emmanuel received the attentions of the vivacious princess.[17]

The princess's attentions were received with enraptured exultation, by the prince's standards at least. She was twenty-three. Her dark-skinned body was rich with the qualities that Goya liked to paint, and though she had learned how to contain life's essences behind the sinuous tensions called *majesty*, the vivifying air of the dark mountains blew freshly through her pores. She was something less than beautiful, her nose perhaps a bit too capable, a fleshiness too close to class images of peasantry and toil, but she had had the good fortune of having been taken at an early age in tutelage by Marie Fedorovna, empress of Russia and wife of Czar Alexander III. The czarina had performed Pygmalionesque wonders on the back-country princess. Educated at the Romanov court and in the ways of her splendorous and exceedingly gay benefactress, Elena was reputed to be a poetess and a polyglot, well attuned to the glitter, the swirl, and the myths of her day. She was hardly up to the charm of the empress, however, or even her future mother-in-law; indeed, in contradiction of it all, she was possessed of a certain treelike stolidity, and it was doubtless this blend which made Victor Emmanuel heady with love for young "Yela"—her name in Serbo-Croatian.[18]

Four unrecorded days of the brew made his cup run over, and on

June 5, taking leave of the Romanovs and the Montenegrin princess, he inscribed in his scratch-pad diary again, mysteriously, in underscored English: "*I decide.*"

He went home to tell his mother and father. One might have expected to hear Humbert say, "The princess of Monte—who?" Or Margherita: "I don't care what kind of Negro she is. . . ." But it seems not to have happened that way at all. As Margherita wrote to the colonel in August: "My dear Osio, how content I am! I am so happy about the Engagement of my Son that I did not believe before that I could still feel such pleasure past the age of forty!"[19] It did not quite make sense grammatically, but perhaps that was because of her excitement. Humbert, too, was shortly to remark, "My House and that of Montenegro mean freedom and independence."[20]

There were even political advantages to be plucked. Crispi in fact years back had suggested a Montenegrin for the prince, but nothing ever came of it, at least until now. The little state, like its princess, was watched over by Russia, and the wedding would mean that Italy, to a certain extent, would be taken into the Slavic family, which, it was imagined, would be good for Italian imperial designs on Albania. Moreover, coming at this time, just after the Ethiopian disaster at Adowa, a royal marriage would be a welcome diversion. Victor Emmanuel was being hailed in court circles as having had a "stroke of genius," auguring well for his political future.[21]

To be sure, there were also heavy regrets. It was as if he were marrying an Apache princess, or the daughter of an eastern potentate. Elena's father was more a chief than a king, a distinction at any rate he was yet to earn, and short-lived Montenegro was one of the smallest and youngest states in the world, nestled north of Albania in a poor corner less than one-twelfth the size of Luxemburg or Rhode Island. Its history was unknown, its people were uncounted (the Montenegrins claimed to be 130,000 strong, but only guessed at the numbers of the other ethnic groups in the region), and its laws were sparse and "quaint," as Article 72 of its penal code exemplifies:

> If it should happen that a wife be unfaithful and a Montenegrin . . . catches her in the act he is permitted to kill the man and the woman. If the woman escapes, she will not be allowed to live in our State.[22]

The Savoyard dynasty, more than six hundred years the senior of the Petrovich clan, would have to make all kinds of excuses for their poor future relatives, and this was undertaken at once. To compensate for the obscurity and the relative backwardness of the

Petroviches and their countrymen the fine language of Vico was summoned, and so the Montenegrins were suddenly a "poetic" people. Much was made in Rome of alleged Montenegrin virility, especially that which was imagined about Elena and more or less known of her father, who had sired at least ten oversized children. To redress the balance of the Petroviches' political and dynastic shortcomings, as well as their failings in power and prestige, it was argued that Italians do not think of such things. Only love and romance were all. As one courtier explained it at the time:

> We Italians, fundamentally speaking, have in our hearts a pronounced inclination for all that is poetic and mild. And the image of this Prince, destined to one day wear one of the most splendid Crowns of Europe, but who seeks out his lifelong companion according to the dictates of his heart, has captured us all. The thought that the bride belongs to one of the most miniscule Principalities in our part of the world, and a Dynasty which counts but two hundred years against the eight hundred and more of the House of Savoy does not even enter our head.[23]

That was the public stance. In private, the Petroviches, who, as might be surmised, were overjoyed by the Italian affections, had to fulfill one overriding condition: yield to Margherita's demand that Elena would have to leave the Orthodox Church and convert to Catholicism *before* the wedding could take place. This was highly irregular with regard to royal conversions for marriage purposes, and in laboring the point Margherita was being "holier" than the pope; he had already let it be known that he would be quite content with the post-marital conversion of whomever the Savoyard prince might choose. No self-respecting royal house would accept the Italian queen's terms (as Margherita well knew from an earlier refusal of her son by a princess of Britain's royal house), and it created considerable difficulties for the Petrovich family. But love and necessity conquered all.

And so, as that summer drew to a close, with all but the most formal consents well given, there seemed nothing for the prince to do but board one of his yachts, and go off to collect his princess. Crossing a stormy Adriatic, he made his way to the Montenegrin capital, Cetinje, to meet Elena's eight brothers and sisters, and to ask her father, the not-quite-enlightened despot Nicholas I, for his daughter's hand.

Upon arrival, the Italian was embraced by his future brother-in-law, the Herculean heir apparent, Prince Daniel (it was said he had once strangled a bear), and was accepted with heart at the Petrovich court. He was feted superbly and taken to hunt, where he dined on freshly slain antelope, and sat for a photograph in the lap of the multitudinous family decked out in their full native regalia. When beseeched, big Nicholas gave the princess away, and Elena, pale and replete with love's callings, composed a lyrical poem to her diminutive Roman prince:

> He came from the sea
> from the sea came he.
> He is blond like his mother
> full of grace like his mother is he.
> He has a noble appearance about him
> an appearance of pride has he.[24]

He came again from the sea one month later, this time to take her home to Italy. They arrived in Bari in mid-October; a cold, driving rain dampened nothing, neither the cheering crowds nor the penned ecstacies of Carducci, D'Annunzio, and a thousand lesser poets. Elena first went to a church, where at the proper pause in the priest's incantations, she said, "I believe," and was so rendered a Catholic. Two special trains, one for the bride and one for the groom, sped them and their parties to Rome, where they were received by Humbert and Margherita, who kissed the Montenegrin princess and called her *daughter*.

The people, it is said, loved Elena, being genuinely taken by the story-book qualities of the romance. The aristocracy, however, generally disapproved; they scorned her low social station, spread nasty persiflage about her being "twice" the size of her lover, and made invidious comparisons between Victor Emmanuel and his cousin Emmanuel Philibert, duke of Aosta, the cadet line of the Savoyard dynasty. The tall, handsome, and very ambitious duke, whom the crown prince detested, had recently married the daughter of the count of Paris, Hélène of Orleans, one of the most illustrious houses of Europe. The republicans protested the expenses being incurred by the royal marriage, while in government and court circles the reaction to the Montenegrin was mixed. Senator Farini, seeing Elena for the first time, found her "beautiful, well built, and *simpatica*. . . . Her smile is very sweet, but she has neither the splendor nor the robustness for which she has been so praised."[25] And Foreign Minister Visconti Venosta, a hard-nosed aristocrat, was unimpressed with the alleged political gain. He commented wryly, "When you have pretensions about an advance conversion, like now, you have to settle for second-best, like now."[26]

They were married in Saint Mary of the Angels, the church Michelangelo had carved of the *frigidarium* in the ruins of a public bath. The wedding party had arrived in six coaches, followed by five thousands guests, who assembled in a piazza, which was soon to be named for the five hundred young men lost at Dogali, before entering the specially decorated church. Someone who was there said later:

> Everyone looked with curiosity at Nicholas and the Montenegrin princesses, who were dressed in their national costumes. Nicholas was corpulent and tall, with handsome features and scintillating, very black eyes . . . the entire family was very beautiful and of a stature taller than normal. . . . Princess Elena remained kneeling for the entire ceremony, Victor Emmanuel, with his plumed helmet placed beside him, remained on his feet.[27]

Alas, the future king was a prisoner of his size, and without means of escape; all attempts at adjustments in perspective called only greater attention to the unmentionable difficulty and how painfully it was felt.

The ceremony was very long, but at last the supreme moment arrived, as the marrying priest inquired, "Is Your Royal Highness Victor Emmanuel of Savoy, Crown Prince of Italy, content to receive as your legal wife Princess Elena Petrovich, according to the rites of the Holy Mother Church?" The prince turned to Humbert, and asked, "Father, do you permit me?" to which the mustachioed, good-natured, sinner king, with tears in his olive-oil eyes, replied, "Yes," and then a *yes* from the prince and his bride made them man and wife. Margherita, who had succeeded in containing her emotions behind her queen's mask, was more than happy nonetheless, and immediately after the ceremony, she found Colonel Osio, drew him into a quiet corner, and bursting into joyous weeping, she sobbed, "Thanks, for all your work."[28]

The prince wrote in his home-made diary: "Our wedding," and that night the lights of Rome burned until dawn in nuptial celebrations. But for the first time in centuries there was no royal wedding ball; someone had wisely decided that it was as yet too soon after the slaughter at Adowa for such abandon.

The young couple went off on what amounted to a four-year honeymoon. They sailed on Victor Emmanuel's newly christened *Yela* touching all the waters that washed the shores of their Europe.

They were felicitous years, sublime, adventurous, worth a lifetime by any measure. He took her from the blue Gulf of Naples to the dark waters of the North Sea, and on to the Arctic Ocean, advancing boldly along the explorer's route to the eternal summer sun and the then unconquered lure of the pole. In the dazzle of sparkling floes, they crossed the eightieth parallel—further north than any Italian flag ship had ever been—touched Spitzbergen and came down at Coal Bay, where they collected fossils which old ice had stolen in one of its primeval invasions of southern lands. They climbed down from the top of the world and sailed to green islands. He wrote an article for the Italian geographic society, and she, who had taken some excellent photographs of their Arctic journey, sent them along.

When they tired of the south, they went north again, then south once more. They shouted *hurrahs* as they passed the duke of Abruzzi's *Stella Polare*; Victor Emmanuel's younger cousin Louis Amadeus of Savoy had embarked on an expedition which was to bring him closer to the pole than any man before. They boarded the yachts of Kaiser Wilhelm II and Prince Albert of Monaco, and sailed for a while on the *Thistle*, which belonged to the empress-widow of Napoleon III. The *Yela* went home briefly, then to the isle Montecristo, and a summer cruise in the Aegean: Solonika, Mount Athos, and on through the Dardanelles to Constantinople to dine with the sultan and receive his gifts and good graces; now the more eastern ports, the Holy Land, cross country to the heights of Jerusalem and Bethlehem; now Rhodes and on to Piraeus. It was "hurrah" all the way and doubtless it seemed it would be so foreever.[29]

But, as all earthly paradises must end, Gaetano Bresci, of Paterson and Prato, shot Humbert to death, and Victor and Elena came home to be Italy's king and queen.

13

THE "SOCIALIST MONARCHY"

ASSASSINS ARE AMONG OUR SOCIAL TRIMMERS. THEY LABOR WHERE THE ORGANISM HAS GROWN too long or shows a too prominent protuberance. The too successful or the too disruptive must be denied at some moment before all is lost. Humbert the Good had been too disruptive. His Italy had been run like an occupied hostile territory, with all the wickedness of a conquering army. Given the unitary idea, this had been essential for many years, but no longer. By the century's end, at the price of social progress, unrelieved repression of body and soul, and the exploitation of labor to the outermost limits of human tolerance, substantive changes had taken place, and rule by the mace was suddenly on the defensive.

The day of the socialists was at hand, and only the liberals were their match. Now liberalism (which is society's most profligate big spender, for it must indulge the fancies of both the left and the right) is a luxury not every country can afford. But Italy, having traded for decades on flesh and tears, had accumulated at least some of the necessary capital, and, under Humbert, lacked only the will to employ it in the comfortable, liberal style. Fact and sound argument had made it ever more clear to the governing class that liberalism and social reform were the most peaceful road, although to where they might lead no one could really know.

To the good fortune of the pacific and the lovers of monarchist rule, Victor Emmanuel III appeared at this most propitious time. The new king, if he disliked almost everything his mother believed, deplored almost all for which his father had stood. He understood the savage lesson Humbert's slayer had taught, and had every means and intention to proceed therefrom.

There was, however, much to be done. In the midst of economic ascent, the country, when Victor Emmanuel took the throne, languished in sorry political decline.

The state of the Risorgimentalist union was keenly surveyed by Englishmen Bolton King and Thomas Okey in their insightful turn-of-the-century study, *Italy To-Day*. Reviewing in 1901 the condition of the unified state, which in the making had so captured the imagination of their countrymen, they found "chaos and decay," and among the political class, "a selfish struggle for office, a blind resistance to forces that they cannot understand and cannot assimilate, and therefore fear." As for the House of Savoy and the outlook for crown rule, very much a contemporary all-European concern, they reported:

> The prestige and popularity of the throne, so great under Victor Emmanuel II, fell low under Humbert. The late king had none of his father's force of character or knowledge of men. He moved in a narrow Court circle, and listened to men and women who were quite out of touch with the country. . . . To the Democrats he was the head of a faction, the centre of all the reactionary interests, of the army, of the big landlords and capitalists. Whatever truth there may have been in this, he certainly had no sympathy with the new social movement.[1]

The future of the dynasty was entirely in the hands of his successor, said the Britons, but the new sovereign was a great unknown. They sketched this portrait of the man:

> Of the present king, Victor Emmanuel III, it is too early yet to say much, but what little is known of him, is mostly to his good. He has been carefully, too carefully educated, and at one time he suffered from over-study. He has the tastes of an old man or a book-worm, but he is a keen student of history and economics. His politics, so far as he has declared them, are thoroughly liberal, and he seems to have kept surprisingly clear of the prejudices of his father's Court. He was not a friend of Crispi, and it is rumoured that he wanted him to be prosecuted after the Bank revelations. He was opposed to the recent policy of coercion, and since his accession he has bravely refused to have any reaction, in spite, no doubt, of considerable pressure. He probably favours a comprehensive social programme. He is a hard and conscientious worker, with a high ideal of his kingly office, and demanding the same thoroughness and diligence in his Ministers. It is said that he is firm, and if he has sufficient physical strength and force of character, his Liberal sympathies may allow him to recover the ground that his father lost.[2]

All the elements for success were present. King and Okey correctly detected a "startling change" in Italy's economic growth rate. There was, they said, "every sign that Italy is at the commencement of a remarkable industrial expansion."*

> At all events [they concluded], the fate of the Italian monarchy is in its own keeping. If it takes in hand the social movement, as it took in hand the national movement, it has one of the safest thrones in Europe. If it sets itself against progress, if it stands for reaction, for a heavy military expenditure and an adventurous foreign policy, it is doomed, and perhaps at no distant date.[4]

The first public sign to be interpreted as an indication that things were to be different under Victor Emmanuel III was seen in his coronation speech, which he wrote, or at least rewrote himself.** Speaking in the senate at Rome, two days after Humbert's funeral, the monarch addressed his very first words in support of a "liberal monarchy." He paid ample tribute to the past, to religion, and the army, and he promised to vigorously defend the nation's "glorious institutions," but this included a rededication of the throne to parliament and the constitution—court-hated commitments which the right and his father had been trying furiously to dissolve. There were none of the usual threats about law and order; rather, he went so far as to say, "I will never be lacking in the serenest faith in a liberal order."[6]

The speech was applauded on all sides of the senate, but on reflection there seemed cause for preoccupation. The boisterous republicans, whose vitality had by now been lost to the socialists, said the

* Their forecast was admirably borne out. In the first decade of the twentieth century, Italy experienced an economic boom, paralleled only in late post-World War II years. As a result of the sacrifices mentioned above, the disappearance of the spendthrift Crispi, an end to the tariff war with France, and high emigration in a period of rapid technological advance throughout the western world, Italy in the years 1896 to 1908 showed an industrial growth rate of 6.7 percent a year and 12 percent in key industries. Rapid expansion took place in the automobile industry following the establishment of the Fiat plant in 1899 (Fiat stock went from 25 lire to 1,885 lire within a few years after it began production) and the all-important electric power industry, which partially emancipated the country from its dependence on coal imports (from 100 million kilowatt hours generated in 1898, production of electric power rose to more than 2.5 billion kilowatt-hours by 1914). Industrial wages increased considerably, too, but not without a bloody increase in strikes, and even farm wages went up, although the neglected agricultural south continued to pay far more than any other part of Italy for industrial prosperity in cheaper labor, heavier taxes, the proletarianization of farm families and emigration.[3]

** There were earlier, behind-the-scenes indications. On his arrival at Monza, the new king was asked by his father's minister Saracco for the royal signature on various government decrees, and Victor Emmanuel is said to have objected to certain details. "But the King only signs," said the veteran Saracco with astonishment. "The King is willing to sign his own errors, but not those of others," Victor Emmanuel replied.[5] From the man whose signature was to appear, as will be seen, on some of history's most infamous documents, these words ought not to be lost.

king was off to a bad beginning, but it was the conservatives who
worried hardest. At first Victor Emmanuel did nothing, and they took
this as a good omen. He went with Elena on a holiday in Naples, and
then spent time preparing sparsely furnished living quarters in a
few modest rooms of the Quirinal, Victor and Elena doing much of
the housework. The king's simplicities, however, were regarded by
the watchful court as a bad omen, and when his uncle the duke of
Genoa, Margherita's brother, Thomas, saw his spartan surroundings,
he ruefully remarked, "I am more and more convinced that you
want to be a democratic king."[7]

His intentions, however, remained somewhat of an intriguing
mystery until February, 1901, when a government crisis developed as
a result of a paralyzing strike in Genoa. Saracco, Humbert's last minister, who had stayed on in these first months of the new reign, sided
against the strikers, and he resigned his post putting the royal confidence to the test. Victor Emmanuel seized the opportunity. Instead
of returning Saracco or summoning the generals, alternatives for which
his father no doubt would have opted, he reached far to the mod-
erate left and called on the incorrigibly liberal Zanardelli, Humbert's latter-day foe.

The conservatives felt lost, particularly when Zanardelli proceeded
at once to ensure proper parliamentary practices, decrease soak-the-
poor taxes, and withdraw the army's private strikebreaking and anti-
labor services to the owning classes. "Restrictive laws are unnecessary," Victor Emmanuel had told his ministers with Cavourian
wisdom, and that had worked wonders. Even the republicans marv-
eled, allowing themselves to comment circumspectly that the House of
Savoy "has conducted itself correctly; the new king is *simpatico*."[8]

That a new era was dawning was seen further in Zanardelli's choice
of liberal Giolitti for the law-and-order ministry of the interior. Giolitti
had come far as a reformer since his brief ministry ten years earlier,
in another century. He had learned to talk the brand-new language
of Bernsteinian social democracy. In a famous speech made during
the parliamentary debate over the Genoese crisis, he declared that
a new historical period was beginning, and anyone could see that
socialism was "invincible." The question was how to deal with this
reality. Said Giolitti:

> For a long time now attempts have been made at trying to impede
> the organizing of workers. . . . That is absolutely impossible. . . . No
> one can hope to stop the popular classes from gaining their share in

economic and political influence. It is, above all, the duty of those who wish to preserve the present institutions to persuade these classes, and to persuade them by deeds, that they can hope for much more from our institutions than from those who dream about the future. . . . It is mainly up to us whether these classes turn out to be a conservative force, a new element for prosperity and greatness, or a revolutionary storm overthrowing the fortunes of the Fatherland.[9]

The king liked that kind of talk. When old Zanardelli withdrew, Giolitti in 1903 was called up for the job—which is how the celebrated Giolittian era got started and the "socialist monarchy" was made.

Giovanni Giolitti is fourth next to Crispi on the chronological table of united Italy's six extraordinary government chiefs (Cavour and Depretis before them, Mussolini and De Gasperi yet to come); he is third, following Cavour and Depretis, in the tradition of rule by parliamentary dictatorship and "gentle" persuasion; and he is second to no one in paucity of principle and abundance of cynicism.

He was a cold-souled creature, who came from the north. He was born in 1842 in Piedmont, under the reign of Charles Albert. On his paternal side, his father was a bureaucrat, his grandfather was a bureaucrat, and, he says, his grandfather's grandfather, the first remembered Giolitti, was a "democrat." His mother came from a family "which had distinguished itself for its liberalism," and among its members had been bureaucrats, democrats, revolutionaries, soldiers, politicians, and stanch admirers of the House of Savoy. Giolitti himself was or wished to be every one of these things at one time or another, but above all he was the latter.[10]

He was a man without a past, or so he said. "The memories of my family life, of my youth, and of my education, he wrote in the very first sentence of his autobiography, "are very simple and of a common type, devoid of anything particular or exceptional." He acted like a man without a future, one of the first of a new breed which resides permanently in the nonexistent present. His policy, as Mack Smith observes, "was to patch up each leak in turn, to placate the most noisy of his opponents, but only taking care of day-to-day problems as they arose."[11]

Colorlessly, amorphously, nondescriptly, like a passerine bird at times, he had gone through life in an upward way. Civil servant until the age of forty, administrator, and parliamentarian, he had no taste for Crispian rhetoric or D'Annunzian bombast; he liked arithmetic and the bookkeeping crafts. This helped render him sensitive to subtle variations of human greed and other people's weaknesses in a manner in which they might be debited or credited to his own advantage.* He was prone to making mathematical analogies of his liberalism, like the church and state being parallel lines which ought never to meet.

His liberalism was of the purest, simplest kind. It was uncluttered with ideals and pretensions about humanism. The old politics had failed. The country was sick, he said; "the cause of its sickness is that the classes in power have been spending enormous sums on themselves and their own interests and have obtained their money almost entirely from the poorer sections of society." Therefore, reaction no longer made economic sense. It made the majority of the people enemies of the state at a time when their friendship could be bought with their own money. "A period of social justice inaugurated by the government," said Giolitti, "would recall the common people back to their affection for our institutions."[13] He correctly perceived that there remained only two kinds of politics, at least for a while. Traditional Italy had either to inaugurate the "socialist" monarchy or revolutionary socialism and an angry mob of unheard-of proportions would sweep it away, beloved institutions, noble houses, and all.

His method was to mount, not resist, the socialist bronco, and ride until bust. Tortuously, with an air of grand compromise concealing all weaknesses, he met the demands of the movement's "minimum program,"** hoping to prove to the proletariat that all capitalist regimes were not a priori their class enemies, but could also be their class friends. In this way he wished, as he later claimed to have succeeded, to put "Marx in the attic."[15] Indeed he was eminently effec-

* He actually kept a ledger for this purpose. In 1943, fifteen years after Giolitti's death, Victor Emmanuel revealed this to Count Ciano, who recorded the king's reminiscences in his diary as follows: "He talked at length about Giolitti, extolling his callousness and ignorance. No one else in the whole world could manage parliament like Giolitti. He kept a book in which every page was dedicated to a deputy, where he wrote the life, death, and miracles of every man. After having undergone a careful reading in his book, no one could escape his blackmail. The king himself had personally read the page on Eugenio Chiesa [a republican member of parliament], easily threatened because of an old bankruptcy of dubious legality."[12]

** The "minimum program" was the tabernacle in which the Bernsteinian revisionists in Italy sought refuge on their "evolutionary" road to socialism. Consisting of important but conventional reforms, such as the right to organize and strike, a more equitable taxation, and universal suffrage, it was adopted in 1900 at the Socialist party congress in Rome along with a "maximum program" for revolution, necessary to placate the radicals and hold the party together. The "minimum program"—a victory for the persecution-weary Turati, Bissolati, and other old leftists—allowed socialists for the first time to collaborate in parliament and elsewhere with their "class enemies."[14]

tive in driving the liberal wedge far in the socialist party, splitting off to the camp of sweet reason whole legions of erstwhile firebrands. Moreover, practicing old-fashioned *trasformismo* and casting aside traditional discriminations, he opened the cool center of politics to all the forces in the country. With a broken left and a sound economy, he was at various times in a position to give war and imperialism to the bellicose right, honor and influence to the offended Church, and the prospect of greater power and profit to the owning class.

His style was *laissez faire*; he let a hundred flowers bloom. When in 1904 the socialists for the first time tried Georges Sorel's tactic of the general strike, Giolitti tethered his angriest capitalists, and shunning all the old skull-cracking ways of the Humbertine age, waited peacefully for the strike to wilt in conspicuous failure. When the Catholics were antagonized by liberalism's plans to institute divorce, he turned against divorce and invited the Catholics to join him in his opposition to all that was distasteful to the Church. When the nationalists wanted colonial *Lebensraum* and a soul-purging blood bath, Giolitti, the anticolonialist pacifist, gave them the dirty Libyan war and stole their victory for his own.

His enemies called him an "evil hypnotist," a worker of wicked miracles, and he had few friends beyond his young master. The Genoese deputy Raimondo, speaking in parliament, tells how it was at its worst:

> The parties which fight one another in the country at large once again embrace each other in the Chamber. To what do we owe this miracle? We owe it, like all other miracles, to the policy of the Honorable Giolitti. He has had, and still has, an overwhelming personal majority. The Democrats are with him for the laws he grants them, the Conservatives are with him for the application they hope to see of those same laws. . . . With this formidable power of his—let us all recite our *mea culpas*—he has done the work of drawing parties together by means of reforms and of drawing individuals together by means of personal attention. Now, Honorable Giolitti, when parties forget their programs, when those who come here leave at the doors the rags of their political convictions, it means that a majority must be achieved by other means, as all personal powers are forced to do: with trickery and corruption.[16]

His thaumaturgical qualities notwithstanding, the Giolittian system was not always maintained with guile. Historian Salvemini explains that under Giolitti's rule government interference in elections "reached unprecedented heights of brutality."

If an election had to be carried out [he said], the police, in league with the Government supporters, enrolled the scum of the constituencies and the underworld of the neighboring districts. In the last weeks before the polls, the opponents were threatened, bludgeoned, besieged in their homes. Their leaders were debarred from addressing meetings, or even thrown into prison until election day was over. Voters suspected of upholding the opposition were refused polling cards. Those favoring Government candidates were given not only their own polling cards, but also those of opponents, emigrants, deceased voters, and were allowed to vote three, five, ten, twenty times.* The Government candidates were always the winners. Any deputy who dared Giolitti, had to confront a bad time at his next election. . . . Giolitti was not the first to "manage" elections. But he "managed" one after another three national elections (1904, 1909, 1913) and he surpassed all in clarity of purpose and lack of scruples.[17]

Giolitti himself was by no means a violent man. Quite the contrary, he was a benevolent, fatherly figure. Tall and broad shouldered, wearing a *t*-shaped white mustache and goatee, he lacked, when as almost always he appeared in his broad-brimmed fedora and his Uncle Sam coat, only a porch and a tumbler to complete his resemblance to a Kentucky colonel. It is said in his favor that he rigged elections "only" in the backward south and permitted the politically conscious north to run its affairs at will. But it would have been superfluous, if not impossible, to do otherwise. Men such as Salvemini, who coined the adhesive Giolittian epithet, "prime minister of the underworld," would repent their *antigiolittismo* when in darkest times they were to look back with longing at pre-Mussolini Italy, but the "liberal experiment," as Giolitti liked to call it, was, nostalgia aside, only another post-Risorgimento phenomenon preceding the "Fascist experiment."

Indeed, in the end, the "liberal experiment," or the "socialist monarchy," for all the Crocean praises, was a colossal failure, bringing on, as will be seen, slaughter and war on a scale grander than ever before. This is a self-evident truth when looked at from every perspective save one—that back alley view from the House of Savoy. Here, Giolitti was exceedingly successful for as long as a man may be expected to be. An American who has studied the Piedmont minister

---

* Giolitti's electorate consisted not only of voters dead or alive or missing. Also casting ballots was a category to which the franchise had not yet been extended—as evidenced by Mussolini's father's recounting of how the names of fifty local cows were registered at the polls of his home town Predappio. The cows of course voted unanimously for Giolitti and liberalism.

said a generation ago that Giolitti "found a country gathered under a monarchical flag and ruled by a Piedmontese dynasty. He accordingly governed as a faithful servant of his master and King."[18]

The House of Savoy asked no more; that others did is a cause for much lament.

14

ROMA DEMOCRATICA

SO GREAT AND SO EFFECTIVE WAS GIOLITTI'S SERVICE TO THE HOUSE OF SAVOY THAT THE head of the dynasty for the first time in easy memory was able to draw back from the political scene. Receding with him was the old plaguing question of the survival of monarchist rule. "Why should anyone hope for a republic," asked the popular Neapolitan journalist Scarfoglio, "while no one can tell we have a monarchy?"[1]

This was the kind of national mood for which past Savoyard monarchs had been willing to die. Thanks were due Giolitti, and Victor Emmanuel was not ungrateful. "My son," said Queen Mother Margherita, now grown too brittle in her ways to be anything but disparaging of even self-salutary liberalism, "has two manias: his coin collection and his prime minister."*[2] The king had much in common with Giolitti in taste and temperament, an obvious fact so painful to Margherita (although she would live to see her kind of man in the fore). Their relations were extremely cordial and of mutual admiration. They spoke to one another in the clipped dialect of the Piedmontese aristocracy, which made for intimacy, but not the kind that could ever go beyond the duties of state and office. Both men were closed to true friendships; no one would ever penetrate Victor Emmanuel's shut-in soul.

In the first period of his reign, the king had been resolute, determined to lift the monarchy from the morass and secure it on firmer ground. He had read all the important state papers, let his wishes be

---

* That was a neglected "mamma's" way of disapproving. There is another version of what Margherita said, expressive of even greater disapproval: "My son has two manias: his prime minister and his Elena."

known, and gained a quick reputation of possessing the energies required to make big things move. But with Giolitti solicitous and capable of doing the heavy work, Victor Emmanuel felt free to attend to purely dynastic affairs, and he sought to refit the oversized monarchy to his small frame.

The first thing he did was proceed to dismantle the opulent and often offensive trappings of court life. In keeping with the egalitarian character of his government he swept away in a few irreverent strokes almost all the regality Humbert and Margherita had labored so assiduously to erect. Simplicity was the order of the day, and everything that was not considered utilitarian was dispensed with, pure comfort and beauty being first to go.

Court balls were still held, on a reduced scale, but gone were the opening quadrille, the three deep bows before the king and queen, and gone too were the sensualities and the vaporous gaieties which made the outside world so hard to see. The older generation of aristocrats and foreign visitors of exalted rank were not at all pleased. Madame Waddington, daughter of the American statesman Rufus King and the wife of a French minister, visited Rome in 1904 after an absence of nearly a quarter of a century and found the court which had so enthralled her in Humbert's and Margherita's day greatly changed.

She could recall a royal audience with the queen in 1880 as a "pleasurable visit with a fascinating woman in a gracious salon adorned with beautiful paintings and *bibelots*." But when she was received by Elena, in a "rather barren room which showed no sign of being lived in," she was stopped in mid-bow by a queen who seemed tired and "bored at having to find words to say to foreigners she would never see again."[3]

The carnival ball in February, 1904, was "extraordinarily simple, if not democratic"—even by Madame Waddington's American standards. "If I had not known that I had gone to the royal palace," she said, "I would have thought that I was in the wrong house . . . ."[4]

Only the queen mother retained the old elegance, and Victor Emmanuel kept the sort of conspicuous distance from her that public men reserve for notorious relatives. With the money he saved or acquired from the disposal of such extravagances as his father's stable of horses and noblewomen, he bought his mother a palace all her own in Via Veneto, the baked-red villa which would one day become the American consulate in Rome. It was known as "Villa Margherita" in those days, and she held court there (although the members of her old circle of intellectuals were all dead), receiving her visitors in the style being lost to the ages. "There is much more formalism in an audience with the Queen Mother than in those given by the King," an English traveler reported authoritatively, observing that the former experience was "just like what happens when one is in the presence of the Pope."[5]

As for the king, he bought a villa too, far more modest than his mother's and well removed from the urban center. Like his illustrious grandfather, he always felt uneasy in the Quirinal, haunted as it was by popes and periwigs, and at the very first chance he moved out. He made his new home in the rather cramped dwelling space of Villa Ada, which lies high on the ancient Salarian road in a huge grove far outside the city walls. The house had once belonged to his grandfather, but the Savoys, when straitened by the *re galantuomo's* indulgences and Humbert's philanthropy, had had to sell it, and now the little king repurchased it for himself and his queen. It was hardly fit for a king, with its squat, rustic appearance, but it was surrounded by tens of acres of thicket, forest, and undulating meadow, all enclosed by a foot-thick wall of stone.

He called it "Villa Savoia."* There, he could, coming home from "the office" (which is how he regarded the Quirinal), peel off his epaulets, unhitch his sword (two adornments he especially hated), and sit back in a chair not a throne.

Royal life was astonishingly plain. The king and queen had few servants. Elena liked to cook dinner and clean house. Victor picked flowers for his wife, puttered with his hunting rifles, and above all played with his coins. Every morning at an early hour a car with a chauffeur and an adjutant would appear at his front door to take him to "the office." Often, we have it from one such aide, the king, if the weather and his mood were right, would begin the routine like this:

> Good morning. How are you? No, no, I'll carry my own brief case. I too have two hands like you. What a stupendous day! A pity to have to be closed up in the Quirinal. Much better to take a walk in the fresh air. Man was made to travel, to go hunting, and make war. Don't you think so? To shut himself in somewhere and gab all day long is the final degradation of man.[6]

Twice weekly the queen would go "downtown" and give her audiences, and when occasion demanded, both king and queen would attend a ball. "The queen," a contemporary guest would recall, "re-

---

* Today Villa Ada again, one of Rome's finest public parks.

mains seated all alone, hardly speaking to anyone for the first two or three dances; then there is a general moving about and finally she holds court walking around the ballroom talking almost to all. The king, however, remains near the diplomatic corps gathered to one side, conversing only with the men, for it is said he rarely ever speaks to the ladies."[7]

"Yes," Victor Emmanuel would one day confide, "I am an anti-feminist. Not that I think a woman who has gone through college knows less than a truck driver. God no! I mean a woman can't do what a man can do. There have been women who have done something, but they have always been modest things. . . . A woman can't go beyond that. Her brain doesn't have the capacity of a man's."[8]

More frequently he would put it this way: "Women are good for two things only: darning socks and going to bed with."[9]

The king's attitudes and the queen's housewifelyness did not make for popularity at court, less so among the Roman aristocracy, which made the social seasons all the more dry. Victor Emmanuel was not insensitive to the discomfiture of the nobility, deprived as it was of the time-honored means of displaying, if not vaunting, its privileged position. Rank, like the cactus, needs a place in the sun, else the prick cannot be felt. But the king, perhaps with the malice which sometimes afflicts little men with power, simply did not care about the old aristocrats. The continuity of his own highness could be extended only in the new, "democratic" world, and the "socialism" in his monarchy, like his later fascism, disdained the baubles and gewgaws of the idle.

Once, years later, returning from the royal hunting grounds at Castel Porziano, the king expounded at length in this regard. He had shot fifty-nine pigeons and ducks in a mere two hours of that afternoon, and in the car going back to Villa Savoia he was feeling unusually garrulous. He chatted to his driver and his aide, and hummed incessantly. Finally the one-sided conversation fell on the subject of his unsociability. He said:

> When my poor father was alive we used to come here to Castel Porziano quite often. Many people came. In Rome, too, he received guests much more than I do. There were always ambassadors, ministers, and high personages around. I myself don't like receptions very much. Those ambassadors are all spies, more or less. I don't mean it in a bad sense. All they are interested in is snatching your words and your ideas to report them back to their Governments. That's their trade. I understand that very well, but it bores me. . . . Now, as for so-called "high

society," that I can't stand at all; they know it, and I know that they find me lacking in this respect. But I don't care about that in the slightest. Up there, in that group, there are too many people who don't do a thing, who are of no use to the country, nor to society. It doesn't matter what an individual does: whether he be a mechanic, a streetcleaner, a professional, a magistrate, an officer, etcetera, as long as he does something.

Confidentially, I think that there's a great deal of truth in Lenin's words, "Whoever does not work, does not eat." I am very much in favor of that theory.

In this so-called "high society," all you hear speak of are divorces, who's cheating on whom, horse racing, and every sort of gossip. All the things which get on my nerves. I never listen when I hear these kind of stories. I know that they find me lacking, but I detest that "society"; it is too frivolous. It is empty-headed.

I detest people who do nothing. To tell you the truth, nowadays [under Mussolini] the number of these good-for-nothings has decreased; it is harder for them to exist these days . . . but let us speak of joyful things.[10]

"High society," in the shock of the first years of Victor Emmanuel's colorless reign, was rapidly being drawn around the king's glamorous cousin Emmanuel Philibert, duke of Aosta, and his wife, Hélène of Orleans. The duke and his Lady Macbeth of a wife coveted the throne with salivating intensity. As long as Victor Emmanuel and Elena remained without a son, Emmanuel Philibert was the legitimate heir to the crown. The duke had not a tenth of Victor's intellect, but he maintained a lively court in the style of his uncle, Humbert the Good, replete with all the reverences and the obligatory *baciamano*. His palace, which he obtained from his royal rival in an unguarded moment, was at Capidimonte near Naples, looking on Vesuvius and out at the sea.

Comparisons between the two Savoyard couples were as unavoidable as they were perennial. Needless to say they rarely did justice to the king and queen, which seems cause enough to recall a generous paragraph from the memoirs of Francesco Nitti, one of Victor Emmanuel's later prime ministers.

The little king [he wrote] was unaffected, taciturn, dedicated to scholarly pursuits, modest and without any pretensions, yet intelligent and very erudite. But the Duke of Aosta appeared much more imposing and majestic, although he never found a way to demonstrate his own intellectual accomplishments, which in fact were strictly non-existent. The Queen, although born in a small Balkan village, the daughter of a very minor, luckless prince, was beautiful, regal, and modest, while the

Duchess of Aosta, who believed herself the heiress to the grandeur of the Bourbons of France and proudly signed her name *Hélène de France* (even though she was an Italian princess) was affected and loved to behave as if she were the real sovereign.[11]

For eight years Emmanuel Philibert and Hélène, or "the other Elena," as she was known by her Italianized name and rank, cherished the hope that they or one of their two sons would be called upon to ascend, and they groomed themselves and their brood accordingly. Their crossed-fingered waiting was to go unrewarded, however, whereupon they would turn later to the cloak and the dagger.

Victor Emmanuel, the great detester, reserved ample loathings for his ambitious cousins, who flaunted their virility, their handsome selves, and their hopes with rude ostentation. Louis XIV used to call the Orleans braggarts of their wickedness, and the old blood ran in Hélène. Descended from the guillotined Philippe "Égalité" and the bourgeois king, Louis Philippe, she played queen of Naples like the Bourbon side of her race and plotted like a true Orleans. She called the real queen a "shepherdess" and for every step forward into the twentieth century taken by the sovereigns in Rome, Emmanuel Philibert and the countess of Paris took a trumpeted two to the rear.

The heirless little king, undertaking the primary dynastic activity, tried without surcease to thwart the aspiring of the duke and duchess of Aosta, but Elena, for all her famous mountain hardiness, seemed wanting in her genes. Her capacity to make up for the biological losses suffered by her innocent husband failed for years each time it was put to the old-fashioned test—although we learn from Margherita that Elena's efforts were valiant and no less fervid than Victor's. Indeed "Mamma" had worried from the start that the children were trying *too* hard. In 1897, when they had been married not yet a year and Margherita was still queen, she had written, in confidence, to Colonel Osio:

> If you could only see how much they love each other. They are much more in love than at first, and they live entirely for one another. She is a real angel, a wife well suited for my Son. Both of them ardently desire to have a child, the King and I are no less desirous of being grandparents, and the whole country shows that it desires an heir. I feel, however (strictly between you and me), that perhaps the two most interested parties to the affair perhaps [sic] desire it a little too actively, and under such circumstances, sometimes, too much thinking about it (let us put it that way) is harmful to the realization of the desire! But, God willing, we hope to hear the good news before long. . . .[12]

Time went on, and month after month the news was not "good." Humbert left the scene, King Victor Emmanuel, the gossipers stage-whispered, was not getting any younger, and the fruitful Aosta swaggered with no more grace than a block toughy. The queen mother grew impatient and less generous with her daughter-in-law, expressing her doubts about the quality of Elena's bodily organs. When at last she could bear it no longer (she was torn between her admiration of the "other Elena's" regality and the loyalties of familial hierarchies), "Mamma," of all people, went shamelessly and conspicuously to see a gynecologist-obstetrician.

It was shortly afterward that Queen Elena had the good fortune of conceiving. The child was born in June, 1901, but it was "only" a girl, which did not dash the hopes of the Aosta, and did not entirely satisfy the queen mother, even when the baby was baptized Yolanda *Margherita*. The king and queen were radiant. They sent gifts to twenty-eight boys and girls born in Italy on Yolanda's day of birth; they released 750 message-bearing pigeons from the terrace of the Campidoglio to announce the happy event to the world; and then proceeded to try again. The following year brought another child: another girl, beautiful, ill-fated Mafalda. The next year another pregnancy was discovered; the laws of probability were being gloriously exhausted in defense of the crown.

Victor and Elena were serene, but Margherita continued to see excited images in her mind's eye of "a handsome little grandson, very, very dark, because boys resemble the mother."[13] It pleased her to think that the family would return to a properly Italian swarthiness, as it had been, she erroneously believed, until Charles Albert married a fair-skinned Hapsburg.

In September, 1904, the child was born at Racconigi in a tenth-century Piedmontese castle, which had been abandoned by Victor Emmanuel II and reclaimed by Victor Emmanuel III. The king and queen had gone fishing that day in the Maira, and Elena before sundown had shot several rounds at target practice. No one knew her time was near, but in the evening the event took place with nonchalance and calm. The infant, once inspected, gave cause for the sounding of the nation's biggest guns, and 30,000 electric bulbs were turned on to light a corner of the Racconigi nighttime sky.

Victor Emmanuel rushed to telegraph his mother, who had been unable to come because of a nationwide general strike touched off when a Sardinian worker was shot to death by the police. "Mamma," the king wired, "I have had a son. His name will be Humbert."[14] He was *bello*. He resembled his mother, and he weighed a good ten pounds, which was interpreted as auguring well for his health and his height.

Little Humbert, "Bepo," was to be Margherita's favorite. She would smother him with kisses. She would live to see him grow to manhood, the sturdy substance of her dreams: tall, handsome, genteel, "elegant by instinct," as Casalegno says. She would die in good time not to hear the cruel allegations of his homosexuality, his profligacy, and every kind of weakness. And so he would conquer her entirely, stroking the hurt she felt as the mother of the strange, forbidding little king; for even when he was very young, Humbert was so much the figure of the ideal prince. He enchanted Margherita, and was the fount of her greatest pleasure.

"He's a rascal," she used to say, "he's a real Savoy."[15]

He was the new prince of Piedmont, the future king of Italy—an honor he would hold in the thirty-four days before the fall of the House of Savoy.

These Giolittian, prewar times were the "good old days" of Victor's and Elena's reign, Italy's *belle époque* as much as it was all the expanding bourgeois world's. The supercilious aristocracy might despair of its king and queen and give aid and comfort to the Aosta cabal (which did not cease its machinations for possession of the crown), but they were growing old and ever fewer. Their children, who knew less of yesterday's splendor, found the new times not without patrician pleasures all their own.

To Madame Waddington and her generation, *Roma democratica*, spreading beyond her bounds like a beautiful woman grown fat, was an eyesore ("It could have been Wiesbaden, Neuilly, or any other city where businessmen repose . . ."), and even Kaiser Wilhelm remarked on his visit in 1903 that "Rome will end up being as ugly as Berlin."[16] But the city center remained virtually unchanged, and those who possessed a Richard and Brasier horseless, open "double phaeton," or a Fiat limousine could escape to the distant countryside at a titillating speed men before them never knew.

Giolitti's offers to the Church of influence and power removed one of the last social barriers separating the black and white nobilities. The king, in scaling down the traditional *vie de plaisir*, had done nothing to hinder ambassadors and the resident foreign rich, like von Bülow and the Radziwills in exile, from increasing their galas and their invitations, and the erosion of the old exclusiveness was a liberating force which made for fresh gaieties. Money had vanquished past modes of class distinctions; he who had the most was now the most princely of all. The aristocrats of Rome who had remained aloof from bourgeois society, imagining themselves above the mercantile ruling class, had watched their uncapitalized fortunes dwindle and disappear. When at last they were ready to embrace the new order, they found themselves hopelessly behind, often possessing little more than a frayed brocaded livery and the devalued title it accompanied. Only in marriage with the *nouveau riche*, who were in a buying mood for anything which might ennoble an often vulgar past, could they seriously aspire to rejuvenate their status. This, Victor Emmanuel's *Roma democratica* permitted them to do.

It pained their highborn fathers, but the sons and daughters freely and without self-consciousness followed the imperative of seeking union with the monied common horde. Nevertheless, it was indeed a twilight sadness to see the storied Boncompagni, who had been forced by hard circumstance to sell their magnificent family palace (now Villa Margherita), lose their son the duke of Sora to a certain Nicoletta Prinetti, daughter of a manufacturer of bicycles. And when the Orsini and the Colonna, feuding barons of the Middle Ages and lords of Renaissance Rome, were unable to meet the payments on their many mortgages, only marriage to the children of a Levantine trader, in one instance, and a successful shopkeeper, in the other, saved them from even greater humiliations.

The wedding announcements read like the *Götterdämmerung* or the obituaries: here a Borghese, of the givers of popes, marries the offspring of a Genoese merchant; there a Torlonia, of recent unlimited means, weds Elsa Mackay of the New York Mackays; and then even the grotesque, in the marriage of Prince del Drago at the age of twenty-seven to one Josephine Schmid, a fifty-year-old widow of an American whose "baronage" had been obtained in making and selling beer. She reputedly had been left seventy-five million.

The noblest Roman now was J.P. Morgan. He would come from time to time and stay in many rooms of the new Grand Hotel, amid the neo-splendors of its palm gardens and gypsy orchestras. Sometimes he would arrive at the port of Civitavecchia in the 300-foot yacht, the *Corsair*, flying a half-moon and silver star. Then he would make his entrance into Rome grandiosely, as if the feudal Henrys and the idols of the Ghibellines had reappeared in New World dress. He would receive several hundred persons every day, it is said, and many were hard-up princes and forgotten dukes hoping to sell him a painting or a family heirloom. He died in the Grand Hotel in 1913; he was put in a box, sent home to America in a freight car and the hull of a ship. But the Americans kept coming, as fortune made them more princely every day.

Such was the high society which Victor Emmanuel so despised, and when the inevitable court scandals rushed in, the king's arbitrary dislikes and instinctual sobrieties, which held him above all stigma, were seen as the auspicious return of the imagined wisdom of Savoy.*

The king and queen went on their merry, domesticated way: summers at San Rossore and Montecristo, hunting and fish fries by a guarded riverside, and making little girls. Giovanna, future empress of the Bulgarians, was born in 1907, and in 1914, barely remembered Maria of Savoy. Victor and Elena delighted in their parenthood with the kind of open-mouthed awe often seen in young couples who suddenly discover themselves in possession of the God-like powers in mankind's seed. Crown *principino* Humbert, on his grandmother's coaxing, would soon enough be handed over to his own "Colonel Osio" (the disciplinarian Admiral Bonaldi) to undergo the trauma of reification, but for now Victor and Elena reared their children with a freedom princes and lesser boys and girls rarely know. As a palace dame recorded then:

> The queen's motherhood shines in her in everything she does. . . . She is always speaking about her children, without wondering at all whether or not she might appear to her listener as overdoing it. She thinks about them even more so when they are not around, and then her thoughts inevitably turn to words, sweet, noble discourse, full of tenderness and emotion. . . . She wants them to grow up in the sun and in the wind,

---

* Perhaps the most shocking court scandal in those years was the brutal slaying of the countess of Sant'Elia, one of Queen Elena's palace dames. She was found in a fourth-class hotel in Rome, her body horribly mutilated by her lover Baron Vincenzo Paternò, an officer in the royal cavalry. He had been blackmailing her husband, a fact which had caused her separation, and now she was, it was said, trying to free herself from the baron. An autopsy revealed that at the time of death she had had sexual contact with the murderer and some question remained as to whether before or after. "On that occasion," writes Gerbore, "one saw how sage and far-seeing Victor Emmanuel III had been in giving his court that severe, reserved, and bourgeois character. In fact not a single socialist or republican voice dared to speak against the Quirinal."[17] Public and parliamentary outrage was instead turned against the army. The scandal grew when it was learned that the baron had a history of violence known to his superiors, and Minister of War Spingardi was forced to admit that discipline in the highest ranks was much less than satisfactory. This was a condition which was forgotten when the shock wore away, to the great misfortune of young Italians on the fields of the nation's coming battles. The crown wisdom, as will be seen, ran short in some respects.

and when she sees little Yolanda rolling in a stack of hay, yelping enchantedly for the sheer pleasure of it all, the Queen is full of happiness. She allows her children to run into the greenery in the gardens at Rome and Racconigi, and into the forests of San Rossore, neither repressing nor rigorously braking their little caprices, their leaps, their ramblings, and all their dearest play.[18]

Margherita disapproved of this "Montenegrin" upbringing. When one of her granddaughters showed her the latest bit of fun she had learned, the queen mother replied, "That's all very well. But when are they going to teach you to be a princess?"[19] But her word meant little in the king's household, and there would be time enough for such instruction. The world was full of sadness, Victor and Elena believed, and like many modern young couples they wished to give their children a sheltered, running start in life. "It serves no purpose for them to be alarmed so soon," said the queen. "For now, it is their right and their duty to grow up happy, healthy, and strong so that they can face those sadnesses."[20]

It was difficult for Elena to reconcile this sorry predicament, and she was given to long reflections on life's negation of maternal joy and childhood pleasure. Her own life, and in some respects her husband's, was such a contradiction. "I have always been a mamma," she said in those years, recalling her richly imaginative childhood interest in dolls ("I loved them, raised them, educated them as if they were little living creatures"). She had brought up her youngest brother, and he had slept in her room until her marriage. "I know the soul of children, because I love them," said Elena. "No, I am neither more intelligent nor wiser than other mothers, but I truly love children, all children. . . . I look at a child, the child looks at me, and we understand one another. I know if he is thirsty, if he is hungry, and if he is hungry for love. Oh, how often is he hungry only for love!"[21]

But Elena had come from, and now was queen of, a country which often made wars in which children die and mothers are despoiled, and an old Montenegrin proverb taught that "Death kicks as hard at the hovels of the poor as at the Prince's tower." This, at least in the first years of her long experience as queen, caused her uneasiness, and it seems to have been a subject of private discussion with her husband.

It was in those years that Elena was moved to compose a most ambiguous poem, far more sensitive, if no less awkward, than her romantic scribblings of her courtship. The queen, a descendant of Prince-Bishop Petar, the warrior-poet who wrote the epic *Garlands of the Mountains*, foolishly called "the Serbian *Iliad*" by Italian courtiers but nonetheless a work of some distinction, was accustomed to expressing her thoughts in song. This was the style of her father and her illiterate grandfather, Mirko Petrovich, the family balladeer. Elena, writing under the impact of the Russo-Japanese war, in which her beloved Russia had been humiliated by a people Czar Nicholas often referred to as "monkeys," reveals what we may take to be a rare glimpse of the interior life of the royal couple. While the innermost thoughts of Queen Elena may never be more than a minor curiosity, the philosophy of kings is, or ought to be, enlightening.

The poem, written in Serbo-Croatian, was first published in a Russian magazine toward the end of 1904, and signed "The Blue Butterfly." It was reprinted some months later in a German review, which disclosed the identity of the author, and finally in mid-1905 it appeared in Italian publications, the *Corriere della Sera* for one. Its authenticity by then had been well established. The title is *War* and it is here translated from the Italian and reproduced in full:

To the Prince the Princess said:
Tell me, is war not horrible
Is this strife not horrible
this massacre of men
on soil bedewed with blood
they too bleeding of a thousand wounds
moaning lying abandoned on the field
And life, their life, breathed out
so young, so far from home

Tell me, is war not horrible
Is this death not horrible
And when, oh when, will it ever change
Will there ever come a time
when they will finish up the war
when peace will smile eternally
And the Fatherland, which we love
will ask for victims' blood no more

So to the Prince the young Princess spoke
from the bottom of her heart
And he gave no reply
No other reply gave he
than to take her hands
her white and tender hands
which trembled lightly in his own
and lead her to the window
to the window of his royal palace

looking toward the palace square
where many children played

To the Princess said the Prince
Watch those children how they play
Observe how in peaceful games they jubilate
how their cheeks grow rosy red
how their eyes grow shining bright
their hearts palpitate in joy
See how only noble pleasure
overflows contentment in their soul

But, alas, what do I see
Look, down there, a fight begins
harsh words are being used
Well, do you see then, oh beloved
how until now they played so well together
and here they are pulling one another's hair
Observe how they form themselves in parties
how they strike their former comrades
They are children, and believe me, oh beloved
our people, they too are children
We will not have peace
peace will not be possible

So to the Princess the young Prince spoke
She listened well and then inquired
Look, down there, I see one boy
who stands away, laughing to himself
who remains apart from the relentless struggle
Tell me, why then, oh beloved
why does he not struggle too

Because he is the strongest, says the Prince
So too do we also seek to be
to be the strongest very soon
because only in the strongest Fatherland
the peace will smile eternally[22]

Let the royal pennings remain undisturbed by literary criticism; but it should be noted that "The Blue Butterfly" leaves unknown whether the princess's sentiments have been influenced by a false and pedestrian analogy, and the prince, that is, Victor Emmanuel III, who tries to comfort his beloved, was a man who would one day confide that he never wished to succeed his father, and that he believed in nothing.

15

A "NECESSARY" WAR

AS THE LITTLE KING WISHED FOR BIGNESS AND STRENGTH, SO DID MANY OF HIS COUNTRYMEN, and though he often flagged for love of small, pastoral pleasures, they thrashed him forward. "Open the gates of future dominions to our strength!" was the D'Annunzian imperative to Victor Emmanuel on his accession to the throne. "Arm the prow and set sail to the world!" the poet declaimed flatulently in the fleshy folds of his obscenities, which so fouled the Italian air for more than a score of years. "Paradise," he taught, "lies in the shadow of the sword."[1]

Thus the king could not find the serenity he sought with such tidy devotion. D'Annunzio, he knew, was "right," or at least spoke with oracular authority. The malodorous wind wafting through the poet's soul was nothing less than the coming of the New Times. The Giolittian builders had shaken heaven and earth to save the crown, but in doing so, they had, against the best predictions, stirred the very currents which would blow them away—all, to be sure, except the straw-in-the-wind-reading House of Savoy.

The "socialist monarchy" had permitted the country to flourish relatively freely, thereby to feel strengths which had hitherto been either nonexistent or jammed up in the confines of a single class. But the stronger Italy felt, the more unfitting and unmanly Giolitti's cat-footed, fox-headed system appeared. The more mighty he became, the more numerous were his foes, who yearned to destroy him, in the symbol and even in the flesh. Giolitti's *Italietta*, or "Little Italy," seemed unworthy of a nation which now wished again to march for war and glory.

The old lessons, if they had ever been learned, were forgotten.

Kipling's "four things"—Women and Horses and Power and War—were "greater than all things are" in the new Italy as much as in England and elsewhere on the continent. But what need of Kipling when the Italians had D'Annunzio and his disciples—men such as Papini ("This Italy . . . needs someone to beat her so that she awakens, someone to spur her so that she acts") and Enrico Corradini, who saw war as the "supreme sacred act" of a nation.[2]

The most potent forces engendered or excited by the Giolittian phenomenon were D'Annunzian nationalist imperialism, intransigent and vulgar revolutionary socialism (falling rapidly under the leadership of the young Mussolini), and the old, oppressive conservatism of the owning classes. The new socialism and the old owners contributed much to Giolitti's demise, but it was nationalism whose time had come. The war-loving Nationalists and their "Futurist" following of artists and writers (who endeavored "to free words from the tyranny of syntax and meaning")[3] were giants among their people, for a long unhappy time. They owed some of their ideology to the socialists, more of their solvency to the financial power of the reactionary owners (e.g., the producers of munitions and steel), and all the rest to poetry:

> Towering demon-like above all other Nationalists stood the figure of Gabriele D'Annunzio [writes Salomone]. Poet and dramatist, novelist and artist, imposter and thaumaturge, are mere names that describe the outer manifestations of this man's genius but not the genius itself. For a generation he ruled Italian minds with a completeness hardly equaled by the most ruthless political tyrant. He translated the currents of thought of his time into novels and poems which by the music, the beauty and fascination of his words seized upon the imagination. D'Annunzio declaimed upon the beauty of fire and destruction, the voluptuous attractions of power and glory, he sang of the Nietzschian superman.[4]

The Nationalist movement led by Corradini, Papini, and Prezzolini formed the political arm of this condition. With their master, they were self-declared liberticides, who dreamed aloud of "a second Crispi." They hated all they proclaimed cowardly and pacific, and most cowardly and pacific of all were Giolitti and his "*Italia vile.*"*

Their appeal was to "all who want a vaster, larger, more heroic, more glorious life . . . all who hate the melancholy of resignation, the policy of stay-at-home, and cowardice. . . ." They sang the love of

---

* Caring little about consistency, they had nothing against the monarchy, which was a standing invitation to the king to empower them.

peril, rashness, and rebellion. "We proclaim," went the Futurist Manifesto of 1909, "that the world is the richer for a new beauty of speed, and our praise is for the man at the wheel. There is no beauty now save in struggle, no masterpiece can be anything but aggressive, and hence we glorify war, militarism, and patriotism."[5]

War was gorgeous; holocausts were heavenly. According to Papini, a scholar famous for his *Life of Christ*:

> When lives have to be sacrificed we are not saddened if before our minds shines the magnificent harvest of a superior life that will rise from those deaths. And while the lowly democrats cry out against war as a barbaric residue of ferocious ages, we believe it to be the greatest awakener of the weak, a quick and heroic instrument of power and wealth.[6]

By 1910 the Nationalists felt strong enough to found themselves as a people's party, and they called a congress at Florence for this purpose. Corradini gave them their tenets: Nationalism and imperialism, he declared, were the socialism of the poor. Against "the parliamentary lie," he invoked the sociology of Pareto and the political science of Gaetano Mosca. Against the capitalist system he brandished Marx, Sorelian syndicalism, and even Julius Caesar. He called on Hegel and Vico for ethics, and to fight any desire for peace and brotherhood poor Darwin and Spencer were cited. Garibaldi was their inspiration, but given second place to the greatest Nationalist of them all, Mazzini. Of the theory synthesized by the Nationalists, Mack Smith observes, "Clearly, this was one of the particular scrapheaps where Mussolini was to scavenge in order to clothe his ideological nakedness."[7]

For now, however, Mussolini, the under-thirty Marxist purist, opposed the right-wing movement. Giolitti, on the other hand, being a seasoned man, correctly gauged the force and direction of the flow of the Nationalists' sewage, and managed to stay afloat until a later day. As was his fashion, he sought an opportunity to absorb or capture for himself and his king some of the power inherent in the Nationalist cause, and when the party gained mass support for a war against the enfeebled Ottoman Empire, the prize being Turkish Libya, Giolitti raised their cry for "our promised land" as his own.

The year 1911 was bursting with patriotic excitements. It was the half-century mark of the founding of united Italy and the triumph of the Risorgimento. In March, the king inaugurated the grotesque monument to Victor Emmanuel II and the glories of the *ottocento* battles. The monarch, in his toy-soldier-suit blues, with tall, enigmatic Elena on his arm, mounted the white edifice on the Capitoline hill and declared "irresistible" his resolve to make Italy "the freest, happiest, and most respected [country] in the world."[8]

In September, on the advice of Giolitti, he sent the fleet to redeem the royal oath, and his cousin Louis Amadeus to fire first cannon against the Turks in the name of the House of Savoy. Dogali, Adowa, and other misfortunes were at last to be avenged; Italy would be big, or at least bigger, after all.

Everyone in Italy, save some socialists and many soldiers, loved the war. "The great Proletariat has stirred!" cried the poet Pascoli, who should have known better, and the Nationalists, whom he echoed, were themselves so full of joy they began to beat up their opponents in the streets, as well as the mothers who threw themselves on the tracks to block the trains carrying their sons to the war. Victor and Elena, however, could not but think of war's miseries, even "necessary" wars, as the king believed this war to be ("I who do not love war . . . wanted the Libyan war because . . . it was a necessary war in order not to die of suffocation in the Mediterranean").[9] But no Italian happiness of that day and age can have been greater than Margherita's.

> How proud to be an Italian [said she]! And how singularly and unexpectedly great are the ways in which Providence brings good on earth! War, a word which of itself embraces so much pain and so much carnage, in this, our case, what proofs of bravery it has brought us, what heartfelt faith, what nobility, what lofty sentiments and deeds! It is truly a marvelous thing, for which we can never give enough thanks to God![10]

God and Giolitti. For even the queen mother was willing to concede most of the earthly credit to him. So too went the consensus of home opinion. The Nationalist party was thrown on the defensive, scrambling to show its contribution to having caused the war, but to little avail.

"Giolitti," wrote the influential Florentine review *La Voce*, "the anti-Nationalist *par excellence*, the stay-at-home Piedmontese, the evil hypnotist, by going to Tripoli, has changed the course and tenor of Italian life and has stolen the thunder from the Nationalists."[11]

The Libyan war of 1911–12, hardly remembered now, turned out to be a terrible mistake, not only for Italy but for the entire world. In seriously disturbing the world balance of power alone, it must be regarded as among the primary origins of World War I. The Italians "won," but to compare such a triumph with even the Pyrrhic victory does not help us grasp the enormity of the Libyan liability. "A big sandbox," is what the antiwar factions called the North African territory, and they were not far from the truth, at least until oil was discovered there long after the Italians were driven home. Libya, however, might now better be described as a ruinously expensive cemetery for two generations of Italians.

Forgotten or unheeded from the start was the Cavourian admonition to undertake hateful methods only energetically and grandiosely "so that your government will not appear ridiculous as well as odious." What was to be a Blitzkrieg in which Italy, in a matter of days and "without firing a shot," would present the world with a *fait accompli*, dragged on for a year, resistance and rebellion for twenty more.[12] The king annexed Libya by royal decree, but the royal army bungled every battle and the slaughter mounted. The Italians became the first in history to use aerial bombardment, although with the scarce success it could only have had in bleak desert terrain. Their war crimes against innocent civilians shocked European sensibilities —hypocrisies notwithstanding. Less-than-ingenuous Britons and Frenchmen, Russians and Germans clacked their tongues no less reproachfully, and G.M. Trevelyan, whose ecstatic history of Garibaldi and the Thousand had made Italy Edwardian England's darling, now denounced her conduct of the war as "barbarous and uncivilized" even by imperialist standards.[13]

The trouble was that the "sick" Turks and the "cowardly" Arabs fought back.

"To tell the truth," Italian historian Volpe wrote in apologizing for the Libyan errors, "almost everyone in Italy . . . [was] convinced that the war would not be a long and difficult affair: that the Turkish garrisons, their supply lines to the sea closed by blockade, would very soon be forced to surrender; that the native population, Arabs and Berbers, would remain passive, rather, benevolently passive out of hatred for their old Turkish masters. . . ." But the invaders, though their government had studied the war project for at least ten years, found the local situation otherwise. Volpe continues:

> Now reality began at once to deny these beliefs. . . . After the blockade, [arms and supplies] continued to arrive by sea as well as through the interior from neighboring Egypt and Tunisia. The local people, too, with the exception of some small urban groups, very soon gave signs of bearing sentiments which were not benevolent, whether out of love for

Turkey or suspicion, fear, and hatred of Italy, more the foreigner than
Turkey. The whole complex of social forces entered into the contest,
awakening a very backward but not barbaric people, who were keenly
sensitive to the callings of their religion and capable of their own national
sentiments, which had been lying dormant . . . a people who for us had
always been a mystery. . . .[14]

That Italian bishops proclaimed a crusade against Islam, and that
the jingoists viewed the indigenous population not as a "mystery"
but as a herd of insidious subhuman creatures, did much to make the
Arabs fight. It took the royal navy and more than one hundred thousand troops to subdue one-fourth as many Arabs. There was no conquest, however, only a compromise settlement, as Turkey sued for
peace.* With money and concessions to the Turks, the Italians at the
peace table in Switzerland gained recognition from the big powers of
partial sovereignty in Libya, the sultan at Constantinople being allowed to retain his religious sovereignty and thus substantial political
influence.

In this way the Italians got Libya, and the House of Savoy came
to rule over a territory six times greater than Italy itself, seventy-two
times the size of Piedmont, and many thousand-fold larger than the
Alpine eagle's nest of its most ancient fathers. The war had been
fought for living space for the allegedly overpopulated homeland,
but hardly a fraction of the recklessly predicted emigration took
place, although Italians continued to go abroad to other, more distant lands. The desert, in spite of poetry, did not bloom. Those who
did go to take up the white man's burden, brought with them the
white man's hatreds and lived in fear. The colonial governors built
roads, and those were the roads on which the Italians fled when the
British chased them home in World War II.

Now, however, there seemed cause for celebration. D'Annunzio
wrote his *Chansons de geste from Overseas* ("Tripoli, beautiful land
of love . . ."): The king said privately that the period of monarchical
consolidation had come to a happy ending opening a new phase of
aggrandizement for the kingdom. Giolitti gave thanks to the people.
They were worthy of the highest praise, he said, because "without
regard to social class or conditions they gathered unanimously around

---

* Turkey, showing surprising strength in the Libyan war, was in no hurry to
negotiate; the longer it could hold its distant colonial outpost, the more impressed
were the great powers, particularly those which along with their client states were
planning to devour the remains of the Ottoman Empire. It was primarily the fear
of the imminent attack from its Balkan neighbors (including tiny Montenegro) which
induced Turkey to treat with the Italians. Constantinople, it seems, was more
frightened of the Petrovich clan than the mighty House of Savoy.

the army and the fleet and sent their sons serenely to die for the fatherland."[15]

A few days later an anarchist bricklayer took two shots at the king, as he and Elena drove down the Corso on a visit to his father's tomb. The would-be assassin missed his mark, and the celebrations and unanimity continued all the more, with claims of still another gain for the House of Savoy. The king and queen appeared on their balcony with the living proof of this notion—a *monarchist* bricklayer—and were hailed by a happy throng. Further proof was found in the agonizing of the Socialist party, torn wider than ever before when the leaders of its right wing made an unprecedented call at the Quirinal to wish the assaulted sovereign well. Mussolini had cunning reason to deplore "the incredible spectacle . . . of all democratic and revolutionary Italy prostrating itself before the throne." He was able then to ask, "Why this excessive, hysterical sensibility in the case of crowned heads? . . . There are peoples who have sent their king packing; others even have preferred to take the precaution of sending him to the guillotine, and those peoples are in the vanguard of progress."[16]

But Mussolini, too, would learn to love the little king.

In the end, Libya was a triumph for violent, aggressive nationalism, and a defeat for all who opposed it. This meant the downfall of Giovanni Giolitti. He had succeeded in convincing almost everyone that war was often good, and his miscalculation was that the next war would be regarded by many of his countrymen, particularly his king, as infinitely better than the last. But having had the primary responsibility in conducting the Libyan affair, he had learned that Italy could ill-afford any kind of war. With an election approaching, he lied about the cost of the year-long, "lightning" conflict, which had been promised as an easy victory but had instead emptied his treasury, forcing a return after many years of surplus to dangerous deficits. He said nothing of what he knew to be the country's irremediable weaknesses. When, however, he was sincere enough to resist further aggressions, he was therefore rendered a universal anathema to the New Times, an anachronism like those he in his day had swept away.

The next war was World War I, which Giolitti correctly foresaw as ruinous for the Italians in the event of their participation regardless of the outcome. This placed him in loyal opposition to the House of Savoy, and his was a loyalty which was to endure ruinously in its supremest trial.

16

A GREAT WAR

THE TRIAL OF MANY LOYALTIES CAME WITH THE SUMMER OF 1914. ON AUGUST 1 VICTOR EMMANUEL received a presumptuous telegram from his fourth cousin Franz Josef of Hapsburg befitting a vassal state, not the proud possessor of imperial lands and expectations Italy had just become. Russia had threatened the peace of Europe, said the emperor. *He* had decided to defend the Triple Alliance. He was glad that he could count on Italy and her army, and he expressed his most fervent hopes for victory and glory.[1]

Franz Ferdinand was dead at Saravejo. The Austrian ultimatum had been given. Germany had attacked Russia. The British and French were moving troops. The Great War, as some old men and specialists still call it, had begun.

The little king wrote in his scrap-paper diary for that day, "Franz Josef to me—he asks my support." He dabbed two heavy dots of satisfaction under the word *my*.[2] Before him lay a similar appeal from the Germans. The Triple Alliance had come home. Italy and Victor Emmanuel were being called on to redeem the promises Humbert and Margherita had given so frivolously thirty-two years ago.

The little king had already revealed his attitude toward the Triple Alliance to the American ambassador to Rome. "I am more than ever convinced," he had said, venting earlier anger at Austria, "of the utter worthlessness of treaties or any agreements written on paper. They are worth the value of the paper. The only real strength lies in bayonets and cannon."[3] He had been laboring for years to gain slack in the old commitments made with the Central Powers. He had traveled to London, Paris, and St. Petersburg to strengthen relations with the *Entente Cordiale*, and had received the czar, the president, and the king at home, in spite of German cries of adultery.

He despised fatuous Wilhelm II, who had come to the Quirinal in 1903 with his towering Prussian grenadiers—an incident which had made a laughing stock of the belt-high king, compelled by ceremony to stand beside them. The Kaiser, he was well aware, called him "the little thief" in his kinder moments, and the queen of Italy was but "the daughter of a Black Mountain cattle thief."[4]

He loathed his archaic, condescending cousin in Vienna, all the more for his need of him, for only Franz Josef had stood between Italy and the Italophobic Franz Ferdinand. There were generals in Vienna, Victor Emmanuel knew too, who had campaigned for a preventive war against Rome solely for the taste of easy victory; they, and the whole Hapsburg circle, considered him and his royal subjects not as a conquering people but as "rabbits," in allusion to a supposed quantity or quality of Italian sexual activity.[5]

The little king was not amused by this. He had lately begun referring to Franz Josef as "Cecco Beppe," the diminutive used by the Austrian-hating Irredentists, to whom Victor Emmanuel, having need of his allies, could give only clandestine encouragement. But now it was "Cecco Beppe" and "Willy" in Berlin who were soliciting help from Rome. On August 2 the Italian told them that there would be no help at all forthcoming. From his reading of the *Triplice*, it seemed to him that he need only maintain a "cordial attitude" toward Vienna and Berlin.

Kaiser Wilhelm cried "scoundrel!" and "impudence!" on receiving his reply, and when his diplomats informed him that the extent of Italy's cordiality would be dependent on what territorial compensations it might expect in return, the German replied, "The little thief always wants to swallow something together with the others."[6] He pressed Vienna to give the Italians the *terre irredente*, but the Austrians called that "blackmail" and refused. On August 3, the Italian king declared his neutrality in the war. Nine months later, making scraps of the Triple Alliance, he was fighting on the side of the *Entente* in the war to end all wars.

Why Italy fought a war which cost the nation two million battlefield casualties, including 650,000 dead, has given cause for much retrospection. The Italians were not attacked, nor were they under particular obligation or irresistible compulsion to take up arms against anyone. To be sure, the war, rhetoric aside, seemed to many well worth fighting.* On the other hand, this was an apparent truth only if the Central Powers could be defeated, and the Italian government was never really sure which side would win. Many of Italy's national objectives could have been achieved by peaceful means. More important, a major war threatened to totally exhaust the country's natural resources and bleed the nation white. The little king would not have said with A.J.P. Taylor that his Italy was "a ridiculous imitation of a Great Power, impressive only to diplomats and literary visitors,"[8] but he was not among the wholly blind and self-deceptive.

For every "sensible" argument advanced in favor of the war there was, in its own terms, an equally sound reason for abstention, let alone the queen mother's gloomy prediction that this particular conflict would promote "excessive development of democratic ideas, above all in Germany, Russia, and Austria."[9] That Italy was led to the line of fire was, in fact, the active decision of one man and his singular tradition: Victor Emmanuel of Savoy. Of this not enough has yet been said.

One factor influencing the king's decision was that he felt an overriding need to break free of Giolitti, who was adamantly opposed to the war, and worse, the new times. Liberalism, Victor Emmanuel believed, was dead, but its remains lay above ground, and this was imperiling the health of the monarchy. Now that war and imperialism had forced Italy into deficit spending, it could no longer pay for reforms. A return to Humbertine authoritarianism and regimentation was needed, although only in a manner appropriate to this second decade of the twentieth century. Whatever misgivings Victor Emmanuel might have had were contained; society as yet knows only two kinds of rule: liberal and illiberal totalitarianism. When one fails the other is sure to come.

Nothing impressed the king of this scarcity of alternatives more than the volcanic events of "Red Week," June 7–14, 1914. Giolitti, as a tactic, had resigned, and Antonio Salandra, his replacement, had to employ 100,000 troops—more than six times as many as Crispi had

---

* The secret Pact of London, with which the Allies in 1915 purchased Italy's participation in the war, offered great attractions. To realize the unfinished longings of the Risorgimento Rome, in accord with the Allied principle of self-determination, was to get almost all the Italian-speaking lands held by Austria. In contradiction to the same principle, but to satisfy Italian memories of the greatness of old Venice, much of slavic Dalmatia, the Greek Dodecanese, and bits of the Turkish empire were also to be given to Italy. To uphold the idea of imperialism, Italy's African lands would be enlarged if the German colonies were divided among the victors. The Italians were also to get a portion of any war indemnity, a loan from Great Britain, and exclusion of the pope from the peace conference.[7]

sent to Sicily—to quell the uprising. Cheered by Mussolini, and led by socialist Pietro Nenni and the world-famous anarchist Malatesta, *Settimana Rossa* showed surprising republican sentiment and made the House of Savoy a special target. Royal emblems were torn down, the red flag flew atop Bologna's city hall, and the entire Romagna was declared a "republic." Not in half a century had the monarchy been so assailed.

Victor Emmanuel was very alarmed. Both he and Salandra were convinced that the new times required, as one Italian historian has written, "much more energetic means than those employed by Giolitti, and that it was extremely dangerous to allow, as he had done on various occasions, the revolutionary wave to die down of its own accord."[10] Red Week was more a riot than a revolution; it did succeed, however, in overthrowing the "socialist monarchy."

But the king had other, more fundamental reasons for wanting war. In 1922, he admitted some of them to a confidant:

> Why, then, did I, who like my minister [Giolitti], do not love war, make two very grave wars?* Here is why. . . . With regard to the World War, I had two almost personal reasons for making it. One was my own, traditional motive, that of the House of Savoy: to put an end to the quarrels with Austria, at the same time forming this Italy of ours, thus completing her as she had to be. For centuries the Savoys had been trying to do this; in 1915 the opportune moment arose. I would never have found another occasion equally as good. Second, I was convinced that if I were on the side of England and Russia, I could not lose. Now we see what Russia was. But in those days she seemed a colossus.**[11]

Said another way, Italy and history had to suffer a man desirous of settling ancient family squabbles in the base tradition of his house. His minister Salandra called it candidly a war of "sacred selfishness"; Salvatorelli, "a grand return to Savoyard territorialism,"[13] or the *settecento* formula we have seen expressed in behalf of the House of Savoy by the royalist minister San Tommasso: "to derive gain from all occasions . . . to profit by the conflict of others, and therein draw its advantages." Indeed some days before joining the Allies, the little

---

* The reference is to the Libyan affair and the Italian intervention in World War I. For Victor Emmanuel's view of the former, see above, p. 194.

** Twenty years earlier Victor Emmanuel had returned from a state visit to Czar Nicholas with a somewhat more profound view of imperial Russia. He believed it no less a power then, but, he said quaintly, "In this great country there is a political atmosphere of near gloom, an oppressive police state nightmare. Too many gendarmes; you can't breathe. If I had been born in Russia, I would be a revolutionary."[12]

king, doubtless unwittingly, actually spoke the formula aloud putting it in the words of the pressing moment:

> I don't understand how any of us can hope for the victory of the Central Powers. Austria cannot be but a vassal of Germany, and if Germany wins, she alone will dominate all Europe. If the Triple *Entente* is victorious, there will be three powers with whom we can deal. Some cracks will always appear in a structure like that, and we will be able to profit by it.[14]

As frank as the king's own explanations may be, we may be sure from what we have seen of him that his motives were in part even more personal than he allows. Without attempting mere conjectures, let us rather wonder at the role of kings in other people's lives.

Once the choice of war and allies was made, which seems to have occurred at the beginning of 1915, Victor Emmanuel, the Salandra government, and the interventionists had a difficult time dragging the nation into battle.

The Pact of London, signed on April 26, 1915, stipulated that Italy had to enter the hostilities within one month from that date, and it was in this period that the secretly committed government and crown raced wildly against time to convince the benighted of war's wisdom. The majority of parliament and the people, Rome well knew, were against the war, as was the pope and still powerful Giolitti. All kinds of illegalities and treacheries would be required, and Victor Emmanuel was prepared to abdicate should they fail. For the first time in his reign he had allowed himself to be maneuvered onto a one-way course, and now at any cost he was going down the hellish road.

He had an able traveling companion in Salandra, a southern professor who thought in the Mazzinian idiom. To Salandra it seemed that "the historic moment had arrived for attaining perfect national unity and for extending Italy's boundaries to the limits consecrated by nature and tradition."[15]

Salandra, in turn, had as foreign minister his former mentor, Sonnino. The old *triplicista* had feverishly wanted war on the Austrian side but turned his guns the other way when Victor Emmanuel showed him why. Baron Sonnino, who had so earnestly plotted with Humbert the Good, made up in his devotion to the House of Savoy what he lacked in farsightedness. The son of a Scottish woman and a Tuscan-Levantine Jewish trader, he had twice been prime minister

Victor Emmanuel II, re galantuomo, first king of united Italy, once called the father of his country.

In battle dress.

In the field.

The caption accompanying this old storybook woodcut reads: "After having examined his hand, the witch said: 'You will die in the Quirinal.'"

An unknown artist renders the re galantuomo *on his death bed. Humbert and Margherita are at his side. The man with the long white beard is Depretis. Crispi (with the droopy white mustache) stands behind him.*

Margherita of Savoy, the first queen of Italy, shortly after ascending the throne.

A contemporary engraving shows Humbert about to be kissed by his cousin Franz Josef on the occasion of the Italian royal couple's visit to the Austrian emperor.

Humbert and Margherita at the opera in Vienna. From left, Franz Josef, Margherita, Crown Prince Rudolf (standing), Empress Elizabeth, and Humbert.

Humbert, the hunter. The submissive-looking animal in the foreground was superimposed in the original photograph.

Humbert the Good, shortly before his assassination.

Margherita in 1898.

*Margherita and her only child,
the future little king.*

A contemporary rendering of Humbert's assassination.

The assassin: Gaetano Bresci, of Paterson, New Jersey.

Humbert the Good lies in state; his son, King Victor Emmanuel III, is at his side.

GLI AUGUSTI SPOSI

VITTORIO EMANUELE DI SAVOIA

ELENA PETROVI

A poster celebrating
the wedding of
Victor and Elena.
The overline reads:
"Long live the august
bride and groom."

Elena of Montenegro on the throne
of Italy.

The little king reviewing the
Prussian guard, pictured by a
German pen at the time of
Kaiser Wilhelm II's visit to Rome.

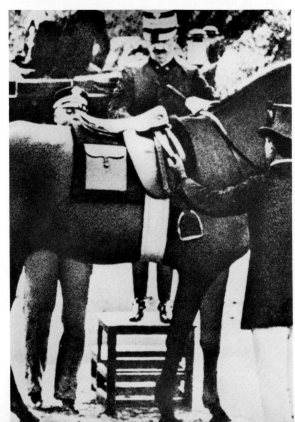

A rare photograph of the five-foot
king of Italy, contending with
the difficulties he faced in
mounting a horse.

Queen Elena first among the millions to give the gold of their wedding rings to be melted down to help pay for the colonial war against Ethiopia.

Victor and Benito, 1934.

The little emperor visits his little empire.

The king and the duce in a solemn moment.

Hitler arrives at a train station
in Rome for his bungled,
infelicitous state visit. The
Fuehrer thought he was calling
on the Duce, but the little
king was his not-very-willing
host.

The Fuehrer in Rome. From
left, Duce, Fuehrer, king, and
queen. Hess and Himmler
stand between and behind
Victor and Elena. The
up-and-coming man with the
feather in his helmet is
Badoglio.

Victor and Elena on their thrones at a ceremony in 1939 dedicating a plaque to Queen Margherita.

The king-emperor, with Mussolini looking on, rewards a young man for his services at the front to the crown and the Fascist state.

Like father like son: Victor
Emmanuel III and Crown
Prince Humbert in 1939.

A political cartoon depicting Victor Emmanuel
III instructing his son during the campaign
for the postwar referendum, in which the
Savoyard monarchy was defeated and
discarded in favor of a republic.

The prince and princess of Piedmont, Humbert and Maria José,
among the people.

during the Giolittian years, each time for one hundred rather insignificant days. Italian and world Jewry considered his achievements a triumph against anti-Semitism, but Sonnino was a declared Protestant.* He had negotiated the Pact of London, and the government believed no one else capable of obtaining so much from the *Entente*, but Victor Emmanuel was to agree with Nitti that the baron was "a bad Christian, a bad Jew, and above all a bad minister."[17]

The interventionists had powerful allies in the Nationalists, who wanted a war on any side. Further, unexpected support came from Mussolini. The future Duce had been expelled from leadership of the antiwar socialists (losing, too, his editorship of *Avanti!* and his party card) because he did not want to be among "the inert spectators to this grandiose drama."[18] Neutralist in September, Mussolini, in November, 1914, had launched his war-thumping newspaper, *Il Popolo d'Italia*, "a socialist daily."**

Of greatest influence, however, was D'Annunzio. When the campaign to intervene began he was in exile in France to escape his creditors, but Salandra, using government funds, cleared up his most pressing debts, and sent for him to thunder for the war. Arrangements were made to dispatch the king to welcome him at Quarto, near Genoa, where Garibaldi on May 5, 1860 ("Oh, night of the fifth of May"), and the Thousand had set sail "to free the slave." On May 5, 1915, D'Annunzio made his famous war cry speech by the rocky shores of Quarto. Victor Emmanuel, who had the day before denounced the Triple Alliance, thought it wiser not to attend, but D'Annunzio was authorized to address his words "to His Majesty the King, absent but present."[20] The significance of this was that while the repudiation of the treaty fell short of intervention, the monarch's "presence" alongside the poet, who had already called for a war on

---

* The less celebrated Luigi Luzzatti, however, another fill-in prime minister for one of Giolitti's tactical retreats, and an accomplished economist, was a full-blooded self-admitted member of the faith, although in a negative way. He maintained his Jewishness, he once declared, only to spite the anti-Semites. "On the day that anti-Semitism ceases," Luzzatti promised, "I will publicly profess [Christianity]."[16] Anticlerical Victor Emmanuel's apparent affinity for Jewish ministers, incidentally, did not escape the Vatican. The only church the king had built, the Catholics complained, was the new main synagogue in Rome. He would strike some sort of balance, however, in 1938, when still feeling "infinite pity" for the Jews, he would decree Italy's anti-Semitic racial laws. See below, p. 301.

** The sterile debate as to whether he received money from the French government to subsidize the newspaper never ends. It is certain enough that he did, beginning with a payment of 100,000 lire. More interesting, and less discussed, however, is the half-million lire extended to the enterprise by such beneficiaries of war as the industrialists Agnelli (Fiat), Perrone (Ansaldo steel), Esterle (Edison electric), and Parodi (munitions).[19]

"slavery and extermination" against the traditional Austrian enemy, signaled his own position.

All this buildup for war was believed necessary primarily to overcome the power and the fear of one man: Giovanni Giolitti. Better judges of the septuagenarian neutralist would have worried not at all, but when Giolitti, after a long stay abroad and in Piedmont, returned to the capital on May 9, Rome trembled. He was greeted at the railroad station by a hostile mob assembled by government agents. Mussolini called Giolitti "the foulest man ever born to the shame of Italy." He said "I would like to put five bullets from a revolver into his stomach."[21] Salandra, stalling for the fever to rise, postponed the opening of parliament, and D'Annunzio beckoned the Romans to burn the parliament building down and literally kill Giolitti.*

But the former prime minister's neutralist majority of some 80 percent of the chamber held firm. As a symbol of this support 300 antiwar deputies—they too under threat of physical violence—managed to leave their calling cards at Giolitti's home within a few hours of his arrival.

The king and his government were faced with an impasse. Victor Emmanuel could exercise his royal prerogative and declare the war as secretly promised, but with parliament against him the conduct of hostilities by a nation so divided would be impossible. The pitch of war hysteria grew ear-splitting. D'Annunzio addressed the Romans:

> No, we are not and do not want to be just a museum, a hotel, a vacation resort, a Prussian-blue horizon where foreigners come for their honeymoons, a gay market where things are bought and sold. Our genius demands that we should put our stamp on the molten metal of the new world. . . . If it is a crime to incite people to violence, I boast of now committing that crime. . . . This war, though it may seem destructive will be the most fruitful means of creating beauty and virtue that has appeared on this earth.[23]

The Nationalists harangued:

> Either Parliament will bring down the Nation and continue to use her palpitating, sainted body plying its trade as pimp, prostituting her to the foreigner yet further, or the Nation will overthrow Parliament, break up the benches and the bars, purify with iron and fire the alcoves of

---

* Under D'Annunzio's incitement to lynch the former minister, the mob proceeded to march on Giolitti's home in Rome and the police, it seems, did nothing to stop them. It took a unit of the royal cavalry and a platoon of *carabinieri* to rescue Giolitti.[22]

the ruffians, and in the face of the world which waits and watches will proclaim the august beauty of her immortal soul.[24]

Yet parliamentary resistance and neutralism in general, as Salandra himself admitted, were on the increase. Mussolini despaired that the king would be too weak to overcome them. "I no longer believe that the war will be made," he said. If that were the case, "the monarchy must pay. Let us redeem ourselves with revolution. My battle cry is either the war or the republic!"[25]

In these circumstances, blocked by Giolitti and lacking a political foundation, Salandra could no longer govern. He would either have to quit or attempt a military *coup d'état*, for which his temperament and the king's were little suited. Only Victor Emmanuel could still act, and on May 13 the Salandra government resigned—although by then this seems to have been a mere formality, the crisis apparently having been resolved in the previous seventy-two hours.

On May 10, however, the king's predicament was soul-deep. There appeared to be no political exit other than abdication. It was this fact which he sought to impress on Giolitti when, in a private audience that morning, he received the old man at the Quirinal.

Giolitti did not know to what extent his king was committed. He therefore restated to Victor Emmanuel his reasons for opposing the war: The Italians could realize much of their territorial ambitions remaining neutral; the army was not as powerful as others including himself had made it appear; the treasury was too fragile to withstand the pressures of battle; there was the danger of destruction and defeat, there was the peril of revolution at home. His return to power, he said, would permit the new government and its overwhelming majority to abrogate any agreement reached with the *Entente* by the Salandra minority.

But the king was an inextricable part of that minority. The Pact of London had been signed in his name. His honor, his house, his monarchy lay indelibly in the mark made by that pen, or so he reasoned. The repudiator of the Triple Alliance would never return to suffer the ridicule of Wilhelm II and the blandishments of his cousin in Vienna. Farini, long gone from the scene, had said it a score of years before: "Like all little men he is firm and has a tenacious will."[26] The *re galantuomo*, Victor Emmanuel II, had led his Piedmontese army in war on Austria, saying, "Either king of Italy, or *monsù* Savoy." Now the third Victor Emmanuel was ready himself to be *monsù* Savoy, but he believed an even graver decision rested with him than had weighed upon his grandfather. Nineteen years later the little king would reminisce:

> I too, in 1915, had to confront the decision to make a war. The political men, you see, were not quite in agreement on what had to be done. It was a very serious thing . . . the drama of 1915 was one of immense proportions, a tragedy involving millions of our soldiers, instead of the hundreds of thousands of the Piedmontese army.
>
> Yes, it is true that my grandfather found himself in an imbroglio at Villafranca, and I myself was in such an imbroglio in 1915. There were those who pulled from one side, those who pulled from the other; everyone wanted his own way. All the same a decision had to be taken.[27]

When Giolitti learned that his king was of one mind, and one mind only, he did the unexpected, but that which all truly faithful men can only do. He did not shield the nation from ambitious men, rise to speak the people's mind, and lead them back from war. Like the canine by the gramophone, he heard his master's voice. ("I expressed the opinion that the Government could not be entrusted to a man known as an adversary of Italy's entry into the war.")[28]

Assured that Giolitti would not resist the royal prerogative, the king and Salandra initiated a sequence of events, most of which were staged in order to influence home opinion and fortify their authority to send the nation's youth into battle. On May 16, ten days before the terms of the Pact of London fell due, Salandra was reempowered by the king. His reinstatement was the equivalent of a public announcement of the withdrawal of Giolitti's opposition, and on the next day Giolitti went home to Piedmont, to his country villa near the town of Cavour ("I considered my mission completed").[29]

For his abjuration, historians and all who hunger for the great still damn Giolitti—the way Mazzini damned his Italy when it yielded only what it could. Even today they call Giolitti craven, malicious, selfish, and a coward, but his own simple self-defense rings truer than all the curses on his name. "I had occasion to speak about the war somewhat later," he wrote in his remembrances. He had been asked to address local officials at a ceremony in his native province of Cuneo. "I expressed myself as follows":

> The sentiments of the representatives of a province such as ours, whose history has for centuries been an uninterrupted series of struggles for independence from the foreigner and of devotion to the Monarchy of the House of Savoy, cannot give cause for any doubt. When the King calls the country to arms, the province of Cuneo without distinction to

parties and without reservation, is unanimous in its devotion to the King, in its unconditional support of the Government, in its unlimited trust in the army and the fleet. . . .[30]

Such were the qualities of the first citizen of Cuneo. On the undulations of like emotions do the fortunes of dynasties and dictators rise and fall.

On May 20, the Giolittian spell broken, parliament opened. The bewildered, leaderless neutralists, turned loose from the sorcerer's spell, had in less than a week been captured by their opposites. Now they lost no time in voting extraordinary powers to the government "in case of war," and when the result was announced they sang the Garibaldian hymn, some among them crying, "Long live the war!"[31]

Victor Emmanuel had trampled down his coronation vow to be true to parliament and Charles Albert's constitution, but in the unseeing eyes of the superpatriots he had saved the nation from perdition.

On May 23, "sacred war" against Austria was declared; on the 24th Italian guns began to roar; on the 26th the little king, "supreme *duce*" of all the armed forces on the land and on the sea, departed for the front.

17

THE WARRIOR KING

✢✢ THE FRONT WAS A NECROPOLIS OF TRENCHES ON
✢✢ THE NORTHEAST FRONTIER. THE WIND AND THE
snow blew over the mountains, the mud wormed into all the creases
of the flesh, and it rained fire and fear. The king, in his ankle-length,
general's gray-green greatcoat, puttees on his spindly legs, was as
present as the firmament. He had appointed his uncle, the duke of
Genoa, regent of the realm, and he remained with his soldiers throughout the war.

Publicists and the faithful called him "the soldier king," but wisely
he did not repeat the military pretensions of his forefathers who had
insisted on commanding every battle. Instead he played the tireless
inspector, the Matthew Brady of the battlefield, and a male "Lady
with the Lamp." He seemed capable of being everywhere. "The king
is like the presence of God," the saying went among the awed recruits, and no one ever knew when the monarch would come by and
ask a boy his name and what he thought about the war.

Every morning at eight, he would emerge from the "Villa Italia"—
as they called his quarters regardless of where the tents were pitched
—and head for the front lines through the fog and the rain and the
snow. A gray open Fiat would take him over the iced mud roads, as
he with his adjutants would hit every position scheduled for the day.
Sometimes the party would stop, and the king would peer through a
field glass on a tripod, his peaked braided cap swung around the way
a baseball catcher wears his hat. Ever present too was his black-box,
plate-back camera, and he would sometimes point it at the enemy,
open shutter on the film, and capture whole armies under silver-
salted glass.

His officers considered him a *pignolo,* a stickler for the rule. They feared his surprise reviews of their front-line installations, which more often brought royal criticism than an understanding of their special plight. At home Victor Emmanuel's detractors maligned "the photographer king," as they dubbed him with malicious intent, but the common soldier, if we are to credit any part of the legend that grew up then, found their king a comfort in the cold.

His courage could not be daunted. He made his daily rounds whatever were the risks. His deep pockets were always filled with cigars, and though he himself had never learned to smoke the smoke of kings, he passed them to his boys when he walked among them in the mud and in the trench. A man fought better and thought more of his king if he were given a good cigar, Victor Emmanuel believed, as had his cigar-smoking father and grandfather. As an abstainer, he could only ape their style, but he more likely than they might have known how King "Bomba" of Naples had won the love of many *lazzaroni* handing his lighted butts to the most insistent beggar—a royal magnanimity, Croce says, "remembered for years, remembered with tears."[1]

The little king ate hard-boiled eggs from a mess tin, nursed stricken peasant boys to health with the magic faith-healers employ, and tended to the dead. The Quirinal became a hospital, Queen Elena in charge, and Margherita, too, gave her villa and a caring hand to the dying and the maimed. Victor caped his son Humbert, twelve years old, in military dress, and he took him near the battlefield to teach him horror and to hate. His own face grew wizened, and his hair turned white from the worries of the war. D'Annunzio immortalized the wartime sovereign on the Mount Rushmore of his pen:

> *The King has given up the purple and the ermine*
> *He wears the army greys and leggings in their stead*
> *And like the infantry's enlisted men*
> *He sloshes through the ditches filled with mud*
>
> *The King who takes his dark bread with*
> *   the fighting man . . .*
> *The King who's quick to give his loving hand . . .*
> *The King whose face is so deeply lined*
> *Yet can be so infinitely kind*
> *   when he dries the sweating temples of a wounded man . . .*[2]

But all the power of the king's tenderness and affection, whatever were their true dimensions, could not replace the power in the barrel of the gun. The army was poorly equipped, poorly trained, and poorly spirited for the fight. The war plans and the rifles were the hand-me-downs of another generation, and the Austrians were tougher than had been supposed by the government in Rome. The war dragged on long beyond the expectations of Salandra and the king. They had thought at the outset that the enemy was already in retreat and had gambled on the conflict not lasting out the year. Now Giolitti's gloomy predictions seemed to have been inspired, as one by one they all came true.

The Italians held the line as well as reality allowed, but the war became a wasting battle for positions, and the Austrian successes, the drain on life and blood, brought defeatism to the land. The pope decried the "useless carnage." He called for peace at the price of victory, and the people felt exhausted, betrayed by men they now believed had used their sons for profit and for fame.

The fighting man, more often than not, was a twenty-year-old farmer's son who could scarcely read, if at all, and knew even less about the reasons for the war. His muddy lot was rendered hell by army Chief of Staff Marshal Cadorna, son of Victor Emmanuel II's famous general. His ignorance was relieved only by a superior ability in maltreating his men.

"Cadorna was a seventeenth-century general," Count Sforza has said, "who understood war as nothing more than a gigantic siege operation—those sieges where the soldier was kept at his post by the whip. His lack of ideas was concealed behind a gruff silence, which was interpreted by Italians as strength. . . . But the millions of soldiers at the front knew the truth, paying with their blood to learn it—like the time Cadorna ordered mass executions of his own men, many of whom were shot although they had been home on leave the day their alleged crime had been committed."[3]

Desertions and draft evasion rose steadily, soon numbering almost as much as the combat forces. Part of the Second Army was on strike, and cries of "Down with the War!" and "Long live the revolution!" were being heard in the fighting zone.[4] Yet, not knowing why, in spite of what Cadorna called the propaganda of the "reds" and clerical "blacks," the Italian soldier held out, as bravely as any Austrian, any Bulgar, or any doughboy from the corn fields of Kansas.

Salandra, who had hazarded most on a speedy war, fell within a year. He was followed by a government of apparent unity, headed by the ancient, nondescript Boselli, and when another year had gone by, peace seemed further in the future than in the past. Czarist Russia had gone down forever; the Bolsheviks would soon be in command. Nearly a dozen battles had been fought against the enemy, and the Italians had advanced less than as many miles.

Then, in October, 1917, came Caporetto, the sudden collapse of the Italian front and the worst single military disaster in the nation's history. Eight hundred thousand troops were scattered, wounded, or slain by fifteen German and Austrian divisions. Three hundred thousand Italians were taken prisoner, and 300,000 fled, many never to return. Milan and Venice were in jeopardy. The front was reestablished at the River Piave line one hundred miles to the west, but ancestral memories of invading hordes terrified the nation.

"What caused it all?" Victor Emmanuel asked his diary in an English-language entry.[5] He spoke again of abdication, but Allied insistence on the dismissal of Cadorna, the timely fall of the Boselli government, and the need for a symbol of national unity saved his crown.

Allied confidence in Italy's fighting abilities was shaken. Entirely unjustified charges of cowardice, strengthened by Cadorna's selfish accusations, attached themselves to the Italian uniform, never to be scraped clean. A conference was held at Peschiera on Lake Garda in which the king stood before England's Lloyd George, Marshal Foch of France, and others, seeking to answer his own question about the causes of Caporetto and to defend Italian honor.

The king at Peschiera became a heroic, if short-lived, legend. His new prime minister, Vittorio Emanuele Orlando, a strongminded Sicilian named for the *re galantuomo*, was later to complain bitterly at the way his master at Peschiera was exalted for deeds "one really owes to me!" Privately, however, he had already written, and had apparently forgotten, "It is well that the Italian people know that the humble and anonymous Italian fighting man, who was later to be glorified as the 'Unknown Soldier,' had in his King [at Peschiera] a stirring and tenacious defender, at a time when it was fashionable to blame him for the causes of the military upset."[6]

So great was the myth that Victor Emmanuel years afterward could afford supreme modesty ("Peschiera? What I did? Much exaggerated. . . . It was nothing"),[7] but in fact, according to Lloyd George's memoirs, he made a spirited stand. He did not take refuge in the defeatist propaganda excuse, although he criticized the pacifism of "the priests." Morale was low in the ranks, but this was primarily because, said the king, "the soldiers coming back from leave brought with them the bitterness of knowing that their personal affairs, their everyday lives at home, were going badly because of their absence."[8] His own faith in his army was unassailable. As for Caporetto itself, the fog had rolled in at the wrong time and circumstances favored only the enemy, but there was no denying it, Cadorna was at fault and had to go.

On this final point the Allies had decided to be adamant, but Victor Emmanuel seems to have taken the step before they could make humiliating demands. Someone had suggested that his cousin Emmanuel Philibert, the covetous duke of Aosta, and wartime commander of the Third Army, be given Cadorna's post, to which the king replied, "Let us not undervalue the duke; we could have need of him elsewhere."[9] Apparently Victor Emmanuel III, in the event of a further, unsalvageable defeat, was prepared to give the throne to the hated cadet, in order that the rule of the House of Savoy might survive. Instead he called on Marshal Diaz, a social-climbing Neapolitan of Spanish blood, who was to play a crucial role in assisting Mussolini's rise to power.

Caporetto was also the last victory of the Austro-Hungarian army and the empire. The threat of invasion galvanized the people as never before, and even some socialists were prepared to fight to the last. A few even went to Russia, after the Winter Palace had been taken at Petrograd, to try to persuade Lenin not to withdraw from the war. The revolutionary leader reviled them; he called them "idiots," agents of imperialism and the bourgeoisie, but nothing could convince Italians that they were not now, in defending their homeland, fighting for the best of all causes.

Exactly one year after Caporetto, the Italians crossed the swollen Piave, registering a spectacular advance as the Austrians in ten days of heavy fighting were driven back on every side. On October 30, 1918, Italian troops arriving on horseback, on bicycles, and on foot reached the village of Vittorio Veneto, splitting the Austrian defense in two, a strategic victory which initiated the total rout of the enemy. On November 3, advance units of the Italian army entered "unredeemed" Trent, while the *bersaglieri* and the navy landed at "unredeemed" Trieste.

On November 4, the Austrians surrendered. An armistice was signed. The Allied forces had lent a helping hand, and denigrators among them frowned upon the sword of Rome. They said, and it is still said, that the Great War was over anyway, as the 11th of that month attests. But the victory of Vittorio Veneto and November 4, remembered today as an Italian national holiday, could not be tarnished at home.

The ancient enemy was in the dust, his empire vanished from the earth. The Italians had won a war.

18

"BLOODY CHRISTMAS"

THOUGH THE LITTLE KING, IN LEADING THE
NATION IN UNEQUIVOCAL TRIUMPH, HAD AT
last achieved the ideal of the Risorgimento, the House of Savoy fared
poorly. The war had meant the end of kingship in the grand style,
and the monarchical principle was now a tower in the sand.

Gone were the Romanovs of Great Russia, slain in a Siberian cel-
lar; gone were the venerated Hapsburgs, their empire drawn and
quartered in nationalist bits; gone were the Hohenzollerns, the pompous Kaiser Wilhelm driven out by his Prussian generals; gone too was
even tiny Montenegro, the Petrovich dynasty fallen and dispersed.
In their place stood lowborn federations and republics, shaky re-
gencies, and, most fearsome of them all, dictatorships of the proletariat. The specter which had haunted Europe since 1848 had
drawn the breath of life, and now its flesh and blood cast a shadow
from Moscow to Madrid.

The remaining monarchies, with the exception of the House of
Savoy, were but autumn leaves of their former selves. Even the
innocuous British crown, in a kingdom where republicanism was
believed to have been buried a half-century earlier, came under assault and felt compelled to make unusual concessions to the threat.*
Victor Emmanuel III, with his royal prerogative left intact, could

---

* A measure of how far the children of Victoria had fallen may be seen in the
following two concessions. Immediately after the fall of czarist Russia, mass meetings
were held in Britain, attacking the monarchy and calling for a socialist revolution.
H.G. Wells urged the establishment of a republic, saying that the time had come to do
away with "an alien and uninspiring Court." "I may be uninspiring," King George
V replied angrily, "but I'll be damned if I'm alien." Nevertheless he was advised by
his counselors to show interest in the working classes in order to convince them that
the monarchy is "a living power for good." They also suggested that, in view of
popular anti-German sentiment at home, the king, grandson of Queen Victoria, change

boast of being the most powerful sovereign in Europe, but he dared not remind anyone at home of this. Italian socialism, with Lenin and the October revolution behind it, was emboldened as never before. The elections of 1919, held without Giolittian violence at the polls, returned the Socialist party as the largest in the chamber. When the king and his newest minister, Francesco Nitti, opened the post-electoral parliamentary session, the socialists walked out as Victor Emmanuel began the speech from the throne. He watched in horror as the entire left wing of the hall withdrew shouting, "Long live the socialist republic!"

All the king's triumphs were bitter. He had gone to the Paris peace conference that year with young Humbert,* and had come home with not all the promises of the Pact of London fulfilled, but with 9,000 square miles of additional territory—another Piedmont or another Sardinia. But as the Germans were to have their "November criminals," the Italians would suffer the myth of the "mutilated victory."

High officers swore they would never accept the terms the king's government had signed at Versailles. The pressure of demobilization in a violently contracting postwar economy (1,000 generals and 100,000 lesser officers believed themselves facing discharge) made any kind of peace an ugly thing. War was their business, and the universal character of the Great War had decisively transformed the royal army. From a dynastic institution, which it had been since the time of the *cinquecento* dukes of Savoy, the army had become a nationalist one, with aspirations not always compatible with subordination to the will of the king. For the first time in a hundred years talk was heard of a non-royalist military *coup d'état* being plotted to tend to the nation's problems. Many officers supported D'Annunzio and his "Thousand" in their cruel and mad assault on Fiume; many more were to follow Mussolini.

---

the name of his house (Saxe-Coburg Gotha), as rumor had it that with a name like that he must be, if not alien, at least pro-German. On the first score, George V began visiting industrial areas and mingling with the workers. On the second, after rejecting such names as Wipper, Wettin, and Fitzroy, in 1917 he formally cast aside Saxe-Coburg and Gotha "and all other German degrees, styles, dignitaries, titles, honours and appellations," taking on the "natural English" name of Windsor.[1]

* The government believed that the king's physical stature would adversely affect Italy's position at the talks and its national image in general. Orlando begged the monarch to permit the handsome crown prince, now a tall and imposing fourteen years of age, to accompany him. The offended king replied that it was not his custom to take the boy with him on travels of state, but he eventually yielded to repeated importunities.

The D'Annunzian episode at Fiume, which was to prove so instructive to the future Duce of Fascism, exposed the moldering innards of the Italian state and crown. The poet-soldier had come home from the war, having served bombastically in the army, the navy, and in the young air force as a daredevil pilot. He had lost an eye, but he had gained a rakish patch, and as many gold medals as the law allowed. Even at fifty-six, the threat of a bloodless respite was still too much for him to bear, and he wished, perhaps more than ever, to "set sail to the world."

Fiume, an Italian-speaking port in newly formed Yugoslavia, had been denied to the Rome government at Paris. The city, which lies fifty miles southeast of Trieste and is known today as Rijeka, had not been included in the Pact of London, but the Italians wanted it anyway. Clemenceau told them "to speak of Fiume is to speak of the moon," a phrase which almost rhymes in French, and Woodrow Wilson boldly drew a line, placing the city on the non-Italian side. Rome was willing to argue peaceably, but D'Annunzio raised the cry of "Fiume or death," and conspired with units of the malcontented army to seize and occupy the disputed territory and claim it for the throne of Savoy.

The king, whatever sympathies he might have had echoing his grandfather's secret encouragement of Garibaldi, wanted no public part of D'Annunzio's aggression. Thus a crisis in military discipline developed. D'Annunzio declared himself regent of Fiume, and moved into the governor's palace. He ran the city like a proconsul of imperial Rome, complete with gladiatorial-like spectacles. Adding enduring personal touches, he made speeches from a balcony, dressed his followers in black shirts, and accepted the title *"duce"* bestowed by his admirers, although he preferred to be called simply *"comandante."*

An enthusiastic Mussolini cried that the nation's capital was in Fiume not Rome, and cashiered officers, runaway schoolboys, adventurers, and thieves by the hundreds rushed to the *comandante*'s side. They called themselves "legionnaires," and with stolen guns and race hatred they hoped to spur the vaunted cause of making *slaves* of the *Slavs*—D'Annunzio's words, unlike the poetaster Clemenceau's, rhymed perfectly in Italian. The army lent its fire power to D'Annunzio's occupation, and eventually the Nitti government, while publicly deploring the affair, gave aid to the poet, hoping to strengthen its position at the bargaining table with the Allies.

The king, his nature repulsed by all flamboyant escapades, tried to ignore D'Annunzio. He hoped the matter, if not the man, would die of natural causes, but D'Annunzio's bravado captured the public imagination. The duke and duchess of Aosta, watching the sovereign's star grow dim at every point, believed again their time was approaching. Victor Emmanuel, apparently defied by the army and rendered politically old-fashioned by the postwar world, was rumored to be "packing his bags." Some people were saying that "the republic is in the air," and the Aosta *camarilla* tried to preempt such an eventuality by plotting with the pro-D'Annunzian elements of the army for a salutary change of faces on the throne.[2]

Nitti, still loyal to his master, warned Victor Emmanuel of reports he had been receiving about the duke and duchess. He later wrote of this affair:

> The behavior of the duke and duchess of Aosta was not very reassuring, especially that of the duchess, who not only talked too much, but acted too much . . . giving rise to the formation of a strong movement against the King. . . . the King often spoke of this to me, with more distrust than worry. The duke went continually to the border zone with no proper motive, and not a few rumors were spread that Italy had need of a warrior King.
>
> The insulting manner in which this was put was: "We don't want a photographer King, we want a soldier King." The inference to be made was simple enough: The duke of Aosta styled himself as a war lord, while the King, too serious and modest to satisfy the tastes of adventurers, was presented as a photographer.
>
> The duchess of Aosta, a spirited intriguer, full of vanity, was no friend of the King and above all the Queen, whom she sought to ridicule on every occasion (*ma cousine la bergère* was the characterization she had spread). The duchess committed gross enormities, such as the ridiculous comedy of her going to Fiume to weep at the grave of a so-called legionnaire who had been killed.[3]

This last gesture infuriated Victor Emmanuel. He asked Nitti to place the duke and duchess under constant surveillance, and said he wished to be informed of all their movements. But Nitti, too, was losing confidence in the durability of the crown. He was halfhearted in attempting to control the Aostas, and he failed to tame D'Annunzio. Neither was he able to deal with the more prosaic problems of the *dopoguerra*, which saw the lire fall from five to the dollar in 1914 to 28.50 in 1920. Every class and party turned against him, and in June, 1920, unable to govern, Nitti grudgingly withdrew.

A southern economist of good intentions and bad judgments, he is remembered with bitterness by the House of Savoy for having taken a fatal step toward dismantling the monarchy.[4] During his ministry he had convinced his already extraordinarily frugal master to set an example to the nation of the need for austerity by surrendering crown properties and wealth to the state. In this way the royal palaces in Milan, Venice, Genoa, Florence, Naples, Caserta, and Palermo, Humbert's and Margherita's beloved villas at Monza and Capodimonte, and other Savoyard real estate were consigned to the national treasury. In addition the king had been induced to make a voluntary cut of the expenditures of the royal house, reducing the civil list by 20 percent, or some three million lire. The funds from income-producing properties, the king decreed, were to go to war veterans' charities.

These measures, which provided for the conversion of the palaces and lands into parks, museums, and libraries, undoubtedly represented the greatest gifts ever given to the Italians by the House of Savoy. Such largess, however, was to bring permanent and inestimable damage to the monarchy. The Aosta couple succeeded with guile and deception in taking hold of the Capodimonte palace, which had been destined to become a public park, and the maintenance funds budgeted for the project were used to finance the duke's continuing intrigues.

Worse, the king was thrown into chronic straitened circumstances, which necessitated increasing economies over the ensuing inflationary years. Victor Emmanuel was apparently too proud or too timid to ask his future ministers, particularly Mussolini, for financial assistance, and whereas in the past he had reduced court functions out of a sense of propriety, now of necessity such affairs all but ceased. The court balls, the yearly carnival, and all the remaining bright lights of the old Humbertine gaiety went out one by one and forever. Worse still, even the royal suppers and galas for the diplomatic corps, the armed forces, and the members of parliament—rituals meant to give visibility to the venerable powers inherent in the crown—had to be dispensed with. Little regality remained, and the king looked littler still. Those who search for telltale moments, mark the disposal of the king's wealth as a sign that the final lowering had begun.

Feeling himself sinking in the thick brought on by the war, the king admitted his error in having led the nation into battle by turning to the man of peace, the apparently immortal Giolitti.

He had not seen Giolitti in five years, not since the slaying of the 650,000, and when he received him, the near-eighty Piedmontese is said to have looked coldly at his master, reprimanding him humor-lessly, "It's not my face that's red."[5]

Giolitti's devotion had not waned, but he was capable of punish-ing ingratitude. Italy, he said now, must never again be taken to war by the will of a single man, even the sovereign, and he proposed the repeal of the royal prerogative, Article 5 of the Savoyard constitution. Only like the stage-prop kings of England could Victor Emmanuel and his heirs henceforth expect to survive, in Giolitti's new view. The *re galantuomo* surely rolled in his grave, but the desperate little king empowered Giolitti, trusting in goodness for what the future might bring.

Giolitti had outlined his new program in a speech at Dronero in Piedmont and had gained therefrom his latest epithet, "the fox of Dronero." But the old craftiness, however undiminished by age, sim-ply no longer worked. Article 5 was not repealed (fortunately so, for the king when all else would be taken from him was to make one last good use of this power against Mussolini), and Giolitti's postwar ministry was a frightful failure. His only success and his final service to the crown, was his speedy dispatch of D'Annunzio.

Giolitti, we have seen, had good reason to despise D'Annunzio, and the pitting of one against the other was a clash of antitheses. Giolitti deplored the occupation of Fiume for what it had done to military discipline, "encouraging soldiers to pay less regard to their oath [to the king] and their duty."[6] D'Annunzio, for his part, had come to identify "sorrowful Italy" with Giolitti.

In November, 1920, Giolitti signed the Treaty of Rapallo with Belgrade, renouncing Italian claims on Slavic Dalmatia, and provid-ing for Fiume as a free city. The self-styled regent of Fiume, while pretending to be the new Garibaldi, did not obey his Victor Emman-uel. His "state," he said, would not recognize the treaty. It seemed like a farce, but the king's government saw no humor when Italian Admiral Millo, military governor of Dalmatia, was unable to dif-ferentiate whether his loyalties belonged to Victor Emmanuel or D'Annunzio. Millo, who was suffering from syphilis of the spinal cord, had publicly given his word of honor that his troops would not be withdrawn from Dalmatia and that he would never abandon the *comandante*.

Giolitti tried to reason with both D'Annunzio and Millo. Millo ad-mitted his regrets at the trouble he had caused but he knew of no honorable way out.

To what extent the confusion of roles had developed can be seen in the record of what next occurred between the prime minister and the admiral, and in the subsequent reaction of the king himself. Each of these men had become, growing old in Savoyard Italy, a burlesque of the titles they bore.

Millo, following the signing of the treaty, had returned from his Dalmatian headquarters at Zara to articulate his dilemma to the prime minister and the question as to which oath he owed priority to was discussed as follows:

> Giolitti: To whom did you swear first?
> Millo: To the king.
> Giolitti: All right, then. Since it is the first swearing that counts, if the king were to ask you to leave Zara, you should obey him, shouldn't you?
> Millo: Yes. You see to it that I get such an order from the king.[7]

The king, of course, in whose name the Treaty of Rapallo had been signed, had already given the order, and it was this which was being disobeyed, destroying forever the feudal-like servitude which the army until World War I had given the House of Savoy. King Charles Felix in 1821 had known how to treat the mutinous officers at Turin, but the little king, knowing that the admiral supported the duke of Aosta's intrigues, feared for his crown. When Foreign Minister Sforza rushed to the Villa Savoia for the royal signature on an order personally drawn up to ease Millo's conscience, the king quite rightly demurred, wondering aloud what would happen "if I am not obeyed."[8]

Sforza advanced several arguments, and the king, as he was wont to do under pressure, gave in and signed. The tabetic admiral, on receiving the order, "burst into tears," says Sforza, "and some months later he thanked me for having saved him from dishonor."[9]

Millo renounced his support of D'Annunzio, and by now all but the die-hard legionnaires, giving up the lost cause, were going home; the smell of blood had shifted to the nascent Fascist movement, and many headed there. But D'Annunzio would not be moved. He threatened a "march on Rome." He held a rigged plebiscite to show the world the popular will, but astonishingly, the Fiumians somehow managed to vote against his rule. The beleaguered port city was being ruined by D'Annunzio's profligacy, and the people, suffering economically more than anything else, prayed he would go away. D'Annunzio, however, announced that the fraudulent plebiscite was fraudulent, and in a final act of lunacy declared war on Italy.

Now Giolitti sent the *comandante* a last warning. Referring to D'Annunzio's most celebrated mistress, the prime minister exhorted: "Tell D'Annunzio that Italy is not Madame Eleanora Duse."[10] Giolitti, obtaining assurances from military and political men who had previously backed or sympathized with the Fiumian escapade that D'Annunzio could not possibly win his war on Italy, sent the fleet in December, 1920, to run the poet out.

Italians called the routing "bloody Christmas," but D'Annunzio was no Custer. The navy's *Andrea Doria* showed its guns in Fiume harbor, fired once or twice on the governor's palace, and D'Annunzio surrendered. Nitti later observed that D'Annunzio "treated Fiume like his lovers, whom he abandoned after exploiting and exhausting them."[11] In any event the *enfant terrible* had been subdued. He came home smiling and rich. He bought a mansion on Lake Garda, decorated it with obscene paintings, and fell out of a window making love, some say, to the chambermaid.* Seriously injured, and apparently having given up his military career, D'Annunzio was made prince of Montenevoso by the king, which in signifying the poet's reentry into the establishment, helped stabilize Italy's eastern frontier.

That the royal army and navy had carried out the order to oust D'Annunzio from Fiume was taken with relief and as an uplifting surprise by the king. The old discipline was never to be restored, and social unrest would grow worse than ever, but Victor Emmanuel at the start of the new year, 1921, felt strengthened by the return of Giolitti.

When the duke of Aosta, foiled by "bloody Christmas," came to him that winter under cover of familial advice with his latest scheme, the king could take pleasure in frustrating his desperate cousin. The duke, on the insistence of the duchess, it seems, now proposed a "Hungarian" solution to Italy's postwar woes. He asked Victor Emmanuel to dissolve all political parties, install a military government, and call upon him to serve as regent. In this way, said the duke, he would bring order to Italy, as Admiral Horthy had done in ousting Bela Kun's communist regime in Budapest. Such a happy turn of events, in the cadet's opinion, would fortify the monarchy and raise high the foundering House of Savoy.

Victor Emmanuel saw through the plot: If such a coup were to succeed, a regency, in his cousin's power, would no doubt be only a halfway seat to the throne; were the attempt to fail, responsibility

---

* There are other accounts of this still more or less unexplained event. These include his being defenestrated by some Fascist thugs, and a suicide attempt.[12]

would fall to the king, and the only possibility of saving the monarchy would be in Victor Emmanuel's abdication in favor—if the plotters were to play their game well—of the duke of Aosta.

The little king sent his cousin home to Hélène of France to try once more, and delighted in telling the tale, at least when he related it to his former minister Nitti.

"The king was laughing as he recounted what the duke had said," Nitti later wrote, "and he told me that even if he were to consider such a reactionary idea, and he had not given it a thought, he would never turn to his cousin."[13]

No doubt it was most amusing at the time. But sober thought of reaction continued to grow very appealing to the king. Never, to be sure, would he turn to the duke and his Hungarian fantasies. Victor Emmanuel's man, history had deemed, was Mussolini.

19

"A NEW WAVE...
OF SAINT-JUSTS"

BY THE END OF THE YEAR THE COMEDY WAS THREADBARE AND THE PILEOUS CLOAK OF TRAGedy was shrouding round. All the elements favoring the investiture of brute reaction with brutish state power were present now, save one: the consent of the little king.

The war had impoverished the poor and enriched the rich, making have-nothings of the have-nots and have-alls of their betters. In industry and banking, many who had fought for the war, as opposed to those who had fought *in* it, had been rewarded beyond the normal confines of imagination.* Some other sectors of the economy, however, had fared badly and failed. The net result was that already highly concentrated and interlocking Italian capitalism came home from the war as giants. "The great trusts," writes historian Procacci, ". . . and the great banks which they controlled . . . had carved out entire provinces of the national economy, to the extent that a liberal economist, Riccardo Bachi, could write in 1919 that the Italian economy was dominated by a 'restricted club whose members were a few big financiers and a few big industrialists.' They were now the authentic baronage with whom the State was forced to negotiate every single day."[2]

The aggrandizement of this class brought with it a new set of problems, denying the new aristocrats their expected due. The war-expanded industry in the peace-contracted economy made the labor

---

* The industrialists who had backed Mussolini's war-calling *Popolo d'Italia* provide a striking illustration: The capital assets of Ansaldo steel and munitions, for example, rose in the two years prior to 1918 from 30 million to 500 million lire; Fiat went from 17 million in 1914 to 200 million in 1919.[1]

force buckle, casting hundreds of thousands among the unemployed, and joblessness rose above 10 percent, which seems to the point where revolutions begin to ferment. But the revolutionaries, for all their half-million strikers and "people's shock-troops," were for whatever reasons simply inept in fulfilling their Marxian-assigned "historic role." They succeeded only in stirring up the venom and the bloodlust of the right. Italy had no Lenin, or Russia had no Mussolini, and so they were bloodied and destroyed by the things they wished to overthrow.

In such circumstances, misfortune and coincidence arranged a fateful encounter. Sorel had predicted that Mussolini was "no ordinary socialist," that he was a *condottiero* who would turn to the right, and on March 23, 1919, the prophecy came true. Mussolini, who adored Sorelian violence and syndicalism, gathered about 150 similarly malcontented souls on that day in a Milan meeting hall in Piazza San Sepolcro, owned by a man who liked to lend his premises to patriots and veterans.

No one, as the organizer later admitted, really knew why the meeting was being held, but Mussolini underscored the pressing need for continuing against the enemy at home the great war Italy had fought against those declared the enemies abroad.* This seemed a righteous, patriotic aim, and the small assembly more or less assented to the formation of a political action group, which, in reviving the structure of an older Mussolinian scheme, was called the *Fascio di combattimento.*** From the start the new movement was violent and anti-Bolshevik, declaring "war on socialism."[3] As unemployed civilians were drawn to the socialists, unemployed soldiers found some of life's meanings in Mussolini's *fasci*. Before long there were *fasci* in many towns. By the end of 1919 there were thirty-one *fasci* with 870 members; by the end of 1920, there were eighty-eight *fasci* and more than 20,000 members, and at the end of 1921, there were ten times as many *fasci* and ten times as many members as the year before. Many of them had conserved the black shirts and sidearms they had worn at Fiume; all of them proudly called themselves *Fascisti*.

The movement went well. The first duty of every Fascist, if we are to judge by what was done, and not what was said, required him to

---

* In his article on fascism in the *Enciclopedia italiana* (1932), Mussolini wrote: ". . . I had no specific doctrinal plan in my mind. My doctrine was the doctrine of action. . . . Fascism was born of a need for action and was action. . . ."

** The group was analogous, in name only, to the Sicilian *fasci* of the 1890s, and had no conscious connection with the later to be vaunted fasces, power symbol of ancient Rome.

break an industrial or agricultural strike, or to kill a "communist," or both. For this purpose "action squads" were formed around local toughs and agitators (Balbo in Ferrara, Farinacci in Cremona, Grandi in Bologna), and the *squadristi* undertook the gory task of carrying out "punitive expeditions" against all those who offended law and order. Thus in the two-year period preceding Mussolini's "March on Rome" in October, 1922, an estimated 3,500 persons were slain. The true figures will never be known, but the above appears reasonable enough judging from the king's own scratch pads, on which he notes only the incidents attracting his attention and records in an "ordinary" month in 1921 about thirty dead and 200 injured.[*4]

The more the Fascists took law and order into their own hands, the more support they received from the authorities and all those who found something to lose or something to hate in the socialist protestations. This at first appears surprising, for people knew no less then than now of the risks in delegating the functions of state institutions to vigilantes. But Mussolini had declared that fascism was merely a "temporary" expedient, and in view of the revolutionary threat and the living Bolshevik state behind it, many who believed themselves democrats at heart were grateful for some temporary relief and assistance.

Sad to say, almost everyone but the victims wished the Fascists well. "The success of the punitive expeditions and the Fascist raids," writes Procacci, "would not have been possible without the *omertà* and, at times, the complicity of the army and the Executive."[6]

Renzo De Felice, Mussolini's latest and most thorough biographer, provides evidence explaining the collusion between the authorities and the Fascists. The reason for the immunity from the law enjoyed by the Fascists, he says, was the "vast sympathy" they had among the rank and file of the public force. This sympathy resulted from "a public opinion which in wide measure sided with them [the Fascists], a magistrature which very often favored them, an army which also frequently sided with the Fascists . . . and in some areas furnished them with weapons and supplies, and finally a central authority which found many difficulties in intervening effectively. . . ."[7]

Some of these difficulties were self-imposed; others were suggested

---

[*] A better indicator perhaps, is a police report on "cases of violence" between Fascists and socialists recorded throughout Italy on a single day, May 8, 1921. The number of such clashes which took place in the sixty-nine cities and towns supplying data totaled 1,073, resulting in 1,817 arrests, of which 1,421 were of persons called socialists and 396 Fascists. The king's calendar, incidentally, records "grave conflicts" on May 8 in a place not even mentioned in the police report.[5]

by the conspicuous struggles of the new baronage against subversion and disorder.

"We did not want a dictatorship," a big industrialist was later to say. "We simply wanted Mussolini, once in power, to restore order and tranquility to the land. After that, we would go back to the old system."[8]

No doubt this was true in some cases, just as there were other Italians who wished bodily harm to every worker yearning for a decent wage. Another group, with Prime Minister Giolitti in the forefront, hoped to use the Fascists to their own gain, and in any case expected that time and *trasformismo* would render them respectable. Giolitti believed fascism "one of the most common phenomena in history." He explained:

> After violent agitations (and what was more violent than the last war?), comes a new wave of very young Saint-Justs, Napoleons, Hoches, and thousands of unknowns. Then the true values reassert themselves and remain in the front ranks, the others disappear, and the world picks up its normal rhythm.[9]

This is the philosophy of Dr. Pangloss. It was the balm rubbed on the conscience of the government, the army, the courts, the owning class, the Vatican, and many an average man. From this derives the comfortable myth that no one knew what fascism was at the outset. But the truth was that it was never anything less than the old-time mace and grapeshot. There never was a moment when fascism did not brandish them against the vital parts of an uppity lower class so that the Old Pyramidal Order might survive another day, another week, another generation.

The year 1921, all who study Italy agree, was decisive for fascism. In January socialism was broken. The communist wing of the Socialist party, intoxicated with self-righteousness, split away from the Turatian right and the "maximalist" center, and founded a party of their own: "the Communist party of Italy, a section of the Third International."*

---

* It is commonplace to regard this event as signaling Moscow's domination of Italian communism. This actually came much later, under Stalin and Togliatti. For now, in view of the Fascist counteroffensive, Lenin energetically disapproved the new party's intransigence toward the socialists. But the Italians, being more-communist-than-thou, had been concerned with little more than exposing the "true" reactionary nature of their former comrades. Further, they argued that the support of a majority was unnecessary, and when Umberto Terracini, the Italian delegate to a meeting of the Comintern in July, 1921, put forward these ideas, Lenin attacked him: "Whoever

In May, Giolitti, hoping to capture the Fascists in the parliamentary net and use them against his opponents, allied with Mussolini. He called elections, campaigned with the future Duce and his *squadristi*, and won thirty-five seats for the Fascists—the one farthest to the right of the chamber has taken by Mussolini.

Giolitti's plan went awry, however, and the following month, when the Fascists and others turned against him, he resigned. His retreat made empty political space for the Fascists to fill, and the new minister, Milquetoastish Ivanhoe Bonomi, could do nothing to stand in their way.

In November, meeting in Rome, the Fascists constituted them-selves as a national political party. Their victories, however, did noth-ing to satisfy their blood lust. By now, under the leadership of Balbo and others, and with the support of the army, their activities had assumed a truly military character. Equipped with the latest weap-ons, including in some cases armored vehicles and, incredibly, artil-lery in the 75 mm. range, they advanced without respite.

The socialists, communists, and trade unionists continued to fight. But it was a losing battle now. The number of strikers fell by nearly 80 percent compared with the preceding year. Fearing for their lives and their jobs, the workers gave up their demands and took sharp cuts in pay instead.

The pope would not lend his support to fascism until later, and D'Annunzio, too jealous of Mussolini to be logical, was as yet defin-ing fascism as "slaveism," invoking his poetic license to call on an awkward, nonexistent word for the sake of meter and rhyme ("*fas-cismo/schiavismo*"). But these were marginal men in this instance, and while appeals were being made for the pope's and the poet's blessings, everyone looked to the king with whom the heavenly and earthly bonds of state power resided.

To be sure, Victor Emmanuel since the war was no longer undis-puted master of all power allegiances, but the mystique of the oath still bound the army to his name. Soldiers and generals, the unruly,

---

does not yet know . . . that we have to win the majority of the working class, is lost to the communist movement, and will never learn anything . . . Here we are at the Third Congress and Comrade Terracini still continues to repeat as before that the problem . . . consists of unmasking the centrists and the semicentrists. Thank you very much! But we have already had enough of this matter." The young Antonio Gramsci, among the founders of the Italian party, saw immediately the gross futility of the split and was first to admit how the party's doctrinaire position was a major factor contributing to Mussolini's rise to power.[10]

syphilitic, or the otherwise disturbed, had strayed with D'Annunzio, as we have seen, and obviously even more of them admired and aided the Fascists. Nevertheless no one imagined that the *entire* army and public force could be swayed; it was the House of Savoy which had to be won.

Later the king would appear to the readers and writers of news magazines and shallow histories as the mere tail on the Fascist carnivore. Mussolini and his party were wiser. Mussolini, writes De Felice, "knew well that in the last analysis the attitude of the sovereign would decide the fate of fascism . . . above all because in terms of the simple arithmetic of politics and power the king meant the army, and against the army the possibility of a Fascist military success was nil."[11] Another Italian of the contemporary thorough-reappraisal school, Antonino Repaci, observes that "the Monarchy was certainly the most serious problem Mussolini had to confront and resolve."[12] And De Felice again, speaking of the Fascist march on Rome which brought Mussolini to power:

> The extent of Victor Emmanuel III's responsibility in the crisis of October 1922 is arguable; it is undeniable, however, that in that crisis the king was a protagonist no less important than Mussolini and certainly more important than all the other *dramatis personae*.[13]

United Italy, in the turn of six decades, was coming full circle. Whereas the red-shirted plebe Garibaldi had surrendered Italy to Victor Emmanuel II, Victor Emmanuel III was now to be asked to give it back to the black-shirted son of a village smith, Mussolini.

20

VICTOR AND BENITO

THE LITTLE KING FIRST HEARD THE NAME MUS-
SOLINI IN 1912, WHEN THE UNSHAVED RADICAL
gained notoriety by publicly characterizing the sovereign as "by definition a useless citizen." In November, 1915, on one of his interminable
tours of the war zone, the king first saw the man himself.

Corporal Mussolini, now the maverick socialist editor who had
gone off to partake in the war he had so vociferously demanded,
had come down with a fever, and the king said a few friendly words
at his bedside to cheer him. In March, 1917, the king saw him again
in a field hospital. On this second occasion, Sergeant Mussolini was
recovering from an injury he had received while being trained to
operate a small caliber artillery weapon. He had been leaning too
close when a shell misfired, and he was cut and burned on the face
and parts of his body. This had earned him a promotion and another
good word from the sovereign whom he had so often reviled.

The Fascist mythmakers, finding all sorts of heroic fictions to explain the "combat origins" of Mussolini's wounds,* were later to entirely forget the first encounter between sovereign and Duce, and
make of the second a modern revival of the meeting at Teano between
the *re galantuomo* and Garibaldi. The old script, however (see above,
p. 34), required a slight alteration:

> The king: Greetings, my dear Mussolini. How are you?
> Mussolini: Not very well, Your Majesty . . .

---

* Mussolini himself made a contribution in his celebrated talks with Emil Ludwig
in 1932. "Is it true," asked Ludwig, "that when they operated on you, you refused
the chloroform?" To which the Duce, nodding a modest yes, replied, "I wanted to
see what the doctors were doing."[1]

Their first serious meeting on relatively level ground took place at the Quirinal on June 30, 1921. Mussolini had been elected to parliament in May, Giolitti had resigned, and the king was engaged in routine consultations with party leaders prior to designating a new minister.

Monarchist sympathies ran high in the Fascist ranks, but Mussolini was still known for his republican sentiments. Summoned to the palace, Mussolini, in tails and white spats, climbed the Quirinal hill, hoping to make a good impression. He told the king that the masses must not be allowed to govern and that only the ruling classes could and should exercise state power.[2] The king was unimpressed. He did not like Fascists then. Bartoli explains the sovereign's attitude at the time:

> Victor Emmanuel had been observing them for quite a while. He had been pleased at first seeing the men of the extreme left humiliated and contained; then he grew preoccupied and anxious. He had no sympathy for Mussolini, a talented adventurer unfaithful to his plebeian origins. The king's personal tastes inclined him toward simpler men, well-prepared, serious, bourgeois. . . . He was a soldier but he did not like their ostentatious uniforms, their military grades, their irregular hierarchies, and he looked on them as civilians dressed as soldiers.[3]

No particular significance ought to be given that first of many hundred royal audiences. Each man afterward went his separate way until, to the misfortune of the multitudes and themselves, they were brought so durably together again.

Nevertheless, it marks a clear beginning to that long, unsung relationship between the two men, a unity of opposites which has, as will be seen, so many of the features of a domestic marriage. No man in Italy, in spite of strut and braggadocio, was to be more awed of the little king than the blacksmith's son. No prince of Savoy ever bathed the feet of the poor with the humility and affection Victor Emmanuel was to find in his prunelike soul and give to Mussolini.

De Felice writes:

> Despite the differences [in their personalities] Victor Emmanuel and Mussolini were obviously made for one another, for notwithstanding the crises and conflicts, notwithstanding Mussolini's fundamental anti-monarchism and the influences of their respective clans, the personal relations between the two men, for more than twenty years, were to be characterized by a reciprocal esteem and respect, even if sometimes spotted with a mutual sense of the other's inferiority. With regard to

Victor Emmanuel, it is not without significance that as late as June 18, 1943, when the situation was dramatically clear, and he was on the threshold of the *coup d'état*, the king, speaking of Mussolini to his adjutant, would observe, "All the same, that man's got a great head!"*⁴

Now, of course, there was no real relationship between them; the two men knew relatively little about one another. Mussolini's knowledge of the king and his history was derived from less-than-disinterested schoolbooks, educated but conflicting hearsay, and fawning or flailing newspaper cuttings. Victor Emmanuel's acquaintance with the sort of man Mussolini was came for the most part from police intelligence. The innumerable biographies of varying authenticity recounting the difficult steps which brought Mussolini from working class obscurity to world reknown were yet to be written. What exactly Victor Emmanuel knew prior to the "March on Rome" of the man to whom he was to yield so much of himself and others would therefore be of considerable interest. Fortunately an approximation is now possible with the recent availability of a famous, but secret, government document known as the "Gasti report."[6]

Giovanni Gasti, inspector general of the public security forces, was a Holmesian policeman with a sense of human behavior which in Mussolini's case was to prove uncanny. In April, 1919, with more than twenty-five years of police and detective work behind him, he was promoted acting chief of police of Milan, a title he secured some months later with his comprehensive investigation of Mussolini and the new *fascio di combattimento*. The results of this undertaking were transmitted by him directly to the prime minister.

His top-secret report, often referred to (usually as "explosive"), but rarely seen, was taken as the fundamental study of the movement and its leader by at least three of the last five of the king's pre-Mussolini prime ministers: Orlando, Nitti, and Giolitti.[7] It is not known whether Victor Emmanuel actually read the 7,500-word report, but his interest in fascism and Mussolini was more serious than that of his ministers, and in any event the information provided to him was taken from this primary document.

* Years later, with the Duce dead, hung, and buried, Victor Emmanuel would repeat the remark with some elaboration revealing a more complex, but substantially unchanged view of the man. Opening his hands in an exaggerated gesture of size, he said, "Mussolini had a head like this. But he was ignorant, a beast."[5] As for Mussolini, it will be seen how he often privately raged against the king, but always folded in spine-curved veneration in his presence. Following his arrest in 1943 by Victor Emmanuel, the Duce would wish "crowning success" to the new government of "His Majesty the King, to whom for twenty-one years I have been a loyal servant, and so will I remain. . . ." (See below, p. 340).

Dated June 4, 1919, the report is divided into two main sections, one of which deals with the founding meeting of the Fascist movement, held a little more than two months earlier, while most of the second part is devoted to Mussolini. There was nothing very new even then in the first part, but the latter contained fascinating, original material, analytical insights which were often prophetic, and a few diabolical suggestions. It therefore seems relevant to our story to examine the second part of this document at length. It begins:

Biographical Notes (Mussolini)

Prof. Benito Mussolini, son of Alessandro, born at Predappio (Forlí) 7/29/1883, residing in Milan at 38 Foro Bonaparte, is a socialist revolutionary with a police record, and an elementary school teacher licensed also to teach in secondary schools. He was formerly first secretary of the Chambers of Labor at Cesena, Forlí, and Ravenna, and later, from 1912, Director of the newspaper *Avanti!*, in whose columns he took violent, suggestive, and intransigent positions.

The report goes on to summarize more or less objectively the events in Mussolini's life which we have already encountered, including his expulsion from the Socialist party, the establishment of his interventionist newspaper, and his brief wartime military career. It continues:

On December 25, 1915, at Treviglio, he married a woman from his home province, Rachele Guidi, with whom he had already had a child —Edda—procreated at Forlí in 1910. He also had a lover, a Trentinian named Ida Irene Dalser . . . Miss Dalser worked at the newspaper *Popolo d'Italia* and had intimate relations with Mussolini. A child was born on 11/11/1915, Benito Albino Dalser, and he was later legally acknowledged by Mussolini . . . .

A detailed account follows of this strange woman who was later to die in a mental hospital, as, still later, was the son she had with Mussolini. Abandoned by Mussolini, says the police inspector, she sought revenge, and eventually, as a result of her harrassment of Mussolini and his family, she was expelled from Milan and the province by the police as a public menace. She continued to seek revenge, however, accusing her former lover of having betrayed Italy prior to World War I by selling himself to France, and she told of a meeting in Geneva between him and a former French prime minister in which a million lire was alleged to have been paid to Mussolini to promote Italian interventionism.

This had led Gasti to investigate these claims. He confirmed that such a meeting had taken place, although he failed to learn what had actually occurred. However, he reported that it was common knowledge that Mussolini had received funds from France via Switzerland for the publication of *Popolo d'Italia*, and that he had also been subsidized by the Pirelli and Ansaldo firms.

Gasti did not possess the documentary proof of this, he said, but the circumstantial evidence was abundant, and he made much of the fact that Mussolini, fired unexpectedly from his editorship of *Avanti!* "without any money, suddenly had large sums of capital constantly at his disposal." Gasti goes on to say:

> It is enough to state that none of his collaborators, all of whom are well paid, and none of his followers, has ever gone to him in vain for financial help; that he has a luxurious apartment in Foro Bonaparte; that he lunches and dines constantly in first-class restaurants; that he goes about in automobiles and taxis; that he has a press secretary; and that . . . he maintains as a bodyguard for himself and the safety of the editorial offices of *Popolo d'Italia* a squad of 25 *arditi*, each of whom are paid fifteen lire a day, amounting to a daily expense of L.375. . . .

Gasti now paints this penetrating portrait of his man:

Physio-psychological Notes

Benito Mussolini has a strong physical constitution, although he has syphilis.

His energy permits him to work continuously.

He sleeps until a late hour of the morning, leaves his house at noon, and does not return until 3 o'clock the following morning. These fifteen hours, less a brief pause for meals, are devoted to his journalistic and political activities.

He is a sensualist, and that is demonstrated by his various relations with women, most notably those with the above-indicated Miss Guidi and Miss Dalser.

He is emotional and impulsive, and these traits render him suggestive and persuasive in his public speeches, although, while being a good speaker, he cannot be said to be an orator.

He is at heart a sentimentalist and as a result he attracts a great deal of sympathy and friends.

He is disinterested and lavish with the money he manages, and this has given him a reputation as being altruistic and philanthropic.

He is very intelligent, perceptive, self-controlled, responsive, a good judge of men and their qualities and weaknesses.

Facile and ready with his likes and dislikes, capable of sacrifice for his friends, he is tenacious in his enmities and his hatred.

He is courageous and audacious; has organizing ability, is able to make quick decisions, but is not tenacious in his convictions and objectives.

He is very ambitious. He is motivated by the conviction that he represents an important force in Italy's destiny and is decided upon making himself count. He is a man who is not content with a second place. He wants to be first and to dominate. . . .

This, according to my investigations, is the moral picture of the man. It contrasts with the opinions of his old comrades-in-faith, and the inner circles of the parties of order, which consider him a sellout, corrupt, and corruptible; and—contrasts with others who consider him firmly welded to his socialist principles of previous times.

How, Gasti implicitly inquired, should this high-tension, seething power be handled? And what in any case might one expect his fate to be?

If a person of high authority and intelligence were to find in his [Mussolini's] psychological make-up the *punctum minoris resistentiae*; if above all such a person were to be congenial to him and subtly infuse himself into his mind without initially opposing his political dreams and expectations; if he were to demonstrate to him what Italy's true interests are (for I believe him patriotic); if, with great tact, showing respect for his personal convictions and tactics, he were to offer him in the interest of a meaningful collaboration the necessary base for a cooperative political action in a way in which this intention would not appear as his capitulation or domestication—either of which would be offensive—Mussolini, little by little, would allow himself to be won.

But, given his temperament, no one will ever be able to guarantee with certainty that as a result of changed conditions and men, he will not suddenly defect. He is, as I said, emotional and impulsive. Nevertheless his collaboration, even if only temporary, could be very useful because of his influence. . . .

Of late (mid-May), he was [but seems to be somewhat less so now] of the opinion that it was expedient to support the Orlando Government and especially the Prime Minister, because a ministerial crisis could compromise the highest institutions. . . .

On the adverse side, it is certain that Mussolini, a man of thought and action, an effective and incisive writer, a persuasive and lively speaker, could become a *condottiero*, a fearsome ringleader.*

* The inspector concluded with a few final farseeing words about the Fascists. Relating widespread but unconfirmed police reports of Fascist plans to overthrow the government and that the movement favored the abdication of the king and a regency of the duke of Aosta, he warned that "these rumors . . . may very well be the expression or the preparatory coefficients of a national mood and the collective state of mind."

Gasti continued to supply the Rome government with intelligence, making the surveillance of fascism and Mussolini his specialty and primary activity. Never did he find anything to alter his original report, and all his facts were later corroborated, all his opinions remarkably justified.

It cannot then be said truthfully, it seems, that Rome and the king were ignorant or misled as to whom and with what they were dealing. Victor Emmanuel, it must be concluded, was more than anyone else advised that fascism was the gang-land antithesis of liberalism and that Mussolini was an unstable renegade suffering from a venereal disease which in its third stage attacks the nervous system and often leads to an insanity accompanied by delusions of grandeur.*

Such were among the several considerations which weighed on the House of Savoy when the ruffian marchers on Rome began to thump on the palace door.

The little king began to pay serious attention to the aspirations of the Fascists toward the end of August, 1922. His first reaction was to oppose them.

Earlier in the month the enfeebled socialists and the worker's movement had been dealt their death blow when a desperation general strike was assailed by Fascist guns and clubs. Mussolini, posing as the sole defender of the state, had unleashed a "column of fire" against the strikers, lighting the nighttime summer sky. Even the black-shirted Italo Balbo was moved to write in his diary:

> It was a terrifying night. Our passage was signaled with high columns of fire and smoke. The entire Romagnan plain all the way to the hills was subjected to the furious reprisals of the Fascists, who were decided once and for all to put an end to the red terror.[9]

The king, the government, and the people had sat as spectators in a Circus Maximus of unprecedented violence, as Mussolini and his *squadristi* gave the "antinationals" forty-eight hours to back down. Confused and isolated, the strikers yielded, but the Fascists advanced all the same, killing and maiming with teeth-gnashing hatred,

---

* In Mussolini's case the disease was apparently arrested before the onset of its worst effects, although this could not have been known in 1922. In 1926, as Duce, he fell seriously ill as a result of gastric ulcers, and rumors spread that his condition was due to syphilis. On hearing of what was being said, he subjected himself with some apprehension to a Wassermann test, which is said to have proved negative. This seems to have been later confirmed, leaving little ground for reports that he continued to deteriorate from this disease.[8]

seizing and wrecking all that stood in their way, and crying for law and order.

The Bonomi government had fallen. The king still hoped that Giolitti had some unused or reusable miracles in his frock coat, but the new distribution of parliamentary power allowed Mussolini and all who believed themselves profiting to check Giolitti's return. Victor Emmanuel had to install a stopgap ministry instead, headed by Luigi Facta, a back-country lawyer whose only qualification for the high office was that he had a political weight of zero.

When at the end of August the first rumors of a Fascist "march on Rome" began to circulate, the king began to take matters of state into his own hands. He was, he told Facta, prepared to resist any Fascist attempt to overthrow the government, if only for dynastic reasons.

He had learned that some months earlier a Mussolinian emissary, the old Nationalist Corradini, had made secret approaches to the duke of Aosta. Corradini had been authorized to declare Mussolini's willingness to uphold the monarchy and the king in exchange for the royal gift of power. He had asked the duke to convey this message to Victor Emmanuel, but, knowing Emmanuel Philibert's lust for the throne, he had let it be understood that if the king were to refuse, and if he "were defeated or were to abdicate, Prince Humbert would be proclaimed King and the duke of Aosta would assume the regency."[10] This had proved irresistible to the duke: eighteen-year-old Humbert seemed scarcely a match for the Aosta guile, which meant that the crown would lie within a few clever twists away. The flush of a sudden affection for fascism on the part of the duke and duchess, however, had apparently lighted Victor Emmanuel's eyes and had stiffened his resolve to snare his slippery cousins once again. He took steps to restrain them.

Even "Mamma" had to be curbed. Margherita, now over seventy, believing that the sum of her years and accomplishments had endowed her with matriarchal wisdom, saw the nation's savior in Mussolini. For her, she said, he was one of Italy's "great *condottieri*," a man with a "marvelous temperament," for whom she had "warm sympathy, maternal affection. . . ."[11]

In October of that year, on the eve of the march on Rome, she received two members of the Fascist quadrumvirate, who revealed their plans for a *coup d'état* and solicited her support. The queen mother said that the projected Fascist assault on the capital "could not but be addressed to the salvation and glory of the Fatherland." When advised by her callers that only by a surrender to fascism could bloodshed and a clash with the army be avoided, she undertook the role of appealing to her son.[12]

But Victor Emmanuel had long ago gone deaf to his mother's jaundiced counsel. Her influence was nil. It was either her awareness of this or an explicit command from her son which kept her from fulfilling her desire to review a detachment of black-shirts and send them on their march on the capital with a stiff-arm Fascist salute.[13]

In the meantime Mussolini groped for ways to win the little king, and the crown showed itself not entirely obstinate and insensitive. Since the late summer Mussolini had made a special effort to resolve the all important problem of the royal army, but without visible success.

In August, an anonymous group of high officers, claiming to speak for the entire army, had published a letter in Sonnino's *Giornale d'Italia* demanding that the Fascists express their intentions toward the monarchy unequivocally. "It is useless to deny that we sympathize with the Fascists, who are fighting against Bolshevism," said the officers. "But today the king and the monarchy are being subjected to polemics. Mussolini must take a very clear stand. Our oath of loyalty cannot be compromised. If the Fascists were to go against the Crown, our commands would be, 'Fire resolutely.' The officers of the Italian army, before they would commit treason, would commit suicide."[14]

To this Mussolini had replied: "The Crown is not in jeopardy, provided that the Crown does not wish to place itself in jeopardy. Is that clear?"[15] Apparently it was not, for on September 20, he made a celebrated speech at Udine, in which he declared to any remaining republicans in his ranks that "you must have the courage to be a monarchist." Alluding to the king, he said:

> Whoever sympathizes with us will not be withdrawn in the shadow. He will remain in the light. . . . The monarchy, therefore, would represent the historical continuity of the nation. A beautiful role, a role of incalculable historical importance.[16]

It was a few days after the Udine speech that Victor Emmanuel made his inquiry of Prime Minister Facta, "This Mussolini, can he be trusted?"

And that was the week in which the future Duce remarked offhandedly, "We have decided to march on Rome."[17]

21

THE OCTOBER REVOLUTION, OR "IF GIOLITTI RETURNS WE'RE . . ."

THE CONCEPT OF A MARCH ON ROME WITH THE AIM OF OVERTHROWING THE GOVERNMENT originated, as has been mentioned, with D'Annunzio at Fiume two years earlier. The *comandante* had in fact drawn up an insurrectionary plan, which was rendered no less an illusion by its length and many details. The Fascists, if anyone, ought to have been the legitimate heirs to such schemes, but when Mussolini began to pick up the threat, the poet is said to have asked in his inimitable fashion, "Roma, alma mater, will you give yourself to a butcher?"[*][1]

When in August, 1922, Mussolini declared that the march on Rome was "strategically possible via the three great arteries: from the Adriatic coast, from the Tyrrhenian coast, through the Tiber valley,"[2] he was merely contributing monumental nonsense to the myth, which was being refurbished mainly for the benefit of those who would have to do the marching. For the truth was that Rome could not be taken; it could only be given, and Mussolini, his war plans show, knew that best of all. Yet he also knew, better than anyone else, that Rome would not be given unless it were asked for in the strongest possible way.

Events were rapidly unfolding a now-or-never situation for fascism. That Mussolini saw this and acted has often been raised in explanation of why some men succeed and others do not, but when placed

---

* D'Annunzio was perpetually troublesome to Mussolini, and many, one wonders why, looked to the former to save them from the latter ("Of the two, the one who kills the other will rule," the saying went). Even Gramsci and the Communist party hoped to play D'Annunzio against the Fascists, but in the end the poet went out the window—possibly with *squadrista* assistance—and in any event promised neutrality in an encounter with Mussolini two weeks prior to the march.

against all the possibilities that might have occurred, we find history and fascism to be a grotesque game of chance. One such possibility was the fact that early in October the pieces of Giolitti's prompt return to power were all but assembled in Rome. The negative side of the Fascist victories was that the greater the movement grew in size and in threat, the more pressure it exerted on the nation's liberal forces to come together again. So compelling was this phenomenon that Mussolini himself was being split into two Mussolinis—which, for the following reasons, was why he was able to decide on the march on Rome. Whereas the Fascist revolutionary Mussolini was dazzling the nation with a widescreen show of brute force, a "liberal" Mussolini, unseen, was secretly negotiating with Giolitti and Facta for a second-place spot in an old-fashioned, democratic-constitutional regime.[3] Not that Inspector Gasti had misjudged his man's will to be first, but Mussolini was perfectly willing to ascend in the traditional manner. This kind of duplicity was part tactic, part strategic, and wholly self-serving.

It was tactical because in dealing with both Giolitti and Facta it was designed to prolong the negotiations and thereby abet the continuance of the chaotic conditions resulting from the presence of the relatively impotent temporary government.*

It was strategic because should the march on Rome be unsuccessful Mussolini would not have closed all the roads to power, and indeed would probably be invited to join any new parliamentary government in order to facilitate the peaceful surrender of any Fascists intending to fight to the last.

It was self-serving because, while most Fascists were to march ready to die for the Good Cause with which their Duce had inflamed them, Mussolini was ready, if necessary, to send them to die for the reinforcement of the very things the Good Cause was against.**

According to De Felice, the decision to proceed with the march on Rome was made by Mussolini on October 12.[4] On the 16th, in a tough turning-point meeting held at Milan, he fought to win the rest of the Fascist leadership to his views. The quadrumvirate, in whom

---

* Another way in which this ploy was used to important advantage may be seen in connection with the Fascist congress in Naples, which opened on October 24 and culminated in the march on Rome. The Facta government had debated whether or not to permit the party to gather in Naples, but decided in favor when led to believe by Mussolini that the conference would authorize him to partake in a new liberal government.

** Of course, even plans with many contingencies could go badly. Mussolini, therefore, on the day of the march on Rome would remain in Milan, that is, close to the Swiss border.

all Fascist military power was to be invested, was divided in half. Retired General De Bono and Cesare De Vecchi, both monarchists, held that conditions were premature, the Fascist forces entirely unprepared; Balbo and party chief Michele Bianchi took Mussolini's side that the critical moment was slipping away. As Mussolini declared:

> The revolutionary act of marching on Rome is either undertaken immediately or never more. The time is ripe and the government is rotted. The specter of Giolitti advances steadily and you know that with Giolitti in power we had better think of doing something else.[5]

This seems to have carried the day. On the 21st, at Florence, a five-part plan was drafted. All that remained to be decided was the date for the action. This was postponed until the Fascist party congress at Naples, to open on the 24th, although it was understood that preliminary mobilization for the insurrection would begin no later than October 28.

A "black point," Mussolini believed, was the king. "He is certainly an enigmatic figure," Mussolini said privately at the time, but this was no reason not to go forward. "There are other mainsprings around him which we will bring into play."[6]

As for the Enigmatic Figure, he was on vacation at San Rossore. He had gone to the Tuscan playground of his forefathers and the grand dukes and archbishops before them, no doubt to escape the *gran pasticcio* in Rome, but not without assurances that the capital was safe. He had no confidence in Facta, and on October 7 he had himself given orders that the army brake the Fascist penetration of its ranks. On the 19th, the minister of war, Soleri, had issued a directive to General Pugliese, which the officer understood as a firm order "to absolutely prevent entry into the Capital by the Fascists."[7] Pugliese, in command of the Rome garrison of 28,400 of the most loyal and disciplined troops in the army, had already informed Soleri of the certainty that his men would obey any order whatsoever issued by the government and the king.[8]

It was this secure, well-equipped military force, backed by the largest part of the entire Italian Army (the marchers on Rome would number some 26,000 men, armed for the most part with billies, small sidearms, and shotguns, in many instances unaccompanied by ammunition), which had permitted Facta to boast that the state was safely in his hands. To a delegation of parliamentary deputies who had become alarmed by an increasing number of rumors of insurrection, the prime minister replied with a broad smile, "March on Rome? In Rome, I'm in charge. I'm here with my regiments and cannons."[9]

The king, though well removed from the city, was far more sober than his minister, given the internal dynamic of things. He had asked for a continuous flow of telegraphed intelligence. On the 24th, Facta wired that the prospect of a march on Rome had "faded away." But the king was already aware from other sources that this was definitely not the case, and he concluded that Facta was sending only the most optimistic news. He demanded that the worst be transmitted in full.

The worst, so far, came on the 26th. This day, and not the much discussed night of October 27–28 (with the royal decision to empower Mussolini located in the smallest hours of the morning following an alleged exchange of telephone calls between the king and his generals), ought to be regarded as fateful for Italy, fascism, and the House of Savoy—if the pursuit of such moments is to be made.

In the course of the 26th an exchange of telegrams took place between Facta and the king, which shows that Victor Emmanuel had by now formulated his own position.

Facta's wire reported:

> Information received unexpectedly indicates possibility of some Fascist attempt. Government will provide energetically [for the defense of the capital]. Mussolini yesterday informed me he would be willing to enter Ministry . . . provided said ministry was presided over by me. So as not to break off I replied that as your minister this was something we had to examine together. . . .[10]

Mussolini, of course, was playing the two-headed game described above. Facta's game was a kind of tic-tac-toe compared with Mussolini's chess. Everyone believed Facta to be a Giolittian foil. But Facta enjoyed being prime minister. Since his stopgap government would have to step down to make room for whatever new combination might issue from the present crisis, he hoped foolhardily to beat all the other contenders, and emerge as the king's choice to head a representative parliamentary regime.[11] This explains his own prolongation of negotiations, for which reason he was a mere pawn on Mussolini's board.

The king's game, however, was on the same board.

Though the sovereign, too, was stalling, a maneuver which has misled many to believe him no less outsmarted than Facta, time was on his side only. He had heard by other means, namely the duke of Aosta, that the Fascists were indeed going to march on Rome, on October 28. The duke, who had happened to be in Turin, had been informed by one of the Fascist quadrumvirate, De Vecchi, and the news had been passed to Victor Emmanuel apparently for the purpose of intimidation and to hasten his surrender. What the king found more alarming, however, was that when as a defense measure he ordered his cousin to remain in the city, the duke disobeyed and moved down the peninsula to his estate near Perugia, the Fascist stronghold city, which had been designated as general headquarters for the insurrectionary assault on the capital. This was dynastic, not to mention military insubordination of a most grievous kind, and the king could not but conclude that his throne was in the line of fire.[12]

This was one of the factors—but not the principle one—influencing the fact that the king had reached his decision: He was going to bring Mussolini to some level of power, one way or another, and the longer he could forestall violence—that is, hope that the Fascists would back down from the threat of conflict with the royal troops—the less power he would need to give away.

Only two days earlier, Mussolini's conversion to monarchism seemed finally to have made some impression on the king. It was on that day that Mussolini repeated at the Fascist congress his assurances that the crown would be venerated and defended, and Victor Emmanuel at last made note of this, jotting on his calendar, "Mussolini at Naples talks monarchy."[13]

The king now envisaged Mussolini in the number-two position of a conventional government. It was no longer a question of whether or not Mussolini, but of *how* Mussolini. For whereas the *re galantuomo* could send the royal troops to trammel Garibaldi's designs on Rome fearing only for the prestige of the crown, the little king could fire on Mussolini only at the risk of the crown itself. It was not the diminished loyalty of the soldiers which determined his position. As General Badoglio is said to have remarked at the time, "On the first shot, all fascism will collapse."[14] That was beside the point. The defeat of the Fascists meant civil war; for who but the Fascists had subdued the "Bolshevik threat"? Were these men to be denied and opposed, the socialists, communists, and worker's movement would hasten their own resurrection, and in the process the entire nation would be plunged into a death struggle between right and left. Undoubtedly the first casualty would be the institution which in engaging these forces had made itself the enemy of all: the House of Savoy.*

Accordingly, on receipt of Facta's dispatch of the 26th, Victor Emmanuel replied, indicating that his position—empowering Mussolini in some secondary way—had been taken. He wired:

> Thanks for your telegram. It seems to me expedient not to lose contact with Hon. Mussolini whose proposal can offer an opportune solution to present difficulties, since *the only effective way of avoiding dangerous shocks is in associating fascism with the Government by legal means.***16

Once the royal decision is moved back to the 26th, the events of the 27th and 28th, about which countless chapters and many books have been written, are perhaps deprived of some of their apparent tension and drama. On the other hand, that gray Sunday, the 29th, when Mussolini was summoned to Rome by the king to form a government, that is, to be in the number *one* position, which is usually regarded as an anticlimax, comes to the fore as the moment of moments. Nevertheless those three or four days taken together certainly form the most memorable weekend in modern Italian history.

In the first hour of Friday, the 27th, Facta telegraphed the king at San Rossore about the advisability of his prompt return to Rome. Facta was now in receipt of hard intelligence about the imminent Fascist advance and had decided that his own hour had come, which is why he believed the king had to be on hand. Emergency conditions developed during the day, as black-shirts in some cities began mobilizing without interference from the paralytic government. The king, in an angry mood, entrained for the capital that afternoon, while bookmakers in Rome were laying odds on the various candidates to head a new ministry. A government with a clear mandate on how to meet or neutralize the Fascist threat seemed in Rome to be an imperative which could no longer be postponed, and as the sovereign journeyed southward, Facta and his cabinet prepared to greet him with their resignations. Facta, of course, foresaw a Facta-Mussolini compromise regime, and indeed he was the odds-on favorite, but during the day former prime minister Salandra, who had been a 100-to-

---

* Victor Emmanuel III and his descendants were forever to insist on a biased rendering of this thesis in explanation of the crown's behavior, but in doing so, they would plait and drape it in so much shiny exculpation and fancy, involuted reason, no one would see or believe the simple truth which lay within.15 Institutions, more than men, want to live.

** The emphasis is added; "dangerous shocks" was the king's euphemism for civil war.

one-shot, emerged as one of the most favored, with Mussolini again in the second position.

It was Giolitti, however, celebrating his eightieth birthday that very day, whom all the contenders feared, Mussolini most of all. Recalling how the old man had sent the navy to fire on D'Annunzio at Fiume, Mussolini had remarked some days earlier, "If Giolitti returns to power we're fucked [*siamo fottuti*]."[17] But Giolitti, he too projecting Mussolini as his number-two man, waited in comfortable Piedmont to be beckoned to the rescue.

Mussolini also, for reasons noted above, preferred to be courted from afar, and while the black-shirts were gathering in mobs for the march, he barricaded himself in the offices of *Popolo d'Italia,* ready to lead the movement to victory, sell it out in a *combinazione,* or like Frederick Barbarossa head for the Alpine passes.

The king arrived in Rome a few minutes past eight o'clock in the evening. For the next thirty-six hours or so the rush of people in high places trying to protect or enhance their personal positions was so frenetic, so interwoven with double and triple dealings, that the truth is garbled hopelessly.

The largest question, which may never be answered, is whether or not the king on the evening of the 27th authorized his government to proclaim a state of siege for the defense of the capital. For if he had, as many say he did, his refusal to sign the decree on the morning of the 28th would indicate a middle-of-the-night turnabout and raise the gravest suspicions about the cause of such erratic behavior. He has, therefore, been variously accused of secret plotting with the Fascists, yielding to threats against his family, and even of having accepted his "mamma's" advice. More plausible, but not very well documented, is the often related story of an after-midnight secret meeting between the king and his highest generals. In this affair pro-Fascist Marshal Diaz, when allegedly asked by the king whether the army would obey a royal order to suppress the Fascist insurgents, is said to have replied, "Your Majesty, the Army will do its duty, but it would be better not to put it to the test."[18]

If, however, Victor Emmanuel had not instructed the government to declare martial law; if he had, in fact, as his telegram of the 26th indicates, decided against the use of force and on giving a measure of power to Mussolini, there is no reason to doubt him when he denies all of the above allegations and gives his own explanation—so characteristically banal in content and momentous in consequence:

I had to call on "these people" [the Fascists] to govern, because every-one else, in one way or another, had abandoned me. For forty-eight hours, I personally had to give orders directly to the chief of police and the commander of the garrison so that the Italians wouldn't slaughter one another.[19]

In any event, the reasonably well established facts of that weekend may be summed up as follows.

Facta and some members of his cabinet were on hand at Termini station when the king's train arrived. Looking grim and preoccupied, the sovereign alighted, and, according to Minister of War Soleri, his first words to his prime minister were that Rome had to be defended. "The Crown must be allowed to deliberate in complete freedom, and not under the pressure of Fascist guns."[20] There was as yet no mention of actually proclaiming a state of siege, but Soleri and Facta seem to have taken it as a likely possibility. After the king had left the station for Villa Savoia, Facta remarked to one of his colleagues: "The king said he is pained . . . by the thought of declaring a state of siege because the state of siege will provoke civil war. But he is aware that he cannot permit Rome to be overrun without defending it. I will see the king again this evening. He wants to meditate on his decision on the basis of the latest news."[21]

The latest news, from Facta's viewpoint, was hopeless. Taking leave of the king, he went to the Viminal, the complex of buildings housing the ministry of the interior, where he learned that the outlawry of the Fascist squads was gaining momentum. Some provincial prefects had been seized by the black-shirts, and the club-bearing, jackbooted row-dies were heading for Rome. More important to the prime minister was the latest political intelligence, which at this hour led him to conclude "that events had overtaken any parliamentary combination on the basis of that which had been hoped for."[22] The hope, of course, had been for the success of his own candidacy, but a talk with the prefect in Milan, Lusignoli, who had been to Cavour to see Giolitti, seemed to him to foreshadow a Giolitti-Mussolini solution. In any case, he was now convinced that his own chances were virtually nil.

With this in mind, Facta went to Villa Savoia and handed in his resignation, in order to give his king a free hand, not to mention full responsibility for whatever might occur. "Facta takes flight," Victor Emmanuel jotted in recording that occasion;[23] nevertheless it re-mained the duty of the Facta government to stay on as the acting executive and this was not contested.

The question of the state of siege arose. The king twice asked

Facta to telephone the Viminal for late reports, and twice he was told that the rebels were growing ever more unruly. Victor Emmanuel, on the eyewitness testimony of his adjutant, General Cittadini, then instructed the minister to propose whatever measures appeared necessary, which of course included the state of siege. The king added: "I will see later what must be done."[24]

Perhaps Facta never heard the final sentence; perhaps it was never spoken. When he returned to the Viminal, however, he told Senator Bergamini, director of the *Giornale d'Italia*, who was waiting anxiously for news about the royal audience, that he had been authorized by the king to take whatever measures appeared necessary, including the proclamation of a state of siege.[25]

Feeling that he had put in a good day's work, Facta went home to sleep. The king too went to sleep, as did almost everyone in Italy except Mussolini and his men.

While the state slept, the nighttime activities of the Fascists grew bolder and bolder. In the absence of any opposition, they proceeded to occupy prefectures, telegraph offices, and even military posts.

Mussolini, however, was still ready to jump either way—for or against his revolution. At 3:00 A.M. he received a telephone call from party leader Bianchi, the quadrumvir positioned in Rome. Bianchi, the hardest-liner, feared the Duce might weaken and be lured into a compromise which would betray the movement. His talk with Mussolini was hardly reassuring. As recorded in Rome, it went:

Bianchi: Benito?
Mussolini: What is it, Michelino?
Bianchi: My friends and I want to know what instructions you have for us?
Mussolini: Instructions? From me?
Bianchi: Yes. What is the latest news?
Mussolini: The latest is that Lusignoli was at Cavour and says that it would be possible to get Giolitti to give us four important portfolios and four undersecretary posts. . . .
Bianchi: Benito, do you want my opinion? Do you want to hear my firm, irrevocable advice?
Mussolini: Yes, yes.
Bianchi: Say no.
Mussolini: Of course. The machine is in motion. Nothing can stop it. . . .
Bianchi: Then we agree. May I communicate this in your name?
Mussolini: Wait. Let's see what Lusignoli has to say. Tomorrow we can discuss it again. . . . Yes, because that way you'll be brought up to date. I'll tell you what Lusignoli reports to me.
Bianchi: All right.[26]

Apparently the machine was not really unstoppable. Here was an instance when perhaps all that was needed was one more portfolio, another undersecretaryship, or a few hard words from the king. But the king, decided as he was that Mussolini had earned some place in some new regime, simply had no grasp of how to bring him along under the crown's control.

The conditions engendered by the march on Rome provide the first example of the behavior pattern which was to characterize the relationship between the king and Duce—a pattern repeated again and again for the next twenty years. There was something about the syphilitic Fascist chieftain which filled the Savoyard prince with awe and fascination, and vice versa. Mussolini was always prepared to submit to the will of the throne, while the king was forever afraid that he would not obey. Even now, incapable of either commanding or resisting this strange creature of action, Victor Emmanuel, like a diffident but nonetheless willing maiden about to be taken, hoped the man would be gentle. Mussolini, however, so often won when obstructed, was always inclined, without instruction and guidance, to be lustful.

While Mussolini kept a lonely vigil, Fascist aggression was getting so out of hand that someone thought the prime minister, if not the king, ought to be awakened. This was done, and Facta hearing the most recent developments, ordered an emergency meeting of his cabinet for 5:30 that morning at the Viminal. An aide went about waking all the ministers, save one who could not be reached, having repaired to an unnamed hotel with a sleeping companion. The king's adjutant Cittadini was also aroused and invited to the meeting, and it seems he in turn waked up the king, for Facta's secretary later said that prior to going to the Viminal the prime minister stopped off for a few minutes to see the sovereign.

Laboring under the apparent misunderstanding that he had been given full powers, Facta emerged from this predawn encounter with his convictions unaltered.

He met with his cabinet at about six o'clock in the morning. They spoke for less than an hour, and after some debate agreed unanimously on proclaiming a state of siege. No one quite knew how to word the decree, and someone got the idea of consulting the text used by Humbert the Good's ministers when they had declared martial law following the events in Milan of 1898. This was judged sound, and while somebody searched the files, a telegram was sent to all the prefects in Italy and to the commander of the Rome garrison advising them of the government's decision to reestablish public order by the use of armed force. They were instructed to crush the insurrectional movement at once. The immediate arrest of the Fascist leaders, not excluding Mussolini, was ordered.[27]

In the meantime, the old decree was found, brought up to date, and rushed to the Viminal's own printing plant, where it was clanged out like an "extra." It was bundled, hurled into the bicycle baskets of the brush and paste men, and by 8:30 that morning of the 28th slapped up on the walls of Rome. It reported that an insurrection was going on in Italy, and that the government was resolute in its decision to end it "by all means and at whatever cost."[28]

The proclamation had not needed much rewriting, but it was immensely effective. Only moments after publication, and before a shot was fired, it began to break up bands of Fascists, tired from having been out all night and anxious to get home to a warm bed. More important, three of the four quadrumvirs showed themselves ready to admit defeat.[29]

The decree, as required by law, had been promulgated in the name of the king, but Victor Emmanuel had not yet actually seen the document, and thus it was to the Quirinal that Luigi Facta went next that morning to collect the royal signature. The king, however, much to Facta's horror, refused to sign. He had already been informed of the acting government's initiative and now berated his minister for having taken a step without the "moral authority" to do so, let alone the sovereign's consent.

The king in the past had often said no to his ministers, but had almost always surrendered to insistence. This trait of Victor Emmanuel's personality was well-known in Rome, and it only furthered Facta's dismay when he found himself unique in being unable to dissuade him. There are those who say he did not argue very forcefully, and when he returned to share the news of the king's refusal with the members of his cabinet, they were so appalled, it seems, that they sent him back to plead once more. In any case, he was unsuccessful, even when he appealed for mercy, pointing out that the decree, if withdrawn, was his political death warrant.

"This is my end as a political man," he said to his master. "I will always remain buried under the charge of having promulgated the state of siege."

Victor Emmanuel replied that issuing the proclamation had been a "very bad" thing to do. "No, no," he said, shaking his head, "I won't sign. . . ."[30] He folded the document and slipped it into his desk drawer.

By noon, news that the king had not signed the state of siege had reached out in every direction with varying degrees of accuracy. Victor Emmanuel, believing that he had spared the nation a blood bath, thought now that his own brand of good sense and moderation would prevail. He saw the way cleared for a new regime with the secondary participation of Mussolini, and when he received the Fascist quadrumvir De Vecchi that afternoon he excluded any possibility of the Duce being given the prime minister's post.[31] The king's choice was Salandra. Salandra agreed, and the evening *Giornale d'Italia* announced the imminent formation of a Salandra-Mussolini government.

Mussolini, however, held another view of the situation, one less obstructed by illusion. He reasoned quite flawlessly that if the power of the state would not be used against the Fascists, then the power of the Fascists by default was supreme. Throughout the evening, Salandra and his friends telephoned and telegraphed Mussolini, imploring him to yield to the king's wishes and come to Rome. Even the Fascists in the capital, namely De Vecchi, Grandi, and the elder Count Ciano, recommended the royal compromise, but Mussolini, from his barricaded office in Milan, was heard on the telephone to reply: "It was not worthwhile mobilizing the Fascist army, causing a revolution and killing people for the sake of a Salandra-Mussolini solution. I will not accept."[32] Nor was there reason now to accept Giolitti or any other man as his superior; he was *de facto* second only to his king.

On the morning of the 29th, Salandra, after making one last unsuccessful try to convince Mussolini, went to the Quirinal and told the king that his mission had failed. Victor Emmanuel scratched him from his calendar ("Salandra takes flight"). There was only one thing he could do. He called in De Vecchi and asked him to send for his Duce; the government of Italy was his. "I order Mussolini," the king recorded, as if the thing summoned were a pizza pie.[33]

"*Va bene, va bene,*" Mussolini affirmed when the telephone call was made. But he feared a last-minute double cross. He said he would not go to Rome unless he received a personal invitation from the palace. "As soon as I receive the telegram, I will leave at once by airplane," he said. He then dictated to the king's aide, General Cittadini, the text of the message he demanded to have in hand.

It was all most irregular, but at 1:38 P.M. the wire duly arrived. Mussolini's brother, Arnaldo, looked on as the Duce read his own words:

HIS MAJESTY THE KING REQUESTS YOUR IMMEDIATE DEPARTURE TO ROME
DESIRING TO ENTRUST YOU WITH THE FORMATION OF THE MINISTRY STOP
REGARDS GENERAL CITTADINI

Benito relaxed. He turned to Arnaldo and exclaimed, "If only our father were alive."[34]

Mussolini did not, as is well known, go by airplane. He could not even get an early train, which may have partially influenced his celebrated program to make them run on time. With a free ticket, he departed that evening on the sleeper and arrived in the capital the following morning, where he declared to those enthusiasts who received him at the station that his first act as *capo* of the government would be to salute the "glorious army," which he proceeded to do. "Long live Italy!" he cried next, adding for the very first time in his life, "Long live the king!"[35]

It had been raining, and now it stopped as he was driven to his hotel—the Savoy—where after a brief rest he was escorted to the Quirinal, and at the stroke of 11.00 A.M. received by the king. The Duce, bareheaded and still wearing his Fascist black shirt, excused his appearance. But Victor Emmanuel, formally empowering him to put together a regime, cared little, grateful that the long crisis was over. When Mussolini left, the king expressed his sense of relief to a palace intimate, Solaro del Borgo.

"I seem, Solaro, to have come out of a long nightmare," he said. "I know that Orlando, Salandra, all the leaders and the best men in the country are pleased. Look, I have here thousands of telegrams from all over Italy and elsewhere which have arrived at the Quirinal to tell me that I have done well."

Asked what he thought of his new minister, Victor Emmanuel replied:

He is really a man of purpose and I can tell you that he will last some time. There is in him, if I am not mistaken, the will to act and to act well. When I told him to put together an administration on a broad basis and with capable men, I felt that he agreed and was close to my views. I had previously formed quite a different impression of him.[36]

Mussolini, too, was favorably impressed. "From that day onward," he later said, "I instinctively had a great deal of faith in him. . . ."[37]

He came back to the palace later that evening, this time properly attired and hatted. The ministry he had assembled was a coalition of the military-nationalist right with Fascist predominance. "I bring Your Majesty the Italy of Vittorio Veneto," he is reputed to have said in presenting his list. He promised to be a "most humble servant" of the House of Savoy.[38]

The next day, the bedraggled marchers on Rome finally arrived. They paraded outside the Quirinal, while the Mussolini government was being sworn in by the king. Then the Duce and the sovereign stepped out on the balcony to watch the Fascists demonstrate the substance of their faith. They were greeted with traditional cries of long life, good wishes, and to blend the old with the vigorous new, they were hailed by the straight-arm Fascist salute.

The little king stood there for more than four hours. Those who saw him say he was full of smiles. This was one time when he could say with his mother, "Mussolini has saved the Nation" and "the House of Savoy must be grateful. . . ."[39]

PART IV

The Fall of The House of Savoy (1922-1946)

I may have made a mistake.
But it's too late now.[1]

—VICTOR EMMANUEL III
MAY 9, 1946

22

"SEPARATE BEDS": THE DIARCHY

ITALY WAS FASCIST. MANY ITALIANS ADORED MUSSOLINI. MANY WENT INTO EXILE. BUT PEOPLE in general, in spite of anthems and airplanes, are not very mobile, and allegiances, in the end, are more often purchased than won. In Italian they say, "*s'arrangia*." Regimes and whole nations live and die with a song; people get by as they can.

An enlightening illustration of one of the unhappy aspects of the period of adjustment which followed the march on Rome was recorded in those years by Emilio Lussu, the Sardinian *fuoruscito*—the name by which the anti-Fascists in exile became known. Lussu was a member of the tiny parliamentary opposition when Mussolini came to power, and before very long he was arrested and sent to a Fascist concentration camp, from where he escaped to France. A founder of the post–World War I social democratic Sardinian Action party, of short duration, Lussu tells most vividly how one of his dear friends and colleagues, a fellow deputy of the Sardinian liberal left, Pietro Lissia, made his personal arrangement with the changing times.

Ten days or so before the march on Rome, Lissia approached Lussu with a proposal to unify their efforts against the Fascist threat, particularly in Sardinia. Lissia, a man much older than the thirtyish Lussu, was a veteran of many radical causes and he had fought for years to improve the conditions of the working class. Now, he said, freedom itself was in danger. The left had to band together, cast aside its differences, "and become soldiers in the same army."

"If fascism triumphs," he told Lussu, "civilization in our country will be rolled back twenty centuries." One could no longer think of his own personal interests and well-being, he said. It had become a matter of morality and dignity. "We have the duty to fight to the last drop of blood. If we don't, it will be to our shame and the shame of our children. . . . Fascism must understand that it can conquer only over our dead bodies." At the mention of Mussolini's name he shuddered with revulsion.

Lussu was basically in agreement with his older friend, if not with his manner of expression, and they took leave of one another with the resolve to coordinate their political actions—"like two soldiers with a date to meet in the trenches."

"You can imagine my surprise," said Lussu, "when immediately after the march on Rome I learned that he had been appointed in the Mussolini ministry as undersecretary of finance."

Shortly afterward, Lissia, the new undersecretary, made an official visit to Sardinia, escorted by a squad of armed black-shirts. Alighting from the train at Cagliari, he flashed the Fascist salute to those who were there to receive him, and when he was catcalled by one of his former supporters, the saluting arm shot forward with a pointing finger at the heckler, as he cried, "Arrest him!"

That evening he spoke at a meeting of the provincial council. "Gentlemen," he declared, "the time of the carnival of democracy is finished. The government of Benito Mussolini is not a government on paper . . . the march on Rome is untouchable. We did it not for ourselves, but for the greatness of the fatherland." With regard to all who oppose this, said the Fascist, "We will be implacable. We will crush them."

Lussu, present at the meeting, tried to speak against the government. He was shouted down by the black-shirts, but managed to deliver his talk. When the meeting was over, he was approached by a police officer and told that the undersecretary wished to see him at once. He was taken to Lissia's apartment, where he found him waiting for him, his hand extended, his face lighted with a friendly smile.

"Don't be surprised by my speech," Lissia said the moment they were alone. "I had to say what I did, for reasons of formality. But you know that I think exactly as you do, about everything."

Lussu seemed perplexed.

"Yes, I repeat, about everything," the undersecretary went on. "The only thing is, and this you have taught me, man in general, and the political man in particular, is forced to wear a mask."

"But I never taught you anything of the kind."

"A mask. But that is nothing but the simple exterior. It is the thought inside that matters. . . . You know that the democratic ideal which has nourished my spirit for my entire life remains unchanged. Only the clothes have changed. But the habit does not make the monk. . . .

"Before accepting a post in the ministry," the Fascist continued, "I suffered. I assure you that I have had moments in my interior life which were truly dramatic. Think of what it meant to me to have had to abandon my friends of twenty years of political struggles. Ah, do you think that's nothing? Do you believe it a pleasant thing to renounce one's dearest friendships? In the end, I asked myself: how can I be most useful to my country? In the opposition or as a Fascist? And, without any selfishness on my part, I made my decision."

"Did you think that the country would come to ruin if you were to retire from political life?" the younger man asked.

"You're joking, not reasoning. . . . Reality, my friend, reality! Let us speak clearly. Times and tempers change at a dizzying pace. Politics is not an abstraction; politics is an art."

At this point, Lussu recalled, the Fascist seemed to grow sure of himself. His earlier embarrassment waned, and he sought to win Lussu to his side, proposing that he collaborate with the regime. Mussolini was like Caesar, he said, who bore no animosity toward his adversaries.

Lussu got up to leave.

"Well?" asked the Fascist. "Friends or enemies?"

"Enemies."

"Good luck to you. But you'll see."

"What does that mean?"

"You'll see."

They parted without shaking hands. Lussu, at the door, looked back for a moment. Lissia was rigid and stared at him severely. He held a cigar in one hand, as the other rose in a proper Fascist salute.[1]

Mussolini would later observe that when the black-shirts marched into Rome on October 31, 1922, he had made "one little mistake," and that was that "instead of passing in front of the Quirinal Palace, it would have been better had they stormed inside."[2] The king would have his own regrets. Now, however, the honeymoon was on.

In the first months, relations between the two men were extremely cordial, characterized by mutual trust and understanding. Mussolini did nothing the king did not first approve, and the king did nothing but approve.

Twice weekly, every Monday and Thursday, at 10:30 A.M., the Duce would repair to the palace, dressed in a derby and *frac*. His detachable white collar displayed his strong chin; the white gloves and cuffs and the spats which bit the dazzling shine on his shoes covered the fire inside. He disliked the formality, and later he would gain enough confidence to discard such rigorous style (saying, "By now there are only three of us still wearing it: me and Laurel and Hardy.") but somehow he had learned to bear the manner and the dress of a bourgeois minister impressively. Adulatory Margherita was somewhat apprehensive about how the great *condottiero*, whose origins were so removed from life's refinements, would take to the high office he had won. "And to my surprise," she said when Mussolini passed the test, "he seemed like someone who had done nothing in life but live at Court."[3]

When exercising this grace, he would enter the Sala del Consiglio at the Quirinal, execute a perfect deep bow before the king, and repeat the performance when backing away to take leave. From the very start until that final audience in 1943 which ended with the king very courteously placing the Duce under arrest, the routine was always the same. Victor Emmanuel, in his threadbare general's clothes, worn from a misplaced sense of economy to shiny, see-through old age, would extend his soft white hand in response to Mussolini's bow. Then he would take his place at the head of a long table draped with red linen and beckon the minister to speak. For his part, Mussolini would sit at the king's right, report in hushed tones, and ask for the royal advice.

His growing intimacy with the king, or at least the court trappings, was a factor which led Mussolini to an early conclusion that fascism was only a roughhewed, second-best thing when held up alongside the House of Savoy. "The monarchy remained," Mussolini later wrote, "but Fascism, almost immediately, felt the need to create its own institutions. . . ."[4] His envy of the Savoyard establishment, and the inevitable pressure on the movement to consolidate its gains, urged the Duce in an effort to make of the monarchy a two-headed beast he would name the "diarchy."

By that, Mussolini said, he meant "government by twos, the 'double command.' . . ." The diarchal system, he explained, "was that of the matrimonial chamber with separate beds."[5]

Everything Victor Emmanuel had been given by ten centuries of dynastic hard, if not honest, labor and by the "grace of God," Mussolini gave to himself. As a result, said Mussolini:

> Little by little the diarchy took on an ever more defined character, even if not always sanctioned by law. At its culmination there was the king

and the Duce, and when the troops gathered to hail them, they did so as equally before one as the other. . . . Alongside the Army, which predominantly obeyed the king, there was the Militia, which predominantly obeyed the Duce. The king had a special bodyguard of Carabineers, and one day Gino Calza-Bini* created the personal guard of the Duce, "the Musketeers."

The Council of Ministers descended from the Constitution . . . the [Fascist] Grand Council came from the [Fascist] revolution. The dashing and martial hymm "Giovinezza" made its appearance at ceremonies beside the long-winded and gaudy royal march. . . .

Even the military salute did not escape the diarchal system: the old salute was retained for heads covered, while the Roman or Fascist salute was used with caps off (as if in the meantime the heads had been changed!).[6]

Somehow, however, Mussolini, though he wrote his title in capital letters and Victor Emmanuel's as a common noun, could never in a formal way gather the courage or presumption to place himself first. He would grow infinitely more powerful than the little king, but for all his vitriolic asides against him, he would remain unable to disbelieve in Savoyard divinity; and so his jealousies would never be relieved. They were to burn hotter instead. Even when fascism had duplicated twice over all the kingly institutions it had coveted, the Duce's discomfiture was not to ease. He might add insult to injury, but there were intangibles the gods would never grant to the lowborn, and in his record of last regrets, Mussolini would recall that whatever he had, the king had something of the same, only better.

The royal "international"—the intermarried family of European kings—was an insidious and inimitable means by which the House of Savoy conducted its own secret diplomacy, the Duce would lament with paranoiac certainty. "There is no doubt that the general staff of the Army above all was 'royal'; it formed a kind of caste which was very circumscribed, if not completely closed, on which the dynasty could count with the most absolute assurance," he complained. The senate, too, was a dynastic force, and the aristocracy, both black and white, constituted another. Pope Pius XI would call him "the man sent from Providence," but Mussolini would remember only that ". . . the curia and the clergy entered into the royal orbit, so much so that in religious ceremonies a prayer for the king became mandatory."**

---

* Calza Bini was a Roman *squadrista*, expelled from the party in 1923 for extremism.

** Mussolini received more than a fair share of prayers in the nation's churches and synagogues, and thus seems here to be quarreling only with the king's prayers having mandatory status.

Everyone was to appear to Mussolini to be against him. He continues:

> The big bourgeoisie—the industrialists, landowners, and bankers—while not exposing themselves in the front ranks, also marched under the royal banner. Freemasonry considered the king one of its "honorary brothers." The same for Judaism. The prince's tutor was the Jewish professor Polacco.[7]

There was, Mussolini would realize at a very late date, no way to overcome so vast a "conspiracy," but now at the outset with retrospectively imagined naïveté and self-proclaimed good will he made his "separate bed," in order that he might lie beside the little king.

Victor Emmanuel naturally did not appreciate the concept of a diarchy, but there was little he could do to oppose it which would not return him to the position in which he had been prior to the march on Rome. Every elaboration of Mussolini's powers seemed to the king only a very small addition and quite necessary for monarchical stability. Besides, the word *diarchy* was never mentioned in his presence nor was it ever elevated beyond being a fashionable catch-phrase which described a political rather than a juridical condition. Thus Italy was to have a monarchy *and* a diarchy, which did nothing to strengthen Mussolini's ego and much to give cause for nasty jokes about the feebleness of the crown.

One such *barzelletta*, which grew in popularity as the Fascist side of the diarchy grew weightier, told of an encounter between the Duce and the king. Advised by Mussolini that he had ordered the king's telephone number changed, Victor Emmanuel asked what was wrong with the old one. "Your Majesty requires a more personalized number," Mussolini replied, "a simpler one which will make it easier for me to communicate with you. The new number is 610." "Six what?" "*Sei uno zero*, Your Majesty." *Sei uno zero*, the numbers "six, one, zero," in Italian also has an entirely different meaning: it is the familiar second person singular form of saying, "You are a zero."

Inch by inch the king grew smaller, the Duce bigger. Fascist government, having come to power in a most dubious manner, began its work on very weak ground. There was still an array of political forces theoretically far superior to fascism, and Mussolini had a parliamentary base of a mere 7 percent of the chamber. He was at some distance from a one-party dictatorship, and probably had nothing of the sort in mind, although he threatened the opposition with such a prospect in his very first parliamentary address as prime minister.

Instead he asked for the not unusual mandate of extraordinary powers for one year to restore law and order at home. This seemed a fair concession, and men such as Giolitti, Salandra, Bonomi, Orlando, and Croce approved, which assured the formal granting of this "temporary" expedient. Mussolini used his time and his influence, however, to strengthen fascism alone. Before his year had passed he had wooed and cajoled the non-Fascist legislators into rewriting the electoral law in such a way as to give his movement the legal foundations it so clearly lacked, and, in the process, he acquired greater and more permanent powers than the extraordinary ones allowed.

This feat was accomplished not without difficulty. There were internal weaknesses and conflicts in the party which had to be resolved, as many restless *squadristi*, unhappy about what appeared to them as parliamentary business as usual, became an armed threat to the Fascists themselves. Mussolini sought to contain them in creating the Volunteer Militia for National Security (MVSN), which allowed the black-shirts ample freedom to discharge their emotions against "communists" and other "subversives," but even this did not satisfy all.* Mussolini, unlike Hitler's handling of his brown-shirted SA, did not have his "night of the long knives." Unmanageable extremist dissension was to endure for years.

Fascist violence with impunity never relaxed for a moment. Indeed it was the unrelenting physical assault on Mussolini's enemies and the threat to life and property regardless of one's social class or political convictions which was an indispensable means of smoothing the Duce's way. Violence had been used by every one of his predecessors, beginning with Cavour, but Mussolini discovered himself living in an age when the more it was used the more useful it was. Moreover in such circumstances his concessions appeared all the more generous, and when in that first year he lifted taxes on the rich, removed restraints on investors, suspended new laws on land reform, and disbanded a commission investigating wartime profiteers, he seemed to some wholly benevolent.

---

* The Fascist militia, as the MVSN was to become generally known, was an armed force which for the first time in the history of Savoyard rule was not required to swear allegiance to the king. Although the oath was later added as a concession to the crown, the milita remained Mussolini's personal army. Victor Emmanuel gave his approval for the formation of the MVSN because he was as eager as Mussolini to discipline the black-shirts, but it was no less a significant precedent-setting act in the erosion of the crown's powers which steadily ensued.

In the meantime he enjoyed some successes in his foreign policy—notably the sudden annexation of Fiume—which gained him admiration at home, if not in Fiume. For seizing the Yugoslavian port and, unlike D'Annunzio, getting away with it, Victor Emmanuel bestowed the venerable Collar of the Annunziata on him, which made the Duce an everlasting "cousin" of the king, the queen, and their heirs.

His greatest early victory, however, was the passage of the self-aggrandizing electoral law. This was secured with an assist from the Vatican which withdrew its support of Don Sturzo's Catholic *popolari* in favor of fascism. He was also aided by a commission of former prime ministers, but perhaps more so by the mobs of *squadristi* who filled the parliament galleries during the voting. They picked at their nails with their knives and playfully brandished their guns while the deputies feigned not to notice or reassured one another that Fascist infantilism meant nothing. The bill was enacted overwhelmingly, and the elections of April, 1924—the very last to be held with an opposition slate in Mussolini's Italy—gave the Fascists the majority they had sought. The militia brought out the "Fascist" voters and suppressed the opposition with murderous raids, sackings, and burnings both before and after the polling, but the new law for the first time had really made this familiar activity all but superfluous.

The London *Times*, examining Mussolini's first year in office, viewed events from this perspective:

> It is incontestable that Italy has never been so united as she is today. . . . People have become impressed by the fact that *fascismo* is not merely the usual successful political revolution, but also a spiritual revolution. *Fascismo* has abolished the game of Parliamentary chess; it has simplified the taxation system . . . it has vastly improved the public services, particularly the railways. . . . but the chief boons it has conferred upon Italy are internal security and national self-respect.[8]

Benedetto Croce, whose moral influence in Italy was far greater than that of foreign observers, had this to say at the start of the new year, 1924:

> The heart of fascism is love of Italy, the safety of the state, and the true conviction that the state without authority is no state at all. . . . I value so highly the cure which Italy is undergoing from it that I rather hope the patient will not get up too soon from his bed and risk some grave relapse.[9]

23

MURDER IN ROME

WHEN THE NEW PARLIAMENT, WITH A VASTLY REDUCED OPPOSITION, WAS OPENED BY THE KING on May 24, 1924, it hardly seemed likely, in spite of everything, that one man among the 535 deputies would shortly be premeditatedly murdered for speaking against fascism.

True enough, there had been exceedingly shocking incidents involving assaults on high political leaders in the past few months, and there was talk of a secret Fascist organization called *Ceka* entrusted by Mussolini to "give a lesson" from time to time to his more prominent foes. "Lessons" had in fact been given. Former Prime Minister Nitti had had his home devastated and looted at the hands of Fascist toughs.* Opposition leader Giovanni Amendola, among other deputies (including Emilio Lussu), had been severely beaten on city streets. But these had been defended as regrettable, isolated events. Furthermore there was evidence that Mussolini was trying sincerely to discipline the party extremists and was even hoping for a reconciliation with the liberal left.

Now, however, everything was about to change. As a result of the imminent slaying of the liberal-minded Matteotti, the new government as well as fascism itself would all but topple. Victor Emmanuel would again be thrust into a decisive position, placing the royal house under hazard. Modern Italy would fall victim to a true, enduring, and self-confessed dictatorship. That all this would occur with the turn

---

* Nitti, who was receiving his "lesson" for having criticized fascism in an article appearing in a South American publication, later wrote of this incident to the king. The morning after, he informed Victor Emmanuel, the perpetrators of the crime took part in a fox hunt with the duke of Aosta. There, Nitti had learned, the duke was told, "Your Highness, it is by pure chance that we do not bring you Nitti's head."[1]

of the year would have seemed on May 24, as it does still, an incredible twist of fate, wanted by no one and a bane to all.

The king, in his opening speech from the throne, admitted that some errors had been made in the near past, but they had been overcome, he said, and the country's future had been secured by the "fundamentally new political situation."[2]

It was this very situation, which had come about by the new electoral law, which Giacomo Matteotti of the Unitarian Socialist party took upon himself to challenge. In a quiet moment when the president of the chamber called for a procedural motion to confirm the outcome of the elections, Matteotti rose in protest to deliver the final address of his short life.

Citing violence and coercion, Matteotti contested the legality of the elections and moved that they be declared invalid. This was of course an impossibility because of the composition of the majority. Matteotti's true purpose was to give impetus to a new tone of opposition by taking a stance more resolute than ever before. "I have given my speech," he said half-jokingly to his friends on its completion. "Now it's up to you to write my eulogy."[3]

Matteotti, at thirty-nine, was a rising power in the opposition. He hoped to weld a united stand against fascism. Tall, dark-eyed, and steady in his enmity toward the regime, he possessed many of the qualities of leadership and charisma which made him a formidable figure in life and a national hero in his martyrdom.

His speech represented no immediate danger to the Fascists, though it was shouted down and almost drowned out entirely by catcalls from the center and threats from the right. Victor Emmanuel took note of the incident, jotting on his desk pad, "Matteotti provokes a scene in the chamber challenging the validity of the majority. . . ."[4] He then went off to Madrid to visit the king and queen of Spain. He gave scarce regard to the affair, but Mussolini was infuriated.

Following Matteotti's address, the Duce was heard by his close associates to declare, "After that speech, that man should be put out of circulation. . . ." In his own talk in parliament some days later, the Duce turned in Matteotti's direction and said to the left in general that if the Fascists had not been so lenient, "You would have had a bullet in your back." It was not that they did not have the courage, proof of which would soon be forthcoming. When? "We have plenty of time," said Mussolini, "but it will be sooner than you think!"[5]

That was on June 6. Rumors began now to circulate that Matteotti was preparing a second speech which would implicate high Fascist

THE KINGDOM OF ITALY AT ITS BIGGEST DIMENSIONS, 1925

officials in financial scandals. On the 10th Matteotti did not show up in the chamber. No one took notice, but when he did not return home that evening, his family and friends reported his disappearance. The police were already aware of foul play. Someone had seen Matteotti forced into a car, had taken the plate number, and had notified the authorities. On the 12th it was learned that Matteotti had been kidnaped and on the 13th that he had been brutally murdered. Only the body remained to be found.

The details of the crime came out swiftly, and while most of the world's newspapers were filled with reports of the sensational Leopold-Loeb kidnaping and murder in Chicago, Italians were being shocked by events closer to home. What had happened in Rome may be summarized as follows:[6] At about 4:30 P.M. on June 10, Matteotti emerged from his apartment building in Via Mancini, a small quiet street that runs down from the Tiber embankment. He was on his way to parliament and had not gone more than a few steps when he was seized by three or four Fascists. He was beaten to the ground and carried into a seven-seater limousine which had been waiting at the corner. The car sped north on Via Flaminia, its horn screaming to cover the victim's cries for help.

In the car Matteotti struggled with his abductors, five or six men armed with knives and guns. He smashed the glass partition between the front and back seats, and managed to throw an identity card from the window. He continued to resist until one or more of the kidnapers repeatedly stabbed him until he was lifeless. His mutilated body, stripped naked to hinder identification, was buried in a shallow, hastily dug grave some thirteen miles out of Rome.

That the automobile's license plate had been recorded and reported to the police led rapidly to most of the killers and their closest collaborators. The car belonged to a lawyer named Filippo Filippelli, director of the Rome Fascist daily *Corriere Italiano*. This newspaper was controlled by the ministry of the interior, one of Mussolini's own ministerial portfolios. Filippelli denied complicity prior to the crime, saying that he had lent his car to two friends, Amerigo Dumini and Aldo Putato. They had returned the vehicle, with its interior soaked with blood. Dumini had told its owner that they had bungled an attempt to give Matteotti a "lesson" which had been ordered by the Duce himself through the party treasurer, Giovanni Marinelli. They had asked Filippelli to help them "fix" the damages with Italy's police chief, Senator De Bono, the former quadrumvir and a "cousin" of the king by virtue of the Collar. De Bono's complicity, at least after the fact, was later established, but the crime could not be covered up entirely.

Amerigo Dumini, the chief organizer of the murder, who liked to introduce himself as "Dumini, nine homicides," was the personal assistant to Mussolini's press secretary and confidant, Cesare Rossi. Dumini, when arrested, refused to talk, but his sidekick Putato, captured on the same day, declared, in a statement later corroborated by another thug, that Dumini had told him that Mussolini had wanted Matteotti not beaten but slain.

In the next few days Party Treasurer Marinelli and Press Secretary Rossi were arrested, and while the former made no statement, Rossi deposed that Mussolini had formed a secret organization of assassins around Dumini. Disclosures were also made by Senator De Bono and the number-two man in the Duce's interior ministry, Fascist Undersecretary Aldo Finzi.

De Bono said that following the crime he had met secretly, on the Duce's request, with Rossi, Marinelli, and Finzi. Rossi and Marinelli, he said, had warned that Dumini and his gang could not be expected to remain silent if prosecuted and sentenced to long prison terms. The murderers would reveal, both men told De Bono, that they had acted on orders from Mussolini.

Finzi, who confirmed De Bono's statement, testified that he knew nothing of the Matteotti affair, but agreed that Dumini and his men had the Duce's general approval on matters of Fascist violence. Some time before the murder, he added, Mussolini had ordered him to make a payment to Dumini from secret funds belonging to the interior ministry.

Not all of this was publicly known at the outset of the affair, but suspicion pointed almost at once to the prime minister himself, and as early as June 13 he felt it necessary to go before the nation and state his case. Taking the floor in parliament that afternoon, Mussolini announced the capture of Dumini and Putato, and the imminent arrest of all who were involved. He then went on to say:

> If there is someone in this hall who more than anyone else is entitled to be grieved, and I would add exasperated, it is I. Only one of my enemies, sitting up long nights, could have thought of something so diabolical as carrying out this crime which today fills us with horror and makes us cry with indignation.

He had been seeking a *détente* between the warring elements of Italian society, he said, and now this crime had come along to disturb if not ruin his efforts to bring about a "moral reconstruction." The murder had thus been a "humiliating bestiality," *against* fascism. Calling for national unity, he vowed that justice would be done.[7]

Circumstantial evidence would continue to mount against Mussolini, and justice would not be done until the case would be reopened following World War II, but there remains something to be said of the Duce's own version of the affair. To his dying day he would speak of "the corpse which on June 10, 1924, was thrown between me and the Socialists, in order to prevent an agreement. . . ." The Fascist extremists wanted to break the drift toward parliamentary respectability, Mussolini would insist. They blocked the way to compromise with Matteotti's body, his apologists continue to this day to add, and thus both they and the intransigent opposition forced him into the dictatorship.[8]

This is a rather faulty explanation for the twenty years of Fascist crimes which followed the Matteotti affair. Dictatorships are almost always undertaken only under compelling circumstances. Further, there is nothing to support the notion that the extremists, unsatisfied as they were with government-imposed restraints on their savagery, were so farseeing as to be able to calculate the effects of the crime; on the contrary, they had an earned reputation of being dull-witted brutes. Yet it is probably true, as a close examination of the evidence tends to confirm, that Mussolini did not specifically order the murder, as such a development offered small advantage at tremendous risk. He probably did sanction the physical punishment of Matteotti, however. Marinelli, who had dispatched the Dumini gang allegedly on Mussolini's command, had been present when he had made his angry remark that the deputy ought to be taken out of circulation. In any event Mussolini boldly assumed full responsibility in throwing down the gauntlet months later.

It was the question of responsibility which weighed on Victor Emmanuel when he made his return from Madrid on June 16. He had not yet entered Rome when he was approached on the royal train by the opposition, in the person of Count Vittorio di Campello, a monarchist senator and one of the king's gentlemen-in-waiting. Campello presented him with a document which purportedly demonstrated Mussolini's guilt. Victor Emmanuel read a few lines. When he became aware of the content, he cast it aside, covered his face with his hands, and said, "I am blind and deaf. My eyes and my ears are the Senate and the Chamber."[9]

This bit of royal theatrics was not taken very seriously by the anti-Fascists, however. In the past few days, for the first time in memory, the so-called constitutional parties, that is, the remaining oppositional nonrevolutionary left, had begun to knit into a more or less unified grouping. Led by liberal Giovanni Amendola, they were growing confident that they need do little other than withdraw from parliamentary participation and allow Mussolini, in isolation, to fall by the weight of his own conscience. Failing that, they believed, public outrage, which by now had turned the nation against fascism and had led to open anti-Fascist demonstrations, would convince the king to act, if only for the same reason he had installed the Fascists in the first place: namely, to prevent civil war.

Such was the attitude which in that same month of June led to the "Aventine Secession"—the parliamentary walkout of the Amendola opposition, named for the plebeians of ancient Rome who had withdrawn from the city to the Aventine hill.

Former Foreign Minister Count Sforza, who had resigned in protest when Mussolini had come to power, had suggested more vigorous measures to the *aventiniani*. So great was the national revulsion to the Matteotti crime, he later said, that fascism could have easily been swept away by a less passive opposition. "I proposed," he wrote, ". . . breaking into the Palazzo Chigi and arresting the man behind the murder: Mussolini." No one listened; the Aventine group trusted in the king and the courts, Sforza says.[10]

There was a moment, however, when his plan might have succeeded. In the days following the exposure of the murder, the Duce felt himself completely debilitated and the halls of the Palazzo Chigi, normally swarming with obsequious callers, were cavernously empty. Those who saw him on June 14 and 15 found him in a state of melancholia. He saw himself as having failed in his mission, fallen into ignominy. He had visions of being tried or summarily executed by an anti-Fascist squad, and he considered resigning, suggesting to the king that the old socialist Turati replace him.[11]

"I was so terrifyingly alone in the week after Matteotti's murder," Mussolini would later confess, "that one day . . . I said, 'Twenty men resolved to reach me would find no resistance and no defender.' "[12]

By the afternoon of the 16th, however, as the king was returning to Rome, Mussolini had completely regained his self-confidence—one reason being that his friends or foes gave no sign that his fantasies might come true. The following morning, having worked out his position, he went to see the king. He protested his innocence and outlined the measures he wished Victor Emmanuel would allow him to adopt to restore confidence in the regime.

The ministry of the interior was to be swept clean. The scapegoats were to be Finzi,* Rossi, and Police Chief De Bono, all of whom, he was able to report, had already "resigned." It was a case of criminal matters having taken place behind his back, he said. In proof of his good will he would surrender his interior ministry portfolio to Luigi Federzoni, one of the cabinet's more respectable ministers, who enjoyed Victor Emmanuel's trust.

The purged ministry, Mussolini promised, would see to it that all the perpetrators of the crime would be brought to trial and would generally behave in a most unimpeachable fashion. In this way "normal" times would soon return and fascism could get on with its work.[14]

Mussolini had received no advance indication as to how the king would react, and like the entire nation, he waited now in suspense for the word from the throne. Half of Rome, if not counted, was said to have turned out at Termini station to welcome Victor Emmanuel back from Spain. Many expected him to dismiss, even arrest the Duce precipitously. But he had as yet no intention of doing anything so rash. Indeed he felt obliged to assist in shoring up the sagging regime, at least as long as Mussolini could maintain his innocence, or his political support. He therefore, as a first step, approved the Duce's program to revivify the government, but he conveyed the impression to Mussolini and everyone else that he was keeping an open mind on the developing affair and that Fascist rule did not have his unconditional confidence.[15]

He had, if he wished to defend the House of Savoy, no other alternative. His son Humbert would say as much years later in elaboration of how Victor Emmanuel viewed the matter:

> It should not be forgotten that the producer classes of Italy had hardly yet got over the fear of being overthrown by a Soviet-style totalitarian revolution. A collapse of the government would have certainly produced a collapse of the State.

"The opposition, in principle, was justified with regard to what had happened," Humbert adds. But the Aventinians had nothing to offer

* Finzi was to come to a particularly sad ending. He would never regain his standing among the Fascists, and, as a Jew, would turn to antifascism following the decree of the Italian racial laws of 1939. In 1944 he would be arrested by the Germans for aiding the resistance movement. A few weeks later he would be among the arbitrarily chosen victims of the Ardeatine Caves massacre in Rome.[13]

the House of Savoy; they were in fact suspected by Victor Emmanuel of having ulterior motives. According to his son:

> ... in the totality of Matteotti's actions in Parliament, and then through-out the entire "moral question," there emerged a sense of something "unnatural," something "willed," "prearranged," almost as if they wanted to prepare the ground for a wider action with the aim not only to undermine fascism but to create a crisis in the Italian State. The Fascists said immediately that the Aventine, despite Amendola's loyalty, con-tained an occult program of [Socialist] maximalism and republicanism.[16]

Someone had even heard cries at meetings of the Aventinian sup-porters in Genoa and Milan of "Long live Italy without the king!" The mild-mannered, trusting, ineffectual Aventine secessionists would never think of defying Mussolini's warning to them to disabuse them-selves at once of any notion of passing from words to deeds.[17] But to the little king they were a fearsome bunch.

The real strength of the political opposition was tested on June 24, when Mussolini went before the senate. He promised to set things right and reestablish law and order "forever." Only three senators spoke against him. One of them, Count Sforza, was unaware that earlier in the day his wife had been threatened with the prospect of being a widow by that evening should he make his speech.

More than 90 percent of the senate voted for the Duce, which brought enthusiastic cheers from every bench. One senator was so exuberant he fainted.

The action of the senate seemed to lift all threat to the government, and the Fascist toughs began to emerge from their lying-low places and swagger again through the streets. The secessionists, while re-maining together, were reduced to gossiping about the gastric ulcers which had suddenly afflicted Mussolini. The malady was rumored to be fatal; there was still hope for their cause, it was said among them.

The opposition did in fact regain significance in mid-August with the discovery of Matteotti's partially decomposed body. A new wave of outrage swept the country. The press, which had had heavy re-straints placed on it one month earlier, conducted a memorable anti-Fascist campaign nonetheless, and a measure of public opinion was noted in that the circulation of opposition newspapers rose to unprec-edented levels.

Both Mussolini and the king did nothing, expecting that this too would pass. The Fascist extremists, however, led by Roberto Farinacci, mounted tremendous pressure on the Duce to act with a strong hand

and end the protracted crisis once and for all. Mussolini was accused of weakness and his claim to leadership was put under notice. He was visited by various delegations of *squadristi* from the countryside, who warned that they were tired of crawling in and out of their hiding places and demanded bloody solutions to their frustrations.

This situation, with Mussolini caught between the opposition and the most violent wing of his party, dragged on for months. In late October, when his position seemed to be improving, the hitherto pro-Fascist war veterans organization boycotted the ceremonies commemorating the march on Rome, making the Fascists appear painfully isolated. Then, on November 4, the anniversary of the World War I victory, the celebrations erupted into a day of nationwide anti-Fascist demonstrations. Amendola assured his group that the king would surely act very soon.*

In the same month, with the reopening of parliament, hoary Giolitti threw a bombshell declaring that he had gone over to the opposition. This was regarded as a sure sign that Victor Emmanuel was preparing the way for a traditional Giolittian solution to the crisis.

It looked like the very end of fascism. The movement made preparations to go underground, without the Duce if need be. Early in December, Balbo laid plans with other extremist leaders to seize control of the Fascist militia and along with the *squadristi* oppose the fall of fascism with armed resistance. Mussolini, however, declared publicly on December 5, that if Victor Emmanuel were to tell him to go, he would snap to attention, salute, and obey.[19] Again the nation turned its eyes to the king.

The climactic events took place during the Christmas and New Year holidays. Shortly after the crime, Press Secretary Cesare Rossi, feeling himself persecuted as one of Mussolini's scapegoats, had written a long memoir alleging the Duce's personal involvement in Matteotti's abduction and thus his murder. Rossi's evidence was still circumstantial, but more damning than any other disclosures, particularly because of his extreme intimacy with the Duce. This document had been moving about clandestinely for months, and a copy had been in Amendola's hand since August. In the middle of Novem-

---

* During this period the *aventiniani*, like Mussolini, were marshaling supporters. They made a special effort to win D'Annunzio. The poet had been appalled by the murder, characterizing the affair as a "stinking mess," but he was not going to go against Mussolini. One reason was that the big-spending prince of Montenevoso had sunk into financial difficulties once again, and since the Matteotti crime he was being secretly subsidized by the Duce with state funds. From July, 1924, to October, 1927, in fact, he received directly from Mussolini 5,200,000 lire.[18]

ber, he had arranged for it to be handed to the king by former Prime Minister Bonomi, but Victor Emmanuel had replied, "Don't ask me to read it. I am not a judge. I am not competent."[20]

Amendola, exasperated by the royal attitude and hoping to intensify the increasing pressure on the king to act, finally, on December 27, published a long extract of Rossi's confession in his own newspaper, *Il Mondo*. Almost every other paper in the country reprinted the text, including its dramatic conclusion, "Everything that has taken place, has happened as a result of the direct will, or the approval, or the complicity of the Duce."[21]

This appeared to be the *coup de grâce*. The reaction nationwide, even among the Fascists themselves, as well as among members of the Duce's own cabinet, was that Mussolini was really guilty after all. Many who had previously supported Mussolini, now resolved that he had to go. Some of his ministers proposed that he resign. Deputy Emilio Lussu counted an outpouring of some thirty men who began at once to put forward their own candidatures as the prime minister's successor. Once more it was said that the king was about to act; Amendola counseled all to remain calm.

On December 30 the *Corriere della Sera*, powerful spokesman of the industrial north, declared the entire social fabric in jeopardy. In the light of Rossi's accusations, said the prestigious Italian newspaper with the greatest circulation at home and abroad, Mussolini had the obligation to waive the immunities granted to him by law and place himself at the disposition of the courts. It went on:

> Such are the demands of good custom. Such are the demands of moral law. Wretched is the country in which a notable part of the ruling class, reluctant to admit that it has been grossly deceived, denies these, the highest demands of civilized society and gives the masses an example which can abet the most disturbing teachings.[22]

This opinion, coming from the Milan daily, was mighty. It seems likely, however, that the representative sentiments expressed provided the very reasoning which galvanized the Duce's determination to resist and to adopt the will of the Fascist extremists as his own. Mussolini's biographer De Felice has recently made this insightful observation:

> Things had arrived at the point where to leave [his office and the legal protections it afforded] would have meant exposing himself to the risk of judicial action. The Aventinians would certainly not have given truce, and a trial would have surely resulted in his political

demise and, very probably, his conviction. There was too much that could have been used against him for him to hope of coming out unscathed from such a test.[23]

It was at this point that Mussolini decided to silence all opposition. To a band of black-shirt chiefs from the provinces, who burst into his office on New Year's Eve demanding that the *aventiniani* be shot, he said no more than this, and that they should listen to a speech he would give on January 3. As in 1922, only the king and his army could stop him, but by now he had learned to count on Victor Emmanuel's hysterical fear of the monarchy being crushed in a civil war.* Such were the origins of the Fascist dictatorship.

On the last day of 1924, however, the dictatorship was still seventy-two hours in the future and almost everyone believed Mussolini was through. Italy celebrated the *San Silvestro* holiday believing the new times had come. Some newspapers came out with the headlines that the government had already fallen, the Duce resigned. In Reggio Calabria shops closed, all work was suspended, and people poured into the street to rejoice. The local Fascists went back into hiding.

In Rome the rumor that Victor Emmanuel was on the verge of intervening grew louder than ever. Amendola claimed to have been so informed from the court itself, and Turati said, "I too have news that at Villa Ada [Villa Savoia] they have begun to understand and, in short, have waked up. They speak even of declaring a state of siege as a possible solution."[24]

The sovereign himself remained "blind and deaf"—and more than a little mute. When the war hero Ettore Viola had led a delegation of veterans to the royal hunting grounds at San Rossore to tell the king that the *ex-combattenti* had turned against the Fascists, Victor Emmanuel listened courteously, then replied with a vacuous smile: "This morning my daughter shot two quails."[25]

He had been counseled in recent weeks by some of his former prime ministers that the time had in fact come to act. "Take the situation in hand and dominate it," Orlando, with Giolitti's blessings, had told him.[26] But Giolitti and Salandra had previously given advice to the contrary. Charles Albert had bestowed the constitution, and as long as the constitution was "obeyed" he would adhere to the wisdom of his forefathers. To his faithful Solaro del Borgo, Victor Emmanuel had said, "It is the Chamber, with a clear vote of no confidence, which must drag the Mussolini spider out of his hole, because if they expect the monarchy to do it, they'll have a long wait!"[27]

---

* Reactivating that fear were 10,000 Fascists mobilized in Tuscany at the time and turned loose in an orgy of year-end violence.

Mussolini too held his silence. The tension mounted. By January 3 the king had still done nothing, but Mussolini was scheduled to speak in the chamber of deputies, which reopened that day. There were no advance copies of his speech, nor any information as to what he might say; it was a secret kept from the crown itself. The chamber fell still as the Duce strode down the aisle. There was a hard look of confidence in his face, but fear throbbed in his heart. He was about to make history, and he knew it, though what kind of history it might be the man whose body would one day swing in a Milanese piazza had not the slightest idea.

He began by reading a passage from Charles Albert's constitution. He too was a constitutionalist:

> Article 47 of the constitution says: "The Chamber of Deputies has the right to accuse the king's ministers and summon them before the High Court of Justice." I ask you formally whether there is anyone in this Chamber or outside who would like to avail himself of Article 47?

The Fascists cried, "Long live Mussolini!" The opposition was still. As on one wished to take advantage of this clause, Mussolini went on:

> All right, then. My speech will be very clear. . . . It is I, gentlemen, who in this hall will raise the accusations against myself. It is said that I have founded a *Ceka*. Where? When? In what way? No one knows! . . . It is said that fascism is a horde of barbarians encamped within the nation; that it is a movement of bandits and plunderers. On top of this comes the moral question. . . . All right. I declare here and now, in the presence of this Assembly and in the presence of all the people of Italy, that I assume—I alone—the political, moral, and historical responsibility for all that has happened.

The house Bernini had built before the sundial of Heliopolis shook in a grateful ovation, as many voices roared, "We're all with you! We're all with you!" The challenge continued:

> If a few phrases, which have been more or less distorted, are enough to hang a man, then get out the post and get out the stake! If fascism has been nothing but clubs and castor oil, and not a superb passion of the best of Italian youth, then I am guilty! If fascism has been a criminal organization, I am the chief of this criminal organization.

"We're all with you!" replied the chamber, save the opposition, to whom Mussolini now addressed himself:

> You have had illusions. You thought that fascism was finished because I had compromised it . . . but if I were to use one-hundredth part of the energy that I employed in compromising it to unleash it, then

you would see something! But there is no need to do this, because the Government is strong enough to put a definitive end to the Aventine sedition.

Italy, gentlemen, wants peace and tranquillity. She wants hard-working calm. We will give her this tranquillity, this hard-working calm, with love if possible, with force if necessary. You can be sure that within forty-eight hours after my speech the situation will be cleared up in every area.

Apologizing in advance for what he was about to do, Mussolini concluded:

> Everyone knows that what I have in mind is not personal capriciousness, not government wantonness, not ignoble passion, but only a boundless and powerful love of the fatherland.[28]

Mussolini kept his promise. Within forty-eight hours everything changed. The regime mobilized detachments of the Fascist militia and ordered the police to dissolve all "suspicious" organizations, to place under strict surveillance all "communists and subversives," and to seize all weapons held by non-Fascists. They and their weapons were to be located by "frequent searches." Finally, any attempt to resist these measures was to be suppressed by whatever means.* This was followed by the silencing of the press. The *Corriere della Sera* and Giolitti's *La Stampa* were forced into pro-Fascist hands. Matteotti's murderers were eventually released. A series of "very Fascist" laws were drawn up and decreed over the next year, which signaled the definitive end to parliament and the constitution. Although lip service was rendered at least to the latter, the Duce did not hesitate to declare it a kind of quaint "custom which was all right for little Piedmont," but in need of "perfection."[30]

The opposition was dismissed from politics. Those who could not remain silent were either jailed or exiled; most left Italy of their own accord, giving rise to the *fuorusciti* movement of doubtful effectiveness.

It was only many months after Mussolini's speech of January 3 that his opponents perceived the meaning of his forty-eight hours. In the meantime they looked on with mere disapprobation as the Fascists made their funeral arrangements. Turati at first called Mussolini's

---

* By January 6 the new, "respectable" minister of the interior Federzoni, was able to report the results of the first official Fascist government persecutions: Nearly 400 political organizations had been either shut down or dissolved; 111 "dangerous subversives" had been arrested; and 655 homes had been searched. The prefects, he continued, were making use of their new powers "without hesitation."[29]

speech "the usual bluff." Amendola, who would shortly be molested again by a Fascist squad and later die of his injuries, believed the king would now certainly step in.

"He needs time," Amendola said, "a proper amount of time in which to act."[31]

When, immediately following Mussolini's speech, the remaining non-Fascist members of his cabinet resigned in protest, hoping to give Victor Emmanuel an additional reason to take action, even the more militant Count Sforza could still believe. "Tomorrow," he prophesied on that occasion, "we will have a Giolitti-Orlando-Salandra government, and within three or four months, an Amendola government."[32]

Mussolini too, after January 3, thought for a while that the crown might not remain wholly benign. Speaking afterward with Mussolini, the king, as Victor Emmanuel would later say of himself, "criticized the speech animatedly."[33] The Duce was to corroborate this, admitting that this had been the first "clash" between them. "The king," Mussolini wrote, "felt that from that day forward the monarchy ceased to be constitutional in the parliamentary sense of the word."[34]

But Victor Emmanuel healed readily, affixing his thousand-year-old name on every decree by which Italy was being divested of whatever freedoms she professed. The short-term gains which seemed to bring the law and order apparition nearer the nation's grasp were intoxicating, if not delicious.

He felt relieved of a painful episode, which, as Humbert II has suggested, appeared to portend a crypto-republican plot.* Only two days after the Duce's speech, he seemed to have already got over at least some of the discomforts of conscience Mussolini's arrogation of illegal powers had aroused in him. On January 5, in the presence of the Duce, he swore in the Fascist ministers who had been called to replace those who had resigned, and according to one of them, he was in the best of spirits, especially when chatting with the culprit.[36] No doubt his mood was encouraged by a sense that the future of the House of Savoy lay in the well-being of those whom he was entertaining.

---

* In 1932 Emil Ludwig in his celebrated talks with Mussolini hazarded a question in this connection. Referring to the Matteotti affair, and specifically to the reputed republican undertones, the liberal German journalist inquired leadingly, "So you protected the crown . . . and the crown protected you?" "Certainly," the Duce replied after reflection, but no less unguardedly. "One can certainly say that I protected the crown. It is my duty to defend it, but it is also my ardent desire, because I am full of admiration for the King. I esteem him equally as a patriot and as a man of culture. That's right. One can also say it conversely: The crown has loyally and constitutionally protected my government."[35]

To a member of the outgoing group, however, he expressed what were probably closer to his true feelings. On handing his resignation to the king the liberal minister Count Alessandro Casati, who had led the walkout of Mussolini's three non-Fascist cabinet members, spoke for his colleagues and himself:

"Your Majesty will understand," said Casati, "that we cannot remain in a government in which every constitutional guarantee has been abolished. Permit me therefore to say to you . . . that we await Your Majesty's orders or a clear word."

"My dear count," said the king in reply, "as for what has happened, I personally did not expect it; neither was I informed in advance. I know that it is not good. But when they write in newspapers, or when they send me letters in which it is said to me, 'Your Majesty, act, rise up,' I say that these are mere words, because the situation in which the Parliament placed the Crown three years ago is such that there is nothing left for me to do now other than to defend the structure's foundation: the monarchy."[37]

Thus the king, had, in a sense, acted after all, and from his special view of the world, he had acted correctly.

24

ROMA FASCISTA

THAT SUMMER OF 1925 VICTOR EMMANUEL III
CELEBRATED THE QUARTER-CENTURY ANNIVER-
sary of his reign. The quality of his acquired wisdom—applied most
recently in the Matteotti affair—may be felt in the fact that from the
founding of the dictatorial Fascist state until the onset of the next
world war the House of Savoy enjoyed fourteen years of domestic
tranquillity and stability. Not since the king's diminutive forebear,
firebrand despot Emmanuel Philibert the Iron Head, sat on the ducal
throne of absolutist, *cinquecento* Piedmont-Savoy had such a "golden
age" been paralleled.

It was a span of years in which the children of Humbert the Whitehanded saw their domains expand to their greatest dimensions, their
crown elevated to imperial stature, and their royal name on the
thrones of realms beyond their own. But these were also the years of
profound humiliations, the steady loss of their powers, and the penulti-
mate act of their fall.

Victor and Elena since first they sat upon the throne had watched
their faces wrinkle, their hair grow sparse, and a common look of
sadness set in around their lips and in their dimming eyes. Their
attachment to one another had not diminished, and their eccentric
love of simple and bucolic things had grown. They had seen their
children reach adulthood, their royal acquaintances and elders die,
and many of their fondest hopes curdle in their hearts.

Their oldest child, Princess Yolanda, was already married and a
mother herself. Her wedding in 1923 to a captain in the cavalry had
been blessed but not welcomed by her mother and father. She was
one of the most beautiful princesses in Europe, and they had hoped

for a while that she would marry Edward, prince of Wales, heir to the British throne. Edward, the future duke of Windsor, would also marry "low"—and lose his crown—but when he had visited Rome and had appeared with Yolanda on his arm at a dinner at the Quirinal, Victor and Elena had seen the queen of England in Yolanda. The headstrong princess, however, already once denied the affections of a cobbler's grandson with whom she had become infatuated, had insisted on her captain.

Her captain, Count Carlo Calvi di Bergolo, of the rural *piccola nobiltà*, was neither rich nor handsome, and he was sixteen years her senior. She had met him when he had come to do service at one of the royal villas. When Victor and Elena were told by their daughter that either she be permitted to marry him or she would retire behind the walls of a convent, they were heartbroken. They tried everything to dissuade her. Even Mussolini was called in to talk to her. He reminded her that her great-aunt Princess Clotilde had married Prince Napoleon for reasons of state; she replied that her great-aunt was a fool.

As a last resort, Yolanda was given into the hands of her grandmother. Margherita took the girl into complete isolation and for days tried to convince her of her folly. But to no avail. The wedding was announced. Victor and Elena tried to smile, but their smiles were tried to the utmost when the captain showed up in Rome, and the newspaper *Il Messaggero*, innocently garbling two very different news items, printed the following most embarrassing error:

> Coming from Turin, Count Calvi di Bergolo, fiancé of Her Royal Highness Princess Yolanda of Savoy, arrived in Rome yesterday evening. Count Calvi took lodging at the Hotel Quirinal. Stopped and searched by the police, the poor man was found not to have a single lira in his pockets.[1]

The early-rising king, reading the newspaper at breakfast, sent his men running to the kiosks to buy up as many copies as they could carry, but that of course amounted to only several handfuls, and while Victor and Elena tried again to smile, all Rome laughed.

By 1925, however, that was two years past and forgotten. Now with the silver jubilee of Victor and Elena's reign, the court and its followers were looking to the marriage of the royal couple's second child, Mafalda, but a few months away. On that occasion, though the Savoys were pleased with Mafalda's choice, Prince Philip of Hesse, it was the Vatican which raised objections—concerning the German's Protestantism. The king was furious and raved in his pencil-thin voice about the Church wanting everything its own way and giving nothing. The marriage took place anyway, in the Savoyard castle of Racconigi, and it was a happy event in which some of the old splendors of the Humbertine age were taken down from almost forgotten, cobwebby shelves.

The bride, or "little Muty," as Elena never ceased to call her, had Grandfather Humbert's haunting eyes peering from her strange, dark beauty. Philip, a nephew of exiled Kaiser Wilhelm II, was a dashing groom in his sword and sashes. But the two most captivating royal figures, upon whom all eyes were turned that September day, were Queen Mother Margherita, more regal than ever in her ancientness, and her God-favored grandson, the prince of Piedmont, come to splendid manhood, perhaps the tallest, most handsome of all the Savoys.

In Humbert (and in Mussolini's iron rule) Margherita, at seventy-four years of age, had seen her dearest dreams and her most pious prayers come true. Even now, the twenty-one-year-old crown prince was endowed with many of the qualities of De Meis's (and Margherita's) ideal sovereign: "stately, handsome, and strong . . . magnificent, conspicuous, . . . sensual . . . religious." Margherita and all of royal Europe were or were soon to be charmed. He was already, in Margherita's eyes, the young Humbert drawn by her biographer Casalegno:

> Like his grandmother he loved to live in royal palaces and surround himself with luxury and pomp; like his grandfather he tended to be a lavish spender and made light of financial troubles; like the "father of his country," but with greater refinements, he was sensual and gallant, but his many adventures did not keep him from a religious sentiment very similar to Charles Albert's. All these traits enchanted Margherita. . . .[2]

Such were Margherita's contentments when she appeared in public for the last time at the wedding of Princess Mafalda, her favorite among the daughters of the little king. Having lost much of her grace and beauty waddling plumply through middle age, she had recaptured them in the sundown of her years. The excess flesh had melted in a pearly glow, and her old bones, with an assist from an ivory-handled cane, held her well. The light of the ages shone in the mist on her eyes, that knowing, centurial look of the privileged old. And why not: the Italy that had driven her to tantrums and hatreds had at last been conquered by the Italy that had seethed in her heart. Faith and piety had rewarded her beyond all expectation, and when Mussolini, a little more than a month after Mafalda's wedding, escaped an abortive assassination plot, her rewards were all the more. God had protected his "precious life" and had saved Italy from ruin, she said then. She prayed for the "heroic souls" of the Duce and all those, living or dead, whom she loved in "this land of Martyrs and Heroes"; they were of one voice in invoking "You, Lord, for the future and greatness of Italy."[3]

A few weeks later, on the morning of January 4, 1926, she died in her bed, the king and queen and Prince Humbert by her side. "My adored Mamma has breathed her last," Victor Emmanuel wired Mussolini, and Mussolini, who esteemed Margherita as much as she had him, was genuinely moved. She had named him executor of her estate, and for this service he was given one of Margherita's own medals. He wore it around his neck until his death.

Margherita was buried in the Pantheon, in a vault beneath the remains of Humbert the Good. An unlighted lantern hangs from her tomb.

Victor Emmanuel was no sentimentalist. The flag was rung down on Villa Margherita, and the king lost little time in disposing of the building, selling it to an agricultural organization, simply because its maintenance costs were more than he cared to spend. His mother's death was but a brief, mournful episode in these generally happy years: Another sad interruption, however, occurred some two years later, and though of quite a different nature, it was extremely grave.

In 1928, continuing the process initiated after the Matteotti affair, Mussolini proposed that the grand council of the Fascist party, the only legal party now, be constitutionalized as an organ above parliament, the government, and the crown itself. As such, it would have the power to determine the successor to the throne. The grand council was subsequently to be used by the king in bringing down the Duce, but for now its supremacy stripped him of almost every power guaranteed to the kings of Savoy by Charles Albert in 1848. The king would no longer have the right to choose his prime ministers, and in tampering with the laws of succession, it appeared as if the Fascists were taking Prince Humbert hostage to assure the perpetuity of their cause. "It meant a mortal blow to the Constitution," Mussolini later admitted.[4] The court and the dynasty, with the exception of the Aosta line, were enraged. Victor Emmanuel stood firm, at least for a moment. In one of his biweekly meetings with the Duce, he declared in defense of his house: "The regime must not enter into these matters, which have already been regulated by a fundamental law. If one party in a monarchic system can decide on the succession to the throne, the monarchy is no longer such. Succession can only be that of the traditional cry, 'The king is dead, Long live the king!' "[5]

Mussolini, as always when face-to-face with the "sire," was deferential and humble. But beyond the palace doors he was categorically insistent. The king, as ever, when confronted by this combination of qualities, acquiesced. The law was passed shortly afterward.

"From that day," the Duce would write of himself, "Victor Savoy [sic] began to detest Mussolini and bear a tremendous hatred against Fascism." Mussolini, quite simple-mindedly, thought he knew the reasons why: "The functions of the monarchy were withering away. The recurrent ministerial crises, together with the great national calamities and the New Year's Day ceremonies—later abolished— were the only occasions when the king had been able to do something to show himself to the Italians as not just a collector of old coins. . . . During a ministerial crisis the parade of hopefuls to the Quirinal had been an event in which the king had been in the center. . . . All that had ended."[6]

The king's grudges were never enduring. He was assured that the grand council's powers would be used wisely, and only in times of utter emergency. The rewards of Fascist rule, for Victor Emmanuel's part, were infinitely greater than its demands, and only a few months later all his resentments against Mussolini were again abandoned with good cause. For in February, 1929, Fascist Italy came to terms with the Vatican, resolving the antediluvian "Roman Question," which had so tortured the *re galantuomo* and had plagued his heirs and all their ministers in the half-century since his demise.

Victor Emmanuel III, who had gained notoriety for his anticlericalism, did not believe that the pope would ever bless his house and the unified nation. But with the signing of the Lateran Treaties, Mussolini, "sent by Providence," reconciled the Church, giving it, too, law and order in its relations with the people and the state.

That year Victor and Elena went to Saint Peter's for an audience with Pope Pius XI, the first sovereigns of Italy since the Middle Ages to be so received. The monarchs of both Church and state were jubilant, grateful to fascism for having reinforced their respective institutions. If Savoyard rule had been weakened by the Duce's revolution, it could now permit itself to feel rejuvenated. The king's gratitude did not go unexpressed. It is said that he spoke as follows with the Duce:

> Victor Emmanuel: You have succeeded in a work which others have not attempted and could not have carried out. . . . I do not know how to publicly demonstrate my recognition of your accomplishment. I really don't know. The Collar was given to you after the annexation of Fiume. Perhaps a noble title.
> Mussolini: No. A noble title would immediately make me look ridiculous. I couldn't look at myself in the mirror. I will not say boastfully, *"Roi ne puis, prince ne daigne, Rohan je suis,"* but I pray you will not insist. Everyone must have his own style of life.*[7]

The king understood and respected the Duce's wishes. This was ever the case, while Mussolini never failed to misunderstand the king. He was wrong, for example, in believing that the king had wished to be at the center of the nation's political life and not appear as a mere numismatist. In fact Victor Emmanuel was personally quite content in seeing fascism take over the tiresome duties of state; his only concern was its effect on the viability of the monarchy. He was perfectly happy with a court life reduced by the Fascists to its minimum activity, and could never get his fill of hunting at San Rossore, riverside fish fries, and his coins, about which he suffered not the least dismay in being called—in Mussolini's words—"diligent to the point of fanaticism." He felt himself to be but a dilettante, his 88,000-piece, Italian-coins-only collection just "pretty good." He yearned to be a connoisseur, and for greater slack in the tether to the throne so that he might have more, not less, time to give to his coins. Thus his debt of thanks to the Duce was here too founded in sincerity.

Mussolini was always attributing his troubles and ulterior motives to the king; the king never doubted the Duce's good intentions. Not that any of this took place in a dialogue between them. It was among his intimates that Mussolini would recall the things he *should* have said in meeting with the king ("I wanted to answer him, 'My dear, solemn idiot . . .'"), and it was in like company that Victor Emmanuel would sing his praises of the Duce ("He is a man of heart, that Mussolini. . . . Mussolini is good").[8] The long record of the dictator's

* Mussolini had the motto of the feudal House of Rohan slightly wrong. The actual wording is: *"Roi ne puis, duc ne daigne, Rohan suis."* "King I cannot be, duke I disdain, Rohan I am." In any event, it was a poor choice if it were meant by him to illustrate his true feelings. The Rohans had been falsely modest, discarding their motto for the ducal title and eventually that of prince.

behind-the-back vituperations against the crown stands virtually unrelieved by a single unkind or unfriendly word spoken by the king.

In those halcyon years, everyone but his victims had nice things
to say about the Duce. Abroad, fascism gained the admiration not
only of a promising young man named Hitler, and like-minded souls
in many lands, but it also appealed to many distinguished figures in
the freedom-loving West. The English, who had so thrilled to the
exploits of the Trevelyanesque vision of Risorgimento Italy, found
new heroes in Mussolini and his black-shirts. Baldwin, Lloyd George,
and Anthony Eden all agreed on the Duce's greatness, but it was
Winston Churchill who was impressed most profoundly. The future
British prime minister, then chancellor of the exchequer in the Baldwin government, came to Rome in 1927 and visited twice with Mussolini. Following that, he could have said with Lady Austen Chamberlain, "What a man! I have lost my heart!" but instead he called a
press conference at the British embassy in Rome in order that he
might be more explicit.

Mussolini had fascinated him, said Churchill. "His only thought is
for the lasting well-being of the Italian people. . . . It is perfectly absurd to declare that the Italian government does not rest on a popular base or that it is not supported by the active and practical consent
of the masses."

Then, addressing the Fascist movement, which he said had "rendered a service to the entire world," Churchill declared:

> If I were Italian, I am sure that I would have been with you entirely
> from the beginning of your victorious struggle against the bestial ap-
> petites and the passions of Leninism.

Mussolini, the Briton concluded, had demonstrated that there was
a way, after all, to fight "the forces of subversion."*[9] Victor Emmanuel, if Churchill were any guide, could not but be certain that he had
acted inspiredly at every step along the way.

Mussolini's prestige abroad grew tall, which made Italy and even
the little king look bigger than ever. The Duce himself was the
keeper of his own "image." The former editor spent much of his time
making up the nation's newspapers. One can almost see the green
visor around his brow as he issued such third-person instructions to
the press as: "Put the Duce's words in a box . . . under an eight-

---

* Churchill's press conference in Rome produced some criticism in London from
the Labor party. This prompted Baldwin's "cautious" remark that while he had only
read the newspaper accounts of his minister's statements, "I have seen nothing to
which one may object."[10]

column headline"; "The Duce's speech may be commented on (we will send you the comment)."[11] There were to be no photographs published showing him smiling or otherwise appearing as anything less than an eternally youthful, ever pensive figure; the lights would burn late in the Duce's office, a beacon for all who passed on the street below, but Mussolini would not often be there.

It seemed the millennium had come. The nation began dating the years not just with A.D. but also E.F.—the *Era Fascista*. October 28, 1922, had been the Nativity and the Circumcision all in one. Thus the new year began on the anniversary of that memorable day, and was recorded in Roman numerals affixed to everything from documents of state and daily newspapers to love letters and first-grade compositions. In the eighth year of fascism for example, Victor Emmanuel's sixtieth birthday was written: November 11, 1929-VIII E.F. (the E.F., like A.D., was dropped, once learned by all). The king, who received so much in return, was willing to surrender to these and other Fascist eccentricities, and although he persisted to the last in referring to Mussolini as his *presidente*, even he sometimes called the man *duce* ("He said *duce*!" it was exclaimed triumphantly among the Fascist hierarchy).

That same eighth year was an eventful one for Victor and Elena. They celebrated the marriages of Princess Giovanna to Boris, czar of the Bulgarians, and Crown Prince Humbert to Maria José, daughter of the king and queen of the Belgians.

The prince of Piedmont's wedding relieved many preoccupations of his royal parents. Humbert had gained an unhappy reputation of profligacy, and it was well-known that poor Maria José, who had adored the prince since childhood, was the least among his many loves. The followers of his adventures were calling him the "prince of love" or simply "prince charming." His passions, which took place on both sides of the Atlantic, were said therefore to be wide-ranging, but more so for his rumored, but unproved, impartiality toward either sex.

He had not wanted to marry Maria José. "I wish I were a fireman so that I could marry whom I please," a pouting Humbert is said to have lamented on hearing that his time had come.[12] He had often spoken of being someone else, but he never really deviated from the straight and narrow path to the throne. When he was nine he had made up his mind "to work in an office," but when reminded that he would have to be king and "guide the people through peace and war," he had replied, "Well, we'll see...."[13]

Maria José, though not very beautiful, was the most eligible candidate in Europe, as far as the Savoyard court was concerned. The princess was the homely kind, and while being well educated and cultured, she preferred simplicity to court elegance. Humbert was her opposite, glorying in the latter and disdaining the former. She liked fine music and animals, he liked hunting and martial thumpings. These differences, in combination with the prince's cavalier demeanor, seemed likely, it was feared in Rome, to bring the royal plans to ruin. The princess, Brussels let it be known, was growing exasperated with what she had heard of Humbert's escapades; she might place pride before love and withdraw.[14]

The crown prince was advised to harken to reason. The niece of terrible Leopold II, who had privately owned and bled the Congo, Maria José was immensely rich. She was of superior royal stock, coming from the House of Saxe-Coburg and Gotha, which had given Queen Victoria her virile consort, and as a consequence, princes in almost every reigning, pretending, or exiled royal house in Europe. And she was Catholic.

Humbert remained impassive. He did not have the democratic salt of the *re galantuomo*, who had literally rolled in the hay with an uncounted number of farmers' daughters, but he liked his upper-class good times and women no less unbridled. An American in Rome of the 1920s has told the story of a party Humbert attended in the home of Marquise Bertarelli:

> I arrived in time to watch the launching from the window of all the desserts from the buffet table before the terrified eyes of four houseboys in livery. That was the work of [Prince] Girolamo Rospigliosi. At the same time the telephone was ringing. "Is this the home of Marquise Bertarelli? This is the aide-de-camp of His Royal Highness the Crown Prince speaking. Although he was not invited, he will honor the marquise's party all the same." Imagine the poor woman's emotions. She ran everywhere announcing the happy news. Her daughter, a spicy little provincial, ran into her room to change her clothes. . . . [Prince] Rodolfo del Drago took it upon himself to get a live cow, which was to have been unloaded from a truck and led up the steps as the culminating moment of the party. . . .[15]

If Grandmother Margherita were alive, she might not have approved of the hijinks, but doubtless she would have taken the prince's part in opposing the marriage to Maria José. The queen mother had always included the royal Belgians among those houses which brought "bad luck." For once she had had fact on her side. Maximilian, the imported emperor of Mexico, and Crown Prince Rudolf of Austria, brother and son respectively of Franz Josef, had married Belgian princesses, and both Hapsburg men had suffered ghastly endings. Their wives, mad Charlotte and hapless, dim Stephanie, were Maria José's cousins, and Maria's mother, Queen Elizabeth of Belgium, had still thicker blood ties to the assassinated empress, Franz Josef's Elizabeth.

But Victor Emmanuel III, his late mother's sentiments notwithstanding, simply ordered Humbert to the altar, and the prince, however wide might have been his abandon, never once disobeyed his father. Thus, though the marriage would end in dismal failure, and "bad luck" would indeed be visited on both the bride and the groom, Humbert was duly wed to the Belgian.

It was a grandiose, all-European event, without doubt the grandest royal happening of the postwar world. The future Italian queen would always remember it as "a fairy tale of long ago, times that will never again return."[16] For all its splendor, however, it was but a melancholy stage play of times past. The ceremonies lasted a full week, which gave ample time for a multitude of princely figures to gather in Rome. Though the future King George VI was there, as well as the royal families of Scandinavia and, of course, Belgium, it seemed to be a convening of the dispossessed. The surviving royal exiles of imperial Russia and the once-mighty Central Powers; the former sovereigns of Portugal, Greece, and states no longer mapped; and a cosmopolitan mass of used-to-be courtiers and banished noblemen dragged out their old clothes and ribbons, only to stand naked in Rome.

Their humiliations were salved in the presence of the oldest ruling house in Europe—a dynasty in the tutelage of prestigious Fascist power, and it seemed time was on their side. The winds of reaction blowing from *Roma fascista* stirred thoughts of a great restoration from republican Portugal to the Bolshevik east. But the House of Savoy, functioning at the moment as a kind of field hospital giving shelter to the refugee princes, had paid dearly for its survival, and this simple truth was rendering the self-deluded hopeful mere images in the salts of fading photographs. The old powers, for the real, live dynasty in Rome, had grown flaccid, but at least there was irony. As Bartoli has observed, "That recent court of the Quirinal, that Piedmontese dynasty risen rapidly by fortune and audacity to the throne of Italy, had become the first court and the first dynasty of continental Europe, and the marriage of Victor Emmanuel III's heir the maximum event of the languishing international of kings."[17]

The "international" was not small. Five thousand persons attended the wedding ball at the Quirinal. It was a week long remembered. The kings, past, present, and future, led by Humbert and Maria José, danced the Charleston—save the future George VI, who had been permanently offended at the wedding banquet when assigned a place of lesser importance than the lowly former king of Afghanistan. The bride wore a dress designed by the groom. Queen Elena, and even Humbert, it is said, cried at the wedding. The prince and princess called on the pope. The Romans cheered the young couple. Humbert was captivating in his colonel's uniform, even now surrounded by beautiful women. Maria José, in the flush of bridehood, was almost beautiful, although she—and he—did not think so.

The prince and princess of Piedmont went away to ski on Mont Blanc, and then to live in the royal palaces at Turin and Naples. Knowing his taste in women, she tried hard to please. She gave up her passion for nature, music, and art, and took to gymnastics and dieting. She had her naturally thickly curled hair straightened, her teeth capped, and, while she refused to wear anything but low-heeled shoes, she dressed in the very latest fashions, originals created for her by her husband. As might be expected, that was hardly sufficient.

They had not been married more than a few months when gay Humbert was getting into trouble again—most sensationally, in a rotogravured infatuation between the crown prince and the Hollywood "princess" Jeanette Macdonald. The widely headlined story had Maria José surprising the lovers at their trysting place on the *Côte d'Azur*, where she promptly drew a derringer from her purse and took several shots at the actress, none of which came near to the target. Not a word of it was true, but the real princess suffered, as when Dolores Del Rio had been reported to have admitted herself in pursuit of Humbert, "the handsomest man in the world."[18]

The facts may not have been straight but the gallantry of the wild-driving, prank-playing crown prince continued to be truthfully earned. Before long the couple were all but estranged, and not even his surprise visits to her bedroom (once, disguised as an intruding *carabiniere*, he almost frightened her to death) could alleviate her perennial sadness, or, for that matter, produce any children.

When a child was born in 1934—Maria Pia—the crown princess's gynecologist revealed the royal secret while lecturing at the University of Naples on his experiments with artificial insemination. The gynecologist was dismissed from service at the palace, which did not harm his reputation, nor help the prince's. Humbert, however, grew more subdued as a loving father, and the couple drew close to one another again. In 1937 the birth of an eventual heir to Savoyard rule, Victor Emmanuel IV, was celebrated. The *principino* had arrived as a result of the same technique which had brought Maria Pia into the world, or so it seems from the mother's confessions to Count Ciano. In December, 1939, Maria José, pregnant with her third child, Maria Gabriella, was able to confide to the count that at last she was bearing an infant created by herself and her husband in the old-fashioned way. "She speaks well of the Prince of Piedmont," Ciano did not hesitate to pass on, "saying that he has undergone an unexpected and complete *revirement* of mind and manner, and she has let me know that the child to be born is his, without the intervention of physicians or syringes."[19]

The appearance of a fourth Victor Emmanuel was woeful to Hélène of Orleans, but the duke of Aosta was long out of pain. He succumbed peacefully in the ninth year of fascism, reconciled to his throneless destiny. His testament declared him "certain that a magnificent future will dawn on our fatherland under the enlightened guidance of the king and the wise government of the duce."[20]

To those who heard him and cared little about the means to the end foreseen, the duke's last words were to appear as an inspired prophecy. For in the tenth year of fascism the Wise began preparing the empire and the Enlightened would soon after wear the imperial crown.

25

THE LITTLE EMPEROR

FASCISM WAS UNABLE TO HOLD BACK THE HIGH TIDE OF ECONOMIC HARDSHIP WHICH INUNdated the West after 1929. It tried everything to reduce a sudden threefold increase in unemployment: building a wide boulevard from the Tiber to Saint Peter's; clearing the shantytown which lay between the Colosseum and Mussolini's new offices in the Palazzo Venezia; even draining the malarial Pontine marshes, a project first begun in the 1790s. But per capita income descended, dragging down the Duce's good name. There was mass hunger in Italy, and while Mussolini could boast callously that "fortunately the Italian people are not yet accustomed to eating several times a day,"[1] he was not entirely insensitive to the perils of a failing economy. War, waged well, in many cases does much to ameliorate such conditions, at least in the short run, and it seemed a war on Ethiopia might be one such case.* Moreover, Mussolini could not rest forever on the laurels earned from the Lateran Treaties. He longed for a new victory, and the circumstances were such that his longings seemed realizable in the soil of someone else's kingdom—which is one of the reasons why several hundred thousand Italians were made to fight a dirty war of conquest against defenseless black men.

---

* Historian Federico Chabod gives the statistics by which the economic benefits of the Abyssinian campaign may be measured. An index of the securities market, which in 1932 had fallen to 1.38 below zero began to rise in direct proportion with an increase in the likelihood of war. By 1934 it had climbed to 4.10, and when war actually broke out in 1935 it went to 5.74 that year, and 7.28 in 1936, when the war was won. Chabod, however, correctly rejects the widely held notion that it was the will of the capitalist class alone which led Mussolini into the war. Everyone but the scourged derived something positive from the experience, some more immediately and more tangibly than others.[2]

As early as 1932, three years before Abyssinia's "unprovoked aggression," Mussolini decided that Rome needed an empire. The king, fearful of disturbing the national quiescence, was opposed to the idea, however attractive, and asked his *presidente* to reassure him that no such adventure would be embarked upon. Mussolini advanced the assurances requested, proceeding all the while with his war plans, and when Army Chief of Staff Badoglio joined the king in objecting, the Duce remarked in their absence, "Let them sing."[3] Shortly afterward the inevitable "incident" occurred—this one at a watering hole in the desert—and with Italian "honor" on the line, army and crown united now as one in their resolve to redeem it.[4]

Thus the old rhetoric about a place in the sun was uncrated and displayed before the people, who had either forgotten it or were too young to have heard it before. Haile Selassie went to the League, achieving only the immortality of a length of newsreel footage in which his appeal to the nations is seen but not heard. Then, one day in October, 1935, Mussolini stepped out on his balcony overlooking the throngs in the piazza and announced that the war had begun.

He said it was a solemn and historic moment, of course, and not only was the army marching toward its objective, but forty million Italians marched with them. Why? "Because there is an attempt to commit the blackest of all injustices against them, to rob them of a place in the sun."[5]

The war was immensely popular. Beside the aging myths of yesterday's imperialism and memories of Adowa, old D'Annunzio added fresh scrawlings from his pen, the bishops blessed Italian bombs, and the Italian Jews blessed Mussolini.[6] The favorite song of the day was *Faccetta nera*, or *Little Black Face*, which extolled the highly civilized and extraordinarily amorous qualities of an Italian legionnaire who emancipates a beautiful Abyssinian maiden from her slavery and satisfies her every desire for love and freedom.

The League condemned the Italians wholeheartedly, then voted halfhearted sanctions against them, which were as effective as the League itself proved to be. At home, the so-called sanctions were proof enough that the Italians were victims of Great Power persecution.

Victor and Elena led the nation in rescuing the economy from such iniquity in a show of patriotic selflessness. The queen, on a rainy day in December, stood beside the Tomb of the Unknown Soldier in the center of Rome, and gave her gold wedding band, as well as the king's, to the Fascist cause. Little remained of the war-hating young Elena as she tossed the rings into a makeshift furnace to be melted down for hurried use against the enemy. She prayed aloud for victory and hoped that others too would give their gold to nullify the effects of the "sanctions." Her importunities were heard in many quarters. Some 250,000 women of Rome followed her up the steps of the war monument to the *re galantuomo* with gold tributes that they threw into the flaming receptacle. War widows and mothers of fallen soldiers led campaigns throughout the country calling at every door for an offering. The Jews of Italy, grateful for the freedoms enjoyed under "true fascism," conducted their own, separate-but-equal gold-raising campaign. The small Jewish community of Florence gave eight pounds of gold and silver, and the largest community, that of Rome, was more than generous, giving all sorts of gold artifacts from the main synagogue (built by and dedicated to Victor Emmanuel III), including the solid gold key to the ark of the covenant.[7]

The royal gesture, in initiating the national largess, was most appreciated by Mussolini, who thanked both the king and queen. Victor Emmanuel replied: "No one understands better than I what you, in these hours, are doing for our country. The queen and I are very grateful to you, and we are proud that we too are able to be useful in some way in this difficult undertaking guided by you."[8]

If this was a furtive way of underscoring the Duce's primary responsibility for the war, there was certainly good reason to do so. Exactly what the Duce was doing for his country was hardly a secret. He and the Italian army were committing abominable crimes against an entire people. The Italians, it was being unmercifully confirmed even then, were engaging not only the enemy's armed forces, but were attacking civilian populations far removed from the hostilities. Toward the end of 1935 the Italians began raining poison gas on Ethiopia in indiscriminate assaults on humans, domestic animals, and wildlife, polluting waterways and pastures, and, according to one report, "systematically killing all living creatures."*[9] To the six thousand killed at Adowa in 1896, their latter-day avengers added six thousand black men in a massacre at Addis Ababa—although this hardly fulfilled Mussolini's standing order for "ten eyes for an eye."[11]

One reason for the war's popularity at home was that the half-starved Ethiopians were too weak to fight back. The battles were

---

* Such reports were denied in Rome, but later admitted. In 1947 Italy signed a peace treaty in which it agreed that acts committed in Ethiopia during the Abyssinian war were both "war crimes" and "crimes against humanity," the latter term rendering the hapless Italians the first nation in history to have perpetrated barbarities defined in this way in international law.[10]

therefore prosecuted successfully and, more important, speedily. On May 5, 1936, Marshal Badoglio, who would shortly be titled duke of Addis Ababa, marched his troops into the Ethiopian capital. The negus had taken flight, the city had fallen, and Badoglio telegraphed Mussolini that the war was over.

Somebody rang up the king. He began to cry. "My legs were trembling," he later remembered. "I called the queen to the telephone. . . . Then I communicated the news to my son. That night, though I always sleep soundly, I got up, turned on the light, and went to look at a map of Africa. What a march!"[12]

Two days later Victor Emmanuel received the Duce and made him a knight of the Order of Savoy, the highest military honor of his house. Of Mussolini he said: "He is not only a political genius, but a military genius as well." The Duce accepted all honors and gave his master an "empire" in exchange, while some people, as was proper on like occasions, made allusions to Garibaldi.

On May 9 Mussolini appeared on his balcony. Many tens of thousands of exhilarated Romans stood in the piazza below chanting "Duce, Duce, Duce" in a spellbinding rhythm. Millions more listened on the radio as Mussolini made his celebrated "speech of the empire." Once again the Third Rome had arisen. Italy had her empire, he said, and in himself she had her "Founder of the Empire." But it was to the little king that he gave all, as he read the brief proclamation extending the imperial crown and title to Victor Emmanuel III, and to all his rightful heirs from that moment until eternity.

"Up the standards, oh legionnaires!" the founder proclaimed in resurrection of the long dead past. "Lift your irons and your hearts in full salute! After fifteen centuries the Empire has reappeared on the fateful hills of Rome."[13]

Such was the manner in which the princes of Savoy and of still more ancient tribes became the emperor-inheritors of all that once was Rome; and as emperor is the highest rank an earthly creature can attain, their work was, or should have been, done.

Mussolini, unfortunately, had only just begun. He was later to regret that his stomach ailment had not struck him dead on this the summit of his successes, but now he mistook the summit for the mere foothills and he clambered on. The short-run gains of the war proved to be short indeed. The *Savoia 81* fighter aircraft and the poison gas had been bought on credit, and the notes were falling due. Moreover in defying with impunity the finger-waggings of the League of Nations, particularly Great Britain, Italy had maneuvered itself behind the rose-colored glasses of the final illusions. By far the worst of this affliction was the belief that "imperial" Italy, in giving substance to the Humbertine-Crispian hallucination, had at last achieved the Great Powerhood dreamed by Dante, Machiavelli, and the *re galantuomo*. As a consequence, Mussolini, though he presided over a land which by now had even fewer natural resources than in Cavourian times, was overtaken by the most outlandish pretensions. Filled with visions of redistributing British influence in the Mediterranean in his favor and reclaiming from the French the old territories of Corsica, Nice, and Savoy, Mussolini began to pose as the protector of Islam in the East and an independent imperialist power in the West.

This attitude, in the aftermath of the Ethiopian aggression, led to a disastrous new alignment of Italian foreign policy, which sealed the fate of fascism and the House of Savoy. Installing his thirty-three-year-old son-in-law, Count Ciano, as head of the foreign ministry, Mussolini did nothing to mend damaged relations with the western democracies. He purposefully allowed the further deterioration of the traditional Anglo-Italian *entente*, so long considered essential to Rome's well-being. This isolation led the Italians into increasingly closer ties with rising Nazism. The aggressiveness of both governments found reinforcement in one another's ambitions. Then Ciano, eager to enhance his personal prestige with a Fascist victory all his own, convinced Mussolini to intervene in the Spanish civil war, which had erupted immediately after the Ethiopian affair. Estrangement from the West and entanglement with Hitler's Germany, which was also aiding Franco's revolt, now became all the more accentuated. It helped bring on the Pact of Steel alliance between Rome and Berlin, and it would not be long afterward that the Italians would suddenly discover themselves prisoners in a kind of German extermination camp, when not inside the actual camps.

The Germanophobic king-emperor, beginning with his opposition to Mussolini's intervention in the Spanish war, was to resist the Rome-Berlin friendship at every stage. Were he to have done so more energetically, he might have saved his house. But he was hardly a match for Mussolini, and, as we have seen, was a willing victim of another phenomenon by which he was always being denuded of whatever powers that could prove serviceable in his resistance. Victor Emmanuel was not oblivious to his hastening obsolescence, and Mussolini's continued lack of restraint provoked growing dissension between the monarch and the dictator, though as always it remained more or less covert. The wedges of ill will, however, driven ever deeper by Mussolini's claims on all the state's powers, were ultimately to facilitate the king's final break with the Duce.

The year 1938 was particularly inauspicious in this respect. It bore the terminal cycle in the relationship between the two men.

The king who had so recently called Mussolini a military genius, suddenly found him tampering with the army—the last remaining power behind the badly wasted royal prerogatives. It seemed innocuous at first. On February 1 Mussolini introduced the *passo romano*, or the Roman step, which was nothing but the German goose step by an older name. He declared that the *passo romano* was not for "dead beats," and when criticized of mimicking the Nazis, he rejoined that he would like to Prussianize the army—as if it had not already been Prussianized far too often since Victor Amadeus III undertook the endeavor only to see his efforts crushed by young Napoleon.

The king disapproved of the goose step, but said so only privately. He observed that it was not meant for him, and when asked why by Mussolini, he replied jokingly, "Dead beat."[14]

"It's not my fault, if the king is a physical dead beat," Mussolini told Ciano, but not Victor Emmanuel. "Naturally he won't be able to do the parade step without appearing ridiculous. He will hate it for the same reason he has always hated the horse—given that he cannot mount it without a little ladder."[15]

"It's no use," he lamented on another occasion. "The king is just too little for an Italy on the road to greatness."[16]

Two months after the rather inconsequential goose step affair, a bill was rushed through the Fascist chamber and senate which was taken very seriously by the court. Some saw an emerging pattern, indicating that a Fascist scheme was afoot to wrest control of the armed forces entirely.

The bill, which Mussolini in his audience of May 2 placed before the sovereign for signing, was to establish the rank of "First Marshal of the Empire." In contradiction of itself, it would create two such marshals: the king and the Duce. Mussolini theoretically would be elevated to a position of equality with the constitutional royal commander-in-chief. But in practice supremacy would be given to the Duce alone in all areas except that of the oath of loyalty to the king, which it did not impinge on but certainly confused.

Victor Emmanuel had said nothing about the bill, never really believing, it seems, that it would actually come before him for signing. But when Mussolini handed it to him, for the first time in his life he exploded with fury. The king was white with anger. His facial muscles, which had lately shown signs of palsy, caused his jaw to tremble more than usual, as the following clash took place:

> Victor Emmanuel: After the law of the Grand Council, this law is another mortal blow against my sovereign prerogatives. I would have given you any rank as a sign of my admiration, but this equalization puts me in an unsupportable situation, because it is another patent violation of the Constitution of the kingdom.
>
> Mussolini: You know that I don't care at all about these externals. Those who promoted it believed that in conferring such a rank on me, you, Your Majesty, would automatically bestow it.
>
> Victor Emmanuel: No. The chambers cannot take initiatives of this kind. This is the grossest of all! In view of the imminence of an international crisis, however, I do not want to add more fuel to the fire. But if these were other times, rather than suffer this affront, I would prefer to abdicate. I would rip up these braids.[17]

The king pointed to the gold trimmings on his cap and sleeves. Mussolini was somewhat shocked at the unprecedented outburst. Later, when he saw Count Ciano, he exclaimed, "Enough. I'm fed up. I work and he signs. . . . When the war in Spain is over, we'll take care of this."[18] In the meantime, he sought to placate the king with an opinion on the matter from a "very eminent" professor of constitutional law, a certain Santi Romano. When he presented the expert's report confirming the "legality" of the twin first marshalship, Victor Emmanuel again waxed livid with rage.

"Professors of constitutional law," he cried, "especially when they are pusillanimous opportunists, like Professor Santi Romano, always find arguments to justify the most absurd theses. That's their business. But I continue to have my own opinion. Furthermore, I have not kept it secret from the presidents of the two chambers, so that they can notify the promoters of this insult to the Crown that it will be the last."[19]

Mussolini later conjectured that at that moment Victor Emmanuel "swore to himself to get revenge. It was only a matter of waiting for the right time." The Duce himself was the chief of "the promoters," and it is clear from his own testimony that he was feeling a sense of persecution bordering on a psychotic experience. According to another source, Mussolini is quoted as having said that he had invented first marshalship because he had perceived an attitude of hostility in the king, and worse, a "ridiculous sentiment" of triumph. "Over whom?" asked Mussolini himself. "Over me." They had abused his good nature, he felt, and he had therefore instigated the new law "to make these Savoys understand that respect is one thing and moral courage another," he said.[20]

At the height of this conflict between Duce and king, Adolf Hitler and four special trains filled with the Nazi elite arrived in Rome for an official visit—a week-long event which tore aching hearts all the more.

The carefully timed conferment of the rank of first marshal was undoubtedly aimed at elevating the Duce before the Fuehrer as much as the king. But it did nothing to alter the rigors of diplomatic protocol. Thus when the German chief of state arrived in Rome on May 5, 1938, it was his improbable, but no less authentic counterpart, Victor Emmanuel III, rather than the lowly head of government, Mussolini, who had to play host. This led to a genuine farce embroiling the German dictator in an unholy triangle with the squabbling king and Duce. It also created a permanent trauma for all three men, which once again would find its expression in added sufferings for their people.

The trouble, which was foreseen but not properly evaluated, started at the brand-new Saint Paul's railroad station, an auxiliary terminal in the south of Rome. It had been hastily constructed in the gross Fascist architectural style especially for the Fuehrer's visit. Positioned at a point outside the walls of the city, it gave entry into the heart of the capital along the new boulevards built and named by the Fascists (Via dei Trionfi—Street of the Triumphs; Via dell'Impero—Street of the Empire), and offered the most imposing views of the remains of Caesarean Rome. Preparations for Hitler's state visit had been handled by Ciano, with close guidance from his father-in-law. The young foreign minister had made certain that the Italy which would flicker in the windows of the Fuehrer's south-bound trains would be pleasing to the German eye, and the capital itself was scrubbed and then dressed in fasces, crowns, and swastikas. An appropriate number of Romans were induced by one reason or another to line the route from the station to the Quirinal. Another number of persons of declared or suspected objections to the event, were in a like manner made to spend several nights in Regina Coeli—"Queen of Heaven" jail on the left bank of the Tiber—in order that Hitler might survive the pleasures of Rome.

On the great day, the Duce, the king, and their separate entourages went forth to welcome their guests, as did the bright-smiling, flower-bearing children of Rome who had followed the lead of their school-masters to the terminal outside the walls.

No sooner had the smiling Fuehrer stepped from the train when it became embarrassingly evident to all that the masters of ceremonies had unthinkingly spoiled the day. The smile fell glum, and Hitler, who idolized Mussolini and believed that he was at least as mighty in Italy as he himself was at home, suddenly found that it was the little king into whose arms he was being received. The Fuehrer was as lowborn as Mussolini, but in place of the latter's God-fearing awe of his traditional betters, he had an unhealthy hatred of royalty; he was horror-struck. Though he had been briefed on the requirements of custom, he had apparently paid them scarce mind. He thought he was visiting Mussolini, but the Duce scrupulously obeyed the time-honored constraints and kept a respectful distance from his master.

There was nothing the German could do but follow the colorful ushers to the king's carriage, and go off, thigh-to-thigh with the despised sovereign, leaving Mussolini conspicuously and painfully out in the cold. The hurt was everlasting to Mussolini. Years later he recalled the unhappiness of the crowds along the route to the Quirinal, who had sought in vain to catch a glimpse of him in the procession. He had had to return to his office "by way of the back streets of Testaccio," the laundry-hung, working-class district south of the Jewish ghetto.[21]

Hitler, unlike Mussolini, did not hesitate to allow his feelings to show. He wondered aloud whether the horse-drawn House of Savoy had ever heard of the automobile, and agreed with Himmler that the Quirinal was an eerie, inhospitable place which "smells of cata-combs."[22] Like it or not, he had to sleep six nights in the old papal palace, but not before he created a midnight havoc demanding the services of a chambermaid long past the hours of the normal working day. It seems the Fuehrer could not climb into bed unless it were fluffed and patted in his presence, and a nightshift maid had to be seconded from a nearby hotel to perform the required tasks.

This sort of behavior made a most unfavorable impression on the king, whose natural pout grew steadily more severe. The rooming and boarding of the Fuehrer and his friends went on nonetheless, of course, and the king also had to take his unappreciative guest to all the nicest places in Rome, which he did most unwillingly, mumbling curses under his breath. This gave him an opportunity, however, for close-handed observation of Hitler, and in summarizing the view

afforded, he characterized the man as a "psycho-physiological degenerate," who more often than not was under the influence of nar-
cotics.[23]

To Hitler's bad manners and rudeness the court was united in its
cold reception. The Fuehrer, though he would never again allow himself to be subjected to quite the same kind of thorough disdain from
the House of Savoy, would hate the royal family all the more with the
passage of time. He could not bear the sight of the Duce being "rele-
gated to the rear rank," he would later say, and it was therefore painful to meet with him in Italy. "The joy is always taken out of the
reception he arranges for me by the fact that I am compelled to submit to contact with the arrogant idlers of the aristocracy."[24] In the
end Hitler would wreak awful vengeance on the House of Savoy,
sending Princess Mafalda to die in Buchenwald, and it was the
king's crippling fear of the Fuehrer's wrath which, as will be seen,
would play no small part in striking the mortal blow to Savoyard rule.

In the meantime, however, Hitler contented himself, prior to his
departure, with friendly complaints to the Duce. He wanted him to
know that the court had mistreated him and that the monarchy was
anti-Fascist. Mussolini told Hitler to "be patient. I have been patient
for sixteen years."[25]

It was immediately after Hitler's visit that Mussolini's patience with
the monarchy, and particularly the king, began to run out. The new
political situation in Europe and the events unfolding rapidly therefrom were probably the more forceful determinants in Italy's slide
under German hegemony, but the real souring of the Duce's relations with the king certainly smoothed the way. Mussolini found
warmth in the Fuehrer's embrace and with increasing frequency submitted to him ever more passively; even so there was still something
in his nature which did not allow him to show anything but deference
in the actual presence of the king.

As for Victor Emmanuel, he remained as unchanged in his devotions to his house as he was in his willingness, when tried, to surrender
almost everything else. But the non-negotiability of the crown itself
was the very thorn in the Duce's side before which his hands fell
limp each time he yearned most to remove it. His impotence in the
presence of the littlest man in Italy originated almost entirely in his
own soul. It rendered him as stridulously green as he appears in the
Peter Blume painting, *The Eternal City.* Victor Emmanuel simply
exasperated the Duce, urging him, with the flow of events, closer into
Hitler's arms.

When in September of that year Mussolini drew up Italy's very own anti-Semitic racial legislation, the king as always opposed him at first ("Don't put your hands in that snake pit," he advised).[26] Then as always he backed down, which encouraged Mussolini, under attack as a mere imitator of the Fuehrer, to seek a comforting word from the sovereign. "Twenty thousand spineless Italians feel sorry for the Jews," he complained, to which Victor Emmanuel replied, "I am one of them." The king said he felt "infinite pity" for the Jews, which did nothing to deter him from affixing his royal name for all time to the notorious decrees.[27]

Day after day, when out of earshot of the king, Mussolini raged against him now. Count Ciano's diaries are filled with the Duce's threats and superthreats in this regard, and at the same time they betray the strange, lordlike powers the king unconsciously exercised over Mussolini. In the last months before the outbreak of World War II the intensity of Mussolini's attacks rose to fever pitch. He used every occasion for his *in camera* revilings of the king, the throne, and everything royal.

In January, 1939, according to Ciano, the Duce returned to the theme of the king's height. Victor Emmanuel had diminished the physical prestige of the army, Mussolini said, so that it harmonized with his own "unhappy physique."[28]

In March, when the king opposed Mussolini's plans for the annexation of Albania, he came away from the palace and exploded to Ciano that if Hitler had had "a prickhead of a King he would never have been able to take Austria and Czechoslovakia."[29]

At the beginning of May the Duce inveighed against the crown's use of horse-drawn carriages and said he would put a stop to it; and at the end of the same month, Ciano quotes him in attacking the monarchy, saying: "I envy Hitler. He doesn't have a train of empty freight cars to drag along."[30]

A few days later, an incident occurred which touched off one of Mussolini's most virulent tirades. It had all the ingredients of provoking a second Matteotti affair, with the king, or the crown, as the victim. Albania had already been taken by the Italians, absorbed into the "empire"; a ceremony at the Quirinal was held on June 3, granting the Albanians their new Italian-made constitution. King-Emperor Victor Emmanuel, failing to detect any sign on the Albanian flag which would indicate its being ruled by the House of Savoy, complained in sarcastic tones to Ciano. Ciano did his best to placate the offended monarch, noting that the flag bore the blue Savoyard sash. Ciano then relates:

He agrees but remains in bad humor. I report this to the Duce, who seizes the opportunity to take off like a charging bull against the Monarchy. . . . The Duce says that now he is absolutely fed up with dragging "empty freight cars behind him, which furthermore often have their brakes on," that the King "is a little man, sour and untrustworthy, who worries about the embroidery on a flag, rather than feel pride in seeing the national territory increased by 30,000 square kilometers," and finally that "it is the Monarchy which impedes the Fascistization of the army by its idiotic windbagginess. . . ."

Ciano, recording the presence of party leader Starace, a fawning figure ready at a moment's notice to organize any kind of Fascist violence, goes on to quote Mussolini as follows:

The Duce said: "I am like a cat, cautious and prudent, but when I make my leap I am sure of landing where I want. Now I am beginning to think that the House of Savoy needs to be finished off. All that we have to do to liquidate them is mobilize . . . 250,000 men. Or perhaps simply posting a decree is enough."

"He spoke with such forcefulness," Ciano observed, "that Starace interpreted Mussolini's words as a directive to the party to march into action."[31] The Duce apparently cooled before any such coup could be plotted, but a week or so later he is to be found again pre-occupied with the royal irritant.

Generalissimo Franco, the new chief of state of fallen Spain, was about to visit Rome, and the old problem of protocol was preying on Mussolini's mind. On June 13 Ciano wrote:

The Duce calls me to speak about Franco's visit. He is very annoyed about the inevitable interference of the King, in view of Franco being Chief of State. He says: "I do not, however, intend to repeat the half-for-you-half-for-me sharecropping we had with Hitler's visit. If the King is shameless enough not to withdraw—and he is—then I will. This para-doxical situation must be brought before the Italian people, so that they finally understand that they have to make their choice."[32]

Mussolini's threats were empty. The little king, however, feeling but not articulating the same incompatibility, began now to think in terms of separation, if not divorce. He was about to pick up the all-too-shriveled initiative and tend to its convalescence. This was Europe 1939; momentous events were overtaking the old order. New sides were being drawn, and the choices to be made would mean, as always, the rise of one and the other's fall. If this were a time confus-ing to Mussolini, it was eminently familiar to the House of Savoy.

26

WAITING FOR DIO

KING-EMPEROR VICTOR EMMANUEL III MARKED HIS SEVENTIETH BIRTHDAY IN 1939. NOT FOR two hundred years had a reigning Savoyard prince lived to reach that age, a remarkable genetic achievement for the dying-young first born of the Carignano branch of the family.* His defiance of the laws of longevity and the thin blood of inbred love in his veins was worn on the outside, in his eyes and on the coarse surface of his skin. The lines ran deep across his brow; his hair had fallen, and what remained, arched around his ears and twirled neatly above his lip in the Fascist style, had turned pure white. His jaw trembled more than before, two prunelike pouches hung beneath his eyes, and his mouth held fast in a puckered grimace of vexation, as if all that had gathered up inside him were entangled in a knot of unrelenting pain.

Someone who remembers how people saw and thought about him then has written:

> He went around dressed almost always in a general's gray-green uniform, with the pants poorly tailored and scarcely pressed. . . . The Italians did not esteem him very much, except in those regions of traditional monarchism, especially in Piedmont and around Naples. But he was not hated. Many saw in the king an extreme guarantee; others looked upon him affectionately as a little grandfather, somewhat cold and aloof, who had seen most of us born during his reign. Some, finally, rivaled him with Mus-

---

* Charles Albert died at fifty one; Victor Emmanuel II, as we have seen, was dead before reaching fifty eight, Humbert at fifty six, albeit unnaturally. But even these figures were high in the line founded by Prince Thomas, who was born in 1596, the younger son of Charles Emmanuel the Great. Victor Emmanuel III would survive another eight years, but the firstborn of the firstborn Carignanos who had preceded him had compiled an average age at death of only fifty.

solini, counterposing the sobriety and decorum of the Quirinal to the ostentatiousness of the Palazzo Venezia. To the warlike posture of the latter, they opposed the modesty and reserve of the former. Thus, in '39, there was no one general opinion about him; his figure did not arouse strong feelings, like the unconditional love or deep hatred as in the case of Mussolini.[1]

The king was aware of the differences, and as the prospect of world war drew near and increasingly likely, he began to use them to his advantage. He sought within the closest confines of the court to resurrect the traditional policies of his house, and it seems that sometime early in 1939 he decided to prepare for the possibility of replacing Mussolini, forcibly if need be. Certainly by May of that year, at the time of the formalization of the Rome-Berlin Axis in the Pact of Steel, he had awakened from a ten-year sleep. He had gone over to an offensive, although of the cautious kind which might be expected from the long retired and decrescent.[2]

The private and secret policy he adopted now took no account of the desires of Mussolini, fascism, or, for that matter, the Italians. It was the tiresome Savoyard activity, as old as his house, of playing one power against another—but more dangerous than ever now.

For this reason, the king, in spite of his feelings toward Germans, welcomed the Pact of Steel. The treaty committed the Germans to come to Italy's aid in the event of war, and considering the prevailing European condition, the king feared armed conflict with the West, notably with France and Britain. To be sure, the alliance made equal demands on Rome in support of Germany in war. But this was the king who when Hitler and Mussolini were boys had admitted to the American ambassador to the Quirinal of being "convinced of the utter worthlessness of treaties." In the end, nations, royal houses, and persons, it has often been the case, do what is best for themselves. The true usefulness of treaties and oaths, Victor Emmanuel had learned, lay in the credulity of others. As such, agreements on paper, in skilled and scholarly hands, were the instruments with which new bargains might be struck.

Not for one moment did the king place his faith in the Germans. He allowed Mussolini to have that extravagance, ready himself to accept all rewards should there be any. But the bright lights of the Axis, it was perceived, could fail, and so he began to cut a path from the possible darkness. Whereas Mussolini was becoming too compromised with the Nazis to have utility elsewhere, the king sought to cultivate a potential replacement for the Duce in his son-in-law, the anti-German Count Ciano. Whereas the West feared and appeased Nazi aggressiveness, he gladly strengthened ties with Berlin—to give all the more reason why he ought to be courted by the West with kindness.

Nothing better illustrates the main points of the king's private policy—the royal wooing of the young foreign minister and the *entente* with the unsavory Germans while hoping for *rapprochement* with the West—than the pages of Ciano's diary. Ciano is daily to be found undergoing a kind of Pavlovian conditioning program, taken deeper into the king's confidences, while being increasingly encouraged, flattered, and rewarded at every juncture of agreement between them. Not only Victor Emmanuel, but the entire royal family and the court are seen to be engaged in this labor, which appears as a massive repair operation on the roof and foundations of the House of Savoy, suddenly discovered to be in the path of the approaching storm. The pace of this undertaking was dizzying.

Thus in March, 1939, the count—later duke—of Acquarone, Victor Emmanuel's trusted minister of the royal house, went to Ciano to ask only for "a bit of advice" in the name of the king on a matter of peripheral significance. But within a few weeks, the king, using his gratitude to Ciano for having concluded the Pact of Steel, went to unprecedented lengths to draw him into his circle.

"Since 1900," the king told Ciano after wiring his congratulations, "I have never sent a telegram to a minister. I felt I had to break that tradition in order to express the sentiments I so deeply feel." He had wanted to give him the title of marquis, but Mussolini had instructed Ciano to refuse. The king did not insist. He took him into his confidence instead. "The Germans," he said, "will be courteous to us, and even servile, as long as they need us. But as soon as they get a chance, they will show themselves to be the scoundrels they really are." The day was coming, he prophesied, when Italy, and the Germans too, would reach agreement with Great Britain. "Then peace and progress will truly be assured." It was food for thought. "The King," Ciano wrote, "made a strange prediction." He spoke with "unusual certainty."[3]

A few weeks later Ciano's father died. Victor Emmanuel rushed unceremoniously to pay his respects. "He could not control his emotions," Ciano noted appreciatively, ". . . his eyes were filled with tears."[4] Another few weeks passed and the king made Ciano his "cousin" by virtue of the Collar. Now, even the Duce, preoccupied with trying to keep up with Hitler's dazzling eve-of-the-war footwork, was getting suspicious of the king's intentions toward his son-in-law. He had again told him not to accept, because "the Collar could represent certain compromises. . . ." But as Mussolini was seeking the king's cooperation in the coming war, he conceded, much to Ciano's delight.[5]

That was in August, 1939, the last month of peace. On the 24th the king received "Cousin" Ciano to accept his appreciation, but that was hardly on his mind. Poland had come under the shadow of Nazi aggression, and the whole world knew that if the Germans moved east, the West could no longer idle while Hitler's power grew. World war, as it was known then, was about to break out, and the terms of the Pact of Steel required Italy to fight on the Nazi side. For his part, the king was adamantly opposed to fulfilling the conditions imposed by this section of his treaty with Hitler. He was as yet uninformed of what Mussolini was planning to do, but in fact the royal nurturing of Count Ciano had already found reward. The Duce had at first decided to march with the Fuehrer. His son-in-law, however, had argued forcefully for nonintervention if the war were provoked by a German attack on the Poles, and Mussolini, aware of Italy's unpreparedness, had allowed himself to be convinced. He agreed to adopt a policy of friendly neutrality toward the Germans, to which Hitler later acceded with some magnaminity.

Now Ciano was able to please his royal benefactors immensely by confirming that the king's fondest hopes about the count and the war had come true. Ciano's diary entry for that day is revealing. Immediately after his visit with the king, he wrote:

> . . . little is said about the Collar. He wants news of the situation. I quickly bring him up to date, but with him, I don't have to attack the Germans, since his own state of mind is already in open hostility toward them. I show him the four points agreed on with the Duce about our attitude. He approves, above all, the third: the one about our neutrality.

Relieved of that anxiety, the king then sought to fortify the view that Italy's entry into the war would be disastrous. His assessment of the nation's military failings, a subject in which he was probably Italy's best expert, was not only designed to alarm, but was entirely true. Ciano reported it in the following terms:

> In his judgment we are absolutely in no condition to wage war. The army is in a "pitiful" state. His review of the troops and the recent maneuvers has revealed to the full the sorry state of [our] unreadiness.

. . . Our officers are incompetent. Our equipment and weapons are old and obsolete.* To this must be added the national sentiment, which is decidedly anti-German. The peasants go into the army cursing those "German buggers." In his opinion, we therefore have to keep our weapons at our side, and wait for events. Six months of neutrality will give us time to strengthen our forces.

Then, if the circumstances were favorable, Italy could go to war on Hitler's side. Should this be the case, the king let it be known, war might not be all bad. He said that he hoped Ciano would do all that he could to promote the careers of the "best" soldiers of the House of Savoy. As the foreign minister recorded the king's wish:

> . . . if supreme decisions are to be taken, he would like to be in Rome, in order "not to be left out," and he hopes that the Duce, in case of war, gives a command to the Prince of Piedmont. "Those two imbeciles the Dukes of Bergamo and Pistoia have commands; my son, who has a head as good as the Duke of Aosta's, ought well have one, too."** Then, speaking fatherly, he added that the Prince is fond of me, very fond, and that he always speaks to him about me with trust and with hope.[6]

The king preferred, however, that Ciano work for peace. He sent Humbert bearing little gifts for Ciano, such as a dress pin to be worn with the Collar. The prince used the opportunities to discuss "certain questions" with the count, notably the growing antipathy of the army toward the Germans. Maria José said "nice and friendly things" to him, and told Ciano of her hatred "from the bottom of her heart" for the Germans, calling them "liars and pigs."[7] She worried about a Nazi invasion of her home country, and Ciano, ever requiting the Savoyard advances, affirmed that his best information made the prospect of a German attack on Belgium appear more than likely. He promised to forewarn her, if possible, in order that she might alert her brother Leopold III, who had succeeded their late father to the throne. It was a promise kept.[8]

Victor Emmanuel even called on Elena to help save the peace. Her

---

* The Duce would never tire of boasting about his ability to mobilize "eight million bayonets" at a moment's notice, but the king (and the Duce) knew better. The Italian army was still issuing 1891 rifles to its new recruits, and the artillery was of World War I vintage, much of it captured from the Austrians.

** The Savoyard dukes of Bergamo and Pistoia, Adalbert, forty-one, and Philibert, forty-four, were sons of Queen Margherita's brother, Thomas, duke of Genoa, and thus first cousins of the king, but more the rivals of Crown Prince Humbert. The new duke of Aosta was Amadeus, the forty-one-year-old firstborn son of the late Emmanuel Philibert. Amadeus, who had already proved his soldierliness in the Ethiopian war, was to become a national hero in the African campaign and die a British prisoner of war.

quaint efforts took their precedent from the good works in the year 1529 of the widow of the Savoyard duke Philibert the Fair, and his sister, Louise of Savoy, the mother of Francis I, king of France. They had succeeded in concluding the "Peace of the Two Dames," and so Elena addressed a letter to the neutralist queens, Elizabeth of Belgium, Alexandra of Denmark, and Wilhelmina of Holland, as well as to the Grand Duchess Charlotte of Luxemburg and to her own daughter Giovanna, czarina of the Bulgarians. Mussolini, quite properly, was against the idea, and the letter, calling for a "congress of queens" inspired by the peace-loving dames of old, was never posted.*

Meanwhile, Hitler's war had been launched. But this initial phase was the well-named "Phony War," in which after the Nazi conquest of Poland in nineteen days there no longer seemed reason to fight. Britain and France had declared war on Germany, but one sought in vain to locate the front, and the battles were those of nerves.

In neutralist Rome that *Sitzkrieg* winter of 1939–40 saw the further sharpening of the duality between government and crown, and the tugging on all things between. Uncertainties, ambitions denied, and weaknesses human and otherwise combined with the institutional diarchic phenomenon to cleave the minds of the principals themselves.

Victor Emmanuel remained no less abhoring of the Germans, but Hitler's barely contested successes preyed hard on his earlier views that Nazi power was more myth than fire. Conversely, irresolute Britain and sorely divided France appeared hardly as mighty as of old, and while he continued to wish London well, his Savoyard callings urged him toward the apparent winner. Wracked by an indecisiveness unknown in the House of Savoy since the days of Great-Grandfather Charles Albert's mental ordeals, the king worried well into the spring about how to be or not to be.

In January he told Ciano, after not having seen him for a while, that with the current policy "we risk becoming *a Dio spiacenti ed ai nimici suoi*"—displeasing to both God and his enemies.[10] The great difficulty was that the king could not come to a conclusion as to who was *Dio*: the British Empire or the Third Reich. Thus, months later, Ciano was still writing: "The King recommends that we maintain

---

* This gave Elena, the "pacifist," cause for much heartache. She had hoped to use the letter as a mental purgative. "Even if my appeal had been received by the world as utopian, and as only an illusion," she fretted when disappointed by Mussolini, "my conscience would have said to me all the same: 'You did well!' "[9]

our current position of watchful waiting and preparing as long as possible.[11]

The royal dilemma seemed insoluble. Ciano records the sovereign's sentiments on March 5, 1940:

> Long talk with the King. I found him piqued by the attitude of the English,* although that has done nothing to change his unlimited anti-German obstinacy.

Against this, with the king taking situational soundings, the following conversation ensued:

> Victor Emmanuel: I am on the blacklist in Germany.
> Ciano: Yes, Your Majesty. In the number one spot. And, if you will permit me the boldness to say so, I come right after you.
> Victor Emmanuel: I think so, too. But that does honor to both of us with regard to Italy.

Ciano, by now enjoying a certain camaraderie, felt free enough to state unhesitatingly to the king, "I would consider a German victory as the greatest disaster for our country."

Victor Emmanuel was cautious. If not with the Germans, he wondered aloud, what could be obtained from the Allies? The count replied melodramatically: "The salvation of Italy's freedom, which German hegemony would compromise for centuries." The king agreed.[12]

Now it was Ciano who was giving food for thought. Victor Emmanuel, at this point, began to think the unthinkable: He felt he might have to act boldly against Mussolini "at any moment."[13] A few days later the king took the perilous initiative of exposing to Ciano the most seditious side of the House of Savoy. He dispatched his faithful Acquarone, who was to play a crucial role in the actual overthrow of Mussolini three years later, to see the young foreign minister. It was a rehearsal of the conspiratorial events to come. Ciano, who had less than four years of life remaining before being shot for treason by order of his father-in-law, wrote as follows of his encounter with Acquarone:

> Count Acquarone, Minister of the Royal House, approached me on the golf course. He speaks openly of the situation with a sense of preoccupation, and assures me that the King too is aware of the disquiet

---

* The "attitude" in question refers to a British decision taken a few days earlier to intercept German coal exports. As Italy had grown all but entirely dependent on Hitler's coal, London's escalation of the war was considered in Rome as forcing the Italians closer to the Nazi side.

felt throughout the country. According to him, His Majesty feels that the need may arise at any moment for him to intervene in order to turn things in a different direction. He is ready for it, and is prepared to carry it out most energetically. Acquarone says repeatedly that the King feels "more than benevolence" toward me, "real and true affection and much trust."[14]

Acquarone, according to Ciano, did not wish to let the matter rest there. He wanted to get down to specifics, but the foreign minister, out of fear or design, tried, as he notes, to hold such talk to "generalities." One could never be sure he were not speaking to a Fascist spy. The king's emissary acquiesced. The promptitude of all the conspirators was yet to mature.

The king, in his inability to make up his mind, agonized for another ten weeks or so. He again sent forth Humbert with explicit worries about Italy's increasingly pro-German foreign policy and discouraging words that the army was no better now than it had been last summer. As for himself, the king tried at the same time to win popularity in Berlin by giving the Collar to Goering, who had coveted it literally with tears in his eyes. It was not easily bestowed. "To give the Collar to Goering," Victor Emmanuel confided, "is a gesture which displeases me. To send him a telegram [of congratulations] is repugnant to me for a hundred thousand reasons."[15]

The king's *doppio giuoco* did not escape the Duce, who was suffering doubts equally as tormenting as Victor Emmanuel's but oriented in precisely the opposite direction. He could not bear being left behind by the Nazis, yet he could not be sure his poorly disposed forces would not go down in mortifying defeat. The military commitments he had undertaken in the Pact of Steel, and had been unable to fulfill, had rendered him in his own eyes, in spite of Hitler's generosity, "the laughing-stock of Europe."[16] Still, he told Hitler that they both could gain most through peace, though the more others in Rome, especially the king, spoke of peace while Hitler made war, the more the Duce hated peace.

It hurt most when in the presence of the little king. Returning from his audience of April 11, 1940, Mussolini seemed at wit's end. If it were up to Victor Emmanuel, he complained bitterly, Italy would never know the glory of war.

> The king [he said] would like us to enter only to pick up the broken dishes. Let's hope they won't be broken over our heads first. It is so

humiliating to sit on the sidelines with our hands folded while others write history. It doesn't matter who wins. To make a people great it is necessary to send them into combat, even if you have to kick them in the ass. And that's what I intend to do.[17]

In the event, Mussolini did not have to employ that tactic. Hitler, figuratively speaking, did it for him. At dawn on May 10 he lined up seventy-two divisions on his western frontiers and sent them forward with good wishes and ammunition. One by one the states began to fall like so many tenpins: little Luxemburg on that very day; The Netherlands on the 15th; Belgium on the 25th; "invincible" France in thirty-seven days. The world, watching the Nazi sweep, the flight of kings and presidents, and the collapse of all that centuries had built, was stunned. In London the lone voice of warning, Winston Churchill, was given power by the totally discredited appeasers. In Rome hesitations were burned and war plans advanced.

Now no one would stop Mussolini. If the king would ally with the pope in opposing him, he threatened privately, he would "blow up" both of them at the same time. At the end of May the decision was taken: Italy would go to war within days. The king, who was asked to declare the hostilities, approved. He was relieved of the painful fence-sitting, but not of all his doubts. "He is resigned, nothing more than resigned to the idea of war," Ciano wrote after seeing him on June 1. "He believes that France and England have in fact been hit tremendously hard, but he attributes great importance to the eventual intervention of the Americans...."[18]

Said Victor Emmanuel: "Those who talk of a short and easy war are deluding themselves. There are still many unknowns...."[19]

There were last minute fights between the king and the Duce about the size of their share of the supreme command. Mussolini's private threats against the monarchy grew more ferocious and unbounded than before. The king was also very much annoyed. Finally Mussolini was "entrusted" with the office of commander-in-chief, which was something less than the office itself.

On June 3 Ciano found the king at the ready for war. "Now that the sword is about to be unsheathed," wrote the count, "the King like all the Savoys is preparing to be a soldier and nothing but a soldier."[20]

The date was set for June 11. The king was pleased. Eleven, he believed, was his lucky number. He had been born at eleven o'clock in the evening of the eleventh day of the eleventh month; he was sworn into office on the eleventh, and his serial number in the army was 1111. The declaration of war, however, was actually made twenty-four hours earlier, but the king, taking an overnight train to the front, waited until the 11th to issue the proclamation sending the royal army into battle. And it was on the 11th that Victor Emmanuel telegraphed Adolf Hitler: "I am certain that the glorious armies of Italy and Germany will bring victory and an ever greater prosperity to our two nations, which are united in faith."[21]

But fortune could not be deceived. The official date of Italy's entry into the war was not on the lucky eleventh, but on June 10. Thus the king's path had been crossed by the anniversary of the black day the Fascists killed Matteotti.

27

"THE SITUATION IS GRAVE, BUT NOT DESPERATE"

✦✦ THE WAR DID NOT GO WELL FOR THE ITALIANS.
✦✦ ROME AND THE KING HAD GAMBLED ENTIRELY
on German, not Italian, power. With critics long banished from the
Fascist kingdom, almost everyone believed or at least hoped with
Mussolini, who said Italy needed only "one thousand dead to sit at
the peace table." The Duce predicted that the war would be over by
autumn, and to many who in June saw the newsreels and stills of
German troops marching past the *Arc de Triomphe* and raising the
swastika on the Eiffel Tower, the Duce appeared, as the party slogan
so often maintained, "always right."

The Savoys in war were, as usual, soldiers to the quick. The little
king ran around without rest in his leggings and greatcoat. The crown
prince, promoted to the rank of marshal, was given that important
command. He was made head of the ill-fated Army Group West,
which left its shot or frozen dead on the Alpine peaks ancestral Savoys
once held uncontestedly. The queen and the crown princess wore
white; they were indefatigable nurses, never wearying in their at-
tendance to the multitudes of sick, frostbitten, and maimed brought
back from the front. Elena even took a Jewish doctor into her circle
of court workers for the Italian Red Cross. She asked only that he
change his name from Stuckolz to Stuccoli, and in the alteration was
able to rescue him from the kingdom's racial laws.

But the war did not end as early as many wished it would. It
dragged on wet with blood, and when Maria José in a private talk
with Hitler sought his best estimate as to just how long the fighting
would ensue, he replied: "I hope not more than thirty years."[1]

The king's mood, like the mood of most great men without vision,

changed from day to day according to the news reports. By the end
of the first year, in spite of battlefield humiliations in France, Greece,
and Africa, he still believed in victory. British guns had returned the
negus to the throne of the hard-won Ethiopian empire, but Italian
penetration into the Balkans gave satisfying compensation to the
Savoyard dynasty. Victor and Elena welcomed the forcible dismantling of Yugoslavia, which exhumed in its fullest dimension the
lost and beloved kingdom of Montenegro, and made a new Nazi-
Fascist state called Croatia. The king was "very happy" when the
Croats "decided" in favor of a monarchy with the crown to be given
to a prince of Savoy. Victor Emmanuel chose his nephew Aimone,
the younger son of the late duke of Aosta, a choice which at last permitted Hélène of Orleans to envisage her flesh and blood on a throne.
But this dream too would fade.

Aimone, elected by the king for his task because of his "presence"
and "to a certain extent" his intelligence,[2] accepted with pride, although he worried about losing his princely freedom and mobility.*
The duke of Acquarone complained that when he tried to find
Aimone to tell him the good news "it took twenty-four hours to trace
him: he was hiding in a hotel in Milan with some girl."[5] This annoyed
Victor Emmanuel, but the crown was extended nonetheless to satisfy
the desires of some Croats.

Aimone took the name of Tomaslav II, but was a long time in leaving for his kingdom. Many months later the king had to order his
nephew's speedy departure from Rome. "The behavior of this young
man is really absurd," Ciano wrote of the forty-one-year-old sovereign. He was living with a girl well-known in society, frequenting
taverns of dubious repute, and allowing his drinking to get the better
of him. "A few nights ago," said Ciano, "in a night club near Piazza
Colonna, he twisted a tablecloth around his head, and wore it as if

* He was also preoccupied about his safety in the puppet state, and when he
questioned his royal uncle about this, Victor Emmanuel advised him to face his
future "serenely." Immediately after receiving Aimone, the king confided that he
had advised his nephew not to pay much heed to the "excesses" being committed
by the Croat militia, the Ustachi, against the Serbs. "These are things which in
time fall into place," he said. "The Italian government too had to struggle, and
employ not a little repression against the brigandage of southern Italy. . . . Little
by little the Croat government will grow strong and will be able to rely on a regular
army and police force, and much of the excesses will no longer occur."[3] The crimes
of the Ustachi, which are still in the 1970s being prosecuted by the Yugoslavs, were
so hideous that even their Nazi masters had to restrain them. General Jodl made
this entry in his war diary in June, 1942: "The German field gendarmes have arrested a Ustachi company for atrocities against the civil population in East Bosnia;
they have disarmed and imprisoned them."[4]

it were a crown, amid the applause of the waiters and the owner. The owner, a certain Ascensio, who divides his time between his kitchen and prison, is his best friend. A fine figure of a King!"[6]

Aimone of Savoy managed somehow to never actually set foot in his kingdom; the reign of Tomaslav II was to be a short one indeed. Two years hence his obstinacy in procrastinating his coronation was to be vindicated in his survival of the violent downfall of this Axis "state."

As for reanimated Montenegro, the king insisted that a member of the exiled Petrovich clan be restored to the lost powers. Queen Elena was thrilled, but the trouble was that no one qualified was willing to take the job. The long banished poet-warrior-bishop-princes of the black mountains had all either died or fallen into incorrigible decline. At least one of them, the queen's nephew Prince Michael, found to be living in dire straits near Lake Constance, had the good sense of concluding that both Italy and Germany would come to a bad end, and thus rejected the family's crown as having only ephemeral value.[7]

The collective opinion shifted to Elena. She, if anyone, ought to sit on the Montenegrin throne, it was said in Rome. But Victor Emmanuel was adamant in his opposition to that scheme; the royal couple since first they met in St. Petersburg nearly a half-century before were still inseparable. In the end, the Montengerins resisted both royal and Fascist rule, taking up arms in a forceful underground movement, and though Rome imposed an oppressive regency, Prince Michael's predictions would soon come true.*

The king's dynastic business in the Balkans, which included a visit to his Albanian domains (where he escaped the assassination attempt of an unhappy local poet—"That boy is a pretty poor shot"), occupied nearly half a year. That he took the time out to do so was an act of faith in Hitler and Mussolini, and appreciated as such at least by the latter. His armchair conspiring of the year before was put out of mind, and for a while he took a dislike of Count Ciano and burned warmer toward the Duce.

The second year of the war, however, saw all revert back as be-

---

* Victor Emmanuel was ingenuous enough to believe that outbreaks of armed resistance in Montenegro were Ciano's fault. Only the king understood how proud a people were the Montenegrins. During an assembly to reconstitute the monarchy, he complained bitterly that the Italian foreign minister had permitted a photograph of Elena's late father, King Nicholas, to take second place to one of the Duce's. This had done irreparable damage in infuriating the patriots, said the king. "They didn't want to listen to me," he added in disgust on hearing that rebel bands had attacked Italian detachments. "Here is the result!"[8]

fore, and the palace plotting began anew. Now, at the prodding of enemy bayonets, it was to go forward to the very end. By June, 1942, Victor Emmanuel no longer believed in victory. The surprising endurance of Great Britain and the Soviet Union had forced him to discard the contemporary myth of an imminent collapse of those countries. The developing power of the United States in war was further proof that the stability of the Allies was assured. Though he could not any longer speak of the enemy's fall, he was as yet incapable of articulating the thought of his own defeat. Instead, adopting the sentiments of many who foresee dark times for themselves, he saw such misfortune as happening to others. He was tortured by the notion of an ugly and everlasting stalemate.

"No one is going to win," he said now, "and the peoples of the world, in addition to their war miseries, will have to bear the inevitable unhappiness of many shattered illusions." What was needed now was a "compromise peace."[9]

By the end of November, 1942, however, events had shown even stalemate to be a lie. Italy, the king now knew, was going to lose. The many battles for Bengazi, Tobruk, and El Alamein were done; they had fallen to the British and could never be recovered. The Americans had landed in North Africa; they were building the bases and rolling out the air strips from which the inexorable invasion of the homeland would be launched. The deadlock at Stalingrad had been broken by a massive Russian offensive, which was to roll back the Reich literally to the Fuehrer's front door. The morale of the Italian armed forces and the civilian population was nonexistent. Hardships and bombs had made of an unpopular war hatred for all things Nazi and Fascist. Anti-Fascist resistance was being organized underground. Industrial strikes, pamphleteering, and armed attack were not far off. The sons and daughters of the Fascist generation had grown up. Many of them saw the folly and oppression in the old order. They yearned for the new, and the lesson of the times was that it could only be taken with guns.

Victor Emmanuel was "reassured" by Prince Bassiano, a descendant of the Roman Caetanis who had so stanchly supported Victor Emmanuel II and Humbert the Good, that Franklin Roosevelt would never permit Italy's total destruction. The prince, however, spoke solely on the authority of his marriage to an American socialite; the king found little consolation. If Italy is to be defeated, he replied, "It is better not to have too many illusions and to hang on to useless and false promises."[10]

As for himself, he was certain now of that conviction, but he traded the old pipe dreams for new ones. He thought in terms of the House of Savoy exiting unharmed and unstigmatized from the war, even heroically—if only he conclude a separate peace with the Allies. This meant breaking with the Germans of course and almost certainly with Mussolini. He sought therefore to get the conspiracy in motion again, while trying to remain strategically aloof. "Only in desperate circumstances will the Crown be able to intervene," the king's chief aide-de-camp Puntoni said in explaining the royal position to fellow generals already prepared to rebel. "For now it is best that His Majesty be above it all so that one day he can be the arbiter of events."[11]

The king, while he groped for channels in which the imagined peace might be touched, saw his role as nurturing revolution from the monarchist top and preventing it from occurring at any other level. The royal institutions had to be protected from decisive disturbances which might arise at home from Nazis, Fascists, the Allies, or the people. Thus he began to press for the recall of Italian troops from abroad, complaining to Mussolini that the fatherland, and especially the capital, was sorely unprotected.

The audience given by the king to Ciano on November 19, 1942, one of the last such contacts with the foreign minister, is indicative of the mood and substance of this new beginning. Appropriately, this was the day of Russia's launching of the Stalingrad counteroffensive. Victor Emmanuel received both Ciano and Count Grandi, the Fascist regime's "elder statesman," who had been foreign minister, ambassador to London, and was now minister of justice. Grandi, who would lead the grand council's revolt against Mussolini, was actively seeking allies and developing a conspiratorial relationship with Ciano. The king spoke with Grandi for only a few minutes, but well over an hour with Ciano. The foreign minister recorded afterward that the sovereign was anxious for news about Spain, Switzerland, and Turkey, neutral ground where contacts with the Allies might be made. He went on:

> I find him physically well . . . but above all he is worried about the scarcity of armed forces in Italy, and especially in Rome, where even the grenadiers have been withdrawn. He asks me to pressure the Duce to repatriate some of our troops, at the same time begging me not to tell him that it was he who spoke to me of this "so that he should not have thoughts of secret dealings. . . ." As always, his Germanophobia shows up in his words. About how the war is going he repeats a rather

generic statement of faith, but he asks a great deal about Washington and London, and he advises me to hold preciously any thread which may become useful, "even if it is as frail as the web of a spider."[12]

Nazi intelligence was not unaware of the contacts and sentiments among Ciano, Grandi, and the royal house. The Germans based their mistrust of the Italians, and particularly the side-switching House of Savoy, on historical experience. Grandi, with Ciano's help, had prepared a secret mission to Spain to feel for what terms, if any, the Allies might offer. This aborted, but it seems some insignificant conversations took place in Lisbon, and the German legation there telegraphed Berlin that Ciano and Crown Prince Humbert were behind them.[13]

There were other rumors and reports which tended to corroborate this, and Ciano's locker-room anti-Germanism, defeatism, and ambition were already well-known. His participation in a criminal conspiracy was another matter, which was harder to believe, not as much for his relationship to Mussolini as for its unlikeliness. As the German ambassador in Rome, von Mackensen, told the Wilhelmstrasse: "He may be unclear about the extent of his unpopularity, but he must be living on the moon if he has any illusions that he has behind him the mass of the population in whose eyes he is precisely the champion of the Axis."[14]

Nevertheless the effect of what people were saying about the count almost overnight turned Ciano into a symbol of defeat, compromising his usefulness all around. The king backed away, speaking to him of only the most inconsequential affairs, and Mussolini, assessing the bad reports, prepared his son-in-law's fall. In February, 1943, the Duce sent for Ciano, which gave occasion for one of the final entries in his diary: "As soon as I enter the room," he wrote, "I see that he is very embarrassed, and I know what he is about to tell me. 'What would you like to do now?' he says, adding *sotto voce* that he has changed his whole cabinet. I understand why . . ."[15]

Grandi was dropped, too, as well as others, but only to cloud the reasons for the Ciano-Grandi dismissals and to demonstrate that the Duce was still in command. Given a choice of jobs, Ciano rejected the regency of Albania ("where I would go to be the hangman of those to whom I promised brotherhood and equality"), and chose the ambassadorship to the Holy See ("a sinecure which leaves open however many possibilities for the future").[16] Grandi still held his post as president of the Fascist chamber, and both men in fact did not exit from the conspiratorial scene. Indeed Grandi would win fame for his coming high treason, and Ciano, for his, would be slain.

Among the changes made by Mussolini in purging his regime was the substitution of the armed forces chief of staff, bringing General Vittorio Ambrosio to that high command. This was a triumph of the manipulations of Count Ciano, who had advanced the general's candidacy, believing him to be a man who would "act in the interests of his country." Ambrosio, who was to deliver the armed forces to the royal *coup d'état*, was of a like mind with the king. He wished to recall Italian troops in defense of the mainland and to stand up to the Germans. To be sure, Mussolini, who found himself psychologically impotent in the latter regard, had chosen Ambrosio for that very purpose, but the general would obviously serve his king far better than his Duce.

The loss of the sovereign's man in the foreign ministry was thus more than compensated for by the new situation, and with the deteriorating condition of the war, the underpinnings of the gentlemen's revolt began to stand fast. The king continued to hold himself at a safe distance from the plotters in order to be in a position to repudiate them should any move at any stage go awry. In the style of kings gone by he sent the minister of his house, Acquarone, to do the needed work.

Acquarone, a Genoese nobleman, was well suited for the task. He had come to his office in 1938 and had impressed the king with his loyalty and his ability in handling intricate details, notably the royal finances. He entered into the king's confidences, and very soon began to enjoy a position of influence unseen since the younger Rattazzi held sway in the court of Humbert the Good. Acquarone saw the king incessantly, at least once or twice each day, and repaired with him to his favorite places of repose, where he was constantly at his master's side. When the king went fishing in the streams which passed through San Rossore, it was the duke who held the rod.

Acquarone, a man in his early fifties, was affable, gracious, elegant, and charming, endowed with all the qualities of which his king had none. He was not very much taller than the sovereign, but had twice the bearing of an aristocrat. He frequented the salons of Rome, where he mingled with Nazis and Fascists and gathered all the loose talk of consequence for his king. More important he went forth with exquisite discretion seeking to elaborate the rudiments of the coming coup.[17]

In one sense this was not a very difficult assignment. Almost everyone who had the opportunity was eager, given the crumbling state of affairs, to renew time-worn devotions to the crown. Only die-hards and fools did not try to join the countless number of men in high places who made certain to approach Acquarone or pause at the side of Puntoni and whisper words like those of Undersecretary of War Sorice: "The situation is near tragedy. . . . Our salvation is the Monarchy."[18] Or, like Grandi: "Only the King, at the opportune moment, can put things in order. It will be a very difficult and dangerous operation. I, for my part, am with the King."[19]

With such cooperation, Acquarone was able to perform with excellence. Apart from engaging the most obvious supporters of a royal coup, he succeeded in winning the active loyalty of the chief of the Fascist state police, Carmine Senise. Senise had gained invaluable experience having taken part in the planning against Mussolini's coup two full decades ago. The Neapolitan police chief, who reminded Ciano of an "intelligent and ignorant" Bourbon minister, was a master technician. As early as 1940, on his own initiative, he had begun to take security measures to assure the viability of the police, whether it had to work for or against fascism. Now, on Acquarone's urgings, he was prepared to work against fascism. He began by drafting the plans for Mussolini's arrest.*[20]

By the spring of 1943 all the essential elements were in place. Uninterrupted defeat on the battlefield had reduced matters only to a question of timing. Victor Emmanuel, though the precise moment is obscure,** realized by now that he could no longer afford the luxury of dealing in subtleties and ambiguities. Until March he was doing just that, treating potential friends-in-need with only sly encouragement and radiating a peculiar self-confidence, as if all the celebrated shrewdness of his house were at the royal command.

In late February he could still cut off all seditious talk abruptly, while phrasing his forbiddings in such a way as to open every door he closed. On the 23rd, for example, Senator Zuppelli, his old minister of

---

* In April, 1943, Senise was relieved of his office by Mussolini for his failure to act against the industrial strikes which had occurred in March. But his prestige among the Fascists remained high, and he continued to conspire with Acquarone in an unofficial capacity.

** In a letter to the duke of Acquarone, the king later fixed the date of his decision to act against Mussolini. "As of January, 1943," he wrote, "I decided definitively to put an end to the Fascist regime and revoke the powers of the Head of Government, Mussolini." It was a convenient way of marking the initiation of the great event, but it neglects the agonizing royal doubts, which began some time in 1939 and did not end, as will be seen, until the actual day of the *coup*, July 25, 1943.[21]

war during World War I, came to call and advised the violent over-throw of Mussolini. Victor Emmanuel stopped him cold. In spite of his anxieties about winning the senate to his cause, he all but repri-manded Zuppelli about morality and the need to remain scrupulously faithful to fascism and the Nazis. "The situation is grave, but not desperate," he said from one corner of his perennially pained expres-sion, and then, from another: "In any event, a *coup d'état* against the Duce and the regime at this moment, with the Germans inside our house and at the doors, is absolutely inopportune."[22]

Three weeks later, however, whatever Machiavellian inclinations he might have had could be indulged no more. "His Majesty," Puntoni inscribed following a talk with the king on March 16, ". . . leaving nothing to be inferred, spoke to me of his conviction that by now it is no longer the case of concealing the necessity for a de-cisive move against certain men and institutions. He says that it is only a matter of choosing the right moment, and to absolutely avoid any skull cracking. 'An error in timing,' he adds, 'could be fatal. . . .' "[23]

The royal decision notwithstanding, the king was certainly in no great hurry for "the right moment" to come along. He remained true to the pattern of behavior which had towed him through the days of his life. As he had done at the time of Italy's entry into World War I, Mussolini's march on Rome, and the Matteotti affair, he hoped to post-pone action on his part until it might not be needed at all. It was his fondest wish that Mussolini would act against himself, or at least the Germans, and disengage Italy from the war. He continually brought up the subject with Mussolini, and the latter, as matters worsened, was not entirely averse to the idea. The safest solution to Italy's over-riding problem—that of its being utterly destroyed in war by both friend and foe—would be its speedy exit from its commitments to the Reich with Hitler's blessings. This was not an impossibility, as it could be—and was—argued in Rome and Berlin that Italy had become a military and economic burden to Germany, which could put its ex-ported resources to better use at home. Only Mussolini, Victor Em-manuel believed, was capable of winning Hitler's agreement to a friendly separation. As long as such a possibility appeared tenable "the right moment" suffered delay.

But it was the fate of the House of Savoy which preyed uppermost on the king's mind. He was aware, as Deakin has written, "that any move which he might make would be decisive . . . for the future of the Monarchy. He was conscious of his exclusive and unique role which could be played only once. . . ."[24] To fail was to fall; an abortive *coup d'état* in time of war would almost assuredly mean the spiritual and physical liquidation of the crown, and more than likely, some of its most illustrious members, including himself.

Humbert II, in a later confession of his father's mistakes, would admit, with all due respects, that the king "let himself be frightened by the 'oceanic mobs' and the para-Soviet 'apparatus' of fascism. . . ." His father had committed an "error in judgment," Humbert would concede, in assessing Mussolini's powers of resisting the coup. "Victor Emmanuel III," he was to conclude, "believed too much in Mussolini's influence on the Italian masses and too little in the sincere and intimate loyalty of the Italians to their traditional institutions."[25]

While compounding these errors in his hesitations, the little king in the middle of May drafted a memorandum in his own hand, outlining the course of action the nation should pursue. This document of Talmudic instructions seems to have been intended for Mussolini as guidance on how to get out of the war. It approaches the hysterical.

Italy had to be held together, said the king, getting tough, "and not by making rhetorical and merely Fascist speeches." The government had to maintain close relations with the Axis satellite states Hungary, Rumania, and Bulgaria, which had "little love" for the Germans. More important, "One should not forget to extend all possible courtesies to officials in the governments of England and America." Mussolini ought to "think very seriously about the possibility of unhooking Italy's fate to that of Germany's," and the best reason the king could give was that the ally's "internal collapse could come unexpectedly like the collapse of the German empire in 1918."[26]

Less time was spent in contemplation of the king's memorandum, however, than in the contemporary news of the fall of Tunisia to the Allies, ending the war in North Africa. The Italians had attached supreme importance to holding that territory just a channel crossing from their shores.

The "right moment" would soon be coming from the sea.

28

ET TU, VICTOR?

IN THE EARLY HOURS OF JULY 10, 1943, THE ALLIES WADED ONTO THE BEACHES OF SICILY "TO RID Italy of fascism and all its unhappy symbols," as the president of the United States declared.[1] The war which Rome had sent abroad had come home. The king was at San Rossore. He was awakened immediately and departed at dawn for the capital.

He had considered several options, which ranged from a complete turnabout against the ally in the style of Victor Amadeus II's defection from Louis XIV, to a phased withdrawal based on deceiving the Germans until a separate peace with the enemy might be concluded. But all of his plans hinged on the arrest of Mussolini, which had been carefully prepared by the army and the police. Now, it would seem, the king could not but choose. But he waited still.

He did, however, eliminate several choices, one of which was probably the only course of action that could have saved his house, and one, incidentally, in which Maria José was deeply involved. Quite apart from the conspiracy of the monarchist establishment, and unknown to the king, the crown princess had been facilitating seditious contacts among the liberals of pre-Fascist times, and Victor Emmanuel's former prime minister Ivanhoe Bonomi had emerged as one of the leaders of the group. Bonomi had been to see the king on June 2. He had urged not only Mussolini's arrest, but the immediate denunciation of the Axis alliance. This would mean a dangerous confrontation with Berlin, but the royal forces as yet outnumbered those of the Germans in Italy, and the will to eject them was mighty.

The king was "disappointed" in Bonomi (and angered when he learned of Maria José's intrigues), and on July 12 or 13 he rejected a further liberal, "political solution," which envisaged the reinstatement of a regime of surviving pre-Fascist ministers. He called that a government of "ghosts," and settled now on a "technical" ministry of bureaucrats to mark time, while others would attempt to carry out the idea of piecemeal separation from the Axis partner. The government was to be headed by a general, Army Marshal Badoglio, the seventy-two-year-old "duke of Addis Ababa." Badoglio was the only suitable one left, said the king, "whether I like it or not."[2] The "duke," when informed of Victor Emmanuel's wishes, stood ready to serve.

On the 15th he received the old marshal at Villa Savoia and told him that he could not yet establish a firm date for his coup. The Italians, he explained, were not good at keeping secrets, and in a few hours everyone would know everything. Even that secret was not very well kept. On the following day a German military intelligence agent telegraphed Berlin:

> A completely reliable informant and well-known political personality reported to me yesterday the following, which he had been told by Marshal Badoglio with whom he has close relations. The king has turned to Badoglio with regard to eventually taking over the administration in Italy. Badoglio has explained to the king that [if] . . . ordered that one should continue to fight on the side of Germany, he would carry this out loyally; if the order were to initiate peace negotiations, this he would also undertake; and so on. In any event let the king bear the responsibility: he, Badoglio, was only prepared to carry out the latter's orders, whatever they might be, in the most loyal manner. The king wept, and has not yet come to any decision.[3]

As for the lingering indecisiveness of the king, his chief aide Puntoni noted after the royal audience with Badoglio, "I think that he is about to take grave decisions,"[4] and on July 19 two significant events occurred which impelled him even nearer to taking them.

A little after eleven o'clock that morning, Rome, for the first time during the war, or ever, was bombed. Nine waves of Allied aircraft attacked the marshaling yards around the Tiburtina and Termini railway stations, as well as a neighboring working-class quarter, killing 717 persons and injuring 1,600 more.[5]

The planes flew over Villa Savoia, which was only a little more than a mile from the center of the strike. The queen was alarmed, as the king watched and counted them with the aid of binoculars. He was deeply impressed. ("They were flying in perfect formation").[6] Until now he like many others had believed the "holy city" was im-

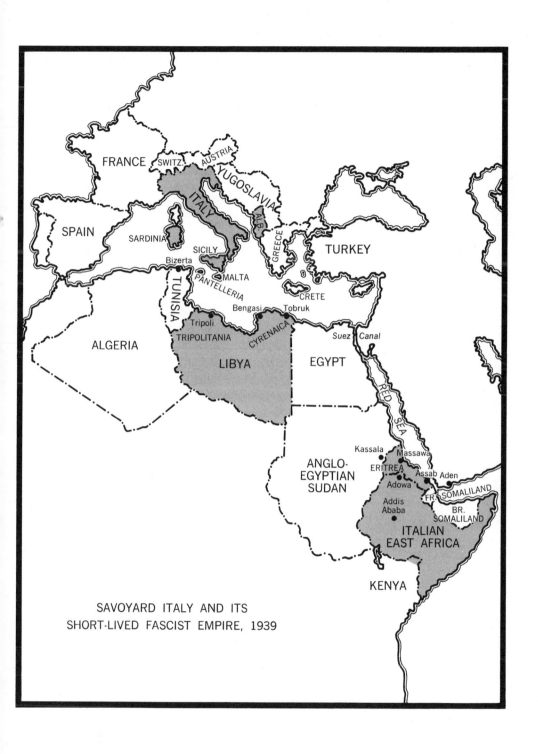

SAVOYARD ITALY AND ITS
SHORT-LIVED FASCIST EMPIRE, 1939

mune from attack, the presence of the pope being its best (and only) anti-aircraft defense.

When the raid subsided some two hours later, the king went with Puntoni to inspect the damages. It was later rumored that the people threw rocks at him as he drove through the devastated districts, but Puntoni's version of the king's reception is undoubtedly more reliable: "The people are mute, hostile," he wrote in his diary. "We go through tears and icy silence. . . . The Sovereign is stricken by this state of affairs"[7]—all the more so when he went to inspect nearby Ciampino airport, a key military installation, and found it literally deserted. The commander, when located, justified this under the phrase "preventive decentralization," but the king thought it abandonment of one's post all the same.

While the bombing had been taking place, Mussolini and Hitler were meeting in northern Italy. The Duce on short notice had flown there early in the day. He was joined by his military and political advisers, including Armed Forces Chief of Staff Ambrosio (who had already secretly ordered the army's plans for Mussolini's arrest). They implored Mussolini to seize the initiative and try to persuade Hitler of Italy's imperative need of exiting from a war which it had lost. Ambrosio went further, demanding that Mussolini get them out within fifteen days.

The Duce was not insensitive to their appeals. By his own admission he was tormented by an "intense agony of spirit." But he felt unable to bring himself to speak face-to-face with the Fuehrer about quitting. "Do you really believe he would allow us our freedom of action?" he asked rhetorically.[8] Indeed, during the conference he said almost nothing at all, other than to paraphrase a message handed to him: He murmured that while they spoke Rome was being bombed. Then, on taking leave of the German, he managed only to affirm, with pretended back-slapping confidence, "We have a common cause, Fuehrer!"[9]

To his advisers, Mussolini lied that he had not had to bring up the matter of ending the war, because the Fuehrer had promised to repair Italy's military failings by dispatching supplies and reinforcements. It was a promise which in the past had often been broken, and now was less likely to be fulfilled than ever, as the Duce well knew ("Naturally our requests must be reasonable and not astronomic").[10]

Ambrosio, when Mussolini was out of sight, suddenly burst forth to his colleagues: "Did you hear what he said . . . after my warning of this morning? He asked him yet again for that war material which they will never send. He still deludes himself, and did not take my words seriously. He is mad, I tell you, mad. What I told him is serious, very serious."[11]

That evening, on his return to Rome, Ambrosio went to see the king. His report appears to have undermined Victor Emmanuel's last hope in the Duce's ability to perform the necessary surgery, for according to Ambrosio, the king at that time conveyed "the decision to liquidate Mussolini."[12]

Close as he may have been, however, Victor Emmanuel had not actually so decided. Perhaps the Duce could still save the House of Savoy, he reasoned. "The regime ceases to function," he told Puntoni the following morning speaking of some disconsolate Fascists who like Ambrosio had beseeched him yesterday to "liquidate" the Duce. "A change must be made at any price. But it's not so easy, for two reasons: first our disastrous military situation; second, the presence in Italy of the Germans."[13]

Even slavishly devoted Puntoni, who really loved the king, believed his master somewhat overly hesitant. That same day Puntoni had a talk with Ambrosio's second in command, who detailed the utter futility of further military resistance, and on July 21, Puntoni "spoke clearly" of this to Victor Emmanuel. He also read him a letter from Dino Grandi, which concluded, "At almost one hundred years since the day King Charles Albert proclaimed the Constitution of the Realm and initiated the Risorgimento—the struggle for freedom, unity, and independence—our fatherland is on the threshold of defeat and dishonor."

The king listened in silence. "Tomorrow," he said, "I will speak frankly about that with the Duce."[14]

Puntoni, however, was unaware of the royal maneuvers which had been undertaken by the duke of Acquarone. As a general, Puntoni was nominally under Mussolini's command, and the king, though he esteemed and trusted his aide, did not wish to subject him to a crisis of conscience. Puntoni therefore did not know that his master had already told Acquarone that he would probably arrest the Duce at the next regular Monday audience, July 26. Further the sovereign had authorized the duke to set in motion the underground machinery assembled for the actual seizure and incarceration of Mussolini. This left open the Thursday audience of July 22, and it was this imminent encounter to which he referred in saying that he would "speak frankly."

Thursday, then, was the Duce's last chance, and as the Monday audience would never actually take place, it was also the last of those traditional Mondays and Thursdays with the king, which had begun well more than a thousand weeks before.

Accordingly, on Thursday, the 22nd, the Duce was ushered into the sovereign's chambers at the Quirinal. "The king was nervous and gloomy," Mussolini later recalled in his version of that final audience.[15]

Said Victor Emmanuel:

> Situation tense. It can't last much longer. Sicily is as good as lost. The Germans are toying with us deceitfully. Discipline among our troops has broken down. The airmen at Ciampino fled as far as Velletri during the attack. They call that "decentralization." I watched the attack the other day from Villa Ada. . . . The history of the "holy city" is finished. We must place our dilemma before the Germans.[16]

The king's account agrees more or less with the Duce's. According to the former, "Mussolini started talking to me of the German secret weapons. I interrupted him: 'The best secret weapons are those which are best known.' He took leave of me."[17]

"At the end of the audience," Puntoni records, "I went to see His Majesty. His face was dark and gloomy. At first he seemed reluctant to speak. Then, finally, as if to free himself from the weight of anguish, he said: 'I tried to make the Duce understand that he alone . . . was the obstacle to our internal recovery . . . He did not understand, or he did not want to understand. It was as if I were speaking to the wind.' "[18]

Mussolini emerged from the king's office subdued and feeling forsaken. The duke of Acquarone was in the antechamber, and Mussolini approached him in a friendly manner. "Why is it that you never come to see me anymore, Acquarone?" he asked.[19] Then, without waiting for a reply, he exited. The valets in their palace reds saluted; the sentinels presented arms. The Duce left the Quirinal in a great black sedan, never to return.

If Acquarone worried whether there was a deeper meaning to Mussolini's question, Mussolini himself suspected nothing, although the rumors of his forthcoming deposal were ample. When Carlo Scorza, secretary of the party, warned him of one report which told of a decision to arrest the Duce and bring Badoglio to power, Mussolini replied, "Don't write detective stories."[20]

In the meantime Acquarone had secured the police and army elements which were to carry out the arrest following the Monday audience. He lacked only the sovereign's final word. Victor Emmanuel still shrank before the ultimate act. The old fears of civil war in which his thousand-year-old house might burn to the ground rattled in his soul. But Mussolini had been as uncomprehending as the wind, and the wind had swept all alternatives away.

"It will be bloodless, Your Majesty," said Acquarone, giving courage to the king.[21]

Neither he nor his master could foresee the rivers of human blood and the mountains of stinking corpses; the uncounted Italians who would have to hand up their very nutrients in redeeming the nation from the pompous follies of their betters.

On the morning of July 24 the duke of Acquarone went to see Badoglio. He brought with him the king's firm decision to replace the Duce with the marshal.[22] Badoglio was handed a proclamation, which he was to read on the radio following the coup. On the same morning the technical details for the July 26 arrest at the Quirinal and the simultaneous capture of several key Fascist chieftains were rehearsed by former Police Chief Senise, Ambrosio's aide General Castellano, and the head of the *carabinieri*, General Cerica. Cerica had been brought into the conspiracy only forty-eight hours or so earlier as a result of his predecessor being killed in the Allied air attack on Rome. This was a time when would-be mutineers were legion.

One unresolved situation hung over the entire affair, exciting natural fears that the king's conspiracy might in some unforeseen manner be laid to ruin. Dino Grandi, who had taken his cue from his last audience with Victor Emmanuel (in which the sovereign had said rather offhandedly, "Help me to obtain the constitutional means),"[23] had been acting more or less independently to secure from his fellow members of the grand council a no-confidence vote against Mussolini. "Our aim," Grandi's emissary had told Acquarone a few days earlier, "is to furnish the King with the 'constitutional clue' which the Sovereign has always declared to be the indispensable condition to induce him to act."[24]

The opportunity had been grasped when Mussolini had agreed to call a meeting of the grand council, which had ceased to function since it last gathered in 1939. The Duce had reluctantly yielded to the appeal of some council members, not including Grandi, who had vague ideas about rejuvenating the supreme body of the Fascist party and state. The meeting had been called for the evening of July 24 at the Palazzo Venezia, and when Grandi had received his invitation, he had set out openly to gather support for the no-confidence motion. It was written as innocuously as he knew how, in order to gain as much backing as possible, for it was meant to be merely the pretext by which the king could act "constitutionally."

The document, which was shown to Mussolini in advance to avoid any charge of intriguing, called for a kind of "return to the constitution." Baron Sonnino had plotted in Humbertine times, when the court had felt liberal government endangering the monarchy. Now, Count Grandi suggested, dictatorial government was the nation's first problem, which could only be solved by a redistribution of the powers fascism had concentrated in the Duce. This required the prompt repair of the traditional political organs, particularly those which would reinvigorate the crown. Grandi's resolution, above all, provided for the return of the command of the armed forces to the king.[25]

Mussolini thought Grandi's document "vile," but did nothing otherwise, and Grandi in the week prior to the meeting marshaled his supporters. Working closely with Ciano, he had gained several backers, but an hour before the meeting began he sent word to the king that he did not know whether he had secured a majority of the twenty-nine council members. He was about to do his duty anyway, he said, and he was confident that the king would do his, which was to "save the country."[26]

The pending meeting of the grand council had stropped men's nerves to a razor's edge. The appointed hour was 5:00 P.M., and on the afternoon of that Saturday, July 24, Rome paled. "Even cities have a face," Mussolini later wrote, "and their face reflects what is on their mind. Rome felt something grave was in the air."[27] Rumors of plot and counterplot whipped around every corner. Again Mussolini was warned of a "thriller" and even a "superthriller" in the making, but he did not respond. The conspiring members of the grand council, on the other hand, were prepared for the worst. Many arrived with weapons bulging in their coats. Grandi, who had been to confession and had left a last letter to his wife and children, brought two hand grenades along. He was stricken with fear as he entered the Palazzo Venezia. This was Mussolini's home ground and it looked like an armed camp of the Fascist militia. Grandi's close collaborator Giuseppe Bottai whispered that they made a terrible mistake. "This," he said, "is our end."[28]

The meeting, though a tempest of recriminations and enduring nearly ten hours, concluded in the early morning of the next day,

Sunday, without incident. Grandi's motion was carried nineteen to seven, whereupon Mussolini dismissed the council, declaring, "Gentlemen, with this resolution, you have provoked a crisis in the regime."[29]

He was advised immediately by the remaining loyalists to arrest the rebels without delay, but he preferred to try to neutralize the internal revolt with the assistance, of all persons, of the king. He believed that there was no doubt whatsoever that Victor Emmanuel would restore whatever confidence had been withdrawn by the Grandi-Ciano circle, and decided at once to advance his customary Monday audience to later that day.

"My relations with the King are perfect," he had said during the grand council meeting. "No later than last Thursday the King said to me: 'My dear Mussolini, you are being attacked from all sides, but I am at your side to defend you.' "[30]

According to Grandi, Mussolini had also said: "Yes, the King is still in favor of me. I have never had friends, but the King is my friend, and I wonder what those who oppose me tonight will think tomorrow." He told those Fascists "who seem to wish to get rid of me" that he could have them arrested, but that was unnecessary for Victor Emmanuel was behind him.[31]

A few minutes after the meeting, however, while the rebels were anxiously departing (Grandi to a prearranged rendezvous with Acquarone), Mussolini told Scorza that he really had no alternative other than to disregard the rebels and seek reaffirmation of his powers from his "friend" the king. Counseled by Scorza to use force against not only the dissidents but all the conspirators being named in the abundant rumors of recent days, Mussolini replied: "Arrest them all? Occupy Rome . . . with the aid of the Germans? Ask the aid of a foreigner to resolve our internal affairs? And how will the King react? And the Army?"[32]

It was the accommodating little king who had often saved him before; and it was the king to whom now he would turn once again. "They don't like us in there," Mussolini said to Scorza, as they drove past the Quirinal that dawn of the 25th. "But the king is a loyal soldier."[33]

The king awoke at his usual hour. It was a burning Sunday in July, the kind of day from which time had taught the Romans to flee, and the sovereign's presence in the city was something in itself suspect. He was briefed by Acquarone, who had come to Villa

Savoia with the news of the grand council motion. He was pleased with this new development, which in his view constitutionalized the operation planned for the following morning, and he gave Acquarone a signed decree naming Badoglio as his prime minister. The decree was brought to Badoglio, who put a bottle of champagne on ice to await developments.

At 10:50 A.M. General Puntoni went to the king and found him "tranquil and serene"; he inferred from the ensuing conversation that Mussolini's demise had been decided for Monday.

A little past noon, however, Puntoni received a telephone call from the Palazzo Venezia requesting that the Duce's audience at the Quirinal be rescheduled to five o'clock that very afternoon at Villa Savoia. Puntoni sought confirmation from the king, who with the recklessness of someone aching to be done with the ignoble deed, agreed without the advice of the conspirators. Victor Emmanuel, suddenly .closing his eyes to all which had occurred, instructed Puntoni, almost as an afterthought, to notify Acquarone of the change. He then asked that the duke be invited to appear at Villa Savoia at 4:00 P.M., a delay which would preclude the possibility of repairing the plans Mussolini had unwittingly spoiled.[34] The king still pretended that he was simply dismissing one of his ministers, as he had done so painlessly nearly two dozen times before the march on Rome.

Acquarone, however, informed by Puntoni of the Duce's 5:00 P.M. appointment, proceeded with haste to make the necessary adjustments for carrying out the arrest at Villa Savoia. A series of orders were transmitted through the conspiratorial chain of command, and within two hours or so a revised plan was agreed on. Acquarone then reported to the king that the capture of Mussolini was ready in spite of all. Everything was prepared for the operation to take place immediately on conclusion of the royal audience.

The images of the Duce being taken prisoner in the Savoyard residence and of possible violence in his own parlor were repugnant to Victor Emmanuel. Nevertheless he gave his consent, while insisting that the offensive act of seizure occur outside the villa and its grounds. Acquarone agreed, but he had no intention of obeying, as it had already been decided that it was essential to make the arrest within the protective confines of the royal estate. Further the duke felt this was not the time to reveal that the head of the *carabinieri* had demanded and had been promised a direct order from the king before agreeing to his vital role in the scheme—that of actually taking possession of and imprisoning the *corpus profanum*.[35]

While the king looked away, a contingent of fifty trusted *carabinieri* began to take up positions behind the bushes of the royal gardens. An ambulance, the innocuous-looking vehicle in which the Duce was to be spirited away, arrived and halted somewhere out of view. The king paced up and down his living room. He had summoned Puntoni and was awaiting his arrival. Some time before four o'clock, the general finally arrived, and he was briefed by the king.

"I am taking command of the Armed Forces," he said, adding that Badoglio was to head the government. "As far as Mussolini is concerned, I have authorized that at the end of the audience he will be stopped outside Villa Savoia and brought to a military compound." This was to be done for Mussolini's own protection from "over-eager" anti-Fascists, as well as to prevent him from contacting party extremists, who might provoke disorder. Then the king added: "Since I don't know how the Duce will react, I request that you remain outside the door of the drawing room, where we will repair for our talk. In case of necessity, intervene."[36]

At about 4:30 P.M. the king and Puntoni, walking just outside the entrance to the royal villa itself, were approached by Acquarone. The duke said that at the last moment the *carabinieri* commandant had informed him that it was impossible to arrest Mussolini anywhere but on the grounds of Villa Savoia. The king was very annoyed, and at this point an argument broke out, in which Victor Emmanuel demanded that the operation be executed in the "pre-established manner." But time was running out, and, as usual, he gave in. Acquarone, however, could not take leave without bringing up the final, and perhaps most distasteful problem, which could no longer be forestalled. The duke bowed his head before the monarch, then spoke in a broken voice: "The commandant of the Royal *Carabinieri*, General Cerica, desires that Your Majesty confirm the order for the arrest of Mussolini."

The king whitened and frowned. The Duce, then, was to be arrested, not "stopped"; and it was Victor Emmanuel of Savoy, not someone else, who would have to take full responsibility for whatever the consequences might be. His jaw shook more than ever. "All right," said the king.[37]

At five minutes before five o'clock Mussolini's sedan passed through the gates of Villa Savoia. The Duce, dressed in a dark blue suit, was accompanied by his secretary, Nicolò De Cesare, and his driver. His escort, three cars full of Fascist police and other functionaries, waited outside the royal grounds.

Mussolini suspected nothing. His wife, Rachele, had pleaded with him only minutes before not to go to the king's villa, which was less than a mile from his own. "Benito," she implored in her homespun style, "don't go . . . don't trust him. The king does what's good for the king, and if it suits him he'll dump you in the river."[38] But Mussolini was confident. At three o'clock he had told a loyal Fascist, "I have never done anything without his complete agreement. . . . He has always been solidly with me."[39]

Now, precisely at five o'clock, the king welcomed him on the doorstep of Villa Savoia. Victor Emmanuel was wearing his outdated first marshal of the empire's uniform. He greeted the Duce warmly and led him into the appointed room. Mussolini's secretary waited outside with the duty officer. Puntoni took his place at the door. The Duce's driver was asked to move his car away from the front entrance, and was then told that there was a telephone call for him. He left the car, followed the messenger to a distant corner, and was seized.

Mussolini expected royal approval of his view that the Grandi motion was not mandatory since the grand council—with which the Duce had wrested so much power and grief from the king—was really only an advisory body. The worst that could happen, he felt, would be that Victor Emmanuel would reassume his position of commander-in-chief of the armed forces, which, he later said, he had been thinking of relinquishing anyway. Once inside the king's drawing room, however, all expectations faded quickly.

There are three primary sources for what occurred during that last meeting between sovereign and Duce—neither of whom would ever again set eyes on the other: Mussolini's, Victor Emmanuel's, and the fragments collected by Puntoni with his ear at the door. Mussolini said that the king was "in a state of abnormal agitation, his drawn face convulsing, and his words short and choppy," as this dialogue took place:

> Victor Emmanuel: My dear Duce, it's all over. Italy has gone to pieces. The morale of the Army is at ground level. The soldiers don't want to fight anymore. The Alpini sing a song which tells how they won't make war any longer for Mussolini.

Here, the king, who had a reputation of being a collector of anti-Fascist jokes and rhymes, began to sing the lyrics, which were in his own Piedmontese dialect: *"Down with Mussolini/The assassin of Alpini. . . ."* The sovereign went on:

> The vote of the Grand Council is tremendous. Nineteen votes for Grandi's resolution, among them four Collars of the Annunziata. Cer-

tainly you don't have any illusions about what the Italians think of you. At this moment you are the most hated man in Italy. You have only one friend left whom you can count on. Only one remains with you. Me. So you needn't worry about your personal safety. I'll protect you. I think the man to handle the situation at this time is Marshal Badoglio. He'll start with a Ministry of functionaries for administration purposes and for continuing the war. Then in six months, we'll see.* All Rome is aware of the Grand Council's resolution and everyone awaits a change.

Mussolini: You are taking an extremely grave decision. A crisis at this time will lead the people to believe that peace is in sight, if the man who declared war is withdrawn. The blow to the Army's morale will be serious. If the soldiers—Alpini or not—don't want to make war for Mussolini, that has no importance, provided that they are disposed to make it for you. . . . I am aware of the people's hatred. I had no trouble seeing it last night in full in the Grand Council. One doesn't govern for so long without imposing many sacrifices which provoke resentments. . . . In any case, I wish the best to the man who takes the situation in hand.[41]

In the king's abbreviated version, Mussolini at first tried to appear nonchalant, affirming that the grand council's action was not binding. But his hands trembled as he spoke, and when Victor Emmanuel told him that he had replaced him with Badoglio, Mussolini slumped under the blow, murmuring, "Then this is my complete collapse."[42]

The king later implied that Mussolini's bodily collapse was his moment of sweet revenge. Seeing the Duce shrink to nothingness before his own eyes was at least some compensation for twenty years of humiliation.

The jagged account given by Puntoni, which tends to confirm those of both principals, is perhaps the most interesting. He could not hear the conversation very well, he said, because Mussolini was speaking "submissively." After a while the Duce stopped talking, and the king began. As Puntoni recorded it in his diary:

"I like you very much," says the King to the Duce, "and I have demonstrated it many times, defending you from every attack. But this time I must ask you to leave your post and leave me free to entrust the government to others."

The Duce does not respond immediately. A few moments of silence go by, then you could hear him whispering, interrupted from time to

---

* Victor Emmanuel, by his admission, even now believed that "within two or three years" times would be such that he would be able to return Mussolini to power.[40] It would not be years, however, but only weeks later—after a bitter dose of Badoglio as prime minister—that the king would begin to look back with longing for the Duce (see below, p. 359).

time with brief replies from the Sovereign, who says that he is regretful but insists on his decision.

Mussolini intervenes fitfully. Then his words are drowned out by the King who is talking about the wrongs done to him, about times when even formalities were not observed. I hear this sentence clearly: "And I've been told that when it was not yet known whether or not I'd sign the decree, those two beggars of yours, Farinacci and Buffarini, said: 'He'll sign it, otherwise we'll make him do it with a few kicks in the behind!'"

Mussolini listens without making a sound, and now the Sovereign does not let up on him. . . . His Majesty, raising the tone of his voice somewhat, says: "I must intervene to save the country from useless slaughter and try to obtain less inhuman treatment from the enemy." The Duce mutters a few tired words. He asks: "And me, what am I supposed to do now?" I do not comprehend the first part of the King's answer, but I hear this clearly: "I'll take care of it on my own responsibility. You can be sure of your personal safety."

From a few broken phrases, I understand that the Sovereign has informed the Duce that his successor will be Badoglio. Silence overtakes the room, broken only by a sentence the King has repeated many times during the course of the conversation. "I'm sorry, I'm sorry," says the Sovereign, "but there can be no other solution."

His Majesty must have made some sign to the Duce that he had nothing further to say, because I now hear only the sounds of chairs being moved and footsteps coming toward the door.[43]

Puntoni retired from view. The audience had lasted about twenty-five minutes. The king and Mussolini emerged from the room, looking sad, but giving no other indication of what had happened inside. Mussolini later said the king was white, "smaller than ever, almost shrunken." The sovereign said something about the torrid weather. "Actually, it is quite hot," said Mussolini.[44]

Victor Emmanuel shook the Duce's hand. He asked to be introduced to his secretary, who was waiting for Mussolini, and who the king said he had never met before. Then he turned to someone and asked, "Where is the president's car?" Mussolini went down a few steps, headed to where he thought the automobile should be.

He was intercepted by a captain in the *carabinieri*, who nodded toward the waiting ambulance. "His Majesty has charged me with protecting your person," said the officer. "I don't believe it," said the Duce, continuing toward his car. "No," the captain insisted, directing him toward the ambulance, "you must get in here." The Duce obeyed. The secretary asked that he be taken, too. He was accommodated.

The ambulance departed at once speeding through the quiet streets of northeast Rome. Mussolini was under arrest.[45]

The king started back into the house. He saw Puntoni and took him by the arm. They went into his study, but Puntoni withdrew when the queen suddenly entered the room, leaving Victor and Elena to themselves. If they felt free of the rude burden they had borne for so many years, Elena, of whom it is said that she could not hate or harm a living thing, found something lacking in Victor's style. "They could have arrested him where and when they wanted, but not here," she complained. "Mussolini was a guest in our house. The rules of royal hospitality have been violated. This is not very nice."[46]

It was not long before Mussolini's absence was noticed, but the measures planned to prevent a countercoup proceeded smoothly. There was no resistance to the fall of "the most hated man in Italy." Fascists worried more about what would happen to themselves.

Few people that evening were aware of what had occurred, but at 10:45 the Piedmont-accented voice of Marshal Badoglio went on the air nationwide. First, he read a message about Mussolini's departure from the scene. Then came a proclamation from Victor Emmanuel. The king said he had taken command of the armed forces. Everyone now had to do his duty; no "deviation" would be tolerated. The "way to recovery" would at last be found in the valor of the army and in respect for the nation's institutions.

Badoglio then read the decree which had been handed to him by the conspirators to be issued in his name. "Italians," he said, "by order of His Majesty the King and Emperor, I assume command of a military government with full powers. The war continues. . . . Let us close ranks behind His Majesty the King and Emperor, the living symbol of the Fatherland, and an example for all. . . . Long live Italy! Long live the King!"[47]

The celebrations did not really burst forth in full until the next morning, but that night crowds of joyful Romans gathered in the piazza at the Quirinal to wish the new times well. Little mind was given then to the three fatal words of later fame which had been uttered by Badoglio and written by the crown; their watchword was: "The war continues." But the heartfelt cry now resounding in the sticky night was: "Long live the king! Long live the House of Savoy!"

29

"I WILL PUBLISH TO THE WORLD
THE FULL RECORD OF
THIS AFFAIR"

HOURS AFTER THE DUCE'S ARREST THE LITTLE KING STROLLED AMONG THE FLOWER BEDS OF Villa Savoia. The war-imposed double daylight-saving time still held the sun in the evening sky. "This is my eighteen Brumaire," said the sovereign as he faced the tasks ahead.[1] At seventy-three years of age he was suddenly supreme in Italian life. Yet, though he played with visions of Napoleon at thirty, he was more the twilight figure of the man going forth to Waterloo. Napoleon had "One Hundred Days." Victor Emmanuel III was to have but "Forty-Five."

In plucking out the eye which had so meanly offended, he had atoned for all the sins of the crown, and on the morrow of the coup the prestige of his house was as high as the day the *re galantuomo* rode tall on his Arab entering Rome. But the little king, unlike his grandfather who had secured the peace before the war, had only the vaguest notion of what to do next. True enough, he had rescued his house from the absolute certainty of its impending demise. Under no circumstance could Savoyard rule have survived in the Italy about to be conquered by the advancing Allies, although the nation it ruled had infinitely more to gain in defeat than in continuing the war on the Axis side. The arrangement struck by the king for thwarting a personal catastrophe meant, therefore, attaching the fate of more than forty million Italians to his own. Moving from absolute certainty for one to blind uncertainty for all, Victor Emmanuel was, as he proclaimed that night of Mussolini's fall, bound with his people in hurtling toward a common destiny, but, understandably, he phrased the truth perversely. "Italians," spoke the message from the throne, "I am today more than ever indissolubly united with you in an unshakable faith in the immortality of the Fatherland."[2] But on the parchments and on the walls of Rome the king should have inscribed instead: "Italians, you are today more than ever indissolubly united with me in an unshakable faith in the immortality of the House of Savoy."

It was not that he was without *any* plan to lead the nation to high ground. But the king who had preached for half a century to be wary of illusions, harbored now the greatest one of all. His was a plan based solely on a prayer that his dearest dreams might come true. Fearful of Hitler's revenge, he had not had the courage to make a clean break with the Axis. This was a misfortune for his house and the nation. The Germans in the field had betrayed the Italians many more times than Rome could ever sell out Berlin, and the soldiers and the people would have fought with stout hearts to throw the Nazis out the Alpine doors. Fascism, over the years, had consumed its popular base. Italy on July 25 was militarily stronger than Germany on its home ground. It would not have been difficult to cut the *Wehrmacht's* supply lines on Italian soil. Had the war not continued on the side of the Germans, almost assuredly they would have had to go home and swallow all lust for vengeance—a thesis Hitler and his close company have allowed and others have often shown.[3]

But Victor Emmanuel, without the benefit of hindsight and lacking as ever in foresight, had elected to follow the traditional, turtle-step policy of his house in a phased withdrawal from the commitments of the Fascists and the war. And if the overthrow of Mussolini was phase one, the second was now to hoodwink the Germans into believing Badoglio's "war continues" promise of business as usual with Berlin long enough to negotiate a secret separate peace with the Allies "on terms." One of the king's terms was to be the American and British defense of Rome against the German reaction to Italy's eventual "betrayal." This was Victor Emmanuel's "way to recovery," and, if realized, the throne of the dynasty which had taken its people from war to blessed peace would undoubtedly be secured to the marble floors of the Quirinal for many years more.

The flaws in the royal planning were abundant. In the first place, the provocative nature of this policy of deception was bound to multiply the German desire for revenge. Worse, the monarchy had not had the slightest hint from the Allies that such a peace was in any way obtainable, at any price, and no useful contact with them had yet been made, not even one as thin as "the web of a spider." On the contrary, the United Nations forces had declared and made clear that there could be only one, indivisible peace with the Axis, that which would emerge from "unconditional surrender." But the king, relying only on his powers of persuasion and guile, disregarded the demands of the Allies, and once order at home seemed reasonably assured, he proceeded in a hesitant fashion with phase two.

The German embassy in Rome, on the night the Duce was overthrown, waited in vain to give aid and sustenance to the Fascist faithful who, it was supposed, might gather there to prepare a lightning countercoup. But Farinacci alone presented himself, and much to the disgust of the Nazis, he asked only for safe and speedy transportation to Berlin. The following day, the director of the Fascist news agency *Stefani*, in a supreme act of loyalty to the Duce, committed suicide—the only known protest against the collapse of the regime. The rejoicing, on the other hand, was universal, at least among those whose social position was not or did not appear to be downgraded. From the big cities to the *campagna*, Italians everywhere ran the Fascists into hiding and smashed the "unhappy symbols."

Even Mussolini demonstrated his patriotism, sending a friendly message to Badoglio on the night of his arrest. Not only would he not create any difficulties, said the former Duce, but he would extend every possible cooperation. He was thankful and content, he wrote from captivity, and wished "crowning success" to Badoglio. He duly recognized the marshal's authority as originating in the orders of "His Majesty the King, to whom for twenty-one years I have been a loyal servant, and so will I remain. Long live Italy!"[4]

It was immediately quite clear to the new government that there would be no serious "deviation" on the home front. The celebrations and demonstrations had been conducted with surprising moderation and nonviolence. However, the internal security measures adopted by the new government's army chief of staff, General Roatta, were as heinous as they were hysterical ("Whoever . . . *insults* the armed forces, the police, or the institutions will be immediately shot").[5] They baptized the new times in blood. The king took a strategic, if not heartfelt, position that all Italians who were neither Fascists nor monarchists were communists—which was why at least the western Allies had better yield to his terms.

Though all danger at home was quiescent, the threat from the ally Victor Emmanuel was preparing to betray strengthened rapidly with the passage of time. When Hitler received the news of Mussolini's arrest he summoned his generals at once. "Badoglio, our most bitter enemy, has taken over," he announced, and then gave a memorable spot analysis of the situation. He said:

> Undoubtedly in their treachery they will proclaim that they will remain loyal to us, but that is treachery. Of course they won't remain loyal. . . . Although that so-and-so [Badoglio] declared immediately that the war would be continued, that won't make any difference. They have to say that, but it remains treason. We'll play the same game while preparing everything to take over the whole crew with one stroke, to capture all that riffraff.[6]

His first scheme was to "send a man down there . . . to arrest the whole government, the king and the whole bunch right away." He wanted Crown Prince Humbert "above all," then the king, and the "whole gang." "Right into a plane and off with them," he cried.[7]

These desires were not discarded; they were broadened instead and directed against Italians in general. While Hitler played "the same game" as the king, he formulated plans to realize the vengeance steaming in his veins; but he grew less interested in capturing the individual traitors than in punishing Italy as a nation. By July 27 his response to the expected event of Italian betrayal had been conceived in more or less rational terms. They provided, among other things, for the Nazi occupation of Rome and the restoration of fascism. Mussolini was to be reinstated with the honors and powers of which he had been shorn. In the meantime, feigning a measure of acceptance of the new state of affairs in Rome, Hitler began moving twelve new divisions into Italy to assure that his will would prevail.[8]

The king, though his divisions were hardly moving at all, thought that once the Allies would see the light *his* will would prevail. He had only to hold back the Germans. In the first forty-eight hours or so following the coup he was in a state of alarm as to what they might do, and he told Puntoni to pack the royal luggage in the event of the need to take flight. "I have no intention of falling into Hitler's hands to become a puppet with the Fuehrer moving the strings according to his caprice," he said.[9]

But when "nothing" more than the German seizure of the Alpine passes occurred (which guaranteed the free movement into Italy of Hitler's twelve divisions), he gained a dangerous confidence in his reacquired powers. He began in his own phlegmatic style to all but swagger.

He shocked the German ambassador with tough remarks about Hitler's low regard for the king of Italy. He went around philosophizing on the reasons for Mussolini's decline (the main reason was sexual abandon: "When you're sixty years old, you cannot commit certain intemperances"), and he scolded old Badoglio, with whom he was at once and forever dissatisfied, with a schoolmaster's tongue.[10]

Hoping to exercise his native Savoyard cunning at the summit, the king dispatched a general with an invitation to the Fuehrer to meet with him tête-à-tête. When, however, this was rejected by Hitler in a manner reminiscent of Wilhelm II's four-letter interjections invoked at the time of Victor Emmanuel's denunciation of the Triple Alliance, the king's self-confidence was shaken. It was replaced by a renewed state of alarm, for his envoy also reported rumored fragments of the Fuehrer's first-hour oaths about capturing "all that riffraff."

The possibility of having to make a hurried exit from the capital was seriously reconsidered. At the beginning of August the king told Puntoni to orient the affairs of the royal house to the idea of a speedy withdrawal of the crown and government to La Maddalena, the island off the Emerald Coast of Sardinia where poor Garibaldi's remains then as now lay entombed. Puntoni arranged for two destroyers to stand ready in the nearby port of Civitavecchia, while other trusted aides undertook the secret and complex mission of moving the king's funds and precious possessions into Switzerland and locating a safe place for his coin collection, which had grown to 105,000 pieces.[11]

There was nothing untoward in making preparations for a tactical retreat to Sardinia (it was, as will be seen, the unprepared and irresponsible manner in which the royal family and some members of the Badoglio regime actually did take flight which was to discredit them forever). But it did seem an unfair use of the nation's time and money when it was later revealed how many high-ranking, distinguished persons in Rome took advantage of their privileged information and position to remove their relatives, furniture, money, and further personal belongings to Switzerland and other places presumed to be safe.[12]

The main objective, of course, was to render flight unnecessary, and with the Germans appearing to be at least half-deceived the king pressed now for early contact with the Allies. On August 4 the first live touch was made with a handshake in Lisbon between

British Ambassador Ronald Campbell and the newly arrived coun-
selor to the Italian legation, the Marquis Blasco Lanza d'Ajeta,
formerly *chef de cabinet* to Count Ciano at the Italian embassy to
the Holy See. D'Ajeta, who had departed with the royal instructions some forty-eight hours earlier, had been chosen for this vital
mission, all other things being equal, because he was the godson of
United States Undersecretary of State Sumner Welles and he spoke
English. He had carried with him a memorized file of German military secrets to give to the Allies as a peace offering, and a large
suitcase filled, it is said, with documents. The Germans had taken
little note of d'Ajeta's departure, although it was the talk of Rome.
The gossipers had pointed to the diplomat's oversized bag as evidence of the flight of Ciano's wife's jewels.

Within the confines of the British ambassador's home, d'Ajeta in
Portugal proceeded to unfold a horror story which obviously had
been calculated in Rome to frighten the western Allies into signing
almost anything.[13] Campbell passed the tale on to London, which in
turn relayed it to Washington, in a message from Churchill to Roosevelt. Churchill, stanch defender of monarchies, including that of the
House of Savoy, was nothing less than credulous of d'Ajeta's rather
exaggerated report ("It certainly seems to give inside information"),
but bound as he was by the unconditional surrender formula, he
refrained for the moment from advancing recommendations. He related d'Ajeta's story to the American president in the following terms,
which are instructive of the king's regard for Allied intelligence as
well as his self-reputed view of the people's regard for him:

> Fascism in Italy is extinct. Every vestige has been swept away. Italy
> turned Red overnight. In Turin and Milan there were Communist
> demonstrations which had to be put down by armed force. Twenty years
> of Fascism has obliterated the middle class. There is nothing between
> the King, with the patriots who have rallied round him, who have
> complete control, and rampant Bolshevism. . . . If we bomb Rome again
> there will be a popular rising. . . . As many Italian troops as possible
> have been concentrated round Rome but they . . . are no match for
> even one well-equipped German division. . . .
> [D'Ajeta's] whole story, as you will have observed, was no more than
> a plea that we should save Italy from the Germans as well as from
> herself, and do it as quickly as possible.
> He expressed the hope that we would not heap abuse on the King
> and Badoglio, which would precipitate the bloodbath, although a little
> of this would help them to keep up the pretence *vis-à-vis* the Germans.[14]

On the day following d'Ajeta's talk in Lisbon, another Italian diplomat, Alberto Berio, made contact with the British at Tangier. One of his main points was that it was in the interest of the British and Americans to aid the king's government to break with the Germans in order to prevent communism from gaining the upper hand in Italy.*[13]

The trouble with this policy and all others designed to win terms for Rome was that it forced the king into the dubious position of abetting German military pressure on the Allies. This meant that the movement of additional *Wehrmacht* forces down the peninsula was seen, in this sense, as a *favorable*, not a disastrous, development insofar as it demonstrated Italian good will to Berlin and might influence British and American willingness to treat with the Badoglio government. Thus Rome actually began requesting the Germans to send more not fewer troops to Italy, multiplying the nation's vulnerability to the slaughter which would soon enough commence.[17]

Both d'Ajeta and Berio waited anxiously for an official Allied response, and while the former received none at all, the latter was told, after another precious week had gone by, that the only terms possible were those to be dictated by London, Washington, and Moscow. The communist fetish had worked all sorts of wonders in the past (and so it would in the future), but the Red Army's victory at Stalingrad had to be given its due, and it was the poor luck of the House of Savoy that its trial came now, not sooner or later.

Fearing the worst from the efforts of his men in Lisbon and Tangier, the king in the meantime had authorized the dispatch of a third emissary, in the person of General Castellano, Ambrosio's chief of staff. He was followed by General Zanussi, of the office of the army chief of staff. These men carried Italy's terms with them to Madrid, Lisbon, Algiers, and elsewhere. They transmitted the unfounded belief in Rome that an offer to break with the Axis would give the Italians a position from which to bargain. Castellano came home very disabused of this notion, while his colleague (whom he considered his rival) labored on uselessly. Like Zanussi, he had learned that the

---

* The good offices of the Vatican were also employed in the king's secret peace offensive. While the Italians were elaborating the theme of "rampant Bolshevism," diplomats of the Holy See tried to convince Washington and London that the greatest menace to the world was not Nazi Germany, but their partner, Soviet Russia. The Vatican advanced the idea of a demilitarized Italy, agreed to by the Anglo-Americans and the Germans. This accord was seen as the first step toward a *rapprochement* with the West which could lead to a union of powers against the Bolshevik East. The Vatican, in the words of the German ambassador to the Holy See, was engaged in the creation of a "Euro-American-Christian united front against Asia."[16]

Allies were indifferent to Italy's suggestions about switching sides. Churchill did not approve of "harping" on it, but the unconditional surrender was standing fast.

Arriving in Rome on August 27, Castellano could do no more than present the king's government with the bitter "short terms" for Italy's unconditional surrender—military capitulation and loss of national sovereignty. These were but a prelude to the infinitely more painful "long terms," a humbling instrument under which the Italy that had made the Risorgimento and had lived it so boundlessly would, to its later good fortune, never recover.*[18]

The long terms were as yet unknown in Rome, but the shorter document gave occasion enough for grief and ugly, time-consuming recriminations in the clashing circles that had gathered around the king. Counterproposals were hastily drafted, and while Rome was willing now to accept unconditional surrender, Castellano was sent back to argue for the most minimal conditions. The Italians had learned from the Allies that the mainland was to be invaded by Anglo-American forces, and now they asked "only" that at least fifteen divisions be landed north of Rome to assure that the king and his government be spared the German reaction.

The Allies, suspicious and not a little prejudiced, were pitiless. If the king wanted protection, they said, he could come to Allied territory, where he would be treated "with all due personal consideration."[20] As they saw it, the Italians had two choices, and Castellano, joined by Zanussi, heard them placed bluntly on August 31. Rome had to "accept . . . or refuse" the Allied terms, they were told.[21] Moreover, the time for discussion had already exceeded the limit the Allies would allow. American diplomat Robert Murphy, sending the Italians back home, later recalled:

> We impressed upon them that this was their last chance, valuable only if seized quickly. We pointed out that if no surrender agreement were eventuated here and now, three results were indicated: King Victor Emmanuel would lose all consideration; the Allies would be obliged, as a war measure, to incite anarchy throughout Italy; we also would be obliged to bomb all Italian cities, including Rome. . . . At five o'clock that afternoon of August 31, the Italian group flew back to Rome with

* The long terms had been given to General Eisenhower, whose negotiators were dealing with Castellano and Zanussi, by Churchill and Roosevelt. They had instructed him not to show the document to the Italians for fear of frightening them off at this crucial stage. Eisenhower thought this a "crooked deal," and prophesied that the offensive document would be kept secret for a decade after the war.[19] In the event, a score of years went by before the long terms were declassified.

our ultimatum that if the King's Government did not accept the Allied terms by midnight the following day, Rome would be bombed.[22]

The Italians were not to return to the capital entirely empty-handed, however. Unknown to them, the coming invasion of Italy was only the Churchillian probing of Europe's "soft underbelly." The main force was to be directed against France many months later, and only a relatively meager amount of men and supplies was available for the landing on the Italian mainland. Eisenhower therefore worried about its chances of success, particularly in view of the German build-up in the peninsula. He had established the invasion beach at a militarily conservative point well south of Rome, but he was still anxious to conclude the Italian surrender to reduce enemy resistance to his forces coming from the sea.

As an inducement in this regard, he agreed to an operation code named Giant II, which provided for the capture of Rome from the Germans, to be launched simultaneously with the invasion. The strategic and psychological value of this "concession," seen as being carried out in conjunction with the Italian forces assembled around Rome, would be well worth gaining acceptance of the armistice terms. Accordingly, Castellano, prior to his departure to Rome, was told that the Allies were prepared to drop the American 82nd Airborne Division on Rome at the time of the main landings to assist the Italians in gaining control of the city.[23]

On September 1 Castellano met with Badoglio, and later in the same day Badoglio saw the king. Castellano, Badoglio, and the king were satisfied that they had received the best of all possible offers, and while some lower echelon men disbelieved that the airborne division would ever be dropped, Victor Emmanuel III gave the crown's reply, which was then radioed to General Eisenhower: "The reply is affirmative; I repeat, affirmative. . . ."[24]

The surrender was signed ceremoniously in an orange grove in Sicily on September 3. It was agreed that it would be announced by both parties a few hours prior to the Allied invasion. The date of the landing was a military secret, but the Italians were told that it would take place within two weeks and that the precise time would be given to them in advance. The unknown date became a critical issue in the hours and days ahead. It contributed to the impending royal catastrophe, for which the stage was now perfectly set.

Castellano, by involuted and fallacious reasoning, had deduced that the landing would take place "possibly the 12th" of September, and his guess was taken in Rome as fact.[25] Thus, when American General Maxwell Taylor, on a mission behind enemy lines to ascertain the feasibility of the 82nd Airborne's task, appeared at Badoglio's front door in the first hour of September 8 and informed him that the invasion would occur later that very day, the government and the crown were thrown into a mighty panic.

Italian military intelligence in the past forty-eight hours or so had reported correctly that the landing force would strike too far south to be in a position to protect Rome. From this a much less certain conclusion was drawn by men heavily inclined toward hesitation. By now, they reasoned, German strength in and around the capital had been so reinforced that air operation Giant II had become obsolete and would therefore be inadequate. Badoglio told Taylor that the armistice and the invasion would thus have to be postponed, and this surprising message was radioed to Eisenhower.

Even more surprising, Badoglio on the basis of an inconclusive interim reply believed that Eisenhower had acceded to his request, and he sent one of his generals back with Taylor "to clarify issues."[26] One such issue was the viability of Giant II, which Taylor immediately cancelled.

The Italians meanwhile directed much of their energies to deceiving the Germans, who were growing more and more convinced that their ally's betrayal was near. Hitler, in fact, was in the process of preparing an ultimatum, which made eighteen demands considered necessary to reestablish Rome's credit in Berlin. The Fuehrer could barely wait to expose those who had caballed for Mussolini's fall, and all who were in the cabal feared for their throats and their skins. The events of September 8, however, would make Hitler's ultimatum highly irrelevant.

The assiduous and provocative efforts at deception reached their peak on that final day. At noon Victor Emmanuel received the new Nazi ambassador to Rome, Rudolf Rahn. Rahn had met with Badoglio on September 3 (when the armistice was being secretly signed in Sicily), and he had been impressed with the old soldier's apparent sincerity. "I am Marshal Badoglio," the Italian had said, "and I will convince you by my deeds that it is unfair not to trust in me."[27] Now Victor Emmanuel spoke warmly of his admiration for the German army, its fine tradition and "fighting spirit." Italy would never surrender, he said baldly, and at the conclusion of their talk, the ambassador immediately afterward telegraphed Berlin, "the King again underscored his decision to continue the struggle to the end, at the side of Germany, with whom Italy is bound in life and in death."[28]

Rahn had dreamed that morning that he had been strangled in his bed by a stranger, and he had still been upset when he had gone to see the king. But Victor Emmanuel, speaking relaxedly and munificently, had altered the ambassador's mood. It had led him to believe that the Axis without fascism was secure at least for a while longer.

The man who had worked this change in the Reich's representative had seen all that had flourished in July wither in forty-five days. The royal machinations in the futile search for a separate peace had not taken place in a void. The Allies, following Mussolini's overthrow, had publicly affirmed a new policy of applying maximum military pressure to drive Italy out of the war. This had meant the merciless bombing of Milan, Turin, Genoa, Naples, another attack on Rome, and raids on smaller cities and the countryside. It had made refugees and mourners of hundreds of thousands of Italians, and this had flushed away in tears and blood all their good wishes for the House of Savoy. Many now looked with hatred at a king who seemed to be cold-heartedly awaiting the semblance of a *force majeure* to justify a humiliating surrender. Others saw delay as the last refuge of the totally bankrupt, the irrational hope for some earthshaking development to intervene—such as a break between the western Allies and Moscow—and somehow rescue the niggardly crown.

Whatever were the king's intentions, he knew now that they had failed. Empowering Badoglio, he felt, had been his first and worst mistake. "His actions are indecisive and insincere," Victor Emmanuel had remarked only two days earlier. "Badoglio is certainly not the man for this crucial moment."[29] But the king, in his forty-five days, had followed only Badoglio's lead, continuing to refuse all other counsel. Maria José had maintained her relations with the liberal forces in Italian society, but in August Victor Emmanuel had ordered her to retire immediately to the royal estate in Val d'Aosta. "I made her understand clearly," he said after reprimanding her, "that in the House of Savoy women must absolutely never enter into affairs of State."[30] But he was further relieved that now she and her children would be near the Swiss border, which they would very shortly cross and be joined by other princes and princesses of Savoy. In tending to his dynastic self, Victor Emmanuel had also looked after his heirs.

Humbert, that morning of September 8, had been summoned to his father's side from the war zone. The crown prince was unaware of the armistice, as he had known nothing of the king's conspiracy against Mussolini. "My dear Bepo," his father had told him after July 25, "I wanted to keep you out of it all, because if the thing would have gone badly, only I would have been ruined."[31]

Now ruination threatened once again. His bags were packed, although he hoped to stay in Rome. Like a peddler or a broker, he knew that much depended on what this day would bring.

Sometime after five o'clock Badoglio received an unequivocal message from Eisenhower that the Allies would accept no postponement. "I intend to broadcast the existence of the armistice at the hour originally planned," Eisenhower said. "If you or any part of your armed forces fail to cooperate as previously agreed, I will publish to the world the full record of this affair. . . . No future action of yours could then restore any confidence whatever in your good faith and consequently the dissolution of your government and nation would ensue."[32]

The "hour originally planned" for the simultaneous announcement was 6:30 P.M.—some sixty minutes away. The invasion of the mainland would follow. Eisenhower's decision, Badoglio later complained, "upset all our plans and brought us to the brink of ruin."[33] The marshal himself, according to those who watched him read the American general's dispatch, was utterly shattered. Somebody notified the king, and within minutes a conference at the Quirinal was assembled, the purpose of which was to decide whether to accept or repudiate the surrender signed five days ago, and switch from having switched to the Allies back to the Germans.

The meeting of the so-called Crown Council began at about 6:00 P.M. Twelve persons were present: the king, Badoglio, Acquarone, Puntoni, Foreign Minister Guariglia, Minister of War Sorice, Ambrosio and his aide Major Marchesi, General Carboni, in command of the forces defending Rome, the chiefs of staff of the navy and the air force, Admiral De Courten and General Sandalli, and General De Stefanis, representing Army Chief of Staff Roatta. Roatta, totally occupied in trying to mislead the Germans a little while longer, had been unable to attend. Indeed at this very moment he was busy denying with indignation as "a bare-faced lie of British propaganda" an unofficial American radio report heard by Ambassador Rahn that the Italians had surrendered unconditionally.[34]

The king opened the meeting: "Gentlemen, as you know, the British and Americans have decided to advance the date of the armistice by four days."

Several of those present not only did not know this piece of news, but were unaware of the existence of the armistice itself. Admiral De Courten mumbled something to this effect, and the king, believing he was asking for the floor, called on him to speak. "Really?" asked the admiral. "I didn't know a thing."

The king frowned with annoyance. He turned to Badoglio and said sharply, "Will you please bring these gentlemen up to date?" Badoglio, it seems, was in no condition to speak. He was slumped in his chair, his chin buried in his chest. Ambrosio undertook the task instead, beginning with the words, "A great misfortune hangs over our heads. . . ."

Ambrosio went on to say, quite inaccurately, that one of the reasons why some of those present were as yet uninformed was that the armistice, as agreed between the Allies and Rome, was to have been announced not before September 12. Now, he continued erroneously, the British and Americans had decided unilaterally to make the Italian commitment public, and, moreover, to land their invasion force at Salerno and not north of Rome as had been stipulated. This situation, he said, placed the Italians militarily between the German hammer and the Allied anvil, and it was necessary now to decide what to do, as the Allied announcement was but minutes away.[35]

Victor Emmanuel, who knew less of the truth than Ambrosio ("Badoglio never showed me the terms of the armistice, even though I asked him many times to see them"),[36] threw open the floor to discussion.

"Why, this is blackmail!" Air Force General Sandalli exclaimed. He then offered his solution to the dilemma. "Let's reject the armistice."[37]

General Carboni advanced a more sophisticated idea. He said that they ought to *pretend* to reject the armistice. This would help gain a little more time with the Germans, he explained. The Allies should be informed of the ruse, while in the meantime the king would disavow Badoglio, as having signed the surrender without authorization from the crown. At this point, it is said, Badoglio shot up from his slouched position and leered at the general as if he were about to have his throat cut.[38]

Ministers Guariglia and Sorice thought Carboni's plan sound, but Major Marchesi, who had been present at the signing of the surrender, spoke now, describing what he believed the Allies had in store for those who would disavow the agreement. Apart from the military consequences, he recalled the text of Eisenhower's threat to tell "the world the full record of this affair"—a sordid tale the monarchy could scarcely hope to survive. Victor Emmanuel, the junior man later recalled, "listened absorbedly."[39]

The realization that their tergiversations and double dealings would be exposed seems to have had a sobering effect on almost everyone. General Puntoni expressed the opinion that the king had to consider before making any decision that the people of Italy were demoralized, and if the war which had continued after Mussolini's fall were to continue still, the burden of responsibility, in Mussolini's absence, would fall wholly on the crown. The king could not hope, in such circumstances, to escape the wrath of his people.[40]

General Carboni suddenly found himself isolated, and when he rose to continue his argument, the king interrupted, saying, "We know." Someone brought in a news dispatch from Reuter reporting that the Italians had surrendered. Carboni declared that the king should issue an immediate denial.

There were tense moments, staggering in their silence. It was 6:30 now, and Major Marchesi, who had left the room to listen to the radio, returned to announce that General Eisenhower was on the air, broadcasting the news. He read a translation of Eisenhower's message, in which it was said that "the Italian government has surrendered its armed forces unconditionally . . . effective this instant."[41]

"Well," said Victor Emmanuel, "there is no longer any doubt." The king would adhere to his given word, at least that which had been given to the enemy. The meeting was adjourned.[42]

Badoglio, who had remained behind, was instructed to make the announcement. At 7:45 P.M., an hour and fifteen minutes late, he was on Radio Rome. The government, he said, had surrendered "to the overwhelming power of the adversary."[43] A recording was made of his tired, droning message, which was repeated at brief intervals; it would ring vividly forever in the memories of a whole generation of Italians. It came, of course, as a complete and happy surprise, but there was no indication of what would come next. There were no instructions from the leaders to the people, and so the latter waited now for a guiding word.

The Germans received official notice of the surrender from the Italian foreign ministry at about seven o'clock that evening. Field Marshal Kesselring, commander of *Wehrmacht* forces in the southern theater of war, signaled the start of Operation Axis, Hitler's orders to go over to the offensive against the Italians, and, if possible, capture Rome. This second aspect of the plan did not, however, seem realizable as yet. Kesselring expected the Allies to strike the mainland near Rome to protect the Badoglio government and thus assure that the surrender terms would be upheld. His first maneuver, therefore, was to employ his troops in securing the way of withdrawal from Rome and points south, to the north. Berlin could not but agree that the desired seizure of Rome might have to be forgone, and in the early hours of the evening Ambassador Rahn asked the Italians for a train to be put at his disposal for the purpose of evacuating German diplomatic, military, and civilian personnel from Rome. The Italians complied with alacrity, while their military leaders ordered that all Germans wishing to leave the capital be permitted prompt exit without opposition.[44] The general orders given to the Italian armed forces with respect to the former ally were entirely defensive. They derived solely from the ambiguous last words of Marshal Badoglio's surrender broadcast directing Italian troops to lay down their arms before the United Nations and to "react" to attack "from any other quarter."

Immediately after the crown council meeting, the king had been joined at the Quirinal by Elena and Prince Humbert. At nightfall, while awaiting developments, the royal family took temporary refuge in the ministry of war, a well-fortified building about equidistant from the Quirinal and the square which would shortly be renamed Piazza of the Republic.* The fatal errors which had been accumulating since July 25 were now to be compounded in horrifying proportions.

---

* The only other members of the royal family remaining in Rome were the king's son-in-law General Calvi di Bergolo (Princess Yolanda's husband) and two of the king's grandchildren (Princess Mafalda's). Before entering the ministry of war, the king had arranged for the children to be taken for safekeeping in the Vatican. He had also sent a message to Count Calvi to come to him at once, but Calvi, commander of the *Centauro* division deployed in defense of Rome, had replied that in times such as these one does not abandon one's post. The king agreed.[45]

30

THE FLIGHT OF THE DAMNED

WHEN THE ROYAL COUPLE AND THE PRINCE OF PIEDMONT ARRIVED AT THE WAR MINISTRY, THEY found Badoglio and his son taking supper. The prime minister was not at all alarmed, having received early reports that the Germans were apparently in the process of withdrawing from Rome. He conveyed the good news to the king and at about ten o'clock said that he was going off to sleep in a room which had been prepared for him in the ministry. Shortly past midnight, after receiving further assurances, the king and queen went to sleep, too, in the same building, having been given War Minister Sorice's apartment. They did not, however, allow themselves the luxury of undressing; the situation was still too fluid.

Without any clear directives, the Italian forces only weakly resisted the German offensive maneuver, and once Kesselring's lines for a northerly retreat were assured, he was encouraged to begin an encirclement movement around the capital. There were no signs of an Allied landing or air drop beyond Salerno, which further emboldened the German commander to one by one cut the eighteen roads to Rome.[1] This too was hardly resisted. The Italian operation for the defense of the city—Memoria 44—which might have, at this critical moment, driven Kesselring back to opting for a guaranteed departure, was simply delayed by confusion and hesitation, and in the end never issued at all.[2] In a few hours it became apparent to General Roatta that Rome and its nearly two million people were being sealed in a German net.

At 4:30 A.M., with the sound of cannons rumbling in the distant air, Roatta was discussing the changed situation in War Minister Sorice's office with the minister, Badoglio, the crown prince, and Puntoni, when General Ambrosio suddenly appeared and asked for a late report. Roatta observed that the Germans seemed now to be preparing to enter not leave the capital. All of the roads were in their hands, he said, with the exception of one: the east-west Via Tiburtina, which runs from the city across the Apennine Mountains and down to the Adriatic Sea. If anyone had any idea of leaving Rome, he had better do so now, which is precisely what Roatta suggested. It seemed to him, he said, "useful not to expose the King and the Government to the risk of capture."[3]

"Gentlemen," Roatta later admitted as having said at that moment, "if the Germans get their hands on us, they will shoot us all. And why should we let them shoot us?"[4]

The question sank fast and deep. If people in Nazi-occupied Rome were going to be shot—and they were, by the hundredfold—ought it not happen to others, not them? The answer lay with the prime minister, and ultimately with the little king.

Badoglio, and presumably each of those present, put the question to his own mind, in his own way. The septuagenarian marshal said later that he asked himself:

> How would my leaving the place of combat be interpreted by others? Would the public comprehend the need for my departure, or would they give it an outright infamous interpretation?

Fortunately his replies were readily at hand. As he was to admit:

> My internal struggle did not last very long. . . . Every personal consideration had to be put aside. What remained supreme were the interests only of the Fatherland. I declared that of course I approved of General Roatta's proposal, and that I had decided to abandon Rome, taking the Tiburtina.[5]

At the time he expressed it to the others somewhat more succinctly, however. The prime minister said: "I'm going."[6]

The king had to be consulted. Puntoni was sent to wake him. Victor Emmanuel, when informed of the prime minister's views on the matter of taking flight from the threatened city, also underwent a moral crisis. It lasted about as long as Badoglio's. The king's reaction was characteristic of his personality. When later queried whether he opposed Badoglio's insistence on the advisability of escaping, the king wrote a hastily composed, telescopic reply to this the most important decision in his life, and in the life of the House of Savoy. He replied:

Yes. Badoglio rendered necessary—[this phrase was then crossed out]. Much and lively resistance. Badoglio's behavior and decision rendered departure necessary.[7]

His resistance, as usual, waned swiftly, and as Puntoni put it in his diary entry for that day: "The King . . . adheres reluctantly to abandon Rome. His intention is to guarantee the continuity of the government's action in cooperation with the Allies and to prevent that the Eternal City suffer the horrors of war."[8]

This, variously phrased and embellished, was to be the House of Savoy's official position in explanation of the king's subsequent embarrassment at having fled. But it would never be able to explain how the wholly negligent abandonment of the capital to the Nazis might have spared Rome and the Romans the hunger, the fear, the tortures, and the massacres which they were to suffer for the next nine months. As for the need to maintain the "government," Puntoni himself, like everyone else, noted at the time, ". . . In reality only the ministers of the Navy and the Air Force are departing; the other [fourteen] ministers are not even informed that the Head of Government is getting ready to leave Rome."[9]

No one had been ordered to defend the city. No one was left in command. Rome would awaken the next morning as naked and exposed as the twins of Mars had been when first they lay abandoned to the Seven Hills 2,700 years ago.

This, then, was not the orderly retreat of state power to more advantageous ground. These men were not going to a base in Sardinia; they were simply *going*—and to where, they had as yet no notion at all. This was the escape of the compromised and the desperate, of frightened, wretched men, who had no time to leave instructions behind, to destroy secret documents, to take a toothbrush or a comb. This was the flight of the damned, and Victor Emmanuel III would never again see Rome.*

* The investigations into this grim episode of Italian history never cease. Even under Savoyard rule an official inquest was held, and a number of military and civil trials have taken place over the years, dealing for the most part with the neglected defense of Rome and the nature of the king's flight. The documents, testimony, and literature in this regard are voluminous, to say the least, but little justification has been found, and no one argues that the abandonment of Rome was not the most grievous error. On the other hand, the recent suggestion that the flight of the royal party was the result of a "deal" between the Badoglio government and Field Marshal Kesselring—safe conduct for the fleeing group in exchange for Rome—has given rise to a great deal of controversy, as well as further court cases. This hypothesis, propounded most thoroughly by Ruggero Zangrandi,[10] is based solely on rather marginal circumstantial evidence, some of which is illustrated below. At best, the idea remains

At about five o'clock on the morning of September 9, the little king, in his gray-green uniform, carrying a small, inexpensive fiberboard suitcase, entered the courtyard of the ministry of war. He was followed by the queen. A few moments later he was joined by his generals, his aides, two or three servants, and his son.

Day had not yet broken. Rome was still, and while she slept twenty-two men and women boarded seven black cars to make haste for Via Tiburtina. It was an ugly, pathetic sight, and the king's *dolore* was no less than anyone else's, because, as he later confided, "Even Sovereigns are given a heart, and they, like every citizen, love the Fatherland."[13] Prince Humbert shook his head in sadness. As the party struck east for the sea, he murmured repeatedly, "My God, what a scene!"[14]

The intermediate destination was the coastal town of Pescara, 140 miles down the Tiburtina. When the decision to take flight had been made, the king's generals had dispatched communications to their forces on land, sea, and air to assure that one or another mode of transport would be waiting to carry the fugitives farther along.

The final place of regroupment was yet to be determined. It was not even known whether Pescara itself was safe. On Puntoni's counsel, the king therefore decided during the journey to head for the estate of his friend the duke of Bovino, which was off the Tiburtina, about ten miles or so from the Adriatic and almost as near to Pescara. He hoped to be able to remain there while awaiting the results of a scouting mission to Pescara, led somewhat reluctantly by Acquarone, to whom he delegated that task. He then sent Humbert to request hospitality for the weary travelers from the duke and duchess, of whom the prince had often been a guest. Humbert, in his high-powered Alfa 2500, took the lead, and the flight continued.[15]

As is often the case when anxious men hurry, quite a few inelegant incidents occurred. Badoglio, it is said, appeared "destroyed" and

---

unproved and still seems highly unlikely. There is no doubt, however, that when the fugitives departed, the Tiburtina road was in fact controlled by Kesselring's forces and that at least some Germans were aware that the king was in transit. But, as one of Kesselring's commanders, General Student, has said in denying any sort of agreement, "I must admit that as soldiers we were, however, happy to be free of the Savoys and the government in the known way."[11] More important, Hitler himself seems to have been of the same opinion. Victor Emmanuel had already left, but Goebbels in his diary entry for the day of the escape wrote as follows: "The royal family is scheduled to leave Rome this evening . . . The Fuehrer is right in believing that we cannot afford to install immediately the sort of regime [in Italy] that we would really like to have. . . . Nor is this the moment to attack the King personally, for the King is still respected by all Italians."[12] Hitler apparently felt it more politic to let Victor Emmanuel hang himself, rather than do it for him.

muttered obsessively about being decapitated or hanged on a road-side tree if he were captured by the Germans.[16] But the truth was that the party was stopped at least twice by the Germans. They were allowed to pass without further delay when a colonel in Victor Emmanuel's car leaned from the window and shouted, *"Ufficiali generali,"* as if it were a password.[17] Naturally this was to give weight to the charges made by the king's future enemies of his having made a "deal" with Kesselring, and additional significance would be attached to the fact that one of the cars, halted by a detachment of the *Hermann Goering* division, was permitted to continue even after it had struck a soldier in the driver's rush to be on his way.*[18]

Two of the automobiles broke down in transit. This was remedied in one case, but in the second, with Badoglio and Acquarone inside, nothing could be done. When a car carrying two lesser-ranking men and some of the royal luggage came by, the prime minister and the duke used their authority to replace the passengers and the baggage with themselves. Their inferiors remained at the side of the road with facile assurances that they would be picked up by those in the party who were yet to pass. In the event, however, either they were unseen or disregarded, for like Rome, they too, bags and all, were left behind.

The movement of the convoy of black sedans was seen by many people along the way, and as the peasants had once gathered to cheer the passage of "Galibardo" and the unrecognized *re galantuomo*, they stood now in silence, comprehending this day the baneful deed Italy and the world would know tomorrow. A second convoy, composed of high military officials, had left Rome shortly after the king's departure, and so the roadside spectacle was all the more imposing.

At about 10:00 A.M. Humbert reached the castle of the duke and duchess of Bovino. It stood at the end of a service road from the Tiburtina to a village in the eastern foothills of the Apennines called Crecchio. Within the hour the entire party arrived, with the exception of Acquarone. The duke and duchess were staggered by the surprise visit, but, as Puntoni wrote, "they made miracles."[20] The duchess's later indiscretions, however, were to give cause for royal regrets.

Her callers came, according to her revelations, "asking to be

---

* No attempt was made to hide the presence of the royal family. The king's car, a Fiat 2800, flew small pennants on the fenders bearing the five gold stars of the "First Marshal of the Empire." Badoglio himself later admitted passing checkpoints and being allowed to proceed, and Puntoni wrote at the time that the party was stopped by the Germans, "but no one created any difficulties with regard to our freedom of movement."[19]

given shelter and hiding, fearing that they had been followed and would be captured by the Germans, who were occupying Italy and Rome. The king seemed rather tranquil, but the prince was very upset. Marshal Badoglio affirmed that within fifteen days or so he would be able to bring the king back to Rome. When asked whom he had left in Rome as his substitute, he replied evasively, saying that he had given the necessary orders."[21]

While waiting for news from Acquarone and for the duchess to prepare their repast, the visitors camped on the duke's estate. The grounds took on the appearance of a trailer park or a wayside rest of a gypsy caravan. The chauffeurs checked and tuned their cars, the servants drew items from the baggage, and when there was nothing more for either of them to do, they found places to sleep on the seats of the sedans. The queen appeared emotionally and physically exhausted, and she and the king were shown to the duke's bedroom in order that they might refresh themselves before luncheon.

In the meantime the local peasants, who had either come by out of curiosity or had been solicited, had gathered around the grounds bearing baskets of food so that the duke could provide for his company. The guests, who numbered well over fifty persons, were to dine on twenty-eight freshly slain chickens, an unrationed quantity of cheese and salami, and the sort of *casereccio* bread, salad, and fresh fruit one finds only in the *campagna*.

By now Acquarone had arrived with the relatively good news that there were not very many Germans in Pescara, and in any event, the local airport was in Italian hands. Moreover there were more than enough aircraft and pilots available to bring the fugitives farther on in their journey to wherever, within reason, they might choose to go. It was therefore agreed that the airport would be their next stop, and on this high note, the luncheon began.

The diners, many of whom had not had any food in the past eighteen hours, were too numerous to sit at one table. They ate in turns, according to rank. The royal family and the "government" lunched with the duke and duchess, and the conversation at table was less than entirely coherent.

At one point the king sighed in no particular context: "And to think, all this is happening because of an election maneuver!" Since the others, taken by surprise, did not know what the king meant, he explained. President Roosevelt, he said, had ordered the date of the armistice announcement (and the invasion) advanced to September 8 because he was to be present at an election rally. Roosevelt had wished to gain the maximum impact of his appearance by personally publicizing the news of World War II's first unconditional surrender, declared the king. This was wholly untrue, but doubtless earnestly believed. In any event, Victor Emmanuel went on, his departure from Rome would not mean much. "Soon we will be on our way back," he said. He opened his wallet to show that he had taken with him only 1,200 lire.

Badoglio said somewhat abstrusely: "I am a Piedmontese. And if I say something, that's because I'm sure of it. In fifteen days, at the latest, we'll be on our way back."

The queen was less confident. Everyone knew how this had begun, she observed sadly, but no one could tell how it would end, and often affairs such as this end badly.[22]

The diners began to discuss Mussolini. Someone wondered what would become of him. Badoglio, who had committed the government and crown by the long terms of the surrender to deliver Mussolini to the Allies, found the question amusing. Referring to the Germans, he exclaimed jocularly, "They've probably freed him by now!"*[23]

"All in all," said the king, taking aim at the prime minister who had failed him even more than the Duce, "he served me faithfully for more than twenty years."[24]

At three o'clock that afternoon Victor Emmanuel and his party took leave of the duke and duchess of Bovino. The king gave expressions of farewell and gratitude, and was in turn wished good fortune and Godspeed, to the sound of which he departed for the airport at Pescara, a dozen miles away.

More than one hundred airplanes, summoned by Ambrosio, were waiting for the king, but in an abbreviated crown council meeting at the terminal, it was decided to proceed not by air but by sea. This decision was influenced to some extent by what may be described as a

---

* The cavalier way in which Mussolini was discarded by the king and Badoglio was another point later to be underscored in the secret deal hypothesis. Mussolini at that moment was being held in expectation of further orders from Badoglio by the loyalist *carabinieri*. The prisoner was confined at Gran Sasso, only thirty miles from the duke's castle, and thus a few minutes flight from Pescara. No doubt the consignment of Mussolini to the mercies of the Allies, in spite of signed promises, would have been distasteful to those who had overthrown him. But that he was simply left for collection and use by the Germans was to create many months of further suffering for the Italians. The Duce's "liberation" took place on September 12. He was flown to Germany, and later in the month installed at the head of a ruinous new-Fascist, puppet regime in northern Italy, which was nevertheless the country's first post-Risorgimento "republic."

mutiny of a group of air force officers and pilots. They had agreed that morning to protest the royal escape as a cowardly act to which they would lend no support. More than protest, some of the aviators appear to have actually refused to fly the king to safety. The group had gathered around a titled major, Prince Carolo Ruspoli, who had been Humbert's classmate at military school. When Humbert arrived at the airport, Ruspoli appealed to him that, if not the king, at least the crown prince return at once to Rome. Ruspoli and his fellow airmen, who had earlier discussed the use of force for this purpose, said now that they would accompany him, giving armed escort back to the forsaken capital.[25]

Humbert had been suffering painful second thoughts all along about the propriety of the royal behavior. In the past twenty-four hours, through no immediate fault of his own, he had left a sorry personal record in his trail. In answering his father's unexplained call to the Quirinal, he had unwittingly abandoned his post as commander of all forces in southern Italy, only, as it turned out, to be in a position to flee to safety with the king. He had left no instructions to his men, believing that he would return to his command that same evening.[26] At the castle of the duke of Bovino, Humbert had already once suggested that it might be wiser for him to return to Rome. He had been addressing his father, but Badoglio, who had been sitting nearby, had answered instead. This had exploded into a heated argument between the crown prince and the marshal about who had the right to command whom. The king, saying nothing, had taken no position on either the altercation or the problem which his son had posed.[27]

Now, at the airport, Humbert, with Prince Ruspoli at his side, again approached his father. The reasons for his prompt return to the capital grew more compelling with each passing moment. For now not only were the officers threatening insubordination, but a crowd of civilians, who had heard of the king's imminent departure to places unknown, were gathering at the entrance to the airport. They did not appear to be well-wishers, and many were shouting imprecations concerning the royal courage.

This time, although Badoglio again was present, the king spoke. His reasons would be given later, but for the moment it seemed effort enough for him to mutter, "I must respect the decisions of my government."[28] Humbert acquiesced, but no one could guess to what measure the indignant officers and the hostile people might be placated, and the idea of leaving by sea was discussed. Thanks to Ambrosio's comprehensive thinking, three warships were speeding to Pescara to oblige. When one of them, the *Baionetta*, or *Bayonet*, was actually sighted thirty miles off shore, the final decision was made. "Then we're all agreed," said the king again and again to be sure that no one would misunderstand. "Everyone is coming with me."[29]

The point of embarkation was moved to the small port of Ortona, about twelve miles south of Pescara, and the time was set for the darkest hour of that night. General Puntoni's diary gives the reasons why: "In order to avoid attracting any attention during the boarding operations, we set our departure from a pier in Ortona at midnight."[30] But kings, as much as they might like to, can rarely travel unattended by their people, and so this plan too would go awry.

The time was now about 6:00 P.M. Six hours remained with nothing for at least the king, queen, and crown prince to do, and as it was advisable to withdraw from the airport, they went back to call once more on the duke and duchess of Bovino.

Humbert explained that his party had met with a contretemps, but that their next departure would surely be their last. The duke and duchess were as hospitable as ever. They excused the disarray of their castle, but since the mess had been made by their guests, whose return had not been foreseen, no lengthy apologies were needed. As for supper, the royal family and their friends would unfortunately have to take pot luck, and when again no objections were raised, the visitors were redirected to the same rooms they had occupied before.

After supping lightly on bread, fruit, and wine, and as the hour of their last going away drew near, the three highest members of the House of Savoy were stricken as one with the supreme crisis of conscience. Badoglio had been left behind to board the *Baionetta* at an early hour, and so now the drama could be played to the last curtain *in familias*.

The episode began when Humbert was drawn aside by his adjutant Francesco Campello. Major Campello, unaware of the earlier recommendations which had been made to the prince, urged that they fly back to Rome. He began to weep as he sought to impress on Humbert the historical import of his abandonment of the capital. Humbert was sympathetic, but the decision was the king's, not his own. The king had already said no, and, the prince added, repeating the age-old saw, "In the House of Savoy, we reign one at a time."[31]

The delicate matter again seemed ended, but at about 9:00 P.M. Humbert called Puntoni to his room, where the general found him alone. "My leaving Rome," the prince said abruptly, "is without a doubt a mistake. I think I had best go back. I feel it indispensable that a member of my House be present in the Capital in such a serious moment as this."

Puntoni, knowing his master's wish that the crown prince accompany him, sought to dissuade Humbert. "By now," he said, "events are precipitating. Probably they are already fighting in Rome . . . and the German command would like nothing better than to lay hands on a hostage like you. . . . In any case, His Majesty has already decided what you must do. He desires that Your Highness be at his side in the event he decides to leave the throne."[32]

This too, however, was insufficient to turn the prince from what he believed was his dynastic duty. He concluded that he had to beseech his father once more. This conviction was strengthened by the duke and duchess. They were bold enough, at some moment before Humbert went to the king, to urge the prince to return to Rome to organize and lead an armed resistance to the German occupation. This, they said, was the only way to save the monarchy from "extreme peril."

The duchess, a descendant of the courtier Caetanis of Rome, is said to have entreated the crown prince as follows: "Your Highness, you know the sentiments of our family toward His Majesty, the Queen, and your House. But forgive me if I implore you to go back to Rome."

"Thank you, Duchess," Humbert replied. "You comfort me greatly. I have only to convince His Majesty the King."[33]

Now the question was raised for the last time, in the presence of his father and mother. The duke of Acquarone was there, too, pursuing his role as gray eminence. Humbert would surely be captured by the Germans, said Acquarone, and forced by threat and even torture to blacken the name of Savoy. It was a poor argument, unworthy of the prince's courage and his will to save his house, but the king insisted, on "constitutional" grounds, that he had to follow the lead of his government. The mother of the potential victim, on hearing the word *torture*, blurted in her acquired Piedmontese: "Bepo, if they catch you they'll kill you."*[34]

---

* It is neither possible nor really relevant to say what might have happened to Humbert had he been captured by the Germans. But members of the House of Savoy and the Badoglio government—including Badoglio's politically active son, Mario—did fall into Nazi hands, and their fate is known. Badoglio's police chief Senise, who, as has been said, was among the principal conspirators in the overthrow of Mussolini, was arrested and deported to Germany in September, 1943, where he sat

Humbert did not say then, as he did later, that the Nazis could have arrested the entire royal party at almost any time since they had left Rome ("Our column . . . was many times in a position to be easily captured if the Germans had had the mind to do so").[36] He simply obeyed.

When the clock struck eleven, the visitors left the duke and duchess once more, this time forever.

The military men in charge of the evacuation of the royal family had sounded a false air raid alarm so that the people in the area would take to whatever shelters they might have, and thus the last stage of the cross-country flight could proceed without "attracting any attention." But when the king arrived at water's edge, near midnight, it was clear that this tactic had not been successful. A crowd of local fishermen, port workers, women, and children had gathered in the darkness. Some shouted catcalls; others urged the boarding party to make haste so as not to draw the Germans to their town. Puntoni wrote:

> At Ortona we were greeted with a great surprise. Notwithstanding efforts to do everything in absolute secrecy, the portside quays are filled with cars. The Sovereign grows nervous and tells me to find out what is happening. They are the vehicles which have brought almost the entire General Staff down here. Nothing like this was foreseen. Surrounded by generals and high officers, we see Roatta in a business suit, with a submachinegun on his shoulder. The King looks at him and shakes his head. We hear voices and warnings in the dark.[37]

Victor Emmanuel knew then, he himself later said, that the House of Savoy had collapsed.[38]

The *Baionetta*, with its lights spent, slipped out of the little port some time before 1:00 A.M. on September 10. Fifty-seven passengers were on board. The captain, like everyone else on his ship, did not know its final destination. Someone had told him to head "south."

---

out the rest of the war in "a small and decent hotel" in Bavaria. He found himself in the company of the duchess of Aosta, Anne of Orleans (Hélène's daughter-in-law and niece), as well as several foreign princes and political figures. Mario Badoglio and Victor Emmanuel's sons-in-law Prince Philip of Hesse and Count Calvi di Bergolo (to whom had fallen the task of surrendering Rome to the Germans after the king's flight) survived similar experiences. The sad exception was Princess Mafalda, who Hitler thought was the "trickiest bitch" in the House of Savoy, and over whose capture Goebbels gloated that she would now be "taken into the school of hard knocks."[35] Mafalda was sent to Buchenwald, where she was held in a special compound for dignitaries. She died in August, 1944, as a result of wounds she had received in an Allied bombardment in the camp area.

The tired king fell asleep on a deck chair. The queen passed the night unable to sleep; she could hear her son in the darkness nearby, tormented by a hacking cough. In the morning it was decided to attempt to go ashore at Brindisi, the ancient port at the very end of the Appian Way, from where the Romans once set sail to conquer the world. Badoglio had earlier argued that the party try to reach territory already secured by the Allies, such as Sicily or even North Africa. But it was hoped that a place in the Italian sun could still be found where there were neither Allies nor Germans, in order that Victor Emmanuel might rule.

The king's corvette, sailing on the heel of the Italian boot, came within sight of Brindisi that afternoon. It was a moment of great tension. A message radioed to the local naval commander, Admiral Rubartelli, had not been answered, and it remained unknown just who was in control of Brindisi. Not much more of Italy remained south of there. As the intruding *Baionetta* entered the harbor, on-shore guns took her in aim. A motorboat headed toward her. It was flying the Italian flag, and when Admiral Rubartelli was recognized among those on the small craft, the *Baionetta's* passengers and crew were greatly relieved.

The admiral came aboard. He was unaware of the royal family's presence, and he was stunned when he suddenly came face-to-face with his king. They are said to have had this conversation:

> Victor Emmanuel: Are there any Germans in Brindisi?
> Rubartelli: No, Your Majesty.
> Victor Emmanuel: Are there any English?
> Rubartelli: None, Your Majesty.
> Victor Emmanuel: Then who is in command?
> Rubartelli: I am.
> Victor Emmanuel: All right. We're coming ashore.[39]

It was Teano all over again, in pitiful caricature. The House of Savoy had sunk far since Garibaldi rode out of Naples to give Italy to the *re galantuomo*. To the little king, Rubartelli on the *Baionetta* gave the so-called "Kingdom of the South," a realm of brief duration.

31

HUMBERT II THE MAY KING

BY THE END OF SEPTEMBER, 1943, UNITED ITALY HAD BEEN DRAWN AND QUARTERED. THE GERmans held fast in Rome. The Allies were gaining on the old Two Sicilies. Mussolini's puppet republic settled in around Lake Garda, north of Milan. And the little king, by the grace of Washington, London, and Moscow, ruled the "kingdom of the South"—four provinces of the Puglie, and the haunted island of Sardinia. The geopolitical accomplishments of the hundred year war of the Risorgimento had been undone. The power of many foreign lands was spoiling Italy anew. Civil war was in the wings, and Italians by the tens of thousands were about to fall. Indeed the Risorgimento was dead. A second coming, more modest of aim, was gathering in the heart and in the hills. This was to be known as the *Resistenza*—the Resistance—a mood and a gun which would drive out the vainglorious past once and for all.

One of the earliest signs that the events of September had altered the very bones of the body politic was the attitude shared by all classes with respect to Victor Emmanuel III. The king who had abandoned Rome in the dead of night was now abandoned by all in the fullness of day. The outcry for the king's abdication was universal, and even Badoglio, the monarchists, and the crown's well-wishers advised Victor Emmanuel's hasty withdrawal. That the nation could not go forward unless it were purged of the little king was suddenly the fashion which clothed every persuasion.[1]

Six anti-Fascist political parties, from right to left, emerged that autumn to champion the fall of the sovereign, although they divided on the fate of the House of Savoy. Their most eloquent and renowned spokesman was Croce. The aging philosopher had, of course, caressed fascism when it was young, but had consistently opposed it when it grew haggish and arthritic. Now he called for the king's abdication, renunciation of the crown by Prince Humbert, and the accession to the throne of six-year-old Victor Emmanuel IV, under a regency to be headed by Badoglio. Only in this way, he said, could the monarchy hope to survive the opprobrium Victor Emmanuel III and his adult heirs had earned from the people. Croce's plan was presented to the crown as a most generous offer, for the popular sentiment was such that men spoke openly of trying their king and sending him to the wall. There was not the slightest doubt, Croce said at the time, that such a trial would end with the king being condemned. Croce warned that he and all liberals and upholders of the Albertian constitution, who wished to see the monarchy live on, could not oppose high court action against Victor Emmanuel, "the violator of the Constitution," although they would remain against the "form of justice that pleased Cromwell's army and Robespierre's Jacobins."[2]

Peril and dishonor could be averted, however, said Croce, if only the king were to abdicate, as Charles Albert and other Savoys had before him. The sole "impediment" to a democratic Italy, the philosopher insisted, "is the person of the King, Victor Emmanuel III, who opened the door to fascism, encouraged it, supported it, and served it for twenty years . . . and who remains, now that Mussolini has fallen, the true and principal representative of fascism. To say that Italy ought to keep its present King, is to say that someone given a new life should remain in the clutches of a corpse."[3]

The king, in his shabby quarters in Brindisi, resisted—perhaps for fear that the threats against him might come true (Mussolini, it will be recalled, clung to his immunities under similar circumstances during the Matteotti affair). Only a few courtiers stood by him. The army, which had always been the real source of the king's power, was all but disbanded, and the fleet was in the hands of the Allies. The thousand-year-old Savoyard structure lay propped on the authority and prestige of a single sympathetic figure: Winston Churchill.

Franklin Roosevelt told Churchill that "I cannot for the life of me understand why we should hesitate [to support the six anti-Fascist parties]. American public opinion would never understand our continued tolerance and apparent support of Victor Emmanuel."[4] But the British prime minister later wrote that "from the moment when the Armistice was signed and when the Italian Fleet loyally and courageously joined the Allies, I felt myself bound to work with the King of Italy . . . On the other hand, there were the usual arguments against having anything to do with those who had worked with or helped Mussolini, and immediately there grew an endless series of intrigues among the six or seven Leftish [sic] parties in Rome to get rid of the King and Badoglio and take the power themselves. . . . I resisted these movements whenever they came to my notice."[5]

Unhappily for the little king, the "movements" did not always come to Churchill's notice; often they were kept from him by his own men in the field. If the king was reviled by the Italians, he was held in utter contempt by the Allies, presumably with the exception of Churchill. Even King George VI refused to answer Victor Emmanuel's appeals for his fraternal assistance, and when the British monarch came to Naples that winter, the Italian was forced by the Allies to vacate his own villa so that George might be properly accommodated.*[6] Such things happen when kings fail.

Victor Emmanuel's humiliations were bottomless. They were overseen, in one essential sphere, by the head of the Allied diplomatic mission to the king's government, General Mason MacFarlane, British governor of Gibraltar. His abhorrence of Italians in general, and Victor Emmanuel and Badoglio in particular, was, according to the American member of the mission, Robert Murphy, "even more bitter than that of most other British officers at that time. . . . [They] hated the Nazis, but they despised the Italians."[8] The Italians, in MacFarlane's eyes, could do nothing right. They had earned his disfavor by following Mussolini, and when they sought now to demonstrate their will to join the Allied side, MacFarlane observed, "The bloody bastards tried for years to do us in, and now look at them!"[9]

MacFarlane presented himself before the king of Italy in short pants, his sleeves rolled to his elbows. He thought the monarch looked "gaga," and he made the royal family extremely unhappy—so much so that when George VI's visit required their retreat to a house on the cliffs of Amalfi, Victor Emmanuel stared into the green sea one day and wondered aloud, "What if I were to jump from these rocks?"[10]

The little king lived a prisoner's existence. When Murphy saw

---

* George's rudeness was attributed in Italian court circles as stemming from an incident which had occurred in 1930. George, then Albert, Duke of York, had been visibly offended when at Prince Humbert's wedding banquet he had been assigned a place of lesser importance than that of the lowly former king of Afghanistan. The little king, however, was posthumously "avenged." In a book of his conversations with an aide-de-camp, published in 1954, Victor Emmanuel is revealed to have made scandalous remarks about George's behavior during his visit to Rome for the wedding. "One day," said the Italian about the Briton, "he had to receive the English 'colony' in Rome, but the reception had to be canceled because he was intoxicated. He had been to a 'tea' and had drunk a lot. It was said that he had been taken ill, but the English did not believe it. Many of them had also been at that 'tea' and had seen him carried away . . . drunk."[7]

him in September, he asked the sovereign if there were anything he might do to aid him. The king was hesitant, wary perhaps; then he replied: "The Queen has been unable to get any fresh eggs. Is it possible that we could somehow get a dozen eggs?"[11]

Churchill provided, and for months the little king was able to defer the dark future. He knew he would have to exit sooner or later, but the greater the clamor for his departure, the more reinforced was his conviction that he ought to get something in exchange for whatever concessions he might yield. What his "payoff" ought to be remained obscure, connected somehow to a desire for the kind of vindication yearned for by old men who have all their lives always been true to a Good Cause and ever misunderstood by others. But he was apparently willing to suffer any indignity in order to prolong the agony of his enemies. In one sense, it was a puerile (or senile), meaningless game, for his obstructionism obstructed only those who wished to advance yet another new era of class rule. In many instances, however, it was also Victor Emmanuel's supreme act of selfishness. It led to disastrous internal strife, and the most selfish act of all was his unwillingness to declare war on Germany without, as Puntoni put it, "snatching something in exchange."[12] Without such a declaration Italian prisoners, denied any protection from international law, would be subject to summary executions by the Germans. Fortunately the Allies insisted ("the Anglo-Americans have us by the throat," Puntoni observed), and the little king reluctantly gave in.[13]

Churchill wished to postpone the king's fate at least until the Allies took Rome, but by the spring of 1944, the capital still lay at the end of an impassable road, and the royal intransigence had become a political issue in the United States. "Roosevelt was up for reelection that year," Robert Murphy later recalled, "and the status of Victor Emmanuel was troubling American voters of Italian descent." The president summoned Murphy to Washington. "[He] told me that he had consented to the King's retention longer than he believed wise, because Churchill felt so strongly about this matter, but now an abdication must somehow be arranged."[14]

On April 10, 1944, without Churchill's knowledge, Murphy, MacFarlane, and British diplomats Harold Macmillan and Sir Noel Charles went to see the king to tell him he was through. "These four personages," Puntoni recorded in his diary entry of that "tragic" day, "said that the British and American governments believed that by now Italian public opinion is decisively against [Victor Emmanuel] remaining on the throne and that they therefore feel it indispensable that he renounce his powers as Chief of State." He was told that he had to reply by 4:00 P.M. of that same day. "The request," Puntoni added, "has the character of a real ultimatum."[15]

The end of Savoyard glory, it seemed to Victor Emmanuel, was at hand. Murphy describes the scene:

> The tiny King . . . received us while standing before a very large wall map of Italy. I explained the President's position as tactfully as I could, but the King's emotions suddenly overcame him. He continued to stand very erect and dignified, but his chin quivered and tears came into his pale blue eyes as he spoke with pride of the thousand-year history of the House of Savoy. He said mournfully: "A republican form of government is not suited to the Italian people. They are not prepared for it either temperamentally or historically. In a republic every Italian would insist upon being President, and the result would be chaos. The only people who would profit would be the Communists."[16]

Nobody had said anything about a republic (the Allies had asked only that he abdicate in favor of his son), but the king saw himself in a manner like the little Dutch boy with his finger in the dike. Yet there was nothing he could do; he was powerless, and as Machiavelli had taught, "Among other evils which being unarmed brings you, it causes you to be despised."

Monarchists later recounted that in spite of this he stood up strong before his captors, and that it was not Victor Emmanuel who wept but General MacFarlane, overcome as he was by the little king's fortitude and dignity.[17] "MacFarlane, who had come to the King with the air of a master, went out embarrassedly and speechless," says Puntoni.[18] There is reason to doubt that the Anglo-American mission felt much compunction, but the king in fact succeeded in surrendering something less than had been demanded. Within forty-eight hours, to forestall the possibility that the Allies would subject him to "odious blackmail," Victor Emmanuel announced his forthcoming retirement, which fell short of immediate abdication.[19]

"The Italian people know that I have always been at their side in their hours of joy and in their hours of sadness," he proclaimed on April 12. "They know that eight months ago I put an end to the Fascist regime and that in spite of all dangers and risks I brought Italy to the side of the United Nations in the struggle for liberation from Nazism." Giving no explanation, he went on to declare that "I have decided to withdraw from public life, naming my son, the Prince of Piedmont, Lieutenant General [of the crown's powers]. . . . My decision . . . is definitive and irrevocable."[20] ("Even if the whole country begs me on its knees," he added privately, "I won't change my mind.")[21]

His retirement would become effective, he said, on the day the Allied troops entered Rome, and he extracted a promise from the British and the Americans that he would be permitted to return to the capital and ceremoniously transfer his powers (but not his crown) to Prince Humbert.

"Well," Murphy said later, "that was not exactly what President Roosevelt had stipulated. The King had concocted a formula intended to postpone his abdication. . . . Victor Emmanuel thus engineered one more little triumph, but it was his final one."[22]

The western Allies, under pressure from Churchill, and, of all people, Stalin,* felt constrained to fall back before Victor Emmanuel's footwork. His concession did clear the way for the temporary settlement of internal political conflict. They would laugh last later, denying the king access to liberated Rome ("The exuberant Roman crowds did not seem to notice his absence," said Murphy).[24] But the old sovereign and his court believed they had given all. Badoglio cried when the king signed his retirement proclamation, and he tried to kiss the sovereign's hand. The two men had grown to hate one another, but Victor Emmanuel sought to comfort the marshal, patting him on the shoulder. "Your Majesty," said Badoglio, "I have served your house for fifty-five years, and I never thought it would come to this. Let me cry." The king himself, it is said, "was admirably above any emotion."[25] But in the presence of Puntoni, he was "sad, mortified." The business of being king was burdensome, he confided, and he confessed that his active reign of forty-four years had been a protracted sacrifice of his private will. He said:

> It cannot be said that from the time of the formation of Italy things have gone very well for my House! Only my grandfather came out on top. Charles Albert had to abdicate. My father was assassinated. I had no intention to succeed my father, and I had almost convinced him to accept my proposal to renounce the Crown. But he was killed, and I, in that tragic hour, could not refuse to ascend the throne. If I were to have done so, they would have said that I was a coward![26]

Of such foggy substance had nearly a half-century of Italian history been made.

---

* The Russian had suddenly recognized the king's government, thinking he was obstructing "British and American imperialists [who] were out to saddle the European nations with their own administration."[23]

For two years more Victor Emmanuel III remained king in name only, while Prince Humbert exercised all the functions of the throne save the right to wear the crown. They were years which saw the world war end in apocalyptic fire and destruction, and new forces emerge planet-wide eager to dismantle the old. In Italy, in the last year of war, a true reordering of social power had taken place. The *Resistenza*—an Allied-recognized land army of 150,000 partisans and a national spirit which had impelled the people of every large city north of Rome to rise up in civil revolt against the Nazis and the Fascists—had become the *de facto* ruler of Italy.[27] The socialist orientation of the institutions of the *Resistenza* had brought the country to the threshold of a full-scale, Bolshevik-style revolution. Indeed the first phase of the revolution—the coming to power—had already been won, and only the "Whites" remained to be subdued. American historian H. Stuart Hughes has admirably discerned the all but forgotten state of affairs which existed then. He wrote:

> At the end of April 1945, the anti-Fascist forces of the Italian North rejoiced in the exhilaration of a painfully won victory. For a few weeks of glorious spring weather, the members of the Partisan bands and the local Committees of Liberation enjoyed the unfamiliar sensation of being the masters of the country. Few Italians at the time were bold enough to question their authority. By their staunchness in suffering and their courage in battle, the northern anti-Fascists had won the right to lead their countrymen in fashioning a new Italy. For it was primarily through their efforts that Italy had regained a certain standing among the nations: the achievements of the northern resistance had gradually won the grudging respect of the Allies and given the rest of the Italian people something at last of which they could be proud.[28]

Hughes describes the condition of the old ruling class:

> The propertied element was frightened and unsure of itself. Most of the more prosperous Italians had compromised themselves in some fashion with the Fascist regime. As the war ended, and the reckoning seemed at hand, the wealthy, the conservative, and the well-born lay low, hoping without much conviction that the revolutionary storm would pass them by. To save what they could from the wreckage, they were prepared to make the most sweeping concessions to the unfamiliar principles of democracy and socialism.[29]

Only the British and the Americans could contest the rule of the *Resistenza*, and only the brutal nationalism of Stalin and his man in Rome, Communist Party Chief Togliatti, could deny such rule with no contest at all. It was for such reasons—more precisely, the abandonment of the movement by the Soviet Union and the Italian party to the western sphere of influence—that the hard-won gains and the aspirations of the *Resistenza*, as Hughes says, "ended in frustration and disillusionment." But the process took about three years, and it was the misfortune of the House of Savoy that that was the moment of its greatest weaknesses.

The *Resistenza's* so-called "wind of the north" would come and go, fresh air which would carry away much of what Risorgimentalist pretensions had fouled. In its hour of strength it would do much to alter the course Italy had so foolhardily pursued since the time of Cavour, and, in imposing a national referendum to decide whether the Italy of this "second Risorgimento"—as it was called—would be monarchist or republican, it sealed the fate of the House of Savoy.

Savoyard Italy had been sanctioned by the many rigged plebiscites held between 1859 and 1870, and now an honest, final plebiscite—the Allied-overseen referendum of June 2, 1946—would test whether those sanctions could endure. Thus the final months of crown rule in Italy became an election campaign in which the leading members of the House of Savoy were forced to learn and emulate the style of movie queens and politicians on the road. At first Humbert demurred. "I don't want to seem like a candidate who goes looking for votes," he said.[30] But there was no other way, and he went down the trail lesser hopeful men had long before him beaten smooth.

Humbert had got off to a very bad start. Immediately after his father had announced his retirement and the crown prince's lieutenancy, Humbert had given a most unfortunate interview to the London *Times.* He had sought to exonerate his father and cast the blame for the wars and crimes of fascism and Mussolini on the Italian people, a provocative thesis which even the king lamented. His son, he said, had to find someone with "his head on his shoulders" to advise him on public relations.[31] But, with the passage of time, the prince began to recover much of what the king had frittered away. He was catcalled and almost assaulted when in June, 1944, he appeared at public ceremonies honoring the Italians slain by the Germans in the Ardeatine Caves massacre in Rome, but by June, 1946, he had won the admiration and respect of many millions of his countrymen. "He is better than his father," his bitter enemy Count Sforza said, and even the most ardent republicans agreed that they were being treated with royal impartiality.[32]

He developed as a personality in his own right, quite different from, much less forbidding, and far more appealing than his father. Little by little life at the Quirinal, which he had found in absolute desolation, picked up a rhythm and style unknown since the first Humbert strode up and down those halls. The horses and carriages, men in livery, and court galas for the noble and the high were reinstalled. Humbert and Maria José, though they had grown cold toward one another, put on a happy face. They evoked in others a longing for a future composed of the best moments of the past, but understood by all as a future which the mood of the present would never allow. The sadnesses were lightened by the rediscovered splendors of the court, but all the splendors were ponderous, all the gaieties were sad.

Humbert became the spirit incarnate of his milieu. He showed himself to be a mystical creature, his regal composure sustained by the guidelines of tradition but assailed by the callings of the new. The contradiction most easily perceived in Humbert's character, writes Bartoli, "is that between his religious zeal and his erotic crises. He was always coming from or going to a sanctuary or a den. His heart, at Rome, seemed torn between his last great love, a lady who must be nameless, and the Vatican. . . . It is certain that Humbert's religious zeal was no less spontaneous than his sensuality. He had, therefore, to suffer constantly the anguish and the temptation of sin."[33]

No doubt this was a poor use of his energies, but he appeared indefatigable in his efforts to save his house from the final mortification. As much as was possible, he came to dominate the situation, and the real king let him act without restraints. It soon became clear that if the referendum could be postponed, perhaps by a single year, or even six months, memories would fade and the waxing popularity of Prince Humbert would win the day. But the republican movement, led by the energetic minister of the interior, Giuseppe Romita (who was to earn the epithet "father of the republic"),[34] was too powerful, and the Allies, too, with Churchill gone from the scene, favored the monarchy's demise. "A little bit of Republic and a little bit of communism," British ambassador to the Quirinal Noel Charles remarked at the time, "would do some good for the Italians."[35]

The royal campaigners could thus do no more than grasp at the twilight to hold up the setting sun. In June, 1944, for example, the king was shown a letter Count Ciano had written to him shortly before his execution by order of Mussolini six months earlier, and this was retained as a kind of trump card which might restore public faith in the monarchy. For Ciano had said: "Your Majesty knows . . .

how I can testify before God and men of the heroic struggle you conducted to impede that error and that crime which was our war at
the side of the Germans. . . . I have provided that as soon as possible,
after my death, my diary and a documentation which will throw
much light on the truth of many unknown facts will be made
public."[36]

"This letter is important," Victor Emmanuel observed excitedly.
". . . It is a document which at the opportune moment will serve!"[37]
But neither the letter nor the famous diary itself served very well.
When the Ciano papers were published the king gave interviews in
which he confirmed the best of what the count had had to say about
the good deeds of the crown; in the end, however, they were only
fresh reminders of the bad.

On May 9, 1946, with only twenty-three days remaining before
the referendum, Victor Emmanuel III ceded the throne, and the
crown prince ascended as Humbert II. "I abdicate the Crown of the
Kingdom of Italy in favor of my Son Humbert of Savoy, Prince of
Piedmont," wrote the little king on a twelve lire sheet of *carta bollata*.[38] Misdating the document, he copied—with appropriate substi-
tutions—the same sentence penned by Charles Albert in 1849, which
had more or less initiated the chain of events that had brought matters to where they stood now. Victor Emmanuel's abdication was
a surprise, pre-election maneuver worked out secretly between himself and his son. It was designed to give a sudden boost to the candidate's prestige in allowing him to stand before the people as their
king.

Humbert, who had come to the royal villa at Posillipo to witness
the private little ceremony for the abdication, sought his father's
blessings. "Excuse me, papà," he said, "if now I must go forward
and shake the hands of many men who have fought and offended
you." Victor Emmanuel replied: "No, no, do as you must. I may have
made a mistake. But it's too late now." Humbert bowed and kissed
him.[39]

At 7:40 P.M. that same day Victor and Elena set sail from the Gulf
of Naples on the yacht *Duke of the Abruzzi*. Their destination was
Alexandria, Egypt, their place of exile, which had in the meantime
been carefully prepared. They would spend the rest of their life together as guests of King Farouk in a villa the little king named "Yela."
Victor Emmanuel, as his ship carried him away from the homeland
to which he would never again return, looked back twice at Naples.
It was the city of his birth and the best days of his youth. Then,

bearing only his bags and the title Count of Pollenzo, which he had used on his first trip abroad some sixty years before, he disappeared from view.

King Humbert stood at the shore. His place of exile was calling, too.

On June 2, a date which was to become a national holiday, more than twenty-three million Italians stood ready to vote in the first free election in a quarter-century and probably the freest election ever held on the Italian peninsula. Women voted for the first time. Maria José, the third queen of Italy, did not vote for her husband, disqualifying herself as an interested party. But since the referendum was being held in conjunction with political elections, she cast her ballot for the Socialist party, shocking the nation. The queen who had joined the Fascist party in 1940, and the anti-Fascist underground the following year, had become a "socialist" monarch.[40]

The king went to the polls, too. He had tried everything in the past two weeks, taking to the road like a vaudeville star. He had been cheered in the south and booed in the north, for the campaign had split the country along embittered, traditional lines. Indeed Italy, ravaged and starved by war, fractured by political hatreds, banditry, and crime, occupied by foreign powers, and bleeding from the wounds of class struggle, seemed more the Italy of the mid-nineteenth century, rather than the twentieth. The king had campaigned for unity under Savoyard rule, but there were monarchists who even now were preparing to unleash the south against the north in civil war should they fail at the polls.[41] Humbert, it is said, was determined to remain above recourse to violence. He cast his ballot, it is said, blank.

The king never believed he could win. Some weeks earlier he had asked his close friend, journalist Luigi Barzini, Jr., what he foresaw. "I told him," Barzini later recalled, "that no modern dynasty had survived defeat. He bowed his head."[42] It seemed to all a foregone conclusion that the monarchy, unable to postpone the referendum, would be overwhelmingly rejected. "How awful if we only get ten or fifteen percent," said the queen.[43] The dream of the monarchists, including the king himself, was to come close enough to challenge the validity of the referendum, by the threat of force if need be, as a means of winning time until a second polling could take place. If necessary they were ready to go to further extremes.

The voting continued on through June 3 and 4. The first returns came from the south and gave the monarchy a large majority, which continued to mount until the first hours of June 4. Then an avalanche of republican votes rolled in, reducing the monarchist position to a near tie. By noon of the 4th, the newspapers were declaring a republican victory. On the 5th, the prime minister, De Gasperi, went up to the Quirinal to be received by the king, who was awaiting official word. The republic had won, said the minister, twelve million votes to ten million. The royal family would have to depart from Italian soil, never to set foot inside the country again. The Quirinal had to be cleared. The president of the republic, to be elected by a constituent assembly, would soon be moving in.*[44]

The queen, who had reigned for twenty-seven days, departed that very day. But Humbert II, the May King, stayed well into June; he did not go gracefully. The monarchy had received nearly 46 percent of the vote, but more important it had won more than 64 percent of the south, including Rome. Humbert was advised by his most intimate counselors to resist. An entire kingdom—Rome, the Two Sicilies, and Sardinia—was assessed as ready to stand with him. The reconstructed army was still sworn to obey their king.[45]

On the pretext that he was awaiting the official results of the voting due to be handed down by the supreme court, Humbert managed to temporize for a few days. On June 10 the court declared that the republic had been elected, but when it added that it would announce the actual figures on June 18, the king again refused to depart, at least until then. This was accepted by the government, but an argument broke out when De Gasperi stated that the court's decision, regardless of the formality of issuing the final count, was the authority by which the transfer of the powers of the chief of state was to be effected immediately. The king and the monarchists rejected this interpretation. Some hoped to provoke the government to use force, which, it was believed, would ignite a north-south civil war, bring on Allied military intervention, and the annulment of the referendum.[46]

On the evening of June 12, the De Gasperi government invested state power in the prime minister, pending the election of the president of the republic. The news was telephoned to the king by Luigi Barzini, in whose home Humbert was staying incommunicado. A royal plot envisaging a *coup d'état* was hatched by the court at dawn of the next day, and when Humbert received his advisers that morning of the 13th, he was faced with a momentous decision.

---

* Even the Albertian constitution had to be rolled up and carried off with the House of Savoy. A new republican constitution was to be framed by the constituent assembly. It would reduce the powers of the chief of state and expand civil liberties and rights.

The monarchist cabal, led by the minister of the royal house, Falcone Lucifero, had prepared a scheme, which was later revealed by Barzini in the following terms:

The king, declaring that the referendum had been improperly conducted, and in any case, that De Gasperi had exceeded his authority in assuming the powers of the chief of state, would ask that the government resign. Should De Gasperi refuse, Humbert would proclaim the government dissolved, and empower a new minister, possibly Lucifero. The new government would employ the public force to guarantee order, and if the outgoing regime were to resist, De Gasperi and his cabinet would be arrested.* An investigation would be made into the manner in which the referendum had been held, and "if" it were found invalid, a second polling would take place "when conditions allowed."[48]

It was a bold and heinous plot, which was bound as never before to divide the country on both sides of a river of blood. But it was also the only alternative to the fall of the House of Savoy. As the king's adjutant General Infante said that day, "Now either Humbert the warrior mounts his horse, or Humbert the peaceful renounces and departs."[49]

Humbert, in consultation with Lucifero and his other advisers, examined the feasibility of the plot. According to Barzini's account, the king felt he would have to leave Rome and withdraw to his securest stronghold, Naples, from where the inevitable civil war could be directed in relative safety. Then, Humbert asked, what nation would give aid to a king who refused to accept the results of a referendum? Certainly not the pro-republican Allies. Further, such a move would split the armed forces, and turn Italy into a second Spain.[50]

Now Humbert, who apparently had no heart for protracted slaughter which offered scarce hope of victory, is said to have affirmed: "My house united Italy. Going to Naples, I would divide it. I do not want a throne stained with blood. . . ."[51]

To which an adviser rejoined with these high-sounding but no less sophist words: "Your Majesty, you refuse the . . . proposal for noble reasons, of which we are all well aware. Nevertheless it is my

---

* Bartoli, long before Barzini's disclosure, recorded some of the details of the more violent aspects of the plot. He wrote that the *coup* was quite possible, since "in the Rome garrison the monarchist elements prevailed over those loyal to the Government, and that same among the *carabinieri*. An order from the king would have moved those forces as of July 25, 1943. Plans for armed action against the Government had been prepared at the Quirinal. They even provided that an ambulance carry off De Gasperi and his colleagues. . . ."[47]

duty to ask you to consider that your father was harshly criticized because on October 28 [1922] he refused to defend the law by signing the state of siege, in order to save lives and prevent the inevitable bloody clashes which would have broken out among the Italians. I would not like to see it said one day that Your Majesty too accepted an abuse of power against not only his own person but against the State, and that he abandoned his post in order to avert bloodshed."

The king listened attentively. He later said that he was convinced that if he were to resort to force, "I would not have been lacking in men ready to follow me." But he replied that he preferred the criticism his father had earned to having to bear the responsibility of disbanding the nation his Savoyard ancestors had so laboriously helped to assemble under one rule. "I really could not undo," he is said to have remarked, "what my House had done."[52]

This was a decision, whatever the way it was formulated, which brought fortune to those who would have otherwise been uselessly slain.

Nothing remained to do now but leave. Stripped of his powers as head of state and his right to occupy the Quirinal, Humbert II was not going to stay in Italy until June 18 as a common man. He wished to depart with the title of king, and that meant going now. His bags were packed. An airplane stood waiting to carry him to Lisbon and the exile he had already arranged.

A final message to his people was drafted. It was a protest against the treatment which had been accorded the House of Savoy and a wish for the future. Said the last king of Italy:

> Italians, in assuming first the Lieutenancy General of the Realm, and then the Crown, I declared that I would bow to the freely expressed vote of the people with regard to the institutional form of the State. . . . Last night, unexpectedly, flouting the law and the independent and sovereign powers of the judiciary, the Government carried out a revolutionary move, unilaterally and arbitrarily assuming powers to which it has no right. This has placed before me the alternatives of either provoking bloodshed or accepting the [government's] violent act.
>
> Italians . . . I believe it is my duty to do all that I still can to spare the people, who have already suffered greatly, further pain and tears. . . . Not wanting to oppose force to the abuse of power, nor render myself an accomplice to the illegality committed by the Government, I take leave of my country's soil . . .
>
> Performing this sacrifice in the supreme interests of the Fatherland,

I feel it my duty as an Italian, and as King, to raise my protest against this violent act . . .

With my heart filled with pain, but with my conscience serene in having made every effort to fulfill my duty, I leave my Fatherland. The oath of obedience to the king may be considered dissolved . . . I address my thoughts to all who have fallen in the name of Italy, and I salute all Italians. Whatever fate awaits our country, she can always count on me as the most devoted of her sons.

Long live Italy![53]

It was the final arrogance of kings.

At three o'clock that afternoon of June 13, 1946, Humbert of Savoy said his last good-byes to Italy. He left the Quirinal, given the full honors owed to a sovereign. In the courtyard he passed in review of the palace coachmen. His servants and his gentlemen-in-waiting sobbed. He was pale and drawn, but his head was held high, and now and then he managed a smile. He wore a gray flannel suit, and he carried a fedora and a walking stick. He looked tired, enervated, far older than his forty-one years. At Ciampino airport, as he stepped inside the aircraft which was to carry him away, a *carabiniero* came up to him and said, "Your Majesty, we will never forget you."

WHEN A MONARCHY DIES

THE COUNT OF POLLENZO, VICTOR EMMANUEL III, READ OF HIS SON'S DEPARTURE IN THE EGYPTIAN newspapers with "infinite sadness," he said.[1] Such were the remaining days of his life. Villa Yela, at number 31 on a street called Costantin Choremi, was a modest dwelling where the city of Alexandria meets the countryside. It had a garden and a palm tree, and its not very many rooms were decorated with mementos of the House of Savoy: stuffed mooseheads shot by Humbert the Good; a silver nameplate engraved with the family tree; photographs snapped by Victor's queen.

Victor's and Elena's daughters Yolanda and Giovanna, the former czarina of the newly proclaimed republic of Bulgaria, lived now in Alexandria, too, with their families. Old relatives of Elena from Montenegro and imperial Russia resided nearby, among them her older sister, widow of Grand Duke Peter Nicolajevich, a cousin of the slain czar, and Prince Roman Romanov and his family, survivors of the imperial dynasty. Some of them were prospering in the Arab oil business now. Victor and Elena, too (as well as Humbert in Portugal), were reasonably well provided for. The Savoys had ex-patriated several million dollars from their native land, although they claimed the figure to be somewhat less (1.5 million), and had in fact left much more behind in real estate and other property, which was either given to or appropriated by the state.

The little king passed his days going fishing, strolling in the garden with Elena, and collecting Egyptian stamps in a desultory way. He kept a register in the entrance hall to his home for guests to sign when they dropped in. Sometimes he talked to them about times past, expressing judgments on events and men. There was hardly any bitterness in his words. He spoke well of long gone Giolitti and Salandra and some generals of World War I, but he reserved a lingering affection for that giant in his life who had died an ogre hanging upside down.

"Mussolini," the exiled king reminisced one day, "without doubt had a great mind, a man of exceptional intelligence. He was formidable in his politics at home, but not in foreign policy, where he showed himself to be a juggler, too willing to hazard, too trusting in instinct. Many of his errors derived from his inexperience in military matters, and such inexperience encouraged deception on the part of others. What happened after 1943 doesn't make me want to have him bear the cross on his shoulders. The aspects of that situation have to be viewed objectively; much of it was owed to chance."[2]

On the day before Christmas eve, 1947, the little king went fishing on a cold and windy morning. He came down with a chill and a fever, and spent Christmas in bed, disturbed by a persistent cough. A few days later he felt better, and arose very early on the 28th to shave several days growth of beard. He returned to bed suddenly, however. "I have a terrible headache," he told Elena, "and my left arm feels as if it were lead." He had suffered a heart attack and a paralytic stroke. Later in the day he asked his physician, "How long will it last? I have some important things to attend to." "A couple of days," said the doctor, after telling hesitation. Elena was at her husband's bedside; Victor held her hand tightly. He looked up, toward the ceiling. Then he died.[3] Elena, in her anguish, murmured mysteriously, "He was my son."[4]

King Farouk saw to it that Victor Emmanuel was given a funeral that he hoped would be worthy of a monarch. King Zog and his queen, both exiled from Albania, attended. There were many former princes and princesses, and, of course, the deceased's own royal family, including Humbert II. The Egyptian navy band played the royal march of the House of Savoy. The Egyptian army fired its cannons twenty-one times. The little king was laid to rest behind the altar of a Catholic church in Alexandria. The tomb was marked, "Victor Emmanuel of Savoy, 1869–1947." His last wish, denied by the republic of Italy, had been to be buried among his ancestors in the mountaintop crypt Superga, at Turin. Some people are trying still to bring him there.

Elena went to the south of France and lived at Montpellier, near to where her exiled father passed his final years. She died of cancer in 1952. Her last words were, "My children, Humbert, Lord, Lord."[5]

Humbert, king for thirty-four days, is in his twenty-sixth year of exile. He calls himself the count of Sarre. Separated from his wife and his children, he lives in Cascais, outside of Lisbon. He has named his home Villa Italia, and living in it with him are his faithful man-servant and his wife, two Portuguese maids, two chauffeurs, a gardener, and a septuagenarian English woman, Alice Smith, the long retired governess of Humbert's three daughters. The former king is a lonely man. For years groups of Italians came on organized holiday bus tours to visit him. Now it is no longer a profitable venture, and hardly anyone calls on the king. From time to time Humbert's driver takes him for a little ride two miles north along the coast to visit with his sister, former Czarina Giovanna of the Bulgarians.

Maria José left him in 1946. She went to live in Switzerland, very close to the Italian border, in territory once ruled by the dukes of Savoy. She has written a book about the first of them, Amadeus VIII, of fifteenth-century prominence. It has never been published. She is ill and not very happy. "I would like to return to Italy as a private citizen," she said some years ago. "I would not make trouble for anyone. I would not engage in political propaganda."[6] But she cannot come back any more.

Humbert and Maria José have suffered many disappointments in their children. Maria Pia, the oldest, was married in 1955 at the age of twenty-one to Alexander Karageorgevich, of the exiled royal family of Yugoslavia. They had two sets of twins, but their marriage did not last very long; they live apart.

Maria Gabriella, just past thirty, married a financier of Rumanian origin in 1969. Princess Grace and Prince Rainier attended the wedding ceremony in Monaco, and many smiling photographs were taken showing Humbert and Maria José together again with their family. But the matrimony uniting Gabriella of Savoy to a divorced, bourgeois man did not please her pious parents very much, and when the wedding ended, Humbert went his way, and Maria José went hers.

Their youngest, Maria Beatrice, by all called simply "Titti," has been and remains a "problem child," even now at twenty-eight. She left her broken home some years ago. She fell prey to alcohol and drugs. She roomed with an Argentinian diplomat, loved, and almost married—against her father's stern forbiddings—a movie star. Titti three times attempted suicide. She lived on a kibbutz and in a psychiatric ward. She sold her memoirs and the intimate secrets of her pathetic life in the House of Savoy to a scandal magazine. Now she is back with the Argentinian; they are married and in Mexico.

Victor Emmanuel IV, thirty-three-year-old heir to the rule of the fallen dynasty and the pretended throne of Italy, has also caused his father and his mother pain, perhaps the most of all. He cares little about the greatness of his house. Crown prince by dynastic right, prince of Naples by birth, he calls himself merely Victor di Sarre and loves the daughter of a candy manufacturer. His father forbade their marriage, and this has been a factor in the poor relations between the former king and his wayward only son. Indeed a dilemma of succession tortures Humbert now. He feels, intimates relate, that his bachelor heir, in any case, has neither the inclination nor the ability to attend to the interests and the patrimony of the House of Savoy.

Humbert is torn, on the one hand, by the hopes of young Victor's mother and his own, and on the other, by his wish that the millenary tradition live on. Ironically, he is faced with the decision of whether to invest the patronage of the dynasty in Victor Emmanuel or to pass it to the cadet line, in the person of the present duke of Aosta, whose forebears had so brazenly coveted the crown. The duke, grandson of Emmanuel Philibert and Hélène of Orleans, is twenty-seven years old and is himself married to an Orleans, Claudia, daughter of the count of Paris. The duke and duchess have two children, one of them a male. Amadeus has said that he does not wish to succeed his uncle as the Savoyard pretender, but he has also indicated that he would not renounce the role if he were called to serve. It falls to Humbert II, freed from the rules of succession in Charles Albert's constitution, to make his choice.

Humbert is not a well man. He suffers from vaguely revealed internal disorders, for which he has undergone several surgical operations. In 1966 he confided that he had less than three years to live. He has outlasted the prophecy, but he has not regained his health. He spends the time remaining to him trying with scarce success to join together the jagged pieces of the fallen dynasty. He has sought, again without succeeding, to build a wall of silence around the troubles in his house. Behind that porous wall he works unrewardedly every passing day.

His most ambitious labor is the reordering and care of the still secret archives of the ministry of the royal house, which he took with him when he left Rome for the last time. He is preparing his memoirs, which are to be published, he says, long after he is dead. "It would not be fair to make them public while many persons involved are still alive," he recently declared. "I even have the texts of conversations, comments, and confidences written by very well known personalities."[7]

The implication here and wherever the former king alludes to his family papers is that when they are made known they will wipe the Savoyard slate much cleaner than before. This can hardly be the case; indeed it seems rather unlikely that there exists anything significant left to be said in the dynasty's favor, for most assuredly it would have been used at a time when it might have made a difference. The little king too said he would reveal his memoirs posthumously. "Wait until I am dead before publishing them," he declared.[8] At the time, during the pre-referendum campaign, Humbert advised that their disclosure would be "inopportune," and he later denied repeatedly that they ever existed at all.[9] Probably it will be a long time before the hidden archives of Savoy are made known. Doubtless they contain many interesting details, interesting but not flattering.

In the meantime, the fallen, unhappy House of Savoy lies very low. The wasting throne of Italy has been given into the hands of curators and academicians. It stands in an old museum in Turin.

Italy has fared well without the monarchy and its recurrent, restless dreams. The country no longer pretends to great powerhood. A president sits now in the Quirinal. Few people abroad know his name. The republic has no plan to march for glory. Its borders are finite. Its sons do not fight in distant wars. It trades and treats with erstwhile enemies, friends and rivals, and colonies of old. Italy is at peace with the world.

To be sure, class rule still divides and infuriates the nation. The owners still stand high on the dispossessed. (Is there yet any other way?) But the owners tread a little more softly than they did until Mussolini failed, and Italians do not now hunger for the taste of salt, as they did under Humbert the Good. The *Resistenza*, though now just a memory, frightened off the greed of Risorgimento days. There are Fiats, food, and salt for more people than ever before. That, as we know it, is progress.

Postwar Savoyard rule, had it endured, might have made equal gains. Hardly anyone would take that away. Perhaps that is what hurts monarchists most of all: the House of Savoy is relevant no more. Yet, down and out, gone and forgotten as it is, surely it would be less than farseeing to celebrate its requiem. Times change. The Bourbons are coming back in Spain. Kingship lives on its own name and in many more than ever in the past. A tyrant was born today. The quest for glory heaves and slumbers like the tides. History is a continuum from which episodes in folly cannot be excised like a tumor or healed by the goodness of time. The disease is the continuum.

Appendices

APPENDIX I

GENEALOGICAL TABLE OF THE HOUSE OF SAVOY (PARTIAL) *

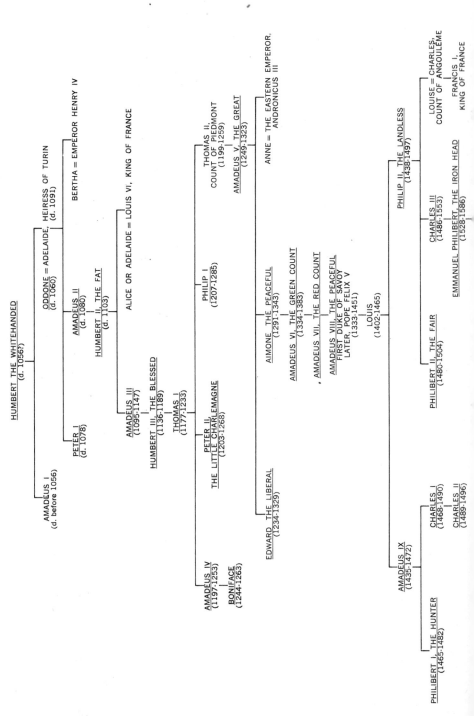

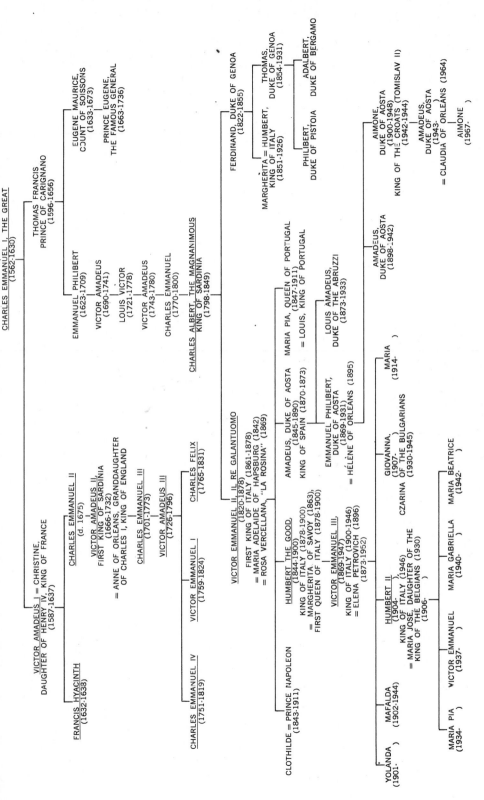

* Underlined names indicate ruling members of the dynasty

APPENDIX II

THE ROYAL PREROGATIVES

(The king's prerogatives were defined by Charles Albert's constitution, proclaimed in the kingdom of Sardinia on March 4, 1848. This was the constitution inherited by united Italy in 1861, and it remained in force until the fall of the House of Savoy in 1946. The following are excerpts from the constitution dealing with the sovereign's powers, which were mighty. Only gods and heads of family-owned businesses may write with such a generous hand. Charles Albert resembled the latter. Nevertheless the royal prerogatives were rarely exercised to the full by the four kings of Italy—oddly enough, a great misfortune for both the kings and the kingdom.)

Article 4. The person of the king is sacred and inviolable.

Article 5. Executive power belongs to the king alone. He is the supreme head of State, commander-in-chief of all forces on land and sea; he declares war, concludes peace treaties, commercial and other alliances, informing the chambers of parliament insofar as the interests and the security of the State allow. . . .

Article 7. The king alone sanctions and promulgates all laws.

Article 8. The king can proclaim amnesties and commute sentences.

Article 9. The king convokes the two chambers every year. He can postpone their sessions and dissolve those of the deputies. . . .

Article 30. No taxation can be levied or withdrawn unless . . . sanctioned by the king.

Article 33. The senate is composed of an unlimited number of members nominated for life by the king. . . .

Article 65. The king nominates and revokes his ministers . . .

Article 68. Justice emanates from the king, and is administered in his name by the judges whom he authorizes to do so.

NOTES

PROLOGUE: WHEN A KING DIES

1. *Gazzetta Ufficiale* (Rome), 10 January 1878.
2. *"Nuove pagine del diario di Alessandro Guiccioli, 1878,"* *Nuova Antologia*, 1 August 1935, p. 417 (diary entry of 6 January 1878). (See bibliographical entry below, p. 421.)
3. *Memorie del re galantuomo* (Milan: 1882), p. 118.
4. *Gazzetta Ufficiale*, 10 January 1878.
5. *Memorie del re galantuomo*, p. 119.
6. Ibid.
7. *Le lettere di Vittorio Emanuele II* (Turin: 1966), 1:774–777 (letter of 28 March 1864).
8. P. Gerbore, *Dame e cavalieri del re* (Milan: 1952), p. 64.
9. Ibid., p. 76.
10. Ibid., p. 79.
11. Ibid.
12. *Memorie del re galantuomo*, p. 119.
13. See L. Salvatorelli, *Casa Savoia nella storia d'Italia* (Rome: 1944), p. 34.
14. The author of this often quoted notion was the eighteenth-century Savoyard king Charles Emmanuel III. See *The Historian's History of the World, Volume IX, Italy* (London: 1908), p. 502.
15. C. J. S. Sprigge, *The Development of Modern Italy* (New Haven: 1944), p. 33.
16. *Gazzetta Ufficiale*, 10 January 1878.
17. *Memorie del re galantuomo*, p. 119.

PART I: THE TRIUMPH OF THE HOUSE OF SAVOY

1. The literature on Humbert the Whitehanded and his times is extensive (see bibliography below) but hardly reliable. By far the best source is F. Cognasso, *Umberto Biancamano* (Turin: 1929).
2. Quoted in ibid., p. 6.
3. Ibid., pp. 9–10.
4. Quoted in ibid., pp. 51–52.
5. Ibid., pp. 83–84.
6. Gibbon, *The Decline and Fall of the Roman Empire*, Low abridgment (London: 1963), p. 488.
7. F. Cognasso, *I Savoia nella politica europea* (Milan: 1941), p. 8.
8. D. Bartoli, *La fine della monarchia* (Milan: 1947), p. 85.
9. Cognasso, *Umberto Biancamano*, pp. 157–160.
10. F. Cognasso, *Il conte verde* (Turin: 1926), pp. 38–89.
11. L. Cibrario, *Origine e progressi delle istituzioni della monarchia di Savoia* (Florence: 1869), 1:379.
12. *Relazioni degli ambasciatori veneti*, Series 2, 1:158.
13. Cibrario, *Origine*, 1:285.
14. Ibid., 1:324–325.
15. Ibid., 1:270 (emphasis in original).
16. A. Bollati in J. Blasi (ed.), *I Savoia dalle origini al 1900* (Florence: 1940), p. 104 (emphasis in original).
17. Quoted in ibid.
18. F. Ercole in Blasi, *Savoia*, p. 153.
19. Processo criminale della casa di Savoia (Turin?, 1797?); see especially pp. 13–15.
20. G. Salvemini, *Mazzini* (London: 1956), pp. 158–159.
21. G. Mazzini, *Ai giovani d'Italia* in *Opere scelte* (Florence: 1957), pp. 446–447.
22. See Salvemini, *Mazzini*, pp. 97–98.
23. Sprigge, *Development of Modern Italy*, p. 34.
24. Quoted in Gerbore, *Dame e cavalieri*, p. 17.
25. See A. Albertini, *La dinastia di Savoia* (Perugia: 1890), p. 155.
26. Quoted in L. Salvatorelli, *Casa Savoia nella storia d'Italia* (Rome: 1944), p. 30.
27. *Neue Rheinischer Zeitung*, 12 August 1848, in E. Ragionieri, *Il Risorgimento italiano nell'opera di Marx e di Engels* (Rome: 1951), p. 610.
28. Cf. Salvatorelli, *Casa Savoia*, p. 30.
29. D. Mack Smith, *Italy* (Ann Arbor: 1959), p. 23.
30. Ibid., p. 22.
31. Salvemini, *Mazzini*, p. 158.
32. E. Crankshaw, *The Fall of the House of Habsburg* (London: 1963), p. 145.

33. *New York Tribune*, 4 August 1859, in P. Alatri, *Orientamenti marxistici sul Risorgimento* (Trieste: 1954), p. 9.
34. G. M. Trevelyan, *Garibaldi and the Thousand* (London: 1965), paperback edition, p. 190.
35. A. Mario, *La camicia rossa* (Milan: 1954), pp. 156–157, in D. Mack Smith (ed.), *Il Risorgimento italiano* (Bari: 1968), pp. 616–618.
36. Mack Smith, *Italy*, p. 42.
37. G. Massari, *La vita ed il regno di Vittorio Emanuele II di Savoia* (Milan: 1922), 2:375.
38. Mack Smith, *Italy*, p. 70.
39. Ibid., p. 75.
40. Proclamation of 20 June 1866, text in Massari, *Vittorio Emanuele II*, p. 438 (my emphasis).
41. Mack Smith, *Italy*, p. 14.
42. Speech of 9 October 1870, text in Massari, *Vittorio Emanuele II*, 2:520.

PART TWO: HUMBERT AND MARGHERITA

1. Humbert to the mayor of Rome, 24 November 1878, in G. Graziano, *Umberto I di Savoja* (Turin: 1902), p. 144.
2. Letter from Margherita to M. Minghetti, 30 July 1882 (emphasis in original), in L. Lipparini (ed.), *Lettere fra la regina Margherita e Marco Minghetti* (Milan: 1947).
3. Speech of 17 February 1880, in Graziano, *Umberto I*, p. 144.
4. Letter from Margherita to Col. Osio, 27 June 1897, in *"Margherita di Savoia a cuore aperto"* (her letters to Osio), in *Oggi*, 16 July–6 August 1953.
5. Speech of 10 December 1890, in Graziano, *Umberto I*, p. 144.
6. Letter from Margherita to Osio, 2 August 1899, in *"cuore aperto."*
7. Speech of 10 December 1890, in Graziano, *Umberto I*, p. 144.
8. Margherita on Humbert's death, 29 July 1900, in C. Casalegno, *La regina Margherita* (Turin: 1956), p. 183.

CHAPTER 1

1. T. Palmenghi-Crispi, *Francesco Crispi: Politica interna* (Milan: 1924), p. 28.
2. Albertini, *La dinastia di Savoia*, pp. 289–290.
3. *L'Opinione*, 10 January 1878, p. 1.
4. The *Times*, quoted in *L'Opinione*, 13 January 1878, p. 1.
5. *L'Opinione*, 11 January 1878, p. 2.
6. Guiccioli, *Diario*, p. 419 (diary entry of 10 January 1878); cf. F. Cusin, *L'Italia unita* (Udine: 1952–1955), 2:64–67.
7. Guiccioli, *Diario*, (diary entry of 15 January 1878).
8. Ibid. (diary entry of 14 January 1878).
9. Ibid., p. 421 (diary entry of 17 January 1878).

CHAPTER 2

1. Ibid., p. 422 (diary entry of 19 January 1878).
2. Letter from Cibrario to Victor Emmanuel II, 6 April 1867, in *Le Lettere di Vittorio Emanuele II*, 2:1174.
3. Ibid.
4. Telegram from Humbert to Cibrario, 7 April 1867, and letter from Victor Emmanuel II to Clotilde, 5 April 1867, in ibid., pp. 1175–1176.
5. Gerbore, *Dame e cavalieri*, p. 123.
6. Letter from Victor Emmanuel II to Humbert, 15 September 1867, in *Le lettere di Vittorio Emanuele II*, 2:1208.
7. P. Vasili, *La société de Rome* (Paris: 1887), p. 14.
8. Letter from Victor Emmanuel II to Humbert, January (?), 1868, in *Le lettere di Vittorio Emanuele II*, 2:1287.
9. Casalegno, *Margherita*, p. 31.
10. O. Savio, *Memorie* (Milan: 1911), 2:183.
11. Bartoli, *Monarchia*, p. 28.
12. Massari, *Vittorio Emanuele II*, 2:484.
13. Letter from Victor Emmanuel II to Humbert, 21 April 1866, in *Le lettere di Vittorio Emanuele II*, 2:868–869.
14. Albertini, *La Dinastia di Savoia*, p. 231.
15. See Casalegno, *Margherita*, pp. 13–26.
16. L. Settembrini, *La culla del principe di Napoli* (Naples (?): 1869 (?)); see also Casalegno, *Margherita*, p. 43.

CHAPTER 3

1. Cf. Gerbore, *Dame e cavalieri*, pp. 141–151; also Cusin, *L'Italia unita*, 1:136–139.
2. F. Gregorovius, *Diari romani* (Rome: 1967), 2:545 (diary entry of 18 June 1871).
3. Ibid.
4. Mack Smith, *Italy*, p. 102.
5. See Cusin, *L'Italia unita*, 1:209.
6. E. Longford, *Queen Victoria: Born to Succeed* (New York: 1966) paperback edition, p. 256.
7. Ibid.

CHAPTER 4

1. Massari, *Vittorio Emanuele II*, 2:557.
2. *Nuova Antologia*, September 1876, quoted in Cusin, *L'Italia unita*, 1:164.
3. C. Morandi, *La sinistra al potere* (Florence: 1944), p. 96.

4. See ibid., pp. 81–84.
5. F. Martini, *Confessioni e ricordi* (Milan: 1929), p. 148.
6. Cusin, *L'Italia unita,* 2:10.
7. See L. Salvatorelli, *La triplice alleanza* (Milan: 1939), pp. 33–37; also Cusin, *L'Italia unita,* 2:52–55, and especially T. Palmenghi-Crispi, *La politica estera di Francesco Crispi* (Milan: 1912) which contains Crispi's diaries.
8. Quoted in Mack Smith, *Italy,* p. 122.
9. Palmenghi-Crispi, *Politica interna,* p. 29.
10. Cusin, *L'Italia unita,* 2:55.
11. Massari, *Vittorio Emanuele II,* 2:589.
12. See Cusin, *L'Italia unita,* 2:47–48.
13. Letter from Crispi to Depretis, 27 August 1877, ibid., 2:50.
14. Ibid., 2:54; cf. Salvatorelli, *La triplice,* p. 54.
15. Crispi's diary, quoted in Salvatorelli, *La triplice,* p. 36.
16. Ibid.
17. Crispi's diary, quoted in Cusin, *L'Italia unita,* 2:52.
18. Bismarck to Saint-Vallier, 29 November 1880, document quoted in Cusin, *L'Italia unita,* 2:54.
19. Letter from Victor Emmanuel II to Depretis, 27 October 1877, in *Le lettere di Vittorio Emanuele II,* 2:1672.
20. Massari, *Vittorio Emanuele II,* 2:590.

CHAPTER 5

1. Quoted in Cusin, *L'Italia unita,* 2:84.
2. A. Bertani, *L'Italia aspetta* (Milan: 1878).
3. Cusin, *L'Italia unita,* 1:151.
4. F. De Sanctis, *Un viaggio elettorale* (Naples: 1876 (?)), pp. 69–70.
5. A. C. De Meis, *Il Sovrano* (Bari: 1927), p. 82.
6. *Atti della Giunta parlamentare per la Inchiesta agraria e sulle condizioni della classe agricola, Rome 1883–1886,* 15 vols.; for a recent critique see A. Caracciolo, *L'Inchiesta agraria Jacini* (Turin: 1958).
7. S. Jacini, *I risultati della Inchiesta agraria* (Rome: 1885), p. 32.
8. Cusin, *L'Italia unita,* 1:68.
9. Ibid., 1:178–179; see also A. Sacchi, *La pellagra nella provincia di Mantova* (Milan: 1967).
10. Jacini, *Inchiesta,* p. 44.
11. Ibid., pp. 44–45.
12. Cusin, *L'Italia unita,* 1:213; see also N. Rosselli, *Mazzini e Bakunin* (Turin: 1967).
13. See R. Romeo, *Risorgimento e capitalismo* (Bari: 1959).
14. Gregorovius, *Diari romani,* 2:600 (diary entry of 21 January 1874).
15. P. Turiello, *Governo e governati in Italia* (Bologna: 1884).

16. See Casalegno, *Margherita*, p. 223; also B. Croce in *Corriere della Sera*, 5 April 1949.
17. Turiello, *Governo e governati*, p. 106.
18. Ibid., p. 298.
19. Ibid., pp. 289–290.
20. Ibid., p. 116.
21. Ibid., p. 303.
22. See Croce's introduction in De Meis, *Il Sovrano*.
23. Ibid., pp. 66–67.
24. Ibid., p. 16.
25. Ibid., pp. 65–66.
26. Casalegno, *Margherita*, p. 152.

CHAPTER 6

1. Cusin, *L'Italia unita*, 2:67–69.
2. Ibid., 2:68.
3. Guiccioli, *Diario*, p. 591 (diary entry for 10 July 1878).
4. See Salvatorelli, *La triplice*, pp. 38–39.
5. Bartoli, *Monarchia*, p. 24; cf. Casalegno, *Margherita*, p. 59.
6. Ibid.
7. G. Carducci, *Eterno femminino regale*, in Casalegno, *Margherita*, pp. 59–60.
8. Quoted in Bartoli, *Monarchia*, p. 25.
9. Casalegno, *Margherita*, p. 62; cf. Bartoli, *Monarchia*, p. 62.
10. Ibid., pp. 62–63.
11. *Resoconto del processo di G. Passanante* (Rome: 1879), p. 45.
12. Guiccioli, *Diario*, p. 599 (diary entry of 17 November 1878).
13. Ibid., p. 598.
14. Ibid., p. 599 (diary entry of 25 November 1878).
15. Cusin, *L'Italia unita*, 2:90.
16. G. Perticone, *L'Italia contemporanea* (Milan: 1968), p. 109.
17. Cusin, *L'Italia unita*, 2:88.
18. Guiccioli, *Diario*, p. 602 (diary entry of 20 December 1878).

CHAPTER 7

1. Casalegno, *Margherita*, p. 159.
2. Salvatorelli, *La triplice*, p. 54.
3. Ibid., pp. 52–60.
4. Cusin, *L'Italia unita*, 2:138; Perticone, *L'Italia contemporanea*, pp. 111–112.
5. Cusin, *L'Italia unita*, 2:140–141; cf. *ibid*.
6. Ibid., 2:139.

7. Ibid., 2:147–151.
8. Ibid., 2:152; cf. Salvatorelli, *La triplice*, p. 60.
9. An intriguing unpublished documentation of this trip is to be found in the papers of P. S. Mancini (then Italian foreign minister), who accompanied the royal party. These documents, hereinafter referred to as the *Mancini papers*, are deposited in the archives of the Istituto per la Storia del Risorgimento Italiano, Rome, catologued as "Mancini: visita dei reali a Vienna."
10. *Mancini papers.*
11. *Neue Freie Presse*, 28 October 1881, quoted in *L'Illustrazione Italiana*, 13 November 1881, p. 306.
12. Crankshaw, *House of Habsburg*, p. 199.
13. *L'Illustrazione Italiana*, 13 November 1881, p. 307.
14. *Mancini papers*; see also Cusin, *L'Italia unita*, 2:152, and Salvatorelli, *La triplice*, p. 60.
15. See Guiccioli, *Diario*, p. 320 (diary entry of 26 November 1881).
16. Speech of 29 November 1881, text in *L'Opinione*, 4 December 1881.
17. Guiccioli, *Diario*, p. 325 (diary entry of 9 December 1881).
18. See Salvatorelli, *La triplice*, p. 61.
19. Guiccioli, *Diario*, p. 320 (diary entry of 26 November 1881).
20. Salvatorelli, *La triplice*, p. 61.
21. Ibid.
22. Ibid., p. 65.
23. See a discussion of the text of the treaty in *ibid.*, pp. 69–71.
24. Ibid., p. 71.
25. Cusin, *L'Italia unita*, 2:169.

CHAPTER 8

1. Cf. Mack Smith, *Italy*, pp. 133–170.
2. B. Croce, *Storia d'Italia dal 1871 al 1915* (Bari: 1967), p. 114.
3. Cusin, *L'Italia unita*, 2:66.
4. Bartoli, *Monarchia*, p. 22.
5. Gerbore, *Dame e cavalieri*, p. 174.
6. Casalegno, *Margherita*, p. 75.
7. Vasili, *Rome*, p. 18.
8. D. Farini, *Diario* (Rome: 1962), 2 vols. (diary entry of 19 February 1897).
9. Graziano, *Umberto I*, p. 110.
10. Telegram from Humbert to mayor of Pordenone, 9 September 1884, in ibid., p. 145.
11. Casalegno, *Margherita*, p. 86.
12. Ibid., p. 88.
13. Bartoli, *Monarchia*, pp. 21–22.

14. J. Bordeux, *Margherita of Savoia* (London: 1926), p. 149.
15. C. Hugo, *Rome en 1886* (Paris: 1886); see Casalegno, *Margherita*, p. 78.
16. "Happemouche" (D'Annunzio) in *Tribuna*, 11 December 1884.
17. Ibid., 29 December 1884.
18. Vasili, *Rome*, p. 21.
19. Croce in *Corriere della Sera*, 5 April 1949.
20. Croce, *Storia d'Italia*, p. 77.
21. Casalegno, *Margherita*, p. 93.
22. Guiccioli, *Diario*, p. 429 (diary entry of 14 February 1882).
23. Letter from Margherita to Marcello, 8 December 1886, in "Lettere di Margherita alla contessa Adriana Marcello" in *Nuova Antologia*, November 1941.
24. Vasili, *Rome*, p. 21.
25. Bartoli, *Monarchia*, p. 28.
26. Casalegno, *Margherita*, p. 178.
27. Guiccioli, *Diario*, p. 190 (diary entry of 20 February 1881).
28. Hugo, *Rome*, quoted in Gerbore, *Dame e cavalieri*, p. 186.
29. *Tribuna*, 11 December 1884.
30. Gerbore, *Dame e cavalieri*, p. 184.
31. Guiccioli, *Diario*, p. 433 (diary entry of 20 March 1882).

CHAPTER 9

1. See Perticone, *L'Italia Contemporanea*, pp. 258–263; cf. Mack Smith, *Italy*, pp. 179–181.
2. See ibid., pp. 183–188; also Mack Smith, *Italy*, pp. 137–140, Croce, *Storia d'Italia*, pp. 157–185, and G. Giolitti, *Memorie della mia vita* (Milan: 1945), pp. 31–59.
3. Cf. Casalegno, *Margherita*, pp. 158–165.
4. Mack Smith, *Italy*, p. 145.
5. Cusin, *L'Italia unita*, 2:54.
6. Mack Smith, *Italy*, p. 160.
7. Ibid., p. 175.
8. Giolitti, *Memorie*, pp. 86–87.
9. Casalegno, *Margherita*, p. 165.
10. Cf. Mack Smith, *Italy*, pp. 167–177, and Giolitti, *Memorie*, pp. 99–129.
11. Palmenghi-Crispi, *Politica interna*, p. 294.
12. Ibid., p. 296.
13. Mack Smith, *Italy*, p. 176.
14. Letter from P. Levi (editor of *La Riforma*) to Crispi, 5 December 1893, text in Palmenghi-Crispi, *Politica interna*, p. 296.
15. Ibid.
16. Ibid., pp. 294–295, Crispi's diary entry of 8 December 1893.

17. Farini, *Diario* (diary entry of 4 March 1894; emphasis in original).
18. Giolitti, *Memorie*, p. 86.
19. See Crispi's diary entry of 23 June 1895, in Palmenghi-Crispi, *Politica interna*, p. 339, and letter from Margherita to Osio, 28 July 1894, in "cuore aperto."
20. Ibid., Crispi's diary entry of 23 June 1895.
21. Casalegno, *Margherita*, p. 160 (emphasis in original).
22. Bartoli, *Monarchia*, p. 31.
23. Mack Smith, *Italy*, p. 184.
24. See W. L. Langer, *The Diplomacy of Imperialism* (New York: 1951), pp. 67–96.
25. G. Murray, quoted in ibid., p. 96.
26. A. Gramsci, *Sul Risorgimento* (Rome: 1967), pp. 73–74.
27. Letter from Menelek to Humbert, undated, but 20 July 1882, in the unpublished Humbert-Menelek correspondence, archives of the Istituto per la Storia del Risorgimento Italiano.
28. Giolitti, *Memorie*, p. 134.
29. See Perticone, *L'Italia Contemporanea*, p. 278.
30. A. Labriola, *Storia di dieci anni* (Milan: 1910), p. 19; cf. Mack Smith, *Italy*, pp. 186–187.

CHAPTER 10

1. Bartoli, *Monarchia*, p. 32.
2. Letter from Engels to Turati, 26 January 1894, text in Ragionieri, *Risorgimento*, pp. 615–616.
3. B. King and T. Okey, *Italy To-day* (London: 1901), p. 284.
4. A. Negri, *Fatalità, tempeste, maternità* (Milan: 1955), pp. 48–49.
5. King and Okey, *Italy To-day*, p. 130.
6. Bartoli, *Monarchia*, p. 62.
7. Labriola, *Dieci anni*, p. 9.
8. A. De Viti de Marco in *Giornale degli economisti*, 1 June 1898.
9. King and Okey, *Italy To-day*, p. 27.
10. S. Sonnino, "Torniamo allo Statuto" in *Nuova Antologia*, 1 January 1897.
11. Labriola, *Dieci anni*, p. 37.
12. Letter from Margherita to Osio, 7 May 1898, in "cuore aperto."
13. See telegrams from the Italian government in *I documenti diplomatici italiani* (Third Series: 1896–1907), Vol. 2: 1 May 1897–23 June 1898, docs. 444–454, pp. 322–325.
14. Letter from Torelli Viollier to P. Villari, 3 June 1898, in the Villari papers, archives of the Vatican, text in *L'Espresso*, 3 November 1968, pp. 16–17.

15. Telegram from Humbert to Bava Beccaris, 6 June 1898, text in Labriola, *Dieci anni*, p. 36.
16. Ibid., p. 49, speech of 4 July 1898.
17. Bartoli, *Monarchia*, p. 37.

CHAPTER 11

1. Statement of 19 July 1900, text in *L'Illustrazione Italiana*, 29 July 1900, p. 71.
2. Graziano, *Umberto I*, p. 146.
3. Letter from Margherita to Osio, 2 August 1899, in *"cuore aperto."*
4. *Corriere della Sera*, 30–31 July 1900, p. 1.
5. See the documents and partial transcript of Bresci's trial in *Corriere della Sera*, 29–30 August and 30–31 August 1900; also A. Petacco, *L'Anarchico che venne dall'America* (Milan: 1969).
6. Bartoli, *Monarchia*, p. 63.
7. *Corriere della Sera*, 31 July–1 August 1900, p. 1.
8. Ibid.
9. Ibid., 30–31 July 1900, p. 1.
10. M. O. Scanzi (E. Osio), *Il generale Osio* (Milan: 1909), p. 145.
11. *Corriere della Sera*, 30–31 July 1900, p.1; cf. Casalegno, *Margherita*, p. 183, and Bartoli, *Monarchia*, p. 60.
12. Letter from Margherita to Bonomelli, 1 August 1900, in *"Lettere di Margherita a mon. Bonomelli* (bishop of Cremona)," in *Nuova Antologia*, February 1940.
13. Ibid.
14. See Casalegno, *Margherita*, pp. 183–185.
15. G. Artieri, *"Il diario di Vittorio Emanuele III,"* in *Epoca*, 14 January–3 March 1968, 2nd installment, pp. 32–33.
16. Labriola, *Dieci anni*, p. 79; cf. Bartoli, *Monarchia*, p. 64.
17. *La Tribuna*, 2 August 1900, p. 1.
18. Ibid.
19. See partial transcript of trial in *Corriere della Sera*, 30–31 August 1900, p. 2.
20. Ibid.
21. Ibid., 25 May 1901; see also Petacco, *Anarchico*.

PART III: THE LITTLE KING

1. G. Artieri, "La vita di Vittorio Emanuele III," in *Storia illustrata*, January–March 1968, 1st installment, pp. 29–30.
2. I. Kirkpatrick, *Mussolini* (New York: 1968), paperback edition, p. 50.
3. E. Ferraris, *La marcia su Roma veduta dal Viminale* (Rome: 1946), p. 52.

4. Speech of 20 September 1922, quoted in R. De Felice, *Mussolini il fascista: La conquista del potere* (Turin: 1966), p. 334.

5. D. Susmel, "Mussolini e i Savoia," in *Tempo*, 20 December 1969–17 January 1970, 1st installment, p. 44.

CHAPTER 12

1. *Supra*, p. 55.
2. A. Robertson, *Victor Emmanuel III: King of Italy* (London: 1925), p. 32.
3. L. Morandi, *Come fu educato, Vittorio Emanuele III* (Turin: 1905), p. 56.
4. C. Richelmy, *Cinque re* (Rome: 1952), p. 160.
5. Morandi, *Vittorio Emanuele III*, p. 65.
6. Casalegno, *Margherita*, pp. 147–148.
7. Morandi, *Vittorio Emanuele III*, p. 58.
8. Letter from Margherita to Minghetti, 3 July 1885, in Lipparini, *Lettere*, p. 178.
9. Morandi, *Vittorio Emanuele III*, p. 56.
10. Bartoli, *Monarchia*, p. 49.
11. Farini, *Diario* (diary entry of 21 October 1896).
12. Bartoli, *Monarchia*, p. 49.
13. Letter from Margherita to Osio, 21 June 1893, in "cuore aperto" (emphasis in original).
14. Bartoli, *Monarchia*, p. 53.
15. Ibid., p. 52.
16. Page reproduced in Artieri, "Il diario," 1st installment, p. 26.
17. Mary, Queen of Rumania, *The Story of My Life* (London: 1924), quoted in Artieri, "Il diario," p. 28.
18. See A. Lumbroso, *Elena di Montenegro* (Florence: 1935); also F. Antonioni, *Due donne nel regno d'Italia* (Rome: 1968).
19. Letter from Margherita to Osio, 29 August 1896, in "cuore aperto."
20. Graziano, *Umberto I*, p. 146.
21. Lumbroso, *Elena*, p. 60.
22. Ibid., p. 13.
23. Quoted in ibid., p. 46.
24. The poem was published in a Russian magazine *Nedelia*; see Casalegno, *Margherita*, p. 152.
25. Bartoli, *Monarchia*, p. 56.
26. Ibid.
27. Lumbroso, *Elena*, p. 62.
28. Scanzi, *Osio*, p. 85.
29. See Artieri, "Il diario," 1st installment, pp. 28–30.

CHAPTER 13

1. King and Okey, *Italy To-day*, pp. 26–27.
2. Ibid., pp. 27–28.
3. See G. Procacci, *Storia degli italiani* (Bari: 1968), 2:456–461.
4. King and Okey, *Italy To-day*, p. 28.
5. Artieri, "La vita," 1st installment, p. 29.
6. Speech of 11 August 1900, text in *Corriere della Sera*, 11–12 August 1900, p. 3.
7. Bartoli, *Monarchia*, p. 73.
8. Ibid., p. 75.
9. Perticone, *L'Italia contemporanea*, p. 348.
10. Giolitti, *Memorie*, pp. 1–9.
11. Mack Smith, *Italy*, p. 287.
12. G. Ciano, *Diario 1939–43* (Milan: 1968), pp. 651–652 (diary entry of 25 January 1943).
13. Mack Smith, *Italy*, p. 217.
14. See A. W. Salomone, *Italian Democracy in the Making* (Philadelphia: 1945), pp. 62–85.
15. Quoted in ibid., p. 42.
16. Ibid., p. 113.
17. G. Salvemini, "Introductory Essay," ibid., p. xiii.
18. Ibid., p. 114.

CHAPTER 14

1. Bartoli, *Monarchia*, p. 103.
2. Ibid., p. 101.
3. Gerbore, *Dame e cavalieri*, pp. 232–233.
4. Ibid., p. 231.
5. R. Bagot, *My Italian Year* (London: 1911), p. 73, quoted in Casalegno, *Margherita*, p. 211.
6. S. Scaroni, *Con Vittorio Emanuele III* (Milan: 1954), p. 52.
7. Gerbore, *Dame e cavalieri*, p. 231.
8. Scaroni, *Vittorio Emanuele III*, p. 38.
9. The king's aphorism was common knowledge in court circles; see, e.g., Susmel, *Mussolini*, 3rd installment, p. 29.
10. Scaroni, *Vittorio Emanuele III*, pp. 65–66.
11. F. S. Nitti, *Rivelazioni* (Naples: 1948), p. 450.
12. Letter from Margherita to Osio, 27 June 1897, in "cuore aperto."
13. Ibid.
14. Casalegno, *Margherita*, p. 217.
15. Ibid.
16. Gerbore, *Dame e cavalieri*, p. 258.

17. Ibid., p. 293.
18. Lumbroso, *Elena*, p. 83.
19. Casalegno, *Margherita*, p. 218.
20. Lumbroso, *Elena*, p. 97.
21. Ibid., p. 93.
22. Ibid., pp. 87–88.

CHAPTER 15

1. See Salomone, *Italian Democracy*, p. 89.
2. Ibid., p. 91.
3. Quoted in Mack Smith, *Italy*, p. 270.
4. Salomone, *Italian Democracy*, p. 88.
5. Mack Smith, *Italy*, p. 270.
6. Salomone, *Italian Democracy*, p. 91.
7. Mack Smith, *Italy*, p. 269.
8. Speech of 28 March 1911, quoted in G. Volpe, *L'Impresa di Tripoli* (Rome: 1946), p. 51.
9. Artieri, "Il diario," 3rd installment, p. 62.
10. Letter from Margherita to Bonomelli, 29 April 1912, in *"Lettere di Margherita."*
11. Salomone, *Italian Democracy*, p. 101.
12. See Mack Smith, *Italy*, pp. 272–281; cf. Volpe, *Tripoli*.
13. Volpe, *Tripoli*, p. 93.
14. Ibid., pp. 66–67.
15. Giolitti, *Memorie*, p. 360.
16. Kirkpatrick, *Mussolini*, pp. 50–51.

CHAPTER 16

1. Artieri, "Il diario," 3rd installment, p. 61.
2. Ibid., page reproduced in 2nd installment, p. 35.
3. W. A. Renzi, "Italy's Neutrality and Entrance into the Great War: A Re-examination," *The American Historical Review*, June 1968, p. 1413.
4. Ibid., p. 1417.
5. Ibid., p. 1422.
6. Artieri, "Il diario," 3rd installment, p. 61.
7. See Renzi, *Italy's Neutrality*, p. 1430, and Mack Smith, *Italy*, p. 298.
8. A. J. P. Taylor, *The Habsburg Monarchy* (London: 1964), paperback edition, p. 237.
9. Bartoli, *Monarchia*, p. 116.
10. Procacci, *Storia degli italiani*, 2:482.
11. Artieri, "Il diario," 3rd installment, p. 62.
12. A. Bergamini, *Il re Vittorio Emanuele di fronte alla storia* (Rome: 1949), p. 9.

13. See Renzi, *Italy's Neutrality*, p. 1415, and Salvatorelli, *Casa Savoia*, p. 43.
14. Artieri, "Il diario," 3rd installment, p. 62.
15. A. Salandra, *La neutralita italiana* (Milan: 1928), p. 191.
16. R. De Felice, *Storia degli ebrei italiani sotto il fascismo* (Turin: 1961), p. 25.
17. Ciano, *Diario*, p. 48 (diary entry of 19 February 1939).
18. B. Mussolini in *Avanti!*, 18 October 1914, text in R. De Felice, *Mussolini il rivoluzionario* (Turin: 1965), pp. 258–260.
19. See ibid., p. 277.
20. Artieri, "Il diario," 3rd installment, p. 62.
21. De Felice, *Il rivoluzionario*, p. 315.
22. Giolitti, *Memorie*, p. 543.
23. Mack Smith, *Italy*, p. 301.
24. Artieri, "Il diario," 3rd installment, p. 64.
25. De Felice, *Il rivoluzionario*, p. 315.
26. Farini, *Diario* (diary entry of 21 October 1896).
27. Scaroni, *Vittorio Emanuele III*, p. 58.
28. Giolitti, *Memorie*, p. 542.
29. Ibid.
30. Ibid., p. 544.
31. Mack Smith, *Italy*, p. 304.

CHAPTER 17

1. H. Acton, *The Last Bourbons of Naples* (London: 1961), p. 70.
2. Bartoli, *Monarchia*, p. 138.
3. C. Sforza, *L'Italia dal 1914 al 1944 quale io la vidi* (Rome: 1945), pp. 46–47.
4. Artieri, "Il diario," 3rd installment, p. 66.
5. Page reproduced in ibid., p. 65.
6. Text in ibid., p. 67.
7. Scaroni, *Vittorio Emanuele III*, p. 58.
8. Artieri, "La vita," 2nd installment, p. 74.
9. Bartoli, *Monarchia*, p. 132.

CHAPTER 18

1. See H. Nicolson, *King George V* (London: 1967) paperback edition, pp. 402–406.
2. See Nitti, *Rivelazioni*, pp. 326–337, 458–460.
3. Ibid., pp. 335–336.
4. Ibid., pp. 561–563.
5. Bartoli, *Monarchia*, p. 151.
6. Giolitti, *Memorie*, p. 582.

7. Sforza, *L'Italia*, p. 123.
8. Ibid., p. 124.
9. Ibid.
10. Artieri, "Il diario," 4th installment, p. 66.
11. Nitti, *Rivelazioni*, p. 342.
12. See ibid., pp. 346–347; also De Felice, *Il fascista*, pp. 283–284.
13. Ibid., p. 459.

CHAPTER 19

1. Procacci, *Storia italiani*, 2:486–487.
2. Ibid., p. 487.
3. Speech of 23 March 1919, text in De Felice, *Il rivoluzionario*, p. 507.
4. See Artieri, "Il diario," 4th installment, pp. 66–67.
5. Document in De Felice, *Il fascista*, pp. 764–765.
6. Procacci, *Storia degli italiani*, 2:501.
7. De Felice, *Il fascista*, p. 147.
8. Quoted in F. Chabod, *L'Italia contemporanea* (Turin: 1961), p. 67.
9. Ibid., p. 68; letter from Giolitti to L. Ambrosini, 1 January 1923.
10. P. Spriano, *Storia del Partito comunista italiano* (Turin: 1967), 1:158.
11. De Felice, *Il fascista*, pp. 311–312.
12. Ibid., p. 310.
13. Ibid., p. 315.

CHAPTER 20

1. E. Ludwig, *Colloqui con Mussolini* (Milan: 1965), paperback edition, p. 67.
2. Bartoli, *Monarchia*, p. 171.
3. Ibid., pp. 170–171.
4. De Felice, *Il fascista*, p. 311.
5. Bartoli, *Monarchia*, p. 197.
6. Document in De Felice, *Il rivoluzionario*, pp. 725–737.
7. See ibid., p. 462.
8. See Kirkpatrick, *Mussolini*, pp. 170–171.
9. I. Balbo, *diario 1922* (Milan: 1932), p. 109 (diary entry of 30 July 1922).
10. De Felice, *Il fascista*, p. 259.
11. Casalegno, *Margherita*, p. 225; cf. Chabod, *L'Italia contemporanea*, p. 73.
12. De Felice, *Il fascista*, p. 313.
13. S. Giuliani, *Interviste* (Milan: 1934), p. 5.
14. *Giornale d'Italia*, 22 August 1922.
15. Mussolini in *Popolo d'Italia*, 23 August 1922.

16. Speech of 20 September 1922, in De Felice, *Il fascista*, p. 335.
17. E. Lussu, *Marcia su Roma e dintorni* (Milan: 1968) paperback edition, p. 48.

CHAPTER 21

1. Ibid., p. 49.
2. Ibid., p. 48.
3. Cf. De Felice, *Il fascista*, pp. 336–339.
4. Ibid., p. 342.
5. Ibid., p. 344.
6. Ibid., p. 343.
7. Ibid., p. 324.
8. Ibid., p. 322.
9. Lussu, *Marcia su Roma*, p. 47.
10. Text in De Felice, *Il fascista*, p. 339.
11. See ibid.
12. See ibid., pp. 360–361, and Artieri, "Il diario," 4th installment, p. 68.
13. Artieri, "Il diario," 4th installment, p. 68.
14. *Il Popolo d'Italia*, 14 October 1922.
15. See Victor Emmanuel III's self-defense in P. Puntoni, *Parla Vittorio Emanuele III* (Milan: 1958), p. 288, and Humbert II in Artieri, "Il diario," 4th installment, p. 69.
16. Text in De Felice, *Il fascista*, p. 339.
17. Artieri, "Il diario," 5th installment, p. 61.
18. Bartoli, *Monarchia*, p. 178.
19. Puntoni, *Vittorio Emanuele III*, p. 40.
20. M. Soleri, *Memorie* (Turin: 1949), p. 150.
21. Bartoli, *Monarchia*, p. 174.
22. Ferraris, *La Marcia su Roma*, p. 95.
23. Page reproduced in Artieri, "Il diario," 4th installment, p. 67.
24. N. D'Aroma, *Vent'anni insieme Vittorio Emanuele e Mussolini* (Bologna: 1957), p. 124.
25. Bartoli, *Monarchia*, p. 174.
26. Ferraris, *La Marcia su Roma*, pp. 88–90.
27. See Lussu, *Marcia su Roma*, p. 54.
28. Artieri, "Il diario," 5th installment, p. 63.
29. See De Felice, *Il fascista*, p. 360.
30. Artieri, "Il diario," 5th installment, p. 64.
31. De Felice, *Il fascista*, p. 372.
32. Kirkpatrick, *Mussolini*, p. 141.
33. See diary page reproduced in Artieri, "Il diario," 4th installment, p. 67.
34. Telegram reproduced in Artieri, "La vita," 2nd installment, p. 76; see also Kirkpatrick, *Mussolini*, p. 144.

35. Susmel, *Mussolini*, 1st installment, p. 38.
36. Kirkpatrick, *Mussolini*, p. 145.
37. Susmel, *Mussolini*, 1st installment, p. 44.
38. Artieri, "Il diario," 5th installment, p. 64.
39. Susmel, *Mussolini*, 1st installment, p. 45; see also Giuliani, *Interviste*, pp. 8–10.

PART IV: THE FALL OF THE HOUSE OF SAVOY

1. Artieri, "Il diario," 8th installment, p. 111.

CHAPTER 22

1. Lussu, *Marcia su Roma*, pp. 63–74.
2. B. Mussolini, *Il tempo del bastone e della carota (Storià di un anno, 1942–1943)* (Milan: 1966) paperback edition, p. 130.
3. F. Crispolti, *Corone e porpore* (Milan: 1936), p. 51.
4. Mussolini, *Il tempo del bastone*, p. 132.
5. Ibid., p. 132.
6. Ibid., pp. 132–133.
7. Ibid., p. 134.
8. *Times*, 31 October 1923.
9. Mack Smith, *Italy*, p. 383.

CHAPTER 23

1. Nitti, *Rivelazioni*, p. 582.
2. Speech of 24 May 1924, quoted in Perticone, *L'Italia contemporanea*, p. 607.
3. Sforza, *L'Italia*, p. 129.
4. Artieri, "Il diario," 5th installment, p. 65.
5. Speech of 6 June 1924, quoted in Perticone, *L'Italia contemporanea*, p. 611.
6. See Kirkpatrick, *Mussolini*, pp. 211–224; also C. Rossi, *Il delitto Matteotti* (Milan: 1965), and De Felice, *Il fascista*, pp. 618–730.
7. De Felice, *Il fascista*, p. 628.
8. See *ibid.*, p. 621; also Kirkpatrick, *Mussolini*, pp. 220–222, and C. Silvestri, *Matteotti, Mussolini e il dramma italiano* (Rome: 1947).
9. Susmel, *Mussolini*, 2nd installment, p. 40.
10. Sforza, *L'Italia*, p. 129.
11. Kirkpatrick, *Mussolini*, p. 227.
12. Ibid.
13. See R. Katz, *Death in Rome* (New York: 1967) pp. 67–68, 118.

14. De Felice, *Il fascista*, pp. 650–651.

15. Ibid.

16. Artieri, "Il diario," 5th installment, pp. 66–67.

17. Speech of 31 August 1924, quoted in Perticone, *L'Italia contemporanea*, p. 616.

18. De Felice, *Il fascista*, pp. 681–682.

19. Speech of 5 December 1924, in B. Mussolini *Opera omnia* (Florence: 1951–1963), 21:194–196.

20. Susmel, *Mussolini*, 2nd installment, p. 41.

21. L. Salvatorelli and G. Mira, *Storia d'Italia nel periodo fascista* (Turin: 1964), p. 351.

22. *Corriere della Sera*, 30 December 1924.

23. De Felice, *Il fascista*, p. 704.

24. Ibid., p. 716.

25. Lussu, *Marcia su Roma*, p. 168.

26. De Felice, *Il fascista*, p. 691.

27. Susmel, *Mussolini*, 2nd installment, p. 41.

28. Mussolini, *Opera omnia*, 21:235–237.

29. Salvatorelli and Mira, *Italia nel periodo fascista*, p. 353.

30. Ibid., p. 367.

31. Bartoli, *Monarchia*, p. 192.

32. Ibid.

33. Puntoni, *Vittorio Emanuele III*, p. 289.

34. Mussolini, *Il tempo del bastone*, p. 135.

35. Ludwig, *Mussolini*, p. 140.

36. Susmel, *Mussolini*, 2nd installment, p. 41.

37. Ibid.

CHAPTER 24

1. *Il Messaggero*, 5 April 1923; see Antonioni, op. cit., p. 146.

2. Casalegno, *Margherita*, p. 217.

3. Ibid., p. 228.

4. Mussolini, *Il tempo del bastone*, p. 137.

5. Ibid.

6. Ibid., p. 135.

7. Ibid., p. 138.

8. Scaroni, *Vittorio Emanuele III*, p. 40.

9. Salvatorelli and Mira, *Italia nel periodo fascista*, p. 414.

10. Ibid., p. 415.

11. Ibid., p. 897.

12. Susmel, *Mussolini*, 3rd installment, p. 28.

13. E. Franco, "La cuccagna non durerà," *Vie Nuova*, 26 December 1968, p. 16.

14. M. Contini, *Maria José: La regina sconosciuta* (Milan: 1955), p. 85; see also Susmel, *Mussolini*, 3rd installment, p. 28.
15. Gerbore, *Dame e cavalieri*, pp. 334–335.
16. Quoted in Contini, *Maria José*, p. 100.
17. Bartoli, *Monarchia*, pp. 284–285.
18. Quoted in Contini, *Maria José*, p. 124.
19. Ciano, *Diario*, p. 231 (diary entry of 30 December 1939).
20. Susmel, *Mussolini*, 3rd installment, p. 29.

CHAPTER 25

1. Speech of 13 December 1930; see *Corriere della Sera*, 14 December 1940.
2. Chabod, *L'Italia contemporanea*, p. 93.
3. Susmel, *Mussolini*, 3rd installment, p. 32.
4. See Mack Smith, *Italy*, pp. 449–450.
5. Speech of 2 October 1935, quoted in Kirkpatrick, *Mussolini*, p. 308.
6. See R. Katz, *Black Sabbath* (New York: 1969), p. 71.
7. Ibid.
8. Susmel, *Mussolini*, 3rd installment, p. 32.
9. United Nations War Crimes Commission, *History of the UNWCC* (London: 1948), pp. 189–190.
10. Ibid.
11. Mack Smith, *Italy*, p. 451.
12. Susmel, *Mussolini*, 3rd installment, p. 32.
13. Speech, of 9 May 1936, quoted in Salvatorelli and Mira, *Italia nel periodo fascista*, p. 882.
14. Susmel, *Mussolini*, 4th installment, p. 27.
15. Salvatorelli and Mira, *Italia nel periodo fascista*, p. 968.
16. Susmel, *Mussolini*, 2nd installment, p. 40.
17. Mussolini, *Il tempo del bastone*, p. 140.
18. Salvatorelli and Mira, *Italia nel periodo fascista*, p. 974.
19. Mussolini, *Il tempo del bastone*, pp. 140–141.
20. Susmel, *Mussolini*, 4th installment, p. 27.
21. Mussolini, *Il tempo del bastone*, p. 139.
22. Kirkpatrick, *Mussolini*, p. 353.
23. Quoted in Salvatorelli and Mira, *Italia nel periodo fascista*, p. 976.
24. Kirkpatrick, *Mussolini*, p. 353.
25. Salvatorelli and Mira, *Italia nel periodo fascista*, p. 977.
26. Artieri, "*Il diario*," 6th installment, p. 68.
27. P. Monelli, *Mussolini piccolo borghese* (Milan: 1968), paperback edition, p. 203; see also Katz, *Black Sabbath*, p. 79.
28. Ciano, *Diario*, p. 35 (diary entry of 30 January 1939).
29. In ital.: "*testa di c[azzo]*"; ibid., p. 76 (diary entry of 27 March 1939).

30. Ibid., p. 118 (diary entry of 25 May 1939).
31. Ibid., pp. 124–125 (diary entry of 3 June 1939).
32. Ibid., pp. 130–131 (diary entry of 13 June 1939).

CHAPTER 26

1. Bartoli, *Monarchia*, pp. 210–211.
2. See Ciano, *Diario*, p. 74 (diary entry of 24 March 1939).
3. Ibid., p. 118 (diary entry of 25 May 1939).
4. Ibid., p. 137 (diary entry of 26 June–2 July 1939).
5. Ibid., pp. 154–155 (diary entries of 6 and 7 August 1939).
6. Ibid., pp. 166–167 (diary entry of 24 August 1939).
7. See ibid., pp. 213, 231 (diary entries of 18 November, 30 December 1939).
8. See Puntoni, *Vittorio Emanuele III*, p. 11.
9. Antonioni, *Due donne*, p. 159.
10. Ciano, *Diario*, p. 246 (diary entry of 29 January 1940).
11. Ibid., p. 292 (diary entry of 6 May 1940).
12. Ibid., pp. 261–262 (diary entry of 5 March 1940).
13. Ibid., p. 267 (diary entry of 14 March 1940).
14. Ibid.
15. Ibid., p. 303 (diary entry of 21 May 1940).
16. Ibid., p. 262 (diary entry of 6 March 1940).
17. Ibid., p. 283 (diary entry of 11 April 1940).
18. Ibid., p. 308 (diary entry of 1 June 1940).
19. Ibid.
20. Ibid., p. 310 (diary entry of 3 June 1940).
21. Susmel, *Mussolini*, 4th installment, p. 29.

CHAPTER 27

1. Contini, *Maria José*, p. 188.
2. Ciano, *Diario*, p. 400 (diary entry of 30 April 1941).
3. Puntoni, *Vittorio Emanuele III* (diary entry of 23 June 1941).
4. E. Davidson, *The Trial of the Germans* (New York: 1967), p. 350.
5. Ciano, *Diario*, pp. 403–404 (diary entry of 8 May 1941).
6. Ibid., p. 470 (diary entry of 17 November 1941).
7. Ibid., pp. 419–420.
8. Puntoni, *Vittorio Emanuele III*, p. 63 (diary entry of 14 July 1941).
9. Ciano, *Diario*, pp. 560–561 (diary entry of 1 June 1942).
10. Puntoni, *Vittorio Emanuele III*, p. 104 (diary entry of 17 November 1942).
11. Ibid., p. 107 (diary entry of 26 November 1942).
12. Ciano, *Diario*, p. 621 (diary entry of 19 November 1942).

13. F. W. Deakin, *The Brutal Friendship* (New York: 1966), paperback edition, p. 124.
14. Ibid., p. 125.
15. Ciano, *Diario*, p. 656 (diary entry of 5 February 1943).
16. Ibid.
17. See Bartoli, *Monarchia*, pp. 221–224.
18. Puntoni, *Vittorio Emanuele III*, p. 127 (diary entry of 3 April 1943).
19. Ibid., pp. 119–120 (diary entry of 12 February 1943).
20. See Deakin, *Brutal Friendship*, pp. 109–112.
21. Letter from Victor Emmanuel to Acquarone, 1 June 1944, text in R. Zangrandi, *1943: 25 luglio–8 settembre* (Milan: 1964), p. 70.
22. Puntoni, *Vittorio Emanuele III*, p. 121 (diary entry of 23 February 1943).
23. Ibid., p. 126 (diary entry of 16 March 1943).
24. Deakin, *Brutal Friendship*, p. 54.
25. Artieri, "Il diario," 7th installment, pp. 99–100.
26. Susmel, *Mussolini*, 5th installment, p. 28.

CHAPTER 28

1. *Foreign Relations of the United States, 1943, Volume 2, Europe* (Washington: 1964), p. 926.
2. Deakin, *Brutal Friendship*, p. 397.
3. Ibid., p. 396.
4. Puntoni, *Vittorio Emanuele III*, p. 139 (diary entry of 15 July 1943).
5. E. Piscitelli, *Storia della resistenza romana* (Bari: 1965), p. 5.
6. Quoted in Mussolini, *Il tempo del bastone*, p. 48.
7. Puntoni, *Vittorio Emanuele III*, pp. 139–140 (diary entry of 19 July 1943).
8. D. Alfieri, *Due dittatori di fronte* (Milan: 1948), p. 315.
9. Mussolini, *Il tempo del bastone*, p. 47.
10. Quoted in Deakin, *Brutal Friendship*, p. 411.
11. Ibid.
12. Ibid., p. 425.
13. Puntoni, *Vittorio Emanuele III*, p. 140 (diary entry of 20 July 1943).
14. Ibid., p. 141 (diary entry of 21 July 1943).
15. Mussolini, *Il tempo del bastone*, p. 48.
16. Ibid.
17. Deakin, *Brutal Friendship*, p. 430.
18. Puntoni, *Vittorio Emanuele III*, p. 141 (diary entry of 22 July 1943).
19. Bartoli, *Monarchia*, p. 228.
20. Deakin, *Brutal Friendship*, p. 434.
21. Bartoli, *Monarchia*, p. 229.
22. Deakin, *Brutal Friendship*, p. 440.
23. Ibid., p. 338.

24. Ibid., p. 432.
25. Ibid., pp. 426–433; the document is reproduced in C. Scorza, "La notte del Gran Consiglio," *Tempo*, 11 June–3 August 1968, 8th installment, p. 30.
26. Kirkpatrick, *Mussolini*, p. 529.
27. Mussolini, *Il tempo del bastone*, p. 49.
28. Kirkpatrick, *Mussolini*, p. 530.
29. Scorza, "Gran Consiglio," 8th installment, p. 31.
30. Deakin, *Brutal Friendship*, p. 451.
31. Kirkpatrick, *Mussolini*, p. 534.
32. Scorza, "Gran Consiglio," 9th installment, p. 53.
33. Ibid., 10th installment, p. 50.
34. See Puntoni, *Vittorio Emanuele III*, p. 142 (diary entry of 24–25 July 1943).
35. Ibid., p. 143; see also Deakin, *Brutal Friendship*, pp. 470–472.
36. Ibid.
37. Bartoli, *Monarchia*, p. 233.
38. Monelli, *Mussolini*, p. 244.
39. Deakin, *Brutal Friendship*, p. 467.
40. Zangrandi, *1943*, p. 411.
41. Mussolini, *Il tempo del bastone*, pp. 64–65.
42. Bartoli, *Monarchia*, p. 234.
43. Puntoni, *Vittorio Emanuele III*, pp. 144–145 (diary entry of 24–25 July 1943).
44. Susmel, *Mussolini*, 5th installment, p. 29.
45. Mussolini, *Il tempo del bastone*, p. 64; see also Puntoni, *Vittorio Emanuele III*, p. 145 (diary entry of 24–25 July 1943).
46. Susmel, *Mussolini*, 5th installment, p. 29.
47. Text in *Il Messaggero*, 26 July 1943, p. 1.

CHAPTER 29

1. Bartoli, *Monarchia*, p. 235.
2. Text in *Il Messaggero*, 26 July 1943, p. 1.
3. See, e. g., L. P. Lochner (ed.), *The Goebbels Diaries* (New York: 1948), paperback edition, p. 468 (diary entry of 27 July 1943); also A. Bullock, *Hitler* (New York: 1961), paperback edition, pp. 638–639, and W. L. Shirer, *The Rise and Fall of The Third Reich* (New York: 1960), p. 999.
4. Letter from Mussolini to Badoglio, 26 July 1943, text in Mussolini, *Il tempo del bastone*, pp. 66–67.
5. Text in P. Secchia and F. Frassati, *Storia della Resistenza* (Rome: 1965), I:12.
6. Bullock, *Hitler*, p. 637.

7. Shirer, *Third Reich*, p. 999.
8. See Bullock, *Hitler*, pp. 638–639.
9. Puntoni, *Vittorio Emanuele III*, p. 147 (diary entry of 28 July 1943).
10. Ibid., p. 148 (diary entry of 29 July 1943).
11. See ibid., p. 150 (diary entry of 1–2 August 1943); see also Zangrandi, *1943*, p. 507.
12. See Zangrandi, *1943*, pp. 506–508.
13. See d'Ajeta's report in R. Guariglia, *Ricordi 1922–1946* (Naples: 1950), pp. 587–599.
14. Churchill to Roosevelt, 5 August 1943, text in W. S. Churchill, *The Second World War* (Boston: 1951), 5:99–100.
15. See A. Garland and H. M. Smyth, *Sicily and the Surrender of Italy* (Washington: 1965), p. 299; also Berio's report in Guariglia, *Ricordi*, pp. 601–605.
16. S. Friedländer, *Pius XII and the Third Reich* (New York: 1966), p. 171; see also Katz, *Death in Rome*, pp. 11–14.
17. See Zangrandi, *1943*, p. 256.
18. See Garland and Smyth, *Sicily*, p. 465.
19. See R. Murphy, *Diplomat Among Warriors* (New York: 1965), paperback edition, p. 216.
20. Garland and Smyth, *Sicily*, p. 457.
21. Ibid., p. 475.
22. Murphy, *Diplomat*, p. 218.
23. Garland and Smyth, *Sicily*, pp. 477–478.
24. Guariglia, *Ricordi*, p. 678.
25. Garland and Smyth, *Sicily*, p. 490.
26. Ibid., p. 503.
27. Telegram from Rahn to Berlin, 11 September 1943, text in Zangrandi, *1943*, pp. 964–966.
28. Ibid.
29. Puntoni, *Vittorio Emanuele III*, p. 161 (diary entry of 6 September 1943).
30. Ibid., p. 152 (diary entry of 9 August 1943).
31. P. Monelli, *Roma 1943* (Milan: 1963), p. 123.
32. Text in Garland and Smyth, *Sicily*, p. 507.
33. P. Badoglio, *L'Italia nella seconda guerra mondiale* (Milan: 1946), p. 105.
34. Telegram from Rahn to Berlin, 11 September 1943, text in Zangrandi, *1943*, p. 965.
35. Ibid., pp. 358–359.
36. Letter from Victor Emmanuel to Acquarone, 17 January 1945, text in *Oggi*, 21 August 1958.
37. Zangrandi, *1943*, p. 359.

38. Ibid., p. 360.
39. Statement by Marchesi, in R. Trionfera and A. Petacco, "Perché Roma si arrese ai nazisti?" in *L'Europeo*, 5 September 1968, p. 23.
40. Puntoni, *Vittorio Emanuele III*, p. 162 (diary entry of 8 September 1943).
41. Text in Garland and Smyth, *Sicily*, p. 508.
42. Zangrandi, *1943*, p. 360.
43. Text in ibid., p. 364.
44. Ibid., p. 365; see also Garland and Smyth, *Sicily*, p. 514.
45. Puntoni, *Vittorio Emanuele III*, pp. 163–164 (diary entry of 8 September 1943).

CHAPTER 30

1. See Garland and Smyth, *Sicily*, pp. 522–523.
2. Ibid., pp. 514–515.
3. Zangrandi, *1943*, p. 366.
4. Interview in *La Nazione* (Florence), 9 September 1963.
5. Badoglio, *L'Italia*, p. 116.
6. Zangrandi, *1943*, p. 367.
7. Document in Puntoni, *Vittorio Emanuele III*, p. 318.
8. Ibid., p. 164 (diary entry of 9 September 1943).
9. Ibid., p. 165.
10. Zangrandi, *1943*, pp. 379–440.
11. Statement of K. Student in Trionfera and Petacco, *Roma*, p. 25.
12. Lochner, *Goebbels*, pp. 501–502 (diary entry of 10 September 1943).
13. Zangrandi, *1943*, p. 383.
14. Bartoli, *Monarchia*, p. 246.
15. Zangrandi, *1943*, p. 404.
16. Puntoni, *Vittorio Emanuele III*, p. 167 (diary entry of 9 September 1943).
17. Zangrandi, *1943*, p. 402.
18. Ibid.
19. Puntoni, *Vittorio Emanuele III*, p. 165 (diary entry of 9 September 1943).
20. Ibid., p. 166.
21. Soleri, *Memorie*, p. 272.
22. E. Caviglia, *Diario*, Milan, 1952, p. 476.
23. Zangrandi, *1943*, p. 411.
24. Ibid.
25. Ibid., p. 417.
26. N. Bolla, *Il segreto di due re* (Milan: 1951), p. 14.
27. See Zangrandi, *1943*, p. 412.
28. Ibid., p. 417.
29. Ibid., p. 419.

30. Puntoni, *Vittorio Emanuele III*, p. 167 (diary entry of 9 September 1943).
31. Zangrandi, *1943*, p. 422.
32. Puntoni, *Vittorio Emanuele III*, p. 167 (diary entry of 9 September 1943).
33. Soleri, *Memorie*, p. 272; see also Zangrandi, *1943*, p. 422.
34. Zangrandi, *1943*, p. 423.
35. Lochner, *Goebbels*, pp. 506, 546 (diary entries of 11 and 23 September 1943).
36. Artieri, "Il diario," 8th installment, p. 107.
37. Puntoni, *Vittorio Emanuele III*, p. 167 (diary entry of 9 September 1943).
38. G. Pillon, "I Savoia nella bufera," *Il Tempo*, 27 June–24 August 1969, 12th installment.
39. Zangrandi, *1943*, p. 439; see also Bartoli, *Monarchia*, p. 250.

CHAPTER 31

1. See, e.g., Chabod, *L'Italia contemporanea*, pp. 118–131.
2. Speech of 14 December 1943, text in A. Degli Espinosa, *Il regno del sud* (Rome: 1946), pp. 215–216.
3. Statement of 20 December 1943, in ibid., p. 220.
4. Telegram from Roosevelt to Churchill, 13 March 1944, text in Churchill, *Second World War*, 5:504.
5. Ibid., vol. 5, p. 188.
6. Artieri, "La vita," 3rd installment, p. 116; see also Bartoli, *Monarchia*, p. 253.
7. Scaroni, *Vittorio Emanuele III*, pp. 109–119; see also Contini, *Maria José*, pp. 101–102.
8. Murphy, *Diplomat*, p. 223.
9. Ibid.
10. Artieri, "La vita," 3rd installment, p. 116.
11. Murphy, *Diplomat*, p. 224.
12. Puntoni, *Vittorio Emanuele III*, p. 176 (diary entry of 13 October 1943).
13. Ibid., p. 175 (diary entry of 7 October 1943).
14. Murphy, *Diplomat*, p. 229.
15. Puntoni, *Vittorio Emanuele III*, p. 218 (diary entry of 10 April 1944).
16. Murphy, *Diplomat*, p. 229.
17. Degli Espinosa, *Il regno del sud*, pp. 333–334.
18. Puntoni, *Vittorio Emanuele III*, p. 219 (diary entry of 10 April 1944).
19. See ibid.
20. Text in Degli Espinosa, *Il regno del sud*, p. 334.
21. Puntoni, *Vittorio Emanuele III*, p. 224 (diary entry of 22 April 1944).

22. Murphy, *Diplomat*, p. 230.

23. G. Deborin, *The Second World War* (Moscow: 1962), p. 323.

24. Murphy, *Diplomat*, p. 231.

25. Degli Espinosa, *Il regno del sud*, p. 334.

26. Puntoni, *Vittorio Emanuele III*, p. 221 (diary entry of 12 April 1944).

27. On the Italian resistance see Secchia and Frassati, *Resistenza*; Salvatorelli and Mira, *Italia nel periodo fascista*; R. Battaglia, *Storia della Resistenza italiana* (Turin: 1964), and C. F. Delzell, *Mussolini's Enemies: The Anti-Fascist Resistance* (Princeton: 1961).

28. H. S. Hughes, *The United States and Italy* (Cambridge: 1965), p. 134.

29. Ibid., p. 133.

30. Bartoli, *Monarchia*, pp. 364–365.

31. Puntoni, *Vittorio Emanuele III*, p. 226 (diary entry of 6 May 1944).

32. Bartoli, *Monarchia*, p. 359.

33. Ibid., pp. 361–362.

34. See his memoirs: G. Romita, *Dalla monarchia alla repubblica* (Pisa: 1959).

35. L. Barzini, Jr., *Le paure d'ieri* (Rome: 1968), p. 32.

36. Letter in Puntoni, *Vittorio Emanuele III*, p. 237.

37. Ibid. (diary entry of 27 June 1944).

38. Document reproduced in Puntoni, *Vittorio Emanuele III*, facing p. 288.

39. Artieri, "Il diario," 8th installment, p. 111.

40. See Contini, *Maria José*, pp. 243–244, and Bartoli, *Monarchia*, p. 329.

41. Cf. Bartoli, *Monarchia*, pp. 369–377; Barzini, *Paure*, pp. 59–65, and Romita, *Dalla Monarchia*.

42. Barzini, *Paure*, p. 38.

43. Bartoli, *Monarchia*, p. 329.

44. On the voting returns see Romita, *Dalla Monarchia*, pp. 193–197; for the official results see F. Etnasi, *2 giugno 1946* (Rome: 1966), p. 315.

45. Cf. Barzini, *Paure*, pp. 67–74, and Bartoli, *Monarchia*, pp. 369–377.

46. Bartoli, *Monarchia*, p. 374.

47. Ibid., p. 376.

48. Barzini, *Paure*, p. 69.

49. Bartoli, *Monarchia*, p. 377.

50. Barzini, *Paure*, p. 71.

51. Ibid.

52. Ibid., pp. 71–72.

53. Ibid., p. 65.

54. Statement of 13 June 1946, text in Etnasi, *2 giugno 1946*, pp. 299–300.

EPILOGUE: WHEN A MONARCHY DIES

1. Puntoni, *Vittorio Emanuele III*, p. 341.

2. Ibid., p. 352.

3. Ibid., pp. 356–357.
4. Antonioni, *Due donne*, p. 173.
5. Ibid., p. 178.
6. Pillon, *Savoia*, 49th installment.
7. *Il Messaggero*, 26 April 1968.
8. Bartoli, *Monarchia*, p. 260.
9. See Pillon, *Savoia*, 32nd installment.

BIBLIOGRAPHY

As might be expected, many documents, monographs, books, and articles have accumulated over the past thousand years which deal with one or another aspect of the House of Savoy. About one hundred years ago a man named Antonio Manno began to make a list of them. He died before he could complete the project, and the work was continued by his assistant, Vincenzo Promis. Promis never finished the job either, but by 1934 ten volumes of the work had been published (see below) listing 42,811 titles. Humbert II is said to be cataloguing the still secret documents he took with him to Portugal (see above, p. 383), and Francesco Cognasso (see below) has done much useful archival and bibliographical research. But a great deal more remains to be done, though it probably never will be.

I have not read all the items on the Manno-Promis list, but it has been necessary for me to examine many of them, as well as others. What follows is a selection of the titles of material I have found particularly useful in preparing this book: it is more or less limited to those works which relate directly to the House of Savoy. Included are documentary, primary, and secondary sources, which are grouped here as general works and in chronological divisions corresponding to the four main parts of this book. This has caused some overlapping, and in such cases, I have placed the books among those with which they seemed to fit best. I have taken the liberty of commenting briefly on some publications.

Most of the material, as well as the unpublished documents cited in the Notes (see above, pp. 389–415), was available at the following research centers, for whose facilities and assistance I am very grateful: Biblioteca di Storia Moderna e Contemporanea (Rome); Biblioteca Nazionale Centrale "Vittorio Emanuele II" (Rome); Biblioteca Reale (Turin); The British Museum; and the New York Public Library.

GENERAL WORKS

Albrecht-Carrié, R., *Italy from Napoleon to Mussolini*. New York, 1950.

Bartoli, D., *La fine della monarchia*. Milan, 1947 (authoritative rev. ed. of Bartoli's *Vittorio Emanuele III*, 1946).

Bonomi, I., *La politica italiana da Porta Pia a Vittorio Veneto, 1870–1918*. Turin, 1944.

Candeloro, G. *Storia dell'Italia moderna*, 6 vols. Milan, 1956–1970 (a continuing work with a Marxist viewpoint).

Chabod, F., *L'Italia contemporanea (1918–1948)*. Turin, 1961.

Cilibrizzi, S. *Storia parlamentare politica e diplomatica d'Italia da Novara a Vittorio Veneto*. 6 vols. Naples, 1939–1943.

Crankshaw, E., *The Fall of the House of Habsburg*. London, 1963.

Croce, B., *Storia d'Italia dal 1871 al 1915*. Rev. ed. Bari, 1967.

Enciclopedia storico nobiliare italiana. Milan, 1928.

Gerbore, P., *Dame e cavalieri del re*. Milan, 1952.

Hughes, S., *The Fall and Rise of Modern Italy*. New York, 1967.

I discorsi della Corona con i proclami alla nazione dal 1848–1936. Milan, 1938.

I documenti diplomatici italiani. Series I–IX (24 vols. have been issued to date covering many of the years between 1861 and 1940).

Mack Smith, D., *Italy*. Rev. ed. Ann Arbor, 1969 (one of the very best of its kind).

Manno, A. and Promis, V., *Bibliografia storica degli stati della monarchia di Savoia*. 10 vols. Turin, 1884–1934 (an unfinished but essential bibliographical work; see above, p. 417).

Morandi, R., *Storia della grande industria in Italia*. Turin, 1966.

Nolte, E., *Three Faces of Fascism*. New York, 1966.

Perticone, G., *L'Italia contemporanea (1871–1948)*. Rev. ed. Milan, 1968 (useful bibliography, chronology, and collection of documents).

Procacci, G., *Storia degli italiani*. 2 vols. Bari, 1968.

Salvatorelli, L., *Casa Savoia nella storia d'Italia*. Rome, 1944 (the best polemical pamphlet of its kind, published clandestinely during the German occupation of Rome).

———, *Sommario della storia d'Italia*. Turin, 1948.

Salvemini, G., *La politica estera dell'Italia, 1871–1915*. Florence, 1950.

Seton-Watson, C., *Italy from Liberalism to Fascism*. London, 1967.

Sprigge, C.J.S., *The Development of Modern Italy*. New Haven, 1944.

Taylor, A.J.P., *The Habsburg Monarchy*. London, 1948.

Taylor, E., *The Fall of the Dynasties*. New York, 1963.

Trevelyan, J.P., *A Short History of the Italian People*. New York, 1956 (good English-language summary).

Volpe, G., *Italia moderna, 1815–1915*. 3 vols. Florence, 1943–1953.

PART I

Acton, H., *The Last Bourbons of Naples*. London, 1961.

Alatri, P., *Orientamenti marxistici sul Risorgimento*. Trieste, 1954.

Albertini, A., *La dinastia di Savoia*. Perugia, 1890 (*"compilata per le scuole primarie"*).

Andrioli, L., *Annali militari dei reali di Savoja*. 3 vols. Turin, 1826.

Berkeley, G.F.H., *Italy in the Making*. 3 vols. Cambridge, 1932–1940.

Blasi, J., ed., *I Savoia dalle origini al 1900*. Florence, 1940 (a collection of monographs).

Brancaccio, N., *Dal nido Savoiardo al Trono d'Italia*. Milan, 1930.

Carutti, D., *Storia della diplomazia della corte di Savoia*. 4 vols. Turin, 1875.

Cavour, C., *Discorsi parlamentari*. Turin, 1962.

Cibrario, L., *Origine e progressi delle istituzioni della monarchia di Savoia*. 2 vols. Florence, 1869 (still an important work).

Cognasso, F., *Il conte verde*. Turin, 1926 (all of Cognasso's works are essential reading).

———, *I Savoia nella politica europea*. Milan, 1941.

———, *Umberto Biancamano*. Turin, 1929.

———, *Vittorio Emanuele II*. Turin, 1942.

Croce, B., *Storia del regno di Napoli*. Bari, 1967.

D'Azeglio, M., *I miei ricordi*. Rome, 1965.

De Angeli, F., *Storia di casa Savoia*. Milan, 1906.

De Meis, A.C., *Il sovrano*. Bari, 1927 (this edition of the work, first published in 1868, includes an introduction by Croce and the early criticisms of Carducci, *et al.*).

De Sanctis, F., *Un viaggio elettorale*. Naples, 1876(?).

d'Ideville, H., *Journal d'un diplomat en Italie*. Paris, 1872.

Gramsci, A., *Il Risorgimento*. Turin, 1949.

———, *Sul Risorgimento*. Rev. ed. Rome, 1967.

Gregorovius, F., *Diari romani (1852–1874)*. 2 vols. Rome, 1967 (first published in 1892).

Guichenon, S., *Histoire de la maison de Savoie*. 3 vols. Turin, 1777–1780 (the uncontested leading work of its kind for at least 100 years, but antiquated now).

Le lettere di Vittorio Emanuele II. 2 vols. Turin, 1966 (selected by Cognasso).

Longford, E., *Queen Victoria: Born to Suceed*. New York, 1965.

Mack Smith, D., (ed.), *Il Risorgimento italiano*. Bari, 1968 (documents, etc.).

———, *Cavour and Garibaldi*. New York, 1954.

———, *Da Cavour a Mussolini*. Catania, 1968 (collected essays).

Maranini, G., *Le origini dello statuto albertino*. Florence, 1926.

Massari, G., *La vita ed il regno di Vittorio Emanuele II di Savoia*. 2 vols. Milan, 1922 (3rd edition, first published in 1878).

Mazzini, G., *Opere scelte*. Rome, 1957.

Memorie del re galantuomo. Milan, 1882 (an anonymous compilation of generally authentic anecdotal material).

Nichols, P., *Piedmont and the English*. London, 1967.

Omodeo, A., *L'Opera politica del conte di Cavour*. 2 vols. Florence, 1945.

Panzini, A., *Il conte di Cavour*. Milan, 1931.

Philippe, G., *I lupi di Savoia*. Florence, 1868.

Processo criminale della casa di Savoia. Turin (?), 1797(?) (this rare document was found in the private library of King Humbert I now in the Biblioteca Reale at Turin).

Ragionieri, E., *Il Risorgimento italiano nell'opera di Marx e di Engels*. Rome, 1951.

Ricotti, E., *Storia della monarchia Piemontese*. 6 vols. Florence, 1861.

Rosselli, N., *Mazzini e Bakunin*. Turin, 1967.

Salvatorelli, L., *Pensiero e azione del Risorgimento*. Turin, 1963.

Salvemini, G., *Mazzini*. London, 1956.

Servion, J., *Gestez et croniques de la mayson de Savoye*. 2 vols. Turin, 1879 (a special edition of Servion's fifteenth-century work on J. Dorievelle's "history" of the House of Savoy).

Spellanzon, C. and Di Nolfo, E., *Storia del Risorgimento e dell'unita d'Italia*. 8 vols. Milan, 1933–65.

The Historian's History of the World, Vol. IX: Italy. London and New York, 1908 (a still useful volume written by a committee of Victorian scholars).

Trevelyan, G.M., *Garibaldi and the Thousand*. London, 1965 (first published in 1909—part of the Garibaldi trilogy).

Yorick, figlio di Yorick (Perrigni, P.C.), *Vittorio Emanuele II*. Rome, 1890 (a curiosity).

PART II

Andreola, A., *Umberto I re buono*. Turin, 1953.

Antonioni, F., *Due donne nel regno d'Italia*. Rome, 1968 (Margherita and Elena).

Atti della Giunta parlamentare per la Inchiesta agraria e sulle condizioni della classe agricola. 15 vols. (in 23 books). Rome, 1883–1886.

Atti relativi alla morte del re Vittorio Emanuele II e all'assensione al trono del re Umberto I. Rome, 1878.

Bordeux, J., *Margherita of Savoia*. London, 1926.

Caracciolo, A., *L'Inchiesta agraria Jacini*. Turin, 1958.

Carducci, G., *Confessioni e battaglie*. Bologna, 1908.

Casalegno, C., *La regina Margherita*. Turin, 1956 (the best biography so far).

Cusin, F., *L'Italia unita*. 2 vols. Udine, 1952–1955 (a useful work by an "anti-historian").

Farini, D., *Diario*. 2 vols. Rome, 1962.

Graziano, G., *Umberto I di Savoja*. Turin, 1902.

Grimaldi, U.A., *Il re "buono"*. Milan, 1970 (the first non-hagiographic biography of Humbert I; a good companion to Casalegno).

Guerra, G.A., *Umberto I*. Turin, 1935.

Guiccioli, A., *"Diario 1876–1917"* in *Nuova Antologia* (the Guiccioli diaries, which begin in 1790 with entries by Guiccioli's grandfather and then his father, appear in issues of this Florentine review beginning 16 November 1932 and conclude with the 1 July 1943 issue; Guiccioli's own diary begins on 1 January 1876).

Hugo, C., *Rome en 1886*. Paris, 1886 (indiscretions of a French countess at Humbert's court).

Jacini, S., *I risultati della Inchiesta agraria*. Rome, 1885.

King, B. and Okey, T., *Italy To-day*. London, 1901.

Labriola, A., *Storia di dieci anni (1899–1909)*. Milan, 1910.

Langer, W.L., *The Diplomacy of Imperialism*. Rev. ed. New York, 1951.

"Lettere di Margherita alla contessa Adriana Marcello" in *Nuova Antologia*, November 1941.

"Lettere di Margherita a mons. Bonomelli (bishop of Cremona)" in *Nuova Antologia*, February 1940.

Lipparini, L., ed., *Lettere fra la regina Margherita e Marco Minghetti (1882–1886)*. Milan, 1947.

"Margherita di Savoia a cuore aperto" in *Oggi*, 16 July–6 August 1953 (letters from the queen to Colonel Osio).

Morandi, C., *La sinistra al potere*. Florence, 1944.

Mosca, G., *Teorica dei governi e governo parlamentare*. Milan, 1925.

Palmenghi-Crispi, T., *Francesco Crispi: Politica interna*. Milan, 1924 (Crispi's papers).

————, *La politica estera di Francesco Crispi*. Milan, 1912 (Crispi's diaries).

Petacco, A., *L'anarchico che venne dall'America*. Milan, 1969 (a work on Humbert's assassin, Bresci).

Reiset, O., *Mes souvenirs*. Paris, 1903.

Resoconto del processo di G. Passanante. Rome, 1879.

Richelmy, C., *Cinque re*. Rome, 1952.

Romeo, R., *Risorgimento e capitalismo*. Bari, 1959.

Roux, O., *La prima regina d'Italia*. Turin, 1901.

Sacchi, A., *La pellagra nella provincia di Mantova*. Milan, 1967.

Salvatorelli, L., *La triplice alleanza*. Milan, 1939.

Savio, O., *Memorie*. 2 vols. Milan, 1911 (memoirs of a baroness at the court of Savoy).

Scanzi, M.O. (Osio, E.), *Il generale Osio*. Milan, 1909.

Settembrini, L., *La culla del principe di Napoli*. Naples (?), 1869(?) (a curiosity).

Stillman, W.J., *Francesco Crispi*. London, 1899.

Turiello, P., *Governo e governati in Italia*. Rev. ed. Bologna, 1889.

Vasili, P. (Adam, J.), *La société de Rome*. Paris, 1887.

Vigo, P., *Annali d'Italia: Storia degli ultimi trent'anni del secolo XIX*. 7 vols. Milan, 1908-1915.

Villari, L., "Quando al Corriere si dimettevano" in *L'Espresso*, 3 November 1968.

Waddington, M.K., *Italian Letters*. London, 1905.

PART III

Alatri, P., *Le origini del fascismo*. Rome, 1956.

Albertini, L., *Le origini della guerra del 1914*. Milan, 1943.

Artieri, G., "Il diario di Vittorio Emanuele III" in *Epoca*, 14 January-3 March 1968 (excerpts from Victor Emmanuel's celebrated "diary").

―――――, "La vita di Vittorio Emanuele III" in *Storia Illustrata*, January-March 1968.

Bagot, R., *My Italian Year*. London, 1911.

Balbo, I., *Diario 1922*. Milan, 1932.

Bertoldi, S., *Vittorio Emanuele III*. Milan, 1970.

Borgese, G.A., *Gabriele D'Annunzio*. Naples, 1909.

―――――, *Goliath: The March of Fascism*. New York, 1938.

Bülow, O. von, *Memorie*. 4 vols. Milan, 1930-1932.

Caracciolo, F., *Victor Emmanuel III intime*. Paris, n.d.

Ciasca, R., *Storia coloniale dell'Italia contemporanea*. Milan, 1940.

Consiglio, A., *Vita di Vittorio Emanuele III*. Milan, 1950.

Crispolti, F., *Corone e porpore*. Milan, 1936.

Da Camino de Simone, N., *I parenti poveri di casa Savoia*. Turin, 1946 (revelations of a descendant of the Mirafiori).

De Felice, R., *Mussolini il rivoluzionario*. Turin, 1965 (volume 1 of the author's monumental biography of Mussolini, a work in progress, of which three of five volumes have appeared).

―――――, *Mussolini il fascista: La conquista del potere*. Turin, 1966 (volume 2 of above).

Ferraris, E., *La marcia su Roma veduta dal Viminale*. Rome, 1946.

Giolitti, G., *Memorie della mia vita*. Milan, 1945 (3rd. edition of 2 volume work first published in 1922).

Giuliani, S., *Interviste*. Milan, 1934.

Gobetti, P., *Risorgimento senza eroe*. Turin, 1926.

Gramsci, A., *Scritti politici*. Rome, 1967.

Grasselli Parni, A., *Vittorio Emanuele terzo*. Rome, 1922.

Hentze, M., *Pre-Fascist Italy*. London, 1939.

Kirkpatrick, I., *Mussolini*. New York, 1964.

Ludwig, E., *Colloqui con Mussolini*. Milan, 1965 (unexpurgated paperback edition of this famous work first published in 1932).

Lumbroso, A., *Elena di Montenegro*. Florence, 1935.

Lussu, E., *Marcia su Roma e dintorni*. Turin, 1945.

Martini, F., *Confessioni e ricordi*. Milan, 1929.

Mary, queen of Rumania, *The Story of My Life*. London, 1924.

Missiroli, M., *La monarchia socialista*. Bologna, 1922.

Morandi, L., *Come fu educato Vittorio Emanuele III*. Rev. ed. Turin, 1905.

Nicolson, H., *King George V*. London, 1952.

Nitti, F.S., *Rivelazioni*. Naples, 1948.

Palmenghi-Crispi, T., *Giovanni Giolitti*. Rome, 1913.

Renzi, W.A., "Italy's Neutrality and Entrance into the Great War: A Re-examination." *The American Historical Review*, June 1968.

Repaci, A., *La marcia su Rome*. 2 vols. Milan, 1963.

Robertson, A., *Victor Emmanuel III, King of Italy*. London, 1925 (one of many panegyrical biographies).

Rossi, C., *Trentatre vicende mussoliniane*. Milan, 1958.

Roth, J.J., "The Roots of Italian Fascism: Sorel and Sorelismo." *The Journal of Modern History*, March 1967.

Salandra, A., *La neutralità italiana*. Milan, 1928.

————, *L'intervento*. Milan, 1930.

Salomone, A.W., *Italian Democracy in the Making*. Philadelphia, 1945.

Salvatorelli, L., *Nazionalfascismo*. Turin, 1923.

Salvemini, G., *Il governo della malvita*. Florence, 1920.

————, "Introductory Essay" in Salomone (see above).

Scaroni, S., *Con Vittorio Emanuele III*. Milan, 1954 (revelations of the king's aide-de-camp, 1933–1935).

Sforza, C., *L'Italia dal 1914 al 1944 quale io la vidi*. Rome, 1945.

Solaro del Borgo, V., *Giornate di guerra del re soldato*. Milan, 1931.

Spriano, P., *Storia del Partito comunista italiano*. Turin, 1967–1971 (volumes 1–3 of a work in progress).

Volpe, G., *L'impresa di Tripoli*. Rome, 1946.

————, *Vittorio Emanuele III*. Milan, 1939.

PART IV

Alfieri, D., *Due dittatori di fronte*. Milan, 1948.

Anfuso, F., *Da palazzo Venezia a lago di Garda*. Milan, 1957.

Badoglio, P., *L'Italia nella seconda guerra mondiale*. Milan, 1946.

Barzini, Jr., L., *Le paure d'ieri*. Rome, 1968.

Battaglia, R., *La seconda guerra mondiale*. Rome, 1960.

————, *Storia della Resistenza italiana*. Rev. ed. Turin, 1964.

Bergamini, A., *Il re Vittorio Emanuele III di fronte alla storia*. Rome, 1949.

Bianchi, G., *25 luglio: crollo di un regime*. Milan, 1963.

Bolla, N., *Il segreto di due re*. Milan, 1951.

Bonomi, I., *Diario di un anno*. Milan, 1947.

Bullock, A., *Hitler*. Rev. ed. New York, 1960.

Capano, R.P., *La Resistenza in Roma*. 2 vols. Naples, 1963.

Carboni, G., *Memorie segrete, 1935–1948*. Florence, 1955.

Cassels, A., *Mussolini's Early Diplomacy*. Princeton, 1970.

Castellano, G., *Come firmai l'armistizio*. Milan, 1945.

————, *La guerra continua*. Milan, 1963.

Caviglia, E., *Diario*. Milan, 1952.

Ciano, G., *Diario, 1937–1938*. Bologna, 1948.

————, *Diario, 1939–43*. 3rd ed. Milan, 1968.

Contini, M., *Maria José: La regina sconosciuta*. Milan, 1955 ("approved" by the former queen).

Croce, B., *Croce, the King and the Allies*. New York, 1950.

D'Andrea, U., *La fine del regno: Grandezza e decadenza di Vittorio Emanuele III*. Turin, 1951.

D'Aroma, N., *Vent'anni insieme: Vittorio Emanuele e Mussolini*. Bologna, 1957.

Deakin, F.W., *The Brutal Friendship*. Rev. ed. New York, 1966.

————, *The Six Hundred Days of Mussolini*. New York, 1966 (revised edition of part 3 of the author's *The Brutal Friendship*, New York, 1962).

De Felice, R., *Mussolini il fascista: L'organizzazione dello Stato fascista*. Turin, 1969 (volume 3 of work cited above).

————, *Storia degli ebrei italiani sotto il fascismo*. Turin, 1961.

Degli Espinosa, A., *Il regno del sud*. Florence, 1955.

Delzell, D.F., *Mussolini's Enemies: The Anti-Fascist Resistance*. Princeton, 1961.

Di Benigno, J., *Occasioni mancate*. Rome, 1945.

Dollmann, E., *Roma nazista*. Milan, 1949.

Etnasi, F., *2 giugno 1946*. Rome, 1966.

Finer, H., *Mussolini's Italy*. London, 1935.

Foreign Relations of the United States, Vol. 2, 1943, Europe. Washington, 1964 (see also *1944* in the same series).

Garland, A., and Smyth, H.M., *Sicily and the Surrender of Italy*. Washington, 1965.

Guariglia, R., *Ricordi, 1922–1946*. Naples, 1950.

Hughes, H.S., *The United States and Italy*. Rev. ed. Cambridge, 1965.

Leonardi, M., *Amadeo d'Aosta*. Rome, 1966.

Lizzardi, O., *Il regno di Badoglio*. Milan, 1963.

Lochner, L.P., ed., *The Goebbels Diaries*. New York, 1948.

Messaggi di Umberto II dall'esilio, 1946–56. Turin, 1956(?).

Moellhausen, E.F., *La carta perdente*. Rome, 1948.

Monelli, P., *Mussolini piccolo borghese*. Milan, 1968.

————, *Roma 1943*. Rev. ed. Milan, 1963.

Murphy, R., *Diplomat Among Warriors*. New York, 1964.

Mussolini, B., *Il tempo del bastone e della carota*. Milan, 1966 (an unexpurgated edition of Mussolini's celebrated unsigned articles in *Corriere della Sera*, 24 June–18 July 1944; also known as *Storia di un anno 1942–1943*).

————, *Opera omnia*. 35 vols. Florence, 1951–1963.

Pillon, G., "I Savoia nella bufera." *Il Tempo*, 27 June–24 August 1969.

Piscitelli, E., *Storia della Resistenza romana*. Bari, 1965.

Puntoni, P., *Parla Vittorio Emanuele III*. Milan, 1958.

Romita, G., *Dalla monarchia alla repubblica*. Pisa, 1959.

Rossi, C., *Il delitto Matteotti*. Milan, 1965.

Rossi, F., *Come arrivammo all'armistizio*. Milan, 1946.

Salvatorelli, L. and Mia, G., *Storia d'Italia nel periodo fascista*. Rev. ed. Turin, 1964.

Scorza, C., *La notte del Gran Consiglio*. Milan, 1968.

Secchia, P. and Frassati, F., *Storia della Resistenza*. 2 vols. Rome, 1965.

Senise, C., *Quando ero capo della polizia*. Rome, 1946.

Shirer, W. L., *The Rise and Fall of the Third Reich*. New York, 1960.

Silva, P., *Io difendo la monarchia*. Rome, 1946.

Silvestri, C., *Matteotti, Mussolini e il dramma italiano*. Rome, 1947.

Soleri, M., *Memorie*. Turin, 1949.

Susmel, D., "Mussolini e i Savoia." *Tempo*, 20 December 1969–17 January 1970.

Tamaro, A., *Due anni di storia, 1943–1945*. 3 vols. Rome, 1948–1950.

————, *Vent'anni di storia, 1922–1943*. 3 vols. Rome, 1954.

Trionfera, R. "Perché Roma non fu difesa." *L'Europeo*, 19 September 1965.

————, "25 anni fa cadeva il fascismo." *L'Europeo*, 25 July 1968.

Trionfera, R. and Petacco, "Perché Roma si arrese ai nazisti?" *L'Europeo*, 5 September 1968 (rebuttal of Zangrandi's work).

Wiskemann, E., *The Rome-Berlin Axis*. Rev. ed. London, 1966.

Zangrandi, R., *1943–25 luglio–8 settembre*. Rev. ed. Milan, 1964. (See above, p. 355 fn.)

Zanussi, G., *Guerra e catastrofe d'Italia*. Rome, 1946.

INDEX

INDEX

Absolutism, 19–20

Abyssinia, Italian Campaign in, 291n, 292, 293, 294

Acciarito, Pietro, 136n

Action Party, in Sardinia, 255

Adalbert, duke of Bergamo, 307

Adam, Juliette, 106, 107, 109, 110, 111

Addis Ababa, Ethiopia, 293

Adelaide, heiress of Turin, 10

Adowa, Ethiopia, 130, 293

Aimone of Savoy, 314–315

Albania, 68, 164, 301–302, 315, 318, 381

Albrecht, Archduke, 50

Alexandra of Denmark, 308

Alexandria, Egypt, 374, 380

Algeria, 92

Allied Powers, 316, 317, 364; Italy and, 338, 339, 340, 341, 342, 343–345, 348, 349, 350, 365; Tunisia and, 322; Victor Emmanuel III and, 367, 370

Alpini, 334, 335

Alps, 8, 341

Amadeus III, 13

Amadeus VI, the Green Count, 16

Amadeus VIII, the Peaceful, 10, 12, 13, 15, 16–17, 382

Amadeus, duke of Aosta (1943–), 383

Amba Alagi, Ethiopia, 129

Ambrosio, Vittorio, 319, 326–327, 344, 349, 350, 354, 359, 360–361

Amendola, Giovanni, 263, 269, 271, 272–273, 274, 277

Andrassy, Minister, 68

Andrea Doria, 221

Anglo-Italian *entente,* 295

Anne of Orleans, duchess of Aosta, 363n

Ansaldo steel, 223n

Anse, Council of (1025), 7

Anti-Semitism, 203n, 301

Aosta, duchess of, *see* Anne of Orleans, Hélène of Orleans

Aosta, duke of, *see* Amadeus, Emmanuel Philibert

Arbessor, Rosa, 54

Ardeatine caves, Rome, 372

Armonia (journal), xx

Assab, Eritrea, 127

Austria, at Berlin Congress, 82; Italy and, 31, 67n, 91–92; in World War I, 212–213

Austro-Hungarian army, 212–213

Austro-Prussian War (1866), 38

Avanti! (journal), 203, 232, 233

Aventine, 276

Aventine Secession, 269

Aventinians, 270–271, 272n, 273

Avogardo, Count, 147, 148, 149

Axis Powers, 338, 340, 348; *see also* Germany

Bachi, Riccardo, 223

Badoglio, Mario, 362n

Badoglio, Pietro, 242, 292, 294, 335, 336, 339, 340–341, 342, 343, 346, 347, 348, 349, 350, 352, 353, 354, 358, 359, 360, 364, 365, 366, 367; brought to power, 324, 328, 329, 332, 333, 337; flight from Rome, 356–357

Baionetta, 361, 363, 364

Bakunin, Mikhail Aleksandrovich, 73

Balbo, Cesare, 31

Balbo, Italo, 235

Baldwin, Stanley, 285

Banks, frauds, 125

Baracco, Baron, 112

Baratieri, Oreste, 123, 124, 129, 130

Barrack-Room Ballads (Kipling), 128

Bartoli, D., 288, 373, 377n

Barzini, Luigi, Jr., 375, 376, 377

Bassiano, Prince, 316

Beccaris, Bavo, 142, 143

Belgium, Germany and, 307, 311

Bengazi, Libya, 316

Bergamini, Senator, 246

Berio, Alberto, 344

Berlin, Congress of, 81

Bernhardt, Sarah, 117

Berold, duke of Saxony, 13–14, 15, 23

Bertani, Agostino, 70, 71

Bertarelli, Marquise, 287

Bianchi, Michele, 240, 246

Bismarck, Otto Eduard Leopold von; at Berlin Congress, 81; Crispi and, 68–69, 119; Italy and, 91–92, 99–100, 101–102

Bissolati-Bergamaschi, Leonida, 134

Blacks, papal sympathizers in Rome, 57, 59, 60, 114, 185

Black-shirts, 261

Blue Butterfly, 189

Blume, Peter, 300

Bolsheviks, 211

Bonaldi, Admiral, 187

Bonaparte, Mathilde, 112

Bonghi, Ruggiero, 112

Bonomi, Milquetoastish Ivanhoe, 227, 236, 273, 323

Borghese, 58

Boris, czar of Bulgaria, 286,

Boselli, Paolo, 210, 211

Bosnia, 82

Boso of Arles, 14

Bottai, Giuseppe, 330

Bourbon, French royal house, 384

Bovino, duchess of, 357, 361–362

Bovino, duke of, 356, 357, 361–362

Boxer Rebellion, 144, 145

Bresci, Gaetano, 143, 146–147, 148, 149, 152, 153

Brindisi, Italy, 364, 366

Bruno, Giordano, 24

Buchenwald, 363n

Buffarini-Guidi, Guido, 336

Bulgaria, 322

Bülow, Karl von, 185

Buzzurri, 61

Cadorna, Luigi, 210, 211, 212

Cairoli, Benedetto, 81, 85, 86–87, 107

Calza-Bini, Gino, 259

Campbell, Ronald, 343

Campello, Major Francesco, 361

Capitalism, 73

Capodimonte palace, 218

Caporetto, Battle of, 211, 212

Carabinieri, 332, 333, 359n

Caracciolo, 158

Carbonari (Charcoal-Burners), 28, 29

Carboni, General, 349, 350, 351

Carducci, Giosue, 79, 82–84, 102, 111, 130

Carta bollata, 37

Carutti, Domenico, 6–7

Casalegno, C., 112, 160, 281

Casati, Count Alessandro, 278

Castellano, General, 329, 344, 345, 346–347

Castle of Porziano, 181

Cateau-Cambrésis, peace of, 18

Cavallotti, Felice Carlo Emmanuele, 137, 140

Cavour, Count Camillo Benso di, xx–xxi, xxii, 36, 54, 261, 372; death, 38; Garibaldi and, 34; influence of, 30–31; Sicily and, 33; United Italy and, 36–37

Ceka, 263, 275

Central Powers, World War I, 202, 203

Cerica, General, 329, 333

Cetinje, Montenegro, 165

Chabod, Federico, 291n

Chamberlain, Lady Austen, 285

Chansons de geste from Overseas (D'Annunzio), 196

Charles, Sir Noel, 368, 373

Charles Albert of Sardinia, xxii, 44, 50, 383; abdication, 30, 366, 374; reforms, 29

Charles Emmanuel I, 20

Charles Emmanuel II, 20, 21

Charles Emmanuel III, 22

Charles Emmanuel IV, 23–24, 25, 29n

Charles Felix of Sardinia, 29, 220

Charlotte, grand duchess of Luxemburg, 288, 308

Chiesa, Eugenio, 174n

Chigi palace, 269

Cholera, in Sicily, 125

Christine of France, 21

Church, Catholic, 58, 185

Churchill, Winston, 285, 311, 343, 345, 346, 366–367, 368, 370, 373

Ciano di Cortellazzo, Count Galeazzo, 174n, 249, 290, 295, 296, 297, 298, 301–302, 304–305, 306–307, 308–310, 311–312, 314–315, 317–319, 320, 330, 343, 373–374

Cibrario, Count Giovanni Antonio Luigi, 50

Circolo (Margherita), 112

Cittadini, General, 246, 247, 249

Civitavecchia, Italy, 342

Claudia of Orleans, duchess of Savoy, 383

Clemenceau, Georges, 216

Clotilde, princess of Savoy, xviii, 280

Coal, 104

Code Napoléon, 25

Cognasso, Francesco, 10

Collar of the Annunziata, 16, 37, 284, 334; to Count Ciano, 305, 306; to Hermann Goering, 310

Communism, 73, 344, 373

Communist party, in Italy, 226, 227, 238n, 261, 276, 340, 343, 369, 372

Congo, 287

Conrad II, emperor of Germany, 5, 8

Conservatism, 192

Constitution, Italian, 275, 376n

Corradini, Enrico, 192, 193, 236

Correnti, Cesare, 45–46, 47

Corriere della Sera (journal), 122n, 142, 189, 273, 276

Corriere Italiano (journal), 266

Corsair, 186

Corsica, 295

Cosenz, Enrico, 127

Cotton, 37n

Coup d'état; royal, 319, 321–322; Fascist, 236–237

Crecchio, Italy, 357

Crispi, Francesco, 43, 44, 45, 47, 49, 65, 66, 80, 86–87, 104, 105, 113, 119, 121–122, 123–124, 125, 127–128, 129, 130, 137, 151, 152, 161, 164, 170, 171n

Critica sociale (journal), 134

Croatia, 314

Croce, Benedetto, 39, 79, 111, 112, 134, 209, 262, 366

Cromwell, Oliver, 21

Crown Council, meeting of, 349–351

Cusin, Fabio, 102–103

Cyprus, 82

Czolgosz, Leon, 152n

d'Ajeta, Marquis Blaso Lanza, 343, 344

Dalser, Benito Albino, 232

Dalser, Ida Irene, 232, 233

Dandolo, 81, 82

D'Annunzio, Gabriele, 109–110, 114–115, 135, 191, 192, 196, 204, 227, 238, 262, 272n, 292; at Fiume, 216, 217, 219–221; poem by, 209; in World War I, 203, 215

Darwinism, 128

D'Azeglio, Massimo Taparelli, 75

De Bono, Emilio, 240, 266–267, 270

De Cesare, Nicolò, 333

De Courten, Admiral, 349, 350

De Felice, Renzo, 225, 228, 230–231, 239, 273–274

De Gasperi, Alcide, 376, 377

del Borgo, Solaro, 250

del Drago, Rodolfo, 287

Del Rio, Dolores, 289

de Marco, De Viti, 134

De Meis, Angelo Camillo, 76–79

d'Orreville, Jean, 13–15

Depression (1929), 291
Depretis, Agostino, 64–65, 66, 67, 69, 80, 102, 114, 120; in Austria, 94, 95, 98; dictatorship, 87–88; death, 104; government crises, 92–93
Depretis, Amelia, 116
De Stefanis, General, 349
De Vecchi, Cesare, 240, 242, 249
Diarchy, 260
Diavolo, Fra, 25n
Diaz, Armando, 212, 244
di Bergolo, Count Carlo, 280, 352n, 363n
di Campello, Count Vittorio, 268
Di Rudinì, Antonio, 133, 137, 140, 143–144
di Sarre, Victor, see Victor Emmanuel IV
Disraeli, Benjamin, 68
Divine Comedy (Dante), 159
Divine Kingship, 3
Divorce, 175
Dogali, Ethiopia, 118, 128
Dreikaiserbund, 91
Dronero, Italy, 219
Duilio, 81
Duke of the Abruzzi, 374
Dumini, Amerigo, 266, 267

Eden, Anthony, 285
Edison electric company, 203n
Edward, prince of Wales, 280
82nd Airborne, U.S. army, 347
Eisenhower, General Dwight D., 345n, 346, 347, 349, 351
El Alamein, 316
Elections, 175–176; (1897), 137; (1900), 144; (1919), 215; (1921), 227; (1924), 262; (1946), 372, 375–376
Electoral law, 261, 262, 264
Elena of Montenegro, 151, 179, 180–181, 182–183, 184–185, 187–188, 189–190, 209, 280, 289, 292–293, 307–308, 313, 315, 337, 352, 359, 364, 368, 374, 381
Elizabeth, empress of Austria, 96
Elizabeth, queen of Belgium, 288, 308
Elizabeth of Saxony, 53–54
Emigration, 196
Emmanuel Philibert, duke of Aosta, xviii, 166, 182–183, 212, 217, 218, 221–222, 234n, 236, 242, 282, 290, 307, 314

Emmanuel Philibert, the Iron Head, 17, 18–19, 23, 279
Enciclopedia italiana, 224n
Engels, Friedrich, 29–30, 134–135
Entente Cordiale, 199
Era Fascista, 286
Eternal City, 300
Ethiopia, Italy and, 119–120, 129, 293–294, 314
Ethiopian army, 129
Eugene, prince of Savoy, 97

Faccetta nera, 292
Facta, Luigi, 236, 237, 239, 240–241, 243, 245–246, 247
Farinacci, Roberto, 271, 336, 340
Farini, Domenico, 103n, 106, 124, 125, 133, 137, 161, 166, 205
Farouk, king of Egypt, 374, 381
Fasci, 121, 126, 224
Fascio di combattimento, 224
Fascism, 73, 74, 226, 238–239, 272, 283, 285, 343
Fascist Republican Party, 131, 329, 340, 375; congress in Naples, 240; early stages, 224–225, 227, 234n, 235–236; government by, 260–261, 262; military power of, 240, 282; militia (MVSN), 261n; origins of, 263–274; resistance to, 316; Risorgimento and, 27
Fascisti, 224
Federzoni, Luigi, 270, 276n
Fedorovna, Marie, empress of Russia, 163
Feudalism, 4, 16
Fiat, 171n, 203, 223n
Filippelli, Filippo, 266
Finzi, Aldo, 267, 270
First Marshal of the Empire, office of, 296–298
Fiume, Yugoslavia, 219, 220, 262, 284
Five Hundred, The, 119
Foch, Ferdinand, 211
Fogazzaro, Antonio, 113
"Four highwaymen," 119, 129
France, 308, 311, 346; at Berlin Congress, 82; Italy and, 39, 99, 121; Mussolini and, 232–233; in Triple Alliance, 102
Francis I, king of France, 308

Francis Ferdinand, archduke of Austria, 198, 199

Francis Joseph I, emperor of Austria, 50, 93, 96–97, 98, 99, 105n, 198, 199, 205

Franco, Francisco, 295, 302

Franco-Prussian War, 39

Franz Josef, *see* Francis Joseph I

Frederick William (Hohenzollern), 46–47, 50

Freemasonry, 260

French Revolution, 23, 86

Futurist Manifesto of 1909, 193

Futurists, 192

Gambetta, Léon, 99, 101

Garibaldi, Giuseppe, xxii, 33, 34–35, 38, 45n, 70, 92, 193, 229

Garlands of the Mountains (Petar), 188

Gascogne, 146

Gasti, Giovanni, 231, 232–233, 234, 235, 239

Gasti report, 231–234

George V, king of England, 215n

George VI, king of England, 288, 289, 367

George, Lloyd, 211, 285

Gerbore, Pietro, 105–106, 116, 187

Germany, 215; Austria and, 202; in France, 313; Italy and, 91–92, 198, 199, 304, 305, 306–307, 318, 321, 322, 324; Poland and, 306; and Triple Alliance, 102; and World War II, 308, 311

Giant II, 346, 347

Gibbon, Edward, 7–8, 22

Giolitti, Giovanni, 122, 126, 129, 176–177, 185, 191, 194, 196, 203n, 221, 226, 230, 231, 236, 239, 240, 244, 245, 246, 249, 272, 274, 381; fall of, 197, 200; Libyan war, 194; life of, 172–173; Mussolini and, 227; politics, 174–175; World War I, 202, 204, 205, 206–207, 218–219, 220

Giornale degli economisti (journal), 136

Giornale d'Italia (journal), 237, 246, 249

Giovanna, czarina of Bulgaria, 187, 286, 308, 380, 382

Goebbels, Joseph, 356n, 363n

Goering, Hermann, 310

Goldman, Emma, 152

Government and Governed (Turiello), 74–76

Gramsci, Antonio, 127–128, 227, 238n

Grandi, Count Dino, 249, 317, 318–319, 320, 327, 329–331, 334

Grand council, 329, 331, 334, 335

Great Britain, 214–215, 295, 308, 339, 350; at Berlin Congress, 82; Ethiopia, 314; Italy and, 295, 305, 344; in World War II, 316

Guariglia, Foreign Minister, 349, 350

Guiccioli, Count Alessandro, xvi, 47, 48, 65, 81, 82, 85, 86, 107–108, 112, 116

Guidi, Rachele, 232, 233

Haile Selassie I (Ras Tafari), emperor of Ethiopia, 292

Hamil Booth Company, 146

Hapsburg, German royal house, 30, 93–99

Hare, Augustus, 61

Helene of Orleans, duchess of Aosta, 166, 182–183, 217, 218, 222, 290, 314

Henry III, the Black, Holy Roman Emperor, 10

Hermann Goering division, German army, 357

Herzegovina, Hungary, 82

Himmler, Heinrich, 299

Hitler, Adolf, 261, 285, 295, 313, 321, 347, 352, 363n; in Italy, 298–300; Mussolini and, 326, 340–341; Victor Emmanuel III, 339, 342, 356n; before World War II, 304, 305, 306, 307, 310, 312

Hughes, H. Stuart, 371

Humbert the Good, *see* Humbert I

Humbert I, king of Italy, 43, 74, 76, 80, 81–84, 87, 88, 90–91, 92, 105–106, 107, 109–110, 113, 114, 119, 120, 145, 146, 170, 282, 319; assassination attempts, 84–85, 136, 148–149, 169; in Austria, 94–99; Crispi and, 124–125, 126, 127, 130–131; early life, 49–50, 51–53, 55, 56–57, 59, 60; Ethiopia and, 129; policies of, 66, 79; romantic intrigues of, 137, 140; Triple Alliance and, 100–101, 102; Victor Emmanuel III and, 159

Humbert the Whitehanded, 5, 6, 7, 8, 9, 10, 59

Humbert II, king of Italy, xvii, xviii, xxi–xxii, 158, 184–185, 187, 209, 215, 236, 270–271, 277, 281, 282, 307, 310, 318, 322, 341, 349, 352, 353, 354, 357, 366, 367n, 369–370, 381–382, 383–384; and election of 1946, 375, 376, 377, 378; flight from Rome, 356, 360–363; as king, 371, 372, 380; marriage, 286–289; in World War II, 313
Humbert III, the Blessed, 14, 150n
Hundred Years' War, 17
Hungary, 221, 322

Imperialism, 118, 127–128
Inchiesta agraria, 71–73
Italian army, 127, 136, 213, 237, 240, 259, 293, 307, 330, 337, 340, 376; in Boxer Rebellion, 144, 145; at Caporetto, 211–212; in Ethiopia, 118, 128–129; Fascism and, 225, 227, 228, 244; at Fiume, 216, 217; Germany and, 353; in Libya, 195; worker revolt in Milan, 141; in World War I, 209–210, 215; in World War II, 316
Italietta, 191
Italy, xxi, 64, 71–72, 73–74, 91, 93, 99, 133–134, 142–143, 269, 295, 323; Austria and, 198–199, 203, 204, 207; in Abyssinia, 294–295; at Berlin Congress, 81–82; dictatorship in, 263; economy of, 114, 121, 171, 217–218; in Ethiopia, 292; Germany and, 67, 68–69, 321, 327; Humbert I, 169; imperialism of, 118–120, 191, 192, 193; industrialization, 37, 104; in Libya, 194, 196; north, 76, 129, 371; in political decline, 170; political parties, 365–366; as republic, 375–376, 377, 384; south, 37, 76, 121, 129, 176; surrender, World War II, 345, 349, 351; Triple Alliance and, 101–102, 104; united, 26–28, 31, 33, 34, 36–37, 40, 86–87, 90, 92; unrest in, xx, 37, 65, 70, 122, 134; and Victor Emmanuel III, 185–186; World War I and, 199–200, 201, 202, 212–213; World War II and, 370–371
Italy To-Day (King and Okey), 170–171
Italy Waits (Bertani), 70

Irredentists, 67n, 95, 101, 105, 129, 199
Islam, 196, 295

Jacini, Count, 71
Jacini commission, 71–73
Jacini report, on agriculture, 104
Jacobins, 23
Jesuits, 19, 124
Jews, 16, 17, 19, 292, 293, 301
Jodl, General, 314

Kaisermesse, 98
Karageorgevich, Alexander, 382
Kekina, see Maria Pia
Kesselring, Albert, 351–352, 353, 355n–356n, 357
Keys to the Mediterranean, 119
King, Bolton, 170–171
King, Rufus, 179
Kingdom of the South, 364, 365
Kingship, 214, 218
Kipling, Rudyard, 128, 192
Krumiri, 92
Kulishov, Anna, 134

Labriola, Antonio, 134
Lamarmora, Alfonso Ferrero, xxi, 38
Lateran Treaties, 283, 291
Law, electoral, 261, 262, 264; of Savoy, 16–17
League of Nations, 292, 294–295
Lenin, Nikolai (Vladimir Ulianov), 70, 182, 212, 215, 226n–227n
Leo XIII, pope, 94
Leopold III, King of Belgium, 287, 307
Liberalism, 104, 169, 174
Liberty league, 126
Libya, 193, 194; annexed by Italy, 195; war in, 175, 196, 197
Life of Christ (Papini), 193
Lisbon, Portugal, 343, 344
Lissa, Pietro, 255–257
Litta, Duchess, 51, 53, 105, 106, 107, 108, 109, 110, 133, 137, 151
Litta-Visconti-Arese, Duke, 108
Little Black Face, 292
Lohengrin, 110
Longford, Elizabeth, 62n

Louis Amadeus, duke of the Abruzzi, 168, 194

Louise of Savoy, duchess of Angoulême, 308

Lucifero, Falcone, 377

Ludwig, Emil, 229n, 277n

Lusignoli (Milan prefect), 245, 246

Lussu, Emilio, 255–257, 263, 273

Luxemburg, Belgium, 311

Luzzatti, Luigi, 203n

Macdonald, Jeanette, 289

MacFarlane, Mason, 367, 369

Machiavelli, Niccolo, 369

Macinato, 74

Mack Smith, Denis, 37, 173

Mackensen, August von, 318

Macmillan, Harold, 368

Maddalena, Italy, 342

Mafalda, 1845, 280–281, 282, 300, 352n, 363n

Malaria, 72

Malatesta, Enrico, 201

Mamiani, Terenzio, 112

Mancini, Pasquale Stanislav, 98, 118

Marcellinus, Amaianus, 6n

Marches (papal state), 33

Marchesi, Major, 349, 350–351

March on Rome, 141, 225, 231, 236, 239, 240–241

Marco Minghetti, 145

Margherita of Savoy, queen of Italy, xvii, xviii, 12, 50, 56, 57–58, 59, 60, 61, 79, 82–84, 85, 89, 91, 93–94, 95–96, 97, 98–99, 105, 106, 107–108, 109, 110–113, 140, 146, 149–151

Margotti, Giacomo, xx

Maria Adelaide, queen of Italy, xix, xx

Maria Beatrice, 382

Maria Gabriella, 382

Maria José, queen of Italy, 286–289, 290, 307, 313, 323, 348, 373, 375, 382

Maria Pia, queen of Portugal, 32, 39, 66, 289, 290, 382

Maria of Savoy, 187

Marinelli, Giovanni, 266, 267, 268

Marx, Karl, 29–30, 73n, 132

Mary, queen of Rumania, 163

Matteotti, Giacomo, 263–264, 266–271, 276, 277n, 312, 366

Mattino (journal), 137, 142

Maximilian, archduke of Austria, emperor of Mexico, 288

Mazzini, Giuseppe, xxii, 26–28, 31, 32–33, 38, 40, 60, 193, 203

Medici, Florentine family, 12

Memoria 44, 353

Menabrea, Count Luigi Federigo, 51, 53

Menelik, emperor of Ethiopia, 129, 130, 133

Messaggero (journal), 280

Mezzogiorno, 37

Michael, prince of Montenegro, 315

Milan, Italy, 31, 140–141, 142–143

Millo, Admiral, 219–220

Minghetti, Laura Acton, 60

Minghetti, Marco, xxi, 112, 116

Mirafiori, Count, 109

Modena, Italy, 32

Monarchy, 136, 144, 170, 171

Mondo (journal), 273

Montenegro, 164–165, 196n, 214, 314, 315, 380

Morgan, J. P., 186–187

Morosini, Francesco, 18

Morra Irpino, 71

Mosca, Gaetano, 193

Murphy, Robert, 345, 367–368, 370

Mussolini, Arnaldo, 249, 250

Mussolini, Alessandro, 232

Mussolini, Benito, xxi, 16, 55, 113, 141, 182, 193, 197, 201, 212, 215, 216, 218, 222, 223n, 224–225, 226, 228, 232, 233–234, 236, 280, 291, 292, 293, 294, 295, 297–298, 299, 300, 305–306, 308, 341, 351, 359, 366, 372, 384; at Fiume, 216; Giolitti and, 204, 227, 239, 241; overthrown, 317–318, 319, 320, 321, 322, 327–333, 334–337, 340, 365, 373; takes power, 238–239, 240, 241, 244, 245, 246, 249, 250, 251, 259–260, 261, 262, 263, 264, 267–269, 270–271, 272, 273–274, 275–276, 285, 286; Victor Emmanuel III and, 230–231, 237, 256, 257–259, 277, 283–284, 301, 304, 309, 310–311, 381; in

World War I, 203, 205, 229; in World War II, 310, 311–312, 313, 326
Mussolini, Edda, 232
Mussolini, Rachele, 333–334
Musketeers, 259

Naples, Italy, 37, 55, 84, 107, 145, 162, 377
Napoleon III, emperor of France, xx, 24–25, 32, 338
Nationalism, 192, 215
Nationalist imperialism, 192
Nationalist party, congress in 1910, 192–193; in Libyan war, 194; in World War I, 203, 204–205
Nazism, 295, 296, 318, 365, 371
Negri, Ada, 135
Nenni, Pietro, 201
Netherlands, falls to Germany, 311
Neue Freie Presse, 94
Nice, France, 295
Nicolajevich, Peter, 380
Nicolajevna, Maria, duchess of Leuchtenberg, xxi
Nicholas II, czar of Russia, 163, 189, 201n
Nicholas I, King of Montenegro, 165, 315n
Nicotera, Baron Giovanni, 61, 65, 85
Nigra, Count Constantino, 121, 124
Nitti, Francesco, 182–183, 215, 217–218, 221, 222, 231, 263
North Africa, 67, 118–119, 133, 316, 322
Nuova Antologia (journal), 63, 64, 92
Nuove poesie (Carducci), 84

Oberdan, Guglielmo, 105n
"Ode to the Queen of Italy" (Carducci), 84
Odi barbare (Carducci), 84
Oddone, 10
Okey, Thomas, 170–171
"On the Late Massacre in Piedmont" (John Milton), 21
Operation Axis, 352
Opinione (journal), 45
Orlando, Vittorio Emanuele, 211, 215n, 231, 234, 274
Ortona, Italy, 361, 363
Oscar I, King of Sweden, 116
Osio, Colonel, 159, 167, 183

Otto III, Holy Roman Emperor, 13–14, 15
Ottoman Empire, 81, 193, 194

Pact of London, 200n, 202, 203, 205, 215, 216
Pact of Steel, 295, 304, 305, 306, 310
Palazzo Venezio, 304, 329, 330
Papini, Giovanni, 192, 193
Parliament, end of, 271
Parma, Italy, 32
Pascoli, Giovanni, 194
Passanante, Giovanni, 84–85
Passo romano, 290
Paterno, Baron Vincenzo, 187
Paul V, pope, 58
Peace of the Two Dames, 308
Pellagra, 72
Pelloux, Luigi, 137, 144
Perugia, Italy, 242
Pescara, Italy, 356, 358, 359
Peschiera, Italy, 211
Petar, ruler of Croatia, 188
Petrograd, Russia, 212
Petrovich, Elena, see Elena of Montenegro
Petrovich, Mirko, 189
Petrucelli, Baron, 105
Philibert, Duke of Pistoia, 307
Philibert II, the Fair, 308
Philip, prince of Hesse, 280–281, 363
Phony War, 308
Piazza of the Republic, 352
Piedmont, 23–24, 25, 29, 31
Pirandello, Luigi, 133
Pisacane, Carlo, 26
Pius IX, pope, xvi, 56, 57n, 70, 90
Pius XI, pope, 259, 283, 326
Poison gas, 293, 294
Polacco, Giorgio, 260
Poland, 306, 308
Ponzio, Count, 149
Popolari, 262
Popolo d'Italia (journal), 203, 223n, 232, 233, 244
Press, Italian, 142, 271, 276
Prezzolini, Giuseppe, 192
Prince of Piedmont, see Humbert II
Prinetti, Nicoletta, 106
Prisoners of war, 131

Puntoni, P., 317, 320, 321, 324, 325, 327, 332, 333, 334–335, 336, 337, 341, 342, 349, 351, 354, 355, 356, 357, 361–362, 363, 368–369, 370
Putato, Aldo, 266, 267

Questione sociale (journal), 147
Quirinal Palace, 114, 180, 209, 230, 251, 257, 288–289, 299, 304, 328, 349, 376, 378

Racconigi, Italy, 184
Racconigi castle, 281
Radetzky, Joseph Wenzel, 30
Radio Rome, 351
Radziwill family, 185
Rahn, Rudolf, 347, 348, 349, 352
Rapallo, treaty of, 219, 220
Rassegna Settimanale (Sonnino), 92
Rattazzi, Urbanino, xxi, 106, 125, 162, 319
Red Army, 344
Red Week, 200–201
Regina Coeli (jail), 298
Repaci, Antonino, 228
Repression; in Italy, 276; in Sicily, 125
Republican movement, 86, 87, 373, 376, 384
Republics, 214, 369
Resistenza, 316, 365, 371, 372, 384
Revolution, 224, 371
Riforma (journal), 124
Rijeka, Yugoslavia, *see* Fiume
Rimbaud, Arthur, 129
Risorgimento, 24–26, 27–28, 35n, 134, 193, 327, 345, 365
Roatta, General, 340, 349, 353–354, 363
Rohan, German royal house, 284n
Romagna, Italy, 37
Romanov, Roman, 380
Romanov, Russian royal family, 214
Rome, 3, 34, 38, 39, 40, 56, 57, 58, 60–61, 63, 114, 115–117, 245–246, 247–248, 324, 326, 339, 341, 346, 352, 353–355, 356–358, 370, 376
Rome-Berlin Axis, 304
Romeo, Rosario, 74n
Römische Tagebücher (Gregorovius), 60
Romita, Giuseppe, 373

Roosevelt, Franklin D., 316, 323, 343, 358–359, 366–367, 368, 370
Roosevelt, Theodore, 96
Rosa Verceillana, La Rosina, xviii, xix, xx–xxi, 57
Rospigliosi, Girolamo, 287
Rossi, Cesare, 267, 270, 272
Rubartelli, Admiral, 364
Rudolf I of Hapsburg, 4, 93, 288
Rudolf III, king of Burgundy, 5
Ruffo, Fabrizio, 25
Rumania, 322
Ruspoli, Prince Carole, 360
Russo-Japanese war, 189
Russo-Turkish war, 46, 67

Salandra, Antonio, 200, 201, 202, 203, 204, 205, 206, 210, 243, 249, 274, 381
Salerno, Italy, 353
Salvatorelli, L., 102, 201
Salvemini, Gaetano, 26, 175–176
Sandalli, General, 349, 350
Santa Fiora, Countess, 133, 137, 140
Saracco, Giuseppe, 144, 151, 171n, 172
Sardinia, 22, 23, 135, 255, 256, 342, 355, 365, 376
Sarzana, Bishop of, 81
Savio, Baroness Olimpia, 52
Savoia 81, 294
Savoy, derivation of name, 6n
Savoy, House of, 6–7, 11–12, 13–15, 16–17, 18–19, 20, 76–77, 78–79, 170, 295, 303n; in Europe, 90–91; Hapsburgs and, 30; in Risorgimento, 24
Scarfoglio, Signora Eduardo, *see* Serao, Matilde
Scorza, Carlo, 328, 331
Second Army, Italian, 210
Securities market, 291
Senise, Carmine, 320, 329, 363n
Serao, Matilde, 109, 135, 137, 178
Serbs, 314n
Settembrini, Luigi, 55
Sfida, 135
Sforza, Count Carlo, 210, 220, 269, 271, 277, 372
Sicily, 22, 37, 135, 328, 346; Allied landing on, 323; fasci of 1890s, 224n; Garibaldi

expedition to, 33, 35n; revolution in, 121–122, 123, 125, 126

Singapore, 145

Smith, Alice, 382

Social democracy, 172

Socialism, 73, 74, 86, 87, 134, 136, 174, 192, 193, 215, 224, 226

Socialist monarchy, 173, 174, 176, 191, 201

Socialist party, 73–74, 112, 126, 140, 169, 175, 197, 203, 215, 226, 227, 232, 235, 268, 371, 375

Solaro del Borgo, 274

Soleri (minister of war), 240, 245

Sommaruga, Angelo, 109

Sonnino, Baron Sidney, 10, 92, 136, 202–203, 237, 330

Sorel, Georges, 175

Sorice (undersecretary of war), 320, 349, 350, 353

Sovereign (De Meis), 76–78

Spain, 264, 295, 297, 302, 377, 384

Spaventa, Silvio, 52–53, 65

Squadristi, 262, 272

Stalin, Joseph V., 370, 371

Stalingrad, Russia, 316, 317, 344

Stampa (journal), 276

Stanley, Sir Henry Morton, 46

Stefani, 340

Stephanie, princess of Belgium, 288

Stella Polare, 168

Stillman, William J., 80

Strikes, 320n

Student, General, 356n

Tangier, Morocco, 344

Taylor, A. J. P., 200

Taylor, General Maxwell, 347

Terracini, Umberto, 226n, 227n

Third Army, U.S., 212

Thistle, 168

Thomas, duke of Genoa, 172, 307n

Times (London), 45n, 62, 262, 372

Togliatti, Palmiro, 371

Tomaslav II, *see* Aimone

Torlonia, Prince Alessandro, 59

Trade unionists, 227

Transformismo, 65

Trentino, Italy, 82, 123

Trevelyan, G. M., 195

Tribuna (journal), 110, 114, 122n

Triple Alliance, Italy, Austria, and Germany (1882), 93, 99, 100–101, 102, 104, 120, 198, 199, 202, 203, 205, 211–212

Tunisia, 82, 92, 322

Turati, Filippo, 134, 142, 152, 269, 276–277

Turiello, Pasquale, 74–76, 79

Turin, Italy, 52

Turkey, 196

Tuscany, Italy, 32

Two Sicilies, 376

Umbria, Italy, 33

Underground, *see Resistenza*

Unemployment, 223–224

Unitarian Socialist party, 264

United Nations, 339–340, 352, 369

Union of Soviet Socialist Republics, 82, 198, 201, 211, 212, 344n, 372

United States, 316, 339, 350, 368

United States Army, 82nd Airborne, 346, 347

Universal Reform of Savoy (1430), 16

Ustachi (Croat militia), 314n

Vaglia, Count Ponzio, 147, 149, 151

Vasili, Count, *see* Adam, Juliette

Vatican, 280–281, 373; Mussolini and, 262; in World War II, 344n

Venice, Italy, 31, 32, 34, 38

Venosta, Visconti, 166

Versailles, Peace Conference, 215, 216

Via Tiburtina, 354, 356

Vico, Giovanni Battista, 76–77

Victor Amadeus I, king of Sicily, 20

Victor Amadeus II, of Savoy, king of Sardinia, 21–22

Victor Amadeus III, of Savoy, 22–23, 296

Victor Emmanuel I, of Piedmont, king of Italy, 25, 28, 29

Victor Emmanuel II, king of Italy, xv–xvii, xxi–xxii, 30, 40, 43, 44–45, 46–48, 51–57, 63–67, 70, 78, 108, 109, 170; Germany and, 295; Mussolini and, 296–297

Victor Emmanuel III, king of Italy, 49, 50, 55, 84, 116, 151, 152, 157–159, 160,

161–168, 169, 170, 171, 172–173, 174n, 178, 179, 180, 181, 182, 185, 188, 191, 193–194, 197, 215, 216–217, 218, 220, 221–222, 227–228, 263, 264, 268, 279, 280, 282–283, 288, 289–300, 302, 303, 306, 308–309, 315, 317–318, 338, 380, 381; abdication of, 369–370, 371, 374, 375; flight from Rome, 356, 358, 360–361, 363, 364, 365–366, 367–368; Mussolini and, 230, 231, 235, 236, 237, 240, 241, 242, 243–246, 247, 248, 257, 258–259, 260, 270, 272, 274, 277, 278, 284, 301, 304, 319, 321, 322, 323–324, 327, 331, 333, 334–337; in World War I, 198–199, 200–203, 205, 206, 208–209, 211–212; in World War II, 311–312, 313–318, 339, 341, 342, 343, 346, 347–348, 349, 350, 353
Victor Emmanuel IV, king of Italy, 290, 366, 383
Victoria, queen of England, xx, 62, 90–91, 106, 213n–215n, 287
Vienna, Austria, 93
Villa Ada, *see* Villa Savoia
Villa Italia, 208
Villa Margherita, 179
Villa Savoia, 180, 245, 331–332, 324, 334, 374
Villa Yela, 380
Villari, Pasquale, 112, 136
Vincenza, Countess of Santa Fiora, 109–110
Viola, Ettore, 274
Violence, Fascist, 261
Viollier, Eugenio Torelli, 142–143
Visconti, Gian Galeazzo, 12, 13
Visconti family, 12, 13
Voce (journal), 194

Volpe, Gioacchino, 195–196
Voltaire, 21–22
Volunteer Militia for National Security (MVSN), 261
Voting rights, 104

Waldenses, persecution of, 19, 21
War (Elena), 189–190
War crimes, 293n
War of Spanish Succession, 21
Wells, H. G., 214n
Welles, Sumner, 343
West Group, U.S. army, 313
Whites, Savoy sympathizers, 57, 59, 60, 114, 185
Wilhelmina, queen of the Netherlands, 308
William II, German emperor, 199, 205, 281, 342
Wilson, Woodrow, 216
Windsor, 215n
World War I, 194–195, 197, 198–200, 202, 207, 208, 214, 215–216, 223
World War II, 196, 301, 304, 306, 308, 313, 316, 317–318, 319, 322, 371

Yela, 167, 168, 374
Yolanda Margherita, princess of Savoy, 184, 279–280, 352n, 380
Yugoslavia, 216, 219, 314

Zanussi, General, 344, 345
Zanardelli, Giuseppe, 81, 82, 86, 87, 123, 124, 137, 172
Zara, Yugoslavia, 220
Zangrandi, Ruggero, 355n
Zog I (Ahmed Bey Zogu), king of Albania, 381